PT
343
.N3
Natan, Alex
German Men of Letters.

GERMAN MEN OF LETTERS

VOLUME III

Twelve Literary Essays

GERMAN MEN OF LETTERS

VOLUME III

Twelve Literary Essays

edited by

ALEX NATAN

OSWALD WOLFF
London
1968

First published 1964
Second impression 1968

MADE AND PRINTED IN GREAT BRITAIN BY
THE GARDEN CITY PRESS LIMITED
LETCHWORTH, HERTFORDSHIRE

CONTENTS

INTRODUCTION

by ALEX NATAN

The impact of Nietzsche's corrosive thought revealed itself as a new departure in German poetry, drama and fiction in opposition to the Naturalist and Neo-Romantic movements. His demand for "the transvaluation of all values" and his heroic pessimism brought to light the growing disintegration of pre-war society and the intellectual dubiety of its beliefs. Furthermore, the philosopher's epoch-making work on *Die Geburt der Tragödie* (The Birth of Tragedy, 1872) laid stress upon the element of wild, unbridled passion in Greek culture. This Dionysiac conception deeply influenced the new movement, which produced works of lasting fame and value, wasted much of its dynamic forces in ecstatic prophecies and caused still more confusion. Its impact on political theory and practice in Germany during and after the First World War was deeply felt, and its revolutionary influences on literature and the visual arts can still be traced right up to Max Frisch and Friedrich Dürrenmatt.

Lothar Schreyer, a member of the avant-gardist "Sturm" circle, defined Expressionism as "the spiritual movement of a time that places inner experience above external life". In a similar way to the evolution of Impressionism the visual artists paved the way for the Expressionist writers. Exhibitions like that of "Die Brücke" in Dresden (1905) and, at a later date, that of the artists around the "Blaue Reiter" in Munich proved a valuable stimulus. These artists expressed in form and colour an art which was to reveal the original idea of the cosmos. "Ich suche", wrote Paul Klee, "einen entlegenen, ursprünglichen Punkt, wo ich eine Art Formel ahne für Mensch, Tier, Pflanze, Erde, Feuer, Wasser, Luft und alle kreisenden Kräfte zugleich. Der Erdgedanke tritt vor dem Weltgeschehen zurück. Die Liebe ist fern und religiös."[1] Franz Marc stated: "Ich beginne immer mehr hinter oder besser gesagt: durch die Dinge zu sehen, ein Dahinter, das die Dinge mit ihrem Schein eher verbergen meist raffiniert verbergen, indem sie den Menschen etwas ganz anderes vortäuschen als was sie tatsächlich bergen. Physikalisch ist es ja eine alte Geschichte; wir wissen heute, was Wärme ist, Schall und Schwere,—wenigstens haben wir eine zweite Deutung, die wissenschaftliche. Ich bin überzeugt, dass hinter dieser noch wieder eine und viele liegen."(2)

It now becomes clearer why Expressionism could not be a unified movement but was merely one of largely individual moods, fluid and very evasive when it came to definition and classification, initially more interested in style than in content. From Naturalism Expressionism assumed a strong feeling of compassion for the fellow-man, enslaved and harassed by the mechanisation and industrialisation of life. This compassion for the "disinherited creature" expanded into an ecstatic confession for an all-embracing brotherhood. From the Neo-Romantic movement the Expressionists inherited the reaction against a materialistic interpretation of life and a metaphysical awareness of God. "The belief in the goodness of man is synonymous with the goodness of God" (Wedekind). To the generation which matured after the turn of the century Nietzsche's dictum: "Today everything is tottering, the whole earth shakes" became the leitmotif of its rebellion against tradition and all established values.

Instinctively Expressionism became the herald of the coming twilight of Western civilisation. Hence, the struggle against the evils, both of society and of life, hence the analytic condemnation of sterile social forms, hence the clarion-call for a new man in a new society, for a new God. Eventually, in defiance of Nietzsche but trusting in the power of the spirit, the beginning of a new golden age was proclaimed, where purified and transfigured Man would find his way back to God. Perhaps nothing explains better the essence of Expressionism than the sentences from Gustav Landauer's "Address to the Poets": "We need the ever-recurring renewal, we need the readiness to shock, we need the loud outcry across all frontiers, we need the trumpet hailing in the great year of jubilation, we need spring, we need delusion, intoxication and frenzy, we need—again and again and again—the revolution, we need the poet!"

"While *Kokoschka* ranks abroad as one of the great artists of our time, there are too many people here who know little of his work. . . . " This statement from the Foreword in the catalogue of the Kokoschka Exhibition of the Tate Gallery in autumn 1962 could have easily continued that there are very few who know that the distinguished painter began his artistic career as a playwright of remarkable merits. It speaks for the close interdependence of art and literature within the range of the Expressionist movement that Kokoschka was able to display his violent love-affair with the visible world through visual and written language, for his formative years coincided with the decades of intellectual and artistic discontent, which the "transvaluation of all values" had caused inside the middle-class mentality before the First World War. In order to prove the possibility of wedding the visual with the spoken art Kokoschka not only produced his play *Hiob* himself, but also painted the illusion of furniture on to the back-drop, in order to abolish the third dimension, a device which wrote a new chapter in the history of the German theatre.

Although Oskar Kokoschka always refused to be type-cast as an "Expressionist", his play *Mörder, Hoffnung der Frauen*, was probably the first Expressionist drama, for it showed a new departure in style, through the violence of subject matter and diction. The play, only ten pages in print, is steeped in colour and light and set in imaginary space. There is an inner conflict—the perennial struggle between the sexes—and an outer one between light and shadow. "Lichtstrahlen kreuzen und suchen sich."(3) It is the light which illumines the inner struggle of the characters: "Die Menschen sprechen, als ob sie sängen. . . . Es gibt keine Psychologie mehr. Die Nähe der Oper ist fühlbar." (4) (Half a century after Kokoschka's first work Friedrich Dürrenmatt wrote his musical *Frank V—Opera of a Private Bank*, which showed distinct affinities with the painter's intentions.) The inner theme concerned the deadly struggle between Man and Woman, a legacy from Strindberg and Wedekind, but also displaying the influence of the sexual psychologist, Otto Weininger.(5) Man and Woman have lost their individuality and have become archetypes, whose traditional polarity modern society has come to question. There is no logical development in this play, because it is set outside the experience of any rational life. The characters are blindly driven by instinct and all-devouring passion, by "senseless desire from horror to horror, insatiable circling in empty space, caused by the splitting of humanity into sexes". The ecstasy of language works its disruptive effects through explosive diction or frantic expression, which, though highly emotionally charged, produces the objectivity of the "Telegram Style". Of his dramas a German critic could write: "Sie erzielen eine Wirkung, als ob Seelen sprächen, die jeden Moment zerfliessen könnten. Sie zerfliessen auch zu Bildvisionen, die den vom Dichter gewollten Sinn noch wesentlich intensiver versinnlichen."(6) Allegory and vision underline Kokoschka's primeval experience: the liberation of the Ego from the taboos of sex. The poet's longing is for a deeper meaning of life. This aspect of Expressionism is very old and yet eternally young. Perhaps it only represented at the time "a late phase of decadent Romanticism".(7)

Albert Ehrenstein, an Expressionist poet in his own right, once proclaimed proudly: "In the beginning was Oskar Kokoschka!"

And yet, one of the earliest and profoundest of German critics of Expressionism attacked Kokoschka in 1921. He charged him with unsatisfied sexual lust, with stooping to bestial bondage, and with writing objectionable texts, open to every base interpretation. "Die Muse einer solchen Brunstorgie kann nur Vagina heissen. Denn was ist die Seele den Erotomanen anderes als das ungebändigte Geschlechtswesen? Kokoschka sieht mit Schmerzenswollust das Schwein in jedem Mann und in jedem Weib."(8) Diebold then poses the question how a painter of recognised merits could thus sin against humanity. He finds the answer in his portraits, which all reveal the animal, the beast: "Mit Meisterschaft ist die Zivillarve der Menschen abgerissen zur Aufdeckung der mit konventioneller Mimik hinweggelogenen Geilheit . . . Das Portrait mag sich mit dem verharrenden Moment eines Menschengesichts begnügen. Das Theaterspiel aber ist Bewegung."(9) Forty years later an English art critic wrote: "Stepping into a room full of Kokoschkas is like getting the full swell of a symphony orchestra after a longish session with a gramophone. . . . A man of extraordinary vision, at once penetrating and panoramic. His portraits—the early ones especially—show us individuals without the wrappings of human defence and disguise through which, at other times, we more or less dimly perceive them."(10) This element which Diebold denounced as an abomination was in truth a deeply felt humanism. Kokoschka has confessed to being a follower of Comenius, the great Czech humanist and pacifist. To show the sufferings or hopes of a human soul, whether in colour or in words, turned into a searching analysis of human possibilities for the painter for the rest of his life.

The shattering trauma of the First World War, the memory of those hours when he lay, pierced by a bayonet, in an open field and was pursued by feverish visions, gave birth to *Orpheus und Eurydike,* regrettably neglected by the modern theatre. The play anticipated much that Jean Cocteau embodied afterwards in his film *Orphée,* and Kokoschka, moreover, wove the Orpheus saga together with the myth of Amor and Psyche. This play is the "fall-out" of a dream of dread and "Lebensangst". The poet himself has admitted that he thought he had "spoken, and whispered in an ecstasy, in a delirium, wept over" the scenes of the play in the agony of approaching death. It is no surprise that Kokoschka opposed tyranny and war, and not without deeper meaning Herbert Read called him "a partisan of anarchism".(11) In *Orpheus und Eurydike,* Psyche speaks the last words: "Ich habe euch lieb". An infinite longing for the ultimate unity of spirit and body, for a last fulfilment, permeates this work. However, it remained only an expression of wingless yearning. "Der Glaube ist dahin and die Seelen frieren. Es bleibt nur der Mut zum umweglosen Feststellen dessen, was ist—ohne alle Literatur."[12]

The erstwhile bugbear of Imperial Vienna may have felt with his last completed play that his task as a poet had come to an end: *individum est ineffabile*. The individual is beyond the reach of words. For in painting and sculpture Man has produced an alternative to evocative language. Kokoschka, as painter, reached the sublimity of Goethe's invocation to the fleeting moment, when he teaches his art pupils: "Open your eyes, look and remember that this particular light, these exact colours and this unique gesture will never, never combine again. Nothing can hold this moment of life unless you seize it with your brush."

Amidst the desiccation of the intellectual life during the decade preceding the holocaust of 1914 *Ernst Barlach* began to make his own way, hardly noticed and still less understood. He presents the rare case of an artist who found expression for his visions through two different media. To write about Barlach the dramatist, is impossible, without paying due regard to his great achievements as a sculptor, for he obtained an almost perfect unity of the dramatic and the plastic arts. The conceptions of the sculptor helped to form the fundamental attitude of the playwright. Barlach was not an artist who shaped the human body to achieve purely aesthetic satisfaction. He created his forms as expressions of the inner man, as the artists of the Romanesque and particularly of the Gothic period had attempted before. All artists who showed some affinity with the tenets of the Expressionist movement perceived an inspiring source in Gothic art. In the case of Barlach it would, however, be wholly erroneous to assume that it was vain ambition which drove the artist to achieve a double distinction. It was an inescapable urge for confession which created his plays out of the spiritual experience of the sculptor.

He opted early for the plastic art, "um eine utopische Existenz auf sich zu nehmen"[13] a rebellious gesture against the accepted tenets of contemporary art teaching. On his journey to Russia (1906) he discovered "die verblüffende Einheit von Innen und Aussen".[14] There he learnt a Christian humility toward all things, out of which his quest for the rediscovery of God was born. It is often asserted that Barlach's artistic vision, which permeated his dramas and novels, was largely moulded by the experience of Russian landscape and people. It is only correct to point to the opposite view that "Barlach erbliche und geistige Anlage rein niederdeutsch, germanisch und 'nordisch' war, allerdings nicht von der strahlend—sieghaften Art, sondern elbisch, trollhaft, spukhaft und spökenkiekerisch, dumpf und sinnlich, grüblerisch und versponnen—das norddeutsche Gegenstück zu den Opfern der böhmischen Nachtmahre von Kubin bis Kafka".[15] Those who know the loneliness of the poet's native Mecklenburg and the superstition of its inhabitants, will understand why Barlach's characters exist against a background of eerie mists, brooding stillness and the rustling wind of the supernatural.

Barlach's very individual "mythos" culminated in the belief that a fully lived and a fully explored life on earth was evidence enough for the existence of a supreme spiritual principle, of God, for whom he longed. He became a Faustian seeker who, earthbound, yearned to touch His hem to save himself from the nihilistic materialism of his evil-boding times. Barlach's first drama *Der Tote Tag* acknowledges the prevailing agnosticism which Nietzsche had bequeathed. But such a dead day must be a day without God, and therefore necessitates the compelling quest for the recovery of the lost relationship to God. Barlach felt the spiritual crisis of his times as a personal challenge which he could only try to meet himself. He began the life of a recluse, engaged in a very personal fight with the good and evil demons in himself. He never became a preacher but an imaginative visionary and prophet. He had to forge his way ahead, toward God. "Er berief sich auf keinen göttlichen Auftrag wie Rilke, er rang mit versiegeltem Mund um die Wiedergabe seiner Gesichte. Er war Gott auf der Spur, aber er sah ihn in keiner verführerisch schönen Gestalt, sondern als ein Wesen, das ihm die Haare zu Berge stellte".[16] For him God remained an eternal wanderer on earth in search of the complete man, while Man, as Barlach understood him, was equally in perpetual quest for God. Barlach blamed the nihilism of the intellect for widening the gulf between God and Man. *Der Tote Tag* ends with the lament : "Sonderbar ist nur, dass der Mensch nicht lernen will, dass sein Vater Gott ist".[17]

This surrealist atmosphere, in a setting for dream figures rather than for realistic individuals, possesses a nightmarish quality which recurs in other haunting plays that, oddly enough, point to many dreamlike, mythical characteristics of the Theatre of the Absurd. The action in Barlach's dramas often dissolves into disputations. His characters discuss philosophical viewpoints. As in his sculptures men in heavy raiments, hampered by falling folds, laboriously pacing the earth, seek for God in agonising quest whence they derived, in his dramas, too, his figures struggle for redemption inside their dull structure of human creatures. Every man born will be once crucified. Ergo : prepare for your Calvary, so that you may be able to glance heavenwards in your cruellest hour and may soar above the world. The father image becomes the mainstay of all spiritual life.

This spirit is identical with God. Therefore Barlach can do without the Son. Human perfection is inborn in any man, because it is his destiny to wear a crown of thorns. Man is for Barlach "der arme Vetter, eine Art misslungene Seitenlinie des Himmels"(18) and his world prison, hell and degradation, where "the blessed and the redeemed need not be the greatest. The sinners and wretched are just as good saints as the saints themselves. There is no difference: we all are damned, banished, the galley-slaves of life."

Out of this statement grew Barlach's longing for the new man, which, in spite of all his disdain for abstract images and a preference for grotesque and humorous situations, places him within the ambience of Expressionist literature. It is the most significant expression of Barlach, the sculptor, to prefer any covering garment, in order to portray Man deeply wrapped in his desolation and loneliness, and veiled before God's countenance. "Das Gewand wird zum Zeichen dafür, dass der Mensch eingeklemmt ist in den Engpass des Lebens."(19) But did Barlach, this suffering Job among modern artists, succeed in coming near or even nearer to God? At the end of his drama *Die Sündflut,* Calan, representing all evil and God-denying principles, is drowning in the Flood. In his last moments he confesses to Noah: "Wie schön ist es, dass auch ich keine Gestalt mehr bin und nur noch Glut und Abgrund in Gott—schon sinke ich ihm zu—Er ist ich geworden und ich Er—Er mit meiner Niedrigkeit, ich mit seiner Herrlichkeit—ein einziges Eins".(20)

With the arrival of the Nazis a realistic flood overtook Barlach. The principle of evil was abroad to kill God once more. Barlach's art was declared degenerate, banned from German museums and threatened with wholesale destruction. He could neither publish nor exhibit his works of art. Poor and in utter loneliness Barlach died in 1938. Was his end symbolic? In his drama *Der Graf von Ratzeburg,* which came only posthumously to light and is regarded as a Protestant equivalent of Claudel's *Le Soulier de satin,* the central figure is run through by pikes wielded by a raving crowd: "Man sieht ihre Spiesse von allen Seiten gegen Heinrich gerichtet, der von ihnen wie von einem Strahlenglanz umgeben steht. Er fällt".(21) Had God deserted his faithful son after all? In his last play the poet stated: "Ich habe keinen Gott, aber Gott hat mich".(22) This indicates a compromise which is not wholly satisfactory.

Any genuine revolution aims at the destruction of the existing social order and at the rebuilding of a new society. In retrospect the events of November 1918 in Germany have proved to be a mock-revolution. Only a very small minority was seriously resolved on destroying the foundations of the class-conscious, imperialist Germany. Within the Expressionist movement a group of Activist writers existed which recognised social and political reform as the goal of their artistic mission. Most of them, convinced of Germany's just cause in waging a defensive war, had volunteered in 1914. The horrible experiences of the ensuing carnage had disillusioned a generation which now hated war and, at its end, hoped for a better world, which would bring justice and social equality. Its principal exponent who first turned pacifist before resorting to direct revolutionary action was *Ernst Toller*. He became the foremost dramatist of the stillborn revolution. To understand his meteoric rise to fame and his subsequent fall into oblivion one must reckon with his Jewish origin and his capitalist parentage, which engendered an inferiority complex from which the poet could never rid himself. It becomes intelligible why Toller, branded as an outcast of society, came to pin all his hopes for a new and better world on the German proletariat. Over and above this, he identified himself with all who suffered from the prevailing social iniquities, and who were prepared to throw off the yoke of injustice, if need be through violence. But Toller never became a Marxian Communist; he remained the idealist, the seer, the visionary, but, nevertheless, ready for action in the street. In the preface to the English edition of his plays (1935) he stated: "The plays collected in this volume are social dramas and tragedies. They bear witness to human suffering, and to fine yet vain struggles to vanquish this suffering. For only unnecessary suffering can be vanquished, the suffering which arises out of the unreason of humanity, out of an inadequate social system. There must always remain a residue of suffering, the lonely suffering imposed upon mankind by life and death. And only this residue is necessary and inevitable, is the tragic element of life and life's symboliser, art."(23)

For his activities in resisting the German counter-revolution, Toller was sentenced to five years' imprisonment. Not a single day of his sentence was remitted; whilst Hitler was let out of prison long before his time was up. Alfred Kerr, Berlin's leading theatre critic, had left us a description of the mature Toller reciting from his own works, for the most part written in prison: "Wie der Mönch von Heisterbach nach langen Schlummer in eine veränderte Welte schritt: so kommt hier ein sich auflehnender Gewissensmensch aus der Haft, um ein halbes Dutzend seiner jungen Jahre von Mächten geringeren Wertes beraubt . . . Der dunkle Toller ist ein weicher Apostelmensch; erfüllt von der Sendung: zu helfen; anklagend zu befeuern."(24) Because Toller, in order to spread the idea of love and humanity by way of merciless social criticism, used drama for propaganda, there was no room for him in the theatre of the moribund Weimar republic. It is, therefore, not surprising that his plays have become better known outside Germany than those of any other Expressionist writer. His gradual fall into oblivion reflected the change of the political climate. Shortly before utter despair drove Toller into committing suicide in New York in 1939 an American socialite gave a party in his honour. Before introducing the poet to her guests she whispered to him: "I say, Mr. Toller, what, by the way, was your profession?" One of the clowns of Wedekind's stamp suffered another crucifixion.

Looking back upon Toller's writings, in which he was so consciously a propagandist, averse not even to rhetoric, the question is often asked whether he can be called a poet. His first drama *Die Wandlung* (Transfiguration) refutes any doubt. This play, divided up in *Stationen* (stages), unfolds on two different levels: realistic episodes alternate with surrealistic scenes and ecstatic dreams of symbolic meaning. While the realistic play shows the actual experiences of the hero in the war, the symbolic represents rather the workings of the subconscious mind. The influence of the later Strindberg is quite evident here. Although *Die Wandlung* anticipates in many ways the modern theatrical trend of analytic introspection, in other ways it remains reminiscent of a mediaeval Dance of Death. The permanent change of scenes—*Stationen*—enables the poet to act as critic, seer, and interpreter of the traumatic experience of war times. The play is full of meaningful allegories, e.g. when rotting skeletons, hanging in barbed wire, swing melancholy in the evening wind. They testify to Toller's poetic inspiration. Its pathos reminds the reader of Georg Büchner, with whom Toller shares his simple message: to feel all the misery of the world, and yet not to send hope to the devil. This is not cheap demagogism but the strongest possible accusation not only against the war but also against the entire outlook of life of the bourgeoisie. This spiritual transformation of the hero towards a new conception of life ends with the ecstatic evocation of love, the strongest of all life-forces: "In the name of love, be our leader. Once more humanity must be vitalised by love. We will bear no more children until love encircles us with radiant hands. Lead us."(25) But the poet realises only too well that love without the blessing of the spirit would be impossible: "You are all of you no longer men and women; you are distorted images of your real selves. And yet you could still be men and women, still be human, if only you had faith in yourselves and in humanity, if only you would grant the spirit fulfilment. . . . "(26) Shades of Dürrenmatt and Frisch are here clearly perceptible. The play ends with a call to revolution: "Go to your rulers and proclaim to them with the organ tone of a million voices that their power is but illusion. Go to the soldiers and tell them to beat their swords into ploughshares. Go to the rich and show them their heart, their heart that was once buried alive beneath their rubbish. Yet be kind to them, for they too are poor, poor and straying. But the castles —these you must destroy; destroy them laughing, the false castles of illusion. Now march! March forward in the light of day."[27] There can be no doubt that Toller was an inspired poet.

However, he realised soon enough that his proclamation of a new brotherhood would prove illusory. And yet he never ceased to fling his rapturous "Even so!" into the face of reality and authority. "And I will pray the father, and he shall give you another Comforter, even the spirit of truth; whom the world cannot receive because it seeth him not, neither knoweth him. Ah, poor dear Son! We must help one another! We must be good to one another!"[28] Old Reaper, another character who seeks God and curses him at the same time, speaks these words at the end of *Die Maschinenstürmer*. In all Toller's plays faith and hope that Man may find his salvation, prevail. Perhaps here the reason, why the German stage neglected Toller so significantly, can be seen. After the collapse in 1945 it did not produce *Die Wandlung*, preferring instead the epitome of hopeless nihilism in Borchert's *Draussen vor der Tür*.

Poetry was the most significant medium of Expressionism. After Kokoschka and Barlach had written the prelude with their dramatic works *Franz Werfel* successfully effected the breakthrough of the movement. His artistic progress was marked by three stages, the first lyric, the second predominantly dramatic, and the third almost exclusively epic. Werfel followed Nietzsche as well as the tradition of German "Sturm und Drang" when he believed in the necessity of overturning all traditional values, which, for him, were epitomised by a father-hatred. The image of the father stood for discipline, for blind subordination, even for the supremacy of the industrial employer. This father-symbol was identical with the satiated *bourgeois par excellence*. What Werfel came to call "Zeitgeist", was the sum-total of what Whitman and Strindberg, Rilke and Tolstoy had proclaimed before him. In his search for a new God Werfel recognised the redemption of the materialistic selfishness of man only made possible by brotherly, self-denying love through a miraculous transformation of the idea of "I am" into that of "We are". His faith in a fraternisation of mankind and his instinctive awareness of the omnipresence of a supreme being helped him to a new conception of reality. The message which the young generation enthusiastically spread as the "dying cry of individualism" consisted in the demand to liberate the "I" and to blend it with the "Thou" to form an invincible "We".

In his poems Werfel did not feel chained to physical gravity. He yearned to drift with the clouds across God's earth, and thus to detect the breath of the creator. In passionate, rhapsodic verses he confessed this all-embracing love. Through it he wanted to reveal the secret of its growing into a redeeming world power through word symphonies of colour and sound. (Music was an early source of inspiration to Werfel which, at a later stage, led to his pre-occupation with the composer Verdi, for Werfel the incarnation of pure music.) Ecstatic visions turned Werfel into a seer, who prophesied the redemption of what is divine in man :

"Mit dem Schreiten des Menschen tritt
Gottes Anmut und Wandel aus allen Herzen und Toren.
Lächeln, Atem und Schritt
Sind mehr als des Lichtes, des Windes, der Sterne Bahn—
Die Welt fängt im Menschen an.
Im Lächeln, im Atem, im Schritt der Geliebten ertrinke!
Weine hin, knie hin, sinke!"(29)

Thus the poet sat in judgment upon the vanity and the madness of the world. The hymns and incantations, satires and visions all aimed at the glorification of the secret of the supreme being, often called God, and of the sanctity of Man.

Werfel's importance for the lyrical phase of Expressionism has not always met with unanimous approval; "Werfel ist kaum Expressionist in seinen Gedichten. Wenn weder die innere Landschaft noch die Vision und Gebärde noch der Aufschrei sind kennzeichnend für seine Verse, sondern die bald trauernde, bald hymnische Aeusserung der reinen, gehetzten, im Frevel noch reuigen und zu Gott heimverlangenden Seele."(30)

Werfel's poetry contained many seeds of drama; protagonist and antagonist, plea and counter-plea. The horrors of the war years turned Werfel to drama and his interpretation of Euripides' *The Trojan Women* underlines the senselessness of war, the disillusionment of Germany's post-war years. The production was an outstanding event in the history of Expressionist drama, for it bore witness to the anti-war feeling in Germany. During this phase as a dramatist the choice of his subject-matter, the intentional effects and calculated constructions did not permit Werfel the attainment of his ultimate goal : the drama of redemption. The exception is his historical play *Juarez und Maximilian,* where a warmth of genuine humanity permeates action and persons. Perhaps the reason why Werfel could only achieve a passing success as a dramatist lies in the very essence of drama: the interplay of human actions and human characters, which leaves little space for the ecstatic manifestations of Pan, the all-embracing world spirit of the Expressionists.

It was through his novels that Werfel achieved international fame and recognition. In the best of his prose fiction the poet who refused any conversion to Christianity out of loyalty to Judaism succeeded in creating a true Catholic atmosphere to such a remarkable degree that he was called "one of the most impressive witnesses to the Catholic creed".[30a] The poet Hans Carossa was moved by the novel *The Song of Bernadette* to say: "Segen und heiliger Fluch der Auserwählten sind in neuerer Zeit kaum jemals leidenschaftlicher nachempfunden und meisterlicher, ja verfeinerter dargestellt worden als durch dieses Buch."[31] His last novel, the Utopian *The Star of the Unborn* was, as so many of Werfel's previous works, concerned with the redemption of man, with the "completeness of the ego". At its centre is the argument with the "Grossbischof" and with the "Ewige Jude" who alone have survived aeons of years, because they have kept faith. Goethe once remarked in the *West-Oestliche Divan*: "The real, singular and most profound theme in the history of the world and of mankind to which all others are subordinated remains the conflict between belief and unbelief." All mature works of Werfel are confessions of faith, the most cherished manifestation of which is the miracle. Franz Werfel remained conscious throughout his life that the sense of everlasting values had been lost and could only be retrieved through a return to faith and love. When the poet died, he at least was once again on the way to God.

Little known outside his own country, *Gottfried Benn* occupies a unique place in German literature. Numerous books were written about him though the body of his work comprises only a few volumes of poems, dramas, essays, prose and confessions, all showing a basic unity. Benn was a practising dermatologist in Berlin. It was medicine that became the mainspring of his creative work, and the daily contact with suffering and death that held up the unfailing mirror of physical decomposition. The impact which dissecting rooms and operating theatres left on Benn produced poetry, which is rightly regarded as one of the highlights of Expressionism. The spectacle of his daily visions produced poetry of an intuitive starkness that was staggering even if diffused into gloom where dream and reality became merged in delirious monologues. It has been suggested that this extraordinary point of departure drove Benn to the arrogant isolation which only permitted the intellectual one alternative of poetic creation: atomisation of his personality or the pursuit of form. Throughout his life Benn followed both courses, oscillating between ecstatic fluidities and submitting to a more controlled discipline that bordered on the hermetic.

After his Expressionist phase and a bout of "Kulturpessimismus" Benn committed the "trahison des clercs" by allowing himself a short but unsuccessful flirtation with the Nazis. Thirty years later an English apologist had this to say: "No writer of the time was more essentially non-political than Gottfried Benn. It was his impatience with politics, an impatience that extended to 'culture' as a department of public relations and half-way house between society and the arts, that made Benn susceptible to the promise of a 'clean sweep' . . . Benn's attempt to see Nazism as the fulfilment of his Neitzschean hopes brings us back once more to the isolation which alone made his blunder possible. Nietzsche, who had declared war on civilisation in the isolation of his last productive years, ranged creative vitality, intelligence and imagination, the very things that had once sustained it, on the opposing side."[32] Admittedly, Benn loved to be called the last acolyte of Nietzsche and to pose as an esoteric nihilist in a well-tailored dinner-jacket. Admittedly, he could write the damaging sentence: "Scharlatan—das ist kein schlimmes Wort, es gibt schlimmere."[33] But could Benn really ever support a new order when he boasted: "Ich blicke nicht über mich hinaus, ich versage mir diese Erleichterung, ich arbeite, ich suche Werte, ich zeichne meine Morphologie, ich drücke mich aus?"[34] This is undiluted egotism triumphant, and in contrast "Verlaine appears as an innocent moralist".[35] In truth, the disillusioned and tired intellectual simply admired the primitiveness of the Nazis which promised a new impetus and uplift for his own work. The Nazis saw through this sort of intellectual opportunism which Benn shared with a number of German writers who, after the war, claimed a retreat into an inner emigration as excuse for their tacit consent to the Hitler régime. Benn was dropped from Hitler's Valhalla for his "amoral, decadent and Jewish works" and retired into literary silence, "an aristocratic form of emigration". After the collapse of the Third Reich Benn endeavoured to explain this alienation from his exiled friends and his personal isolation in Germany in the most revealing and least convincing book *Doppelleben* (1950), which cannot excuse his nasty "open letter" *Answer to the Literary Emigrants* and his essay *The New State and the Intellectuals.*

Those years of error and self-deception served however as a catalyst. For the works Benn published after the Second World War were exciting and recalled the genius of his Expressionist phase. The themes have become broader. Though one meets in them again the cosmic pessimism of the earlier poems, his great obsession is no longer with the death of the individual but with the death of civilisations which slowly disappear into the dusk of history. At that time Benn asserted that six good poems could create the lasting fame of a poet. These he has certainly written.

How high Benn will rank as poet and writer in German literature is very difficult to forecast, for he has his admirers and his severe critics. When he wrote after the Second World War: "Ich finde Gebet und Demut arrogant and anspruchsvoll, es setzt ja voraus, dass ich überhaupt etwas bin, aber das gerade bezweifele ich, es geht nur etwas durch mich hindurch",[36] Walter Muschg answered him brusquely that "the emptiness of a burnt-out world echoes from his existentialism".[37] It is just this detachment from the past which made Benn so popular among the surviving bourgeoisie of Germany which, too, hoped to forget recent events. Benn has never been able to overcome the basic attitude of pessimism which Nietzsche's nihilism had taught him. He remained the sceptical observer on the touchline. The more his curiosity for the enigmatic conditions of human existence drove him in later years to explore the deepest recesses of the unconscious, the more he liked pitting the power of the intellect against the enveloping chaos. Finally, he reached the conclusion that genuine life only existed in art, and that only dedication to art enabled man to withstand chaos. Such art, however, entails the end of centuries of creation, for it becomes the product of an isolated human being, no longer in fruitful exchange with his fellow-man. In this barren vacuum the task of the poet is reduced to making exact statements by adhering to form rigorously and voicing criticism ruthlessly.

The complex personality of Gottfried Benn makes an evaluation extremely difficult. In Germany he is regarded as the greatest German poet since the death of Stefan George, because he combined the verbal audacity of the artist with the objective outlook of the scientist, thus creating an entirely new form of expression.

The search for a new and free man as the architect of a new and free society formed also the main theme of the Expressionist phase in *Fritz von Unruh's* works. The problem of the individual and of the confines of freedom will always tempt a politically minded writer to turn his hero into a tragic character. For personal freedom is usually the antithesis of political freedom, which, however, must control every personal arbitrariness for the sake of safeguarding the interests of the community. The fact that Unruh is today almost forgotten, results partly from his inability to solve the above-mentioned conflict dramatically. He became a *homo politicus* too late. As an Expressionist dramatist he was not interested in the social and political aspects of the revolution, which he preached, but exclusively in the spiritual rebirth of Man from within. When Unruh turned to politics in defence of the Weimar republic, it was too late to embody his creed in a drama. It is, therefore, hardly an exaggeration to see in Unruh a victim of Expressionism, for he had become so steeped in its mentality that he never managed to rid himself entirely of its traces. Unruh, whose promising first plays were produced by nearly every German theatre during the Twenties, has fallen into oblivion since he chose to leave Germany. The writer who will soon be an octogenarian, remained almost unknown in the countries of his exile. His triumphant activity as standard-bearer of freedom and peace has been turned into a legend in Germany. The time will surely come when Unruh's strange career as a writer will attract the attention of a dramatist or a novelist.

Fritz von Unruh, who was the leading exponent of the idealistic trend in Expressionism, was the descendant of a Prussian noble family of ancient lineage. Brought up in the rigid code of military duty and obedience, he soon developed a sharp inclination towards insubordination, when criticising the outworn mentality of his privileged caste. He suffered from the frustration of a profession, which could not be a useful occupation in peacetime and should never become one in wartime. He soon clashed with the stern concept of aristocratic tradition. Faced with the choice of having his second play, *Offiziere,* dealing with a tragic conflict among Prussian officers during the Herero rebellion, produced in Berlin by Max Reinhardt, or to be placed on the retired list of the army, he chose the latter alternative. His next play, *Prinz Louis Ferdinand,* dealing with the modern problem of personal responsibility overriding military orders and containing a forecast of the downfall of the Prussian monarchy, was suppressed by order of Kaiser Wilhelm II.

Under the shattering impact of the retreat from the Marne, Unruh wrote his first passionate disavowal of the war, the dramatic poem, *Vor der Entscheidung.* Two years later, in the thick of the drumfire of Verdun, the officer in a crack Lancer regiment composed the prose poem, *Opfergang,* and the drama *Ein Geschlecht,* which completed Unruh's transformation from a seditious member of an aristocratic caste into a pacifist and a fanatic fighter for peace. Unruh was one among a group of French and German soldiers, who, during a fighting lull at Fort Vaux, raised the corpse of an unknown soldier on a cross between barbed wire, shouting aloud: "Never war again!" The writer attached particular importance to this incident, for it meant to him no longer an individual experience but the experience of a group, the source of inspiration for the large number of subsequent war novels. *Ein Geschlecht* is a one-act tragedy, the first part of a trilogy to be continued with *Platz* (1920) and completed with *Dietrich* (1936), hitherto unpublished. The action is timeless and takes place during a single night. The setting is outside and inside a graveyard on a summit of a mountain. The structure of the play, which has only four characters and a chorus of soldiers, underlines the intention of its author to write an antique tragedy. In the centre of the symbolic action stands the figure of the Mother, who is *mater dolorosa* and *mater gloriosa* at the same time. It was Unruh's intention to stress the evil that is war. War, however, is human civilisation gone wrong. Man must therefore be burdened with guilt, which, in turn, is inherent in existence itself. Its beginning is birth. Unruh's Mother has given birth to five children, who have become the physical and spiritual victims of the carnage. Only she who knows the secret of birth realises the madness of senseless destruction, when the exigencies of the war take one child after the other from her.

> "How can we go on suffering this madness
> Which shatters senselessly and drags to the grave
> The edifice of man that we created!"

She is prepared to atone for her guilt of having borne children unworthy of this earth. Her sacrifice will contain the seed for the rebirth of a new man. In an ecstatic invocation of love and hope she calls for a new world before the powers of darkness silence her once and for all. Only her youngest son, not yet contaminated, survives; he will carry the torch of rebellion and the message of a new Covenant down to the plains. Once more Law and Order triumph over chaos. The shades of Heinrich von Kleist, whose influence was already noticeable in previous plays, seem to be satisfied. But it is interesting to read the dictum of a Berlin critic after the first night: "Schiller is here mated with Antiquity . . . and the fruit is a new Baroque". (Siegfried Jacobsohn in *Das Jahr der Bühne,* 1918.)

The sequence, *Platz,* dealt with the consequences of the victorious rebellion. It is far more realistic and was far less successful. Dietrich, the name of the surviving youngest son, comes to grips with the forces of society. He finally yields to the spirit of opportunism, which dilutes the true meaning of the revolution. He follows a woman, with whom he is in love, renouncing his leadership. From this union the real "new man" will emerge, who will bring about the regeneration of mankind. While Toller's and Georg Kaiser's heroes, like Sorge's *Bettler* and Hasenclever's *Sohn,* blindly believed in their message and mission, and thus avoided the pitfalls of dramatic dichotomy, Unruh, in *Platz,* creates already characters which genuinely doubt the spirit of Expressionism, and even undertakes to parody its style in a subtle way.

One must subscribe to the view that "Unruh, at his best, had something of the white-hot idealism of the young Schiller or Kleist. But his power of translating his vision into convincing characters and action was too weak to reproduce a work of lasting value. Thus his plays have faded with the hour that inspired them."(38)

Lion Feuchtwanger's international reputation was always considered to stand higher outside than inside his native country. And yet, the inclusion of an essay about him in this collection deserves some explanation, as Feuchtwanger, on the surface at least, was not intimately connected with the Expressionist movement. His outstanding contribution to German literature consisted in his new approach to the historical novel. It remains a remarkable fact that he achieved first successes in Britain and America before he could establish his reputation in the country of his birth. In Germany the historical novel always enjoyed much popularity, because this genre enabled both writer and reader to escape from the stark and usually unmanageable reality of the present, by shifting the problems of the present into the past, and, at the same time, glorifying this past in retrospect. Such an oblique interpretation of the present through the medium of the past relieved the author of becoming committed and thus often compromised. Feuchtwanger's treatment of the historical novel did not follow this literary device. He developed a pattern of his own: the historical study was either given a modern psychological interpretation or became openly identical with a study of contemporary events and contemporary society. *Erfolg*, a political *roman à clef*, presents a sociological analysis of some decisive events which occurred in Germany between 1920 and 1924. In distrusting the aims and the stability of the Weimar republic, Feuchtwanger wrote its ruthless criticism combining the objectivity of a Ranke with the narrative style of a Macaulay. His belief in the "Wiedereinbruch der Barbarei in Deutschland und ihren zeitweiligen Sieg über die Vernunft",(39) furnishes perhaps an explanation, why Feuchtwanger is nowadays almost forgotten in Germany, why no biography of him exists, and, worst of all, why even well-known histories of German literature ignore him completely or hardly mention him at all. The late Jethro Bithell, often biased when writing about German authors of Jewish origins, even dared to write that "the historical novels of Lion Feuchtwanger owe their sales to their massed filth; they show little originality".(40)

A further and perhaps more valid reason for the inclusion of Feuchtwanger in this collection of essays can be found in his early plays, which he wrote before he devoted his talents almost exclusively to the historical novel. He began his literary career with a number of adaptations of Greek and Indian plays. Here and in his subsequent historical novels it was the conflict of "Macht und Geist", the clash between power politics and the freedom of the intellect, which attracted the speculative interest of Feuchtwanger. After the first night of *Warren Hastings,* in October 1916, Alfred Kerr, Berlin's feared critic, observed that "Nietzsche stood godfather to this comedy". He objected strongly to the author's detachment and to his lack of personal involvement, which, Kerr alleged, not even a cynic could afford. Another critic, Siegfried Jacobsohn, admitted in *Das Jahr der Bühne* (1917) that "the antithesis was a legitimate and indispensable weapon of the critic. The poet Feuchtwanger remains, however, a critic. Instead of dramatising his characters he prefers juxtaposition and stiff confrontation without committing himself either way." These remarks read as if both critics felt somehow the impact of "alienation effects" without foreseeing the implications for Brecht and the contemporary drama. Curiously enough, Mr. Yuill, in his essay, mentions this "alienation effect" too, but in connection with Feuchtwanger's novels.

This attitude of deliberate non-commitment is of great importance because Feuchtwanger was one of the earliest friends and advisers of Bert Brecht. In fact he helped him with the final shape of *Im Dickicht der Städte* and collaborated in *Das Leben Eduards des Zweiten von England.* Brecht, in turn, assisted his older friend in the revision of *Warren Hastings* in 1925, known in its new version as *Kalkutta, 4. Mai,* while Feuchtwanger helped Brecht during the war to turn his own novel *Simone* into the play *Die Gesichte der Simone Machard.* When *Thomas Wendt,* an early story in dialogues which Feuchtwanger called a "dramatic novel", proved a failure, the writer made, at the time, a special point of stressing his predilection for the "epic theatre", a conception of the drama, also taken up by Brecht at a later date. A further link between the two friends and writers was forged, when Feuchtwanger published his *PEP: J. L. Wetcheek's Amerikanisches Liederbuch,* which contained a number of satirical songs, written in a manner which Brecht favoured at a later stage and which helped him so much towards his international fame. It should prove a rewarding study to examine one day in detail the nature and extent of this literary collaboration. Was Feuchtwanger at one time Brecht's intellectual impresario? To what extent was the older writer guiding the first steps of the younger? How far was Brecht indebted to Feuchtwanger for the incipient stages of his own conception of "alienation effects" in his dramatic writings? A study of Lion Feuchtwanger seems to be fully justified.

Carl Zuckmayer was still a schoolboy when the First World War broke out. As so many of his generation, he welcomed it as an interruption of a *tedium vitae* of dubious value. He joined up as a volunteer, only to return disenchanted and as a rebel against established beliefs. The impact of his war experiences shaped his future intellectual development; in fact, they were never forgotten; only deepened by later exile and further disappointments. During the turbulent years following Germany's defeat, Zuckmayer was caught by the vortex of the intellectual and artistic movements, which became so characteristic of the Twenties. He lived the unsettled existence of a vagrant, sometimes editing a literary review of avant-gardist ideas in the daytime, sometimes singing his own provoking poems in a cabaret in the evening, or peddling cocaine in the murky streets of Berlin by night, for him "the most exciting metropolis of Europe". Out of this hectic life his first drama *Kreuzweg* was born, showing the essence of a belated Expressionism. It was staccato lyric in dialogues, rhapsodic and drunk with pity for a world which had become a lost paradise. The meaning of the drama, however, which was interred after three performances, remained incomprehensible: it was just drowned in a deluge of verbiage. These lines:

"O Brüder! Lasst uns in den Himmel schauen
Und ohne End nach allen Seiten bauen!"[(41)]

were written with the pathos of hymning world-deliverers. The poem *Der Baum* which opens the collection of Zuckmayer's published poems still reflects Expressionist keynotes.

When the poet was awarded the Kleist Prize (1926) for his naturalistic comedy *Der Fröhliche Weinberg,* such a recognition only testified outwardly that Zuckmayer had successfully overcome his Expressionist phase. In fact, he had only succeeded in subduing it, for its potent virus managed again and again to break through works of the future. His later plays, dealing with the problematic nature of political involvement, presume the technique of the Expressionist through the terseness of language and through looseness of dramatic form. As late as 1950 the poet uses allegorical figures—Father Wind, Mother Frost, Brother Mist—in his play *Gesang im Feuerofen.* They serve as a dramatic frame to soften the impact of the crass, realistic action. Throughout his life, Zuckmayer felt a special attraction to the Expressionist motive of Man being redeemed through new religious experience. Later in life he confessed to views in *Pro Domo,* the grass-roots of which are to be found in the impact war and revolution had left on him in 1918: "Wer immer fragt—nur dem Liebenden wird Antwort. Wir wissen, dass es die schöpferische Kraft der Liebe ist, und wir bekennen uns zu ihr. Wir wissen, dass Wahrheit, Schönheit, souveränes Menschentum auf der Erde denkbar und erreichbar sind, und wir bekennen uns dazu. Wir glauben an eine soziale Gerechtigkeit, das heisst: an Befreiung vom Druck und vom Zwang der äusseren Lebensnot—und wir glauben an eine neue, menschen-und geistnahe Religiosität. Wir wehren uns gegen den Untergang, wir kämpfen um unser Dasein, wir wollen leben, aber in einer freien und menschenwürdigen Welt."[(42)]

When Zuckmayer's second play failed on the stage, the poet began to realise that his future as a playwright lay in a different direction. He stood at his own crossroads, and confessed later in an autobiographical sketch :"I had grasped a fundamental fact that a house must be built from the basement up, and not from the roof down; that growth does not begin with the blossoms but at the roots. In poems and prose writings I had instinctively pursued this path, portraying the image of a tree, the life of a moth, or relating the story of a pond with all the creatures that live and breath in it. Now I tried the same in the human realm of drama." This confession to an observant realism made Zuckmayer the most talented successor to Gerhart Hauptmann through the unfailing accuracy of his realistic descriptions. Not without justification, the poet was entitled to the same complaint that E. T. A. Hoffman once uttered: "Ich habe zu viel Wirklichkeit".[(43)] Zuckmayer owed his success to his original strength of being superbly able to portray human beings; to his trust in the positive forces of life; to his compassion for the "little man", untrammelled by the politics of the powers in being. The plays in which he embodied these beliefs, culminated in *Der Hauptmann von Köpenick,* one of the few serious tragi-comedies of German literature. Here the poet sided with the downtrodden little man in the street who defeats his superior orders, which worship the class-structure of the Law and prostrate themselves before the authority-commanding uniform, with his own weapons. The satirical attack against blind obedience to one's superiors revealed Zuckmayer's gift of being able to portray dramatically the problematic nature and dubiety of his own times.

A second group of plays attempted to diagnose political problems of topical interest. He wrote *Des Teufels General,* certainly the most effective drama the poet had so far written. This endeavour to dramatise a chapter from recent German history without following the usual clichés of the day, brought Zuckmayer a tremendous success. Its impact on the uneasy conscience of post-war Germany was deep-cutting. It speaks for the poet's superb flair not to have cast a man of the German "resistance" as the hero of his drama but a General of the Luftwaffe who has sold his soul to the devil—a preoccupation which never loses fascination to the German mind —and who drowns his scruples with the cynical observation: "Wer auf Erden des Teufels General wurde und ihm die Bahn gebombt hat—der muss ihm auch Quartier in der Hölle machen".[44] The perennial conflict of military obedience or resistance against an authoritarian régime fighting for its survival, did not find any satisfactory solution in the play. It is significant that this gripping drama which once belonged to the repertoire of every German theatre was never revived and is forgotten, just as its basic theme has been locked away deep down in the subconscious of every German enjoying the prosperity of an affluent society. Zuckmayer never repeated his success. Perhaps he, after all, did not contribute anything new in theme or treatment to the modern drama.

When *Robert Edler von Musil*—he never used his title of nobility—began to write, the conventional view of life, culminating in the self-complacency of the bourgeoisie at the turn of the century, was already ominously undermined. This progressing fragmentation appeared nowhere so early and was so clearly evident as in the Austro-Hungarian monarchy where Musil was born and educated. In this realm, a "living anachronism", the process of decline of ideas took a synchronous course to the social and political disintegration of a long-established cultural tradition in the very heart of Europe. All that was considered imperishable became brittle, and reality itself most questionable. Robert Musil, "the most important novelist writing in German in this half-century, is one of the least known writers of the age".[45] In spite of the international acclamation of his novel, *Der Mann ohne Eigenschaften,* Musil only enjoys fame with the few and remains unknown to the great reading public, although, or perhaps because, his novel represents the outstanding epic encyclopaedia of our times. The writer was a man of remarkable versatility. He had steadfastly refused all chances open to him through his successful scientific, philosophical and psychological studies, and devoted his life entirely to writing. He died poor and forgotten in Switzerland during the war.

His fame rests upon the lengthy novel, *Der Mann ohn Eigenschaften,* which remained a fragment. Its hero is a man "without qualities" precisely because his talents had to be acquired in the course of the novel. In this respect the work resembles superficially the German type of the *Bildungsroman.* "What distinguishes it from earlier examples is that the hero does not proceed from a given way of life to a different one, either chosen or imposed, but begins with the complete rejection of every existing system and code, and moves on to no predictable solution. It is a Utopian novel in its search for reality so new as to involve the risk of eluding both its hero and his creator."[46] Though Musil is often, and quite erroneously, compared with Proust and Joyce, his narrative does not show the modern obsession with past time or with the stream of consciousness, his diction was sober and factual beside the self-conscious rhetoric or the syntactic escapades of Thomas Mann. Musil was a most painstaking writer who was given to rewriting certain passages more than once. This self-discipline alone separates him from the world of Expressionism. In further contrast to it, Musil used the ambiguous technique of modern scientific studies, that is to say analysis, for reducing *ad absurdum* his chosen time period. The writer worked like a nuclear scientist who demonstrates his results in the field of psychology through the creation of characters unable any longer to burst out through Expressionist spontaneous ignition, simply because his analysis in depth proceeds so thoroughly that no material for combustion was left. Only the world around his figures sometimes seemed to display Expressionist aspects.

In his great novel Musil stated unmistakably: "Der Zusammenbruch der Kultur ist in der Tat das, was der Sommer 1914 eingeleitet hat".[47] This collapse of an epoch is described with passionate sobriety and ironic seriousness. The relatively uneventful action only serves as a point of departure for the unfolding of a tremendous panorama, for a sociological and intellectual *tour de force*, for a critical survey of contemporary culture, for philosophical reflections and essays, for a vast profusion of details and images. The world seems dissolved in incoherence, Man living without any properties, a domineering relativism killing faith and belief. "Es gibt kein Ja, an dem nicht ein Nein hinge."[48] Just as the hero who got rid of his qualities and thus became a man without any properties, is a man potentially with all properties, so, logically enough, the novel comprises every possibility of action and no action—the cancelling out of action in its own futility. Ulrich, the hero, is a man completely disengaged and uncommitted, a man in quest of non-accidental attributes and responsibilities self-chosen—the German counterpart of Gide's "homme disponible".

What then is the meaning of the novel? Is it to be inferred from "die Wendung vom Realismus zur Wahrheit",[49] to a "wesentlichen Leben",[50] to a symbol of genuine, reborn humanity which, beyond the shards of conventional morality, aims at recovering the lost meaning of life? If this is the case, Musil seemed to believe in a positive result of the "transvaluation of all values", in a *vita activa.*

Or does the novelist write a last, an anarchic finale about the frightening error of a time which, with the first shots of the war, falls into the abyss? Some remarks of Musil, set down in his *Nachgelassene Fragmente*, might shed some light on the ultimate intentions of this unfinished novel. Musil speaks of a generation "deren letzte Zuflucht die Sexualität und der Krieg ist",[51] and added: "Ulrich und Agathe sind eigentlich ein Versuch des Anarchismus in der Liebe, der selbst negativ endet. Das ist die tiefe Beziehung der Liebesgeschichte zum Krieg".[52] In other words, Ulrich detected the violence underneath it all which ultimately must condition the pessimistic conception of a *vita negativa*. "The greatest works of art are expeditions into unexplored territory, and in trying to reach the ultimate they may arrive only at a last possibility, their absolute intention summed up by Scott's words from the Antarctic: 'Pretence is useless'.[53] There is no longer a whole man confronting a whole world, but a human something floating about in a universal culture-medium. This is in line with Musil's contention that standardisation and mechanisation are systematically separating man from experience, robbing him of basic qualities, and producing intellectual flotsam. The terseness of Musil's superb handling of the art of language which has been called an interlocking of mathematics and mysticism achieved a breath-taking pith, where finally every sentence embraced the possibility of being reversed in its meaning. Surely, such ironic possibilities and such linguistic "alienation effects" are hardly conducive evidence that the writer discovered a new God or a new man through his amazing gift of handling the transvaluation of all values? His great novel is an epigrammatic and philosophic ideal novel which minutely dissects the foibles and habits of Western man with such incandescent wit and biting logic that it carves for itself an important place among the literary works of distinction of our times.

The collapse of the Third Reich resulted in complete numbness and apathy. Most Germans felt glad to have escaped by the skin of their teeth. Demobilised soldiers, refugees, and millions of other homeless people returned; some of them began to write what is known as "Trümmerliteratur". One of them, Heinrich Böll, defended this mood of writing: "Those people, about whom we wrote, lived amidst the rubble. They returned from the war.... We also wrote about the war, about home-coming and about what we had experienced during the war, and about what we had found at our return: about ruins and rubble". The Germany of 1918 knew a "Heimkehrerliteratur" but no "Trümmerliteratur", because the ravages of war had left her almost intact. The repatriated soldier had also experienced Hell but was, at that time, determined to create a sensible world out of the chaos of war. Those who had survived the Second World War hardly ever found a home which had remained unscathed. They were face to face with utter ruin. They neither possessed hope nor confidence to rebuild a new life. The "Trümmerliteratur" showed every sign of a despairing nihilism. It reflected the cry of distress of a generation which felt cheated out of its right to live. While the Expressionists endeavoured to overcome the trauma of the battlefield through the postulates of their idealist visions, the "Trümmerliteratur" was swamped by a flood of gruesomeness and "Lebensangst". Not without deeper justification Franz Kafka became a poet of international fame after 1945.

A significant writer of this generation reviving an Expressionist style, was *Wolfgang Borchert.* His play *Draussen vor der Tür* proved to be a moving document of the psychosis of an entire generation. Its effect was remarkable, because it influenced the subject-matter and the style of a number of writers who tried to imitate them. Even if *Draussen vor der Tür* has today lost its topicality, it remains a literary testimony of importance because it voiced the burning wrath of an angry young man against a guilty generation, which was responsible for his distress. Dr. Salmon, in a thoughtful introduction to the play, described it as "a study in man's inability to communicate".(54) Reading Borchert's drama, "das kein Theater spielen und kein Publikum sehen will", one can hardly help but compare it with the first-fruits of Toller, Unruh and Hasenclever. They, too, were much concerned with the guilt and responsibility of their elders. However, they were able to communicate. They met with the enthusiastic response of their own generation, they addressed themselves to all peace lovers on earth and to all men of good will, who understood and supported their endeavours to point a way out of chaos and destruction. The Expressionists were certainly not paralysed by the impotence of a hopeless nihilism.

Dr. Salmon admits that Borchert's hero finds himself, *vis-à-vis de rien,* in a nihilist situation. However, he senses ironical undertones, because the hero of the play seems to be confident that, somehow, there will be a future of orderliness and reconstruction. Dr. Salmon's arguments do not sound very convincing, for he does not base them on the play but on a passage from a later work of the writer, *Das ist unser Werk,* which, in turn, sounds hollow and trite to me. After all, it is the inadequacy of Borchert's hero, which makes it impossible for him to master the complications of the post-war situation. Others have been able to do so, e.g. all who manipulated the black market successfully. The "economic miracle" of Germany's recovery, which made itself felt shortly after the writer's death, contradicts the whole tenor of Borchert's assertion, when he proclaims in the above-mentioned passage: "We want to love this Germany as all Christians their Christ: for his sorrow's sake". Borchert himself must have felt that his awareness of nihilism was identical with a confession of utter hopelessness. For in the preface to the radio version of *Draussen vor der Tür* he wrote: "Eine Injektion Nihilismus bewirkt oft, dass man aus lauter Angst wieder Mut zum Leben bekommt".(55) Dr. Salmon sees in this statement an attempt by Borchert to purge himself from nihilism and to grope for a more affirmative approach to life. Again I beg to differ. As seen against the political background of the immediate post-war situation of Germany, Borchert's assertion sounds rather sententious.

I also find it difficult to agree with Dr. Salmon's view about the problem of guilt and responsibility, which is raised in the play, was the central argument in the Nuremberg trials and even today has lost nothing of its topicality. Dr. Salmon writes: "Above all, the whole nation had suffered a traumatic shock from the realisation that the régime for which the Germans had sacrificed their blood and well-being was corrupt and evil. Millions of Germans haunted by guilt, like that of Beckmann for the loss of the eleven men from his 'reconnaissance patrol' ". There exist other opinions, fortified by the documentary evidence of History, that too many Germans gladly sacrificed their blood and well-being to exterminate millions of innocent people of various nations and creeds. Only a small minority really felt genuine guilt and shouldered responsibility for the irredeemable past after 1945, while the majority's shock simply resulted from the painful realisation that the war was lost, the country destroyed, and the overlordship of the "master race" ended. It seems questionable to me whether anything is gained by an interpretation of Borchert's play beyond its purely literary merits.

The play is interesting enough for the reappearance of Expressionist technique and style. Once more we encounter "stages", when the hero wanders between the world of stark reality and between an existence of a dreamlike surrealism. ("Und da erlebt er einen ganz tollen Film.")(56) God, "in whom nobody believes", and Death, in the disguise of an undertaker or of a road-sweeper, bestride the stage. There is the quixotic and schizophrenic figure of the Other Man, a "Doppelgänger" and thus a strange confrontation of the hero with himself, who hovers on the threshold between the conscious and the subconscious. There is finally the dream of Death as a xylophone player, a nightmare which seems to come straight out of Toller's *Die Wandlung*. These scenes born out of the awareness of a haunted imagination seem to be dramatically stronger than the realistic sequences which often lack convincing vitality and their dialogue persuasive power. Above all, there is no hope, no way out. God, admittedly, is not quite dead but reduced to the shape of a lachrymose and doddering old man, too hopelessly compromised to be of any help to a "betrayed generation". Borchert's fame rests on his play though his short stories certainly deserve closer acquaintance. When *Draussen vor der Tür* was revived in Germany in 1957 in memory of the tenth anniversary of the writer's death, it was acclaimed once more as the only play of literary value, written in post-war Germany. "Its justification lies in its subjectivity" commented Heinrich Böll on this occasion. One wonders whether this dictum will still be valid in 1967.

While his Swiss compatriot Dürrenmatt exerts himself to express the gnawing uneasiness of our conscience through daring and often fantastic situations and visions, *Max Frisch* is concerned with the complexity of the human character which must be ultimately held responsible for this uneasiness. A mathematician and architect by training, he pays much attention to balance and form when describing his experiences in our times. His central theme is the questionable or even lost identity of the individual and his self. Frisch enjoys the full support of readers who acutely feel uneasy when considering the dubiety of life in the atomic age, who are inclined to resignation and have grown tired of moral protests. On the other hand, Frisch has met with the opposition of those who still believe they are firmly protected by strong convictions. "The man who has a conviction", says the writer, "is able to cope with everything. Convictions proffer the best safeguard against being drowned in truth and reality". What caused the complete failure of his hitherto most successful play *Andorra* in New York, apart from bad translation and production, was the optimistic belief of an enlightened world in the powers of plain common sense. What Europeans have experienced in human suffering and degradation has never touched the core of the white Americans. The mass seduction of a whole community, and of a whole nation, was considered impossible in the country of maximal consumer seduction.

Stiller and *Faber*, the leading characters in his two best novels, are in search of their own real selves. This quest is a simple attack on the prevailing lethargy and on a resigned attitude to everything which might have nihilistic implications. Frisch, the bringer of new enlightenment, will yet preserve an element of romanticism, Frisch, the dispenser of irony, will always point a clear moral, and Frisch, the rationalist without illusions, will yet retain some strands of vivid imagination. In other words, Frisch undertakes to prove that the true self of a man is not necessarily identical with the image, which history or his fellow-men have given him. In his witty parody *Don Juan oder die Liebe zur Geometrie* Don Giovanni tilts against his reputation of being the eternal lady-killer, because he wants to follow his real passion, the pursuit of mathematics. Because of his real love, he devalues all existing values, and is even prepared to end his life as a "bon bourgeois" with wife and child.

This theme of the true identity behind an artificial mask, the destruction of false conventions, and the freeing of the self from deeply ingrained prejudices, is developed in *Biedermann und die Brandstifter* and in *Andorra*. The former play is a "Morality without a Moral" which shows the influence of Bert Brecht. Who are the wanton fire-raisers : the incendiaries or the bourgeois Everyman who would love to appease the world? The villains serve obviously as foils to the real question of whether a peace-loving good man "in his moral corruption and uncertainty of conviction, can defend himself at all, and indeed whether, being no better than the avowed criminals, he even deserves to be saved".[57] In the end Biedermann confesses what he does not mean and does what he would avoid doing because he is afraid of the truth. The truth, however, is the inability of our world to come to its senses. In *Andorra* Frisch is concerned with pointing the moral that nobody in our present world is really free to use "his" qualities but that certain anonymous impulses exist whose dynamic forces compel him to act at a given moment, irrespective of whether this was his intention or not. In *Andorra* the ostensible innocence of a community is treated with biting irony in the beginning when a house is whitewashed. It becomes the writer's intention to leach the veneer and to reveal the ground-colours. Such an undertaking demands victims. The innocent falls a prey to the delusion, whether of himself or of the society he lives in, for it is always evil delusion which prevents the identification of man with his self and destroys his fundamental goodness and love instinct. Evil is not satisfied with inactivity. It must attack, it must get hold of man, it must feed on human flesh. Even awareness of prevailing evil will no longer stop or change the course of history. Frisch's technique as a writer is the analytical method. His novels and plays usually have a long history to look back upon, which can be traced in his diaries and occasional writings. But Frisch, like Dürrenmatt, is also an inveterate rewriter who is never satisfied with the final result. Once a theme has got hold of him, it proves expandable in many ways. He published reflections on his *Don Juan* play and a postscript to *Biedermann*. It is this variability of approach which is fascinating to the reader and allows the author so many interpretations of his central theme.

Attention has been drawn to the resemblance of Frisch's main characters to the traditional type of the romantic hero in German literature who has lost his identity, e.g. Kleist's *Amphitryon* and Chamisso's *Peter Schlemihl.* The critic has even cited Dr. *Faust,* the archetype of a man who has lost his identity.[58] This analogy appears rather far-fetched, for Frisch's novels and plays are set in a world which has largely become schizophrenic and has thus forced its inhabitants to adapt themselves to such an unusual situation. Amphitryon, Peter Schlemihl and Faust, moreover, consciously part with their selves for material lucre, while Stiller and Graf Oederland, Biedermann and Andri are desperately engaged in distilling their true selves out of the welter of present-day chaos. On their brows is written : Thou shalt not make to thyself any graven image.

The principal problem of the dramatic and narrative work of the two Swiss writers Max Frisch and *Friedrich Dürrenmatt* is the question of how man can hold his own under the pressure of power and guilt of a disintegrating world, and what defensive mechanism is left to him for survival. While Frisch seems rather to continue in the spirit of Georg Kaiser, Dürrenmatt's approach points to the "moralising" tradition of Frank Wedekind. Both writers combine the technique of a probing psycho-analyst with the often exhibitionist effects of grotesque irony and travesty to secure that detachment so necessary for dealing with contemporary problems. Both confirm the thought-provoking fact that a sheltered life in a neutral country does not absolve contemporary man from responsibility but seems rather to increase his uneasiness than to banish it in times of transition like ours. If Europe's predicament is the result of man's evasion of facing squarely his individual responsibility, it certainly transcends all geographical frontiers.

Dürrenmatt has been keenly aware of this uneasiness amidst the soporific smugness of Swiss respectability. To shock his compatriots out of their complacent indolence Dürrenmatt resorted to drastic and acid means to stir up their conscience. Not without deeper significance the playwright is called an "uncomfortable" author by his critics. One recalls Schiller's lines from the Prologue to "Wallenstein" :

> "The outline of the man is blurr'd and dimm'd
> In History's page, by party love and hate."

Therefore one of his Swiss countrymen could pose the question : "Müssen wir uns aber nicht ernsthaft fragen, ob die kritische Zurückhaltung oder gar erbarmungslose Ablehnung wirklich nur auf Missverständnisse beruhe?"[59] Dürrenmatt is on rather bad terms with his critics because he offers them too many facets of his personality without providing the key to it: "I have resigned myself a long time ago to being misunderstood". But the difficulty of evaluating Dürrenmatt's position is inherent in his own chameleon-like conception of his work, for he considers "experiment the only permissible function of the modern playwright and has always been bent on taking his theories to an extreme".[60] Hence his startling habit of rewriting and re-editing his plays apparently with little regard to previous structure or dialogue. Hence, too, the possibility of diametrically opposed approaches to his work.

Dürrenmatt's point of departure was Gottfried Benn's idea of the fragmentation of culture and the isolation of the individual. In an introduction to a comedy, hitherto unpublished, he stated as far back as 1943: "... state, religion, and art are isolated, without interrelation with each other: abstract, inundated by technology, the symbol of the unsubstantial"; therefore his demand for the full reinstatement of the word, because he considers it the flesh of the intellect, the link between its overt manifestations. "Otherwise we will murder each other, for, in this case, everything will turn inward and will wreak destruction." In the urgency of this conviction lies perhaps the explanation why Dürrenmatt prefers an apocalyptic theme in so many of his works. Does it then come as a surprise that his dialogue, which usually takes the form of a conversation, has the effect of an interrogation? But who is the hero, "the Gulliver among the giants", daring to fight against the disintegration of this world? "The world, for me, stands as something monstrous, an enigma of calamity that has to be accepted but to which there must be no surrender." Professor Waidson stresses the importance of the "passive hero, who embodies love and humility, often linked with ridiculousness". Others call him a "negative hero" who will just not acknowledge any further disintegration through sheer refusal to come to terms with the present state of affairs. A German critic mentions "Theaterstücke ohne Helden".[61] But perhaps the executioner or the creature crying out for him is the hero? For it is Dürrenmatt's conviction that man possesses no longer his "own" death, as Rilke once proclaimed, but that external, impersonal forces terminate his empty existence.

To bring home his shock effects, the playwright uses grotesque and burlesque tricks, often bordering on the melodramatic. For in his lecture on *Theaterprobleme* ("Problems of the Theatre") Dürrenmatt has raised considerable doubts whether our contemporary world can be presented at all on the stage: "If art reaches men at all, it reaches only the victims, certainly no longer those in power. The secretaries of Kreon will dispose of Antigone's case. The state has lost its accustomed shape, and as physics is only just able to explain the world in mathematical formulae, this world can only be comprehended in statistics. Power only achieves real, visible form when it erupts in the atomic bomb. . . . One cannot explain the atomic bomb any longer, since one can produce it. In the face of it every art as a creation of man must simply break down, because the bomb too is a creation of man. Two mirrors which are reflected in each other, remain blank". One begins to sense a considerable degree of pessimism and scepticism behind the frivolous mask of mocking and challenging insouciance.

In his "Schiller Oration" in Mannheim (1959) Dürrenmatt already drew some practical conclusions from his theoretical speculations about the nature of the modern stage: "Brecht's demand to change the human conditions must be correlated with Schiller's moral demands. The writer cannot sell himself to politics. He belongs to mankind. Therefore Schiller and Brecht change from being judges who pronounce judgment on us, into our conscience which will now never leave us in peace". In trying to apply these very individualist maxims to his later plays through the medium of "criminal comedies" Dürrenmatt came up against sharp criticism, charging him with "making sport of the most serious problems of our days". But, already in 1955, he had stated: "In the muddle of our century, in this clean-out of the white race, neither the guilty nor the responsible persons exist any longer. This is nobody's fault and it was nobody's intention. . . . Only the comedy can really get at us. Our world has just as much resulted in the grotesque as in the atom bomb".

Wedekind and Sternheim, Brecht and Thornton Wilder may have stood sponsors to Dürrenmatt's beginnings. His present work shows an independence of mind, a wealth of imagination, a degree of purposefulness, which fully justify the sobriquet: the Helvetian Aristophanes. Perhaps it is the acid of Aristophanic satire which is most potent today in neutralising the corroding effects of the virulent nihilism, which Nietzsche applied to unmask the mendacity of our Western society. It throws into sharp relief the human dilemma of our time. It warns us like a soothsayer, but suggests still no reliable course to our salvation.

NOTES AND TRANSLATIONS

1. I search for a distant, original point of departure, where I sense some sort of formula for man, animal, plant, earth, fire, water, air and all revolving forces simultaneously. The concept of our earth gives way to the cosmic idea. Love is remote and religious.

2. More and more I begin to see behind, or better, through all things, that is to say, a "something behind", which things rather hide by their illusions, indeed mostly hide in a cunning way by pretending to hide something quite different which they hide in fact from man. From a purely physical viewpoint this is an old story: we know today what warmth, sound and gravity are . . . at least we have a second interpretation, the scientific one. However, I am convinced, there is still another one behind it and many others behind this one.

3. Rays of light cross and seek each other. (Kokoschka's stage direction.)

4. The human beings speak as if they sing . . . there is no psychology left. The proximity of the opera is perceptible. (P. Fechter: *Geschichte der deutschen Literatur.* Vol. II, p. 145, Mohn Verlag, 1960.)

5. Otto Weininger (1880–1903), author of *Geschlecht und Charakter,* committed suicide.

6. They achieve an effect as if souls were speaking which might dissolve any moment. But they also dissolve in picture visions which symbolise the poet's intended meaning still more intensively. viz. Fechter, p. 146.

7. Soergel-Hohoff: *Dichter und Dichtung der Zeit,* Vol. II, p. 115. Bagel Verlag, 1963.

8. The name of the Muse of such an orgy of rutting can only be Vagina. For what else is the soul of erotomaniacs but unrestrained sexus? Kokoschka, with masochistic lust, sees the swine in every man and in every woman. Bernhard Diebold in *Anarchie im Drama,* p. 319, Frankfurter Verlags Anstalt, 1921.

9. Masterfully the every-day mask of man has been torn away to reveal lechery, otherwise veiled with conventional mimicry . . . the portraitist may be satisfied with the persevering moment of a human face. The play however implies movement. viz. Diebold, p. 320.

10. Jane Stockwood in *Queen,* October 1962.

11. viz. *Frankfurter Allgemeine Zeitung,* October 1, 1962.

12. Faith has vanished, and the souls shiver. Only courage remains to state without prevarication what is—without all literature, viz. Fechter, p. 147.

13. To shoulder a Utopian existence. E. Barlach: Ein selbsterzähltes Leben, 1928.

14. The perplexing oneness of Inside and Outside. *Ibid.*

15. Barlach's hereditary and intellectual aptitude was of a kind which was essentially Low German, Germanic and "Nordic", however not of the radiant-triumphant sort, but troll-like, elfin and eldritch—sultry and sensuous, introspective and wrapt up . . . a North German counterpart of the victims of Bohemian nightmares from Kubin to Kafka. viz. Soergel-Hohoff, p. 359.

16. He did not refer to any divine mission like Rilke. He struggled for the reproduction of his visions with sealed lips. He was on God's trail; he did not perceive him in any seductively beautiful figure but as a being which made his hair stand on end. Walter Muschg: *Tragische Literaturgeschichte,* p. 156, Francke Verlag, Berne, 1957.

17. It is only odd that Man will not learn that God is his father.

18. ... the poor cousin, a kind of unsuccessful side-line of Heaven. viz. Muschg, p. 156.

19. The garment becomes a symbol for Man being wedged in the bottleneck of life. viz. Friedmann-Mann: *Expressionismus,* Rothe Verlag, 1956. pp. 304ff.

20. How splendid it is to have no shape any longer, and only fervour and abyss in God—already I am sinking toward Him—He has become I and I Him—He with my lowness, I with His majesty—a singular One. viz. Friedmann-Mann, p. 304.

21. One sees their pikes directed against Henry from all sides. He stands before them as if surrounded by radiant splendour. (Barlach's stage direction.)

22. I have no God, but God has me.

23. Ernst Toller: *Seven Plays,* John Lane, London 1935. pp. ix–x.

24. As the Monk of Heisterbach came into a changed world after a long sleep: so a rebellious man of conscience, deprived of half a dozen of his young years by powers of lesser value, returns here from prison. This dark-eyed Toller is like a gentle Apostle; filled with his mission: to help; to denounce, to encourage. Alfred Kerr: *Die Welt im Drama,* Kiepenheuer & Witsch, Köln, 1954, p. 162.

25. viz. Toller: *Seven Plays,* p. 98.

26. *Ibid.* p. 105.

27. *Ibid.* p. 105.

28. *Ibid.* p. 54.

29. With Man's strides God's grace and change arise
from everybody's hearts and doors.
Smiles, breathing and strides
are more than the course of the light, of the wind and of the stars—
World begins with Man.
Drown in the smile, in the breathing, in the stride of the beloved!
Cry, kneel down and sink!

30. Werfel is hardly an Expressionist in his poetry. For neither the inner landscape nor the vision or gesture nor the outcry are significant for his verse but the now mourning, now hymnal confession of a pure and hunted soul, penitent in misdeed and longing for God, viz. J. Klein: *Geschichte der Deutschen Lyrik,* p. 824, Steiner Verlag, 1957.

30a. viz. W. Greuzmann: *Dichtung und Glaube,* Bonn, 1952.

31. Hardly anybody in modern times has ever interpreted the blessing and the sacred curse of the Chosen more compassionately and described it with more mastery, indeed with more delicacy, than Werfel in this novel.

32. viz. *The Times Literary Supplement,* August 3, 1962.

33. Charlatan—that is not a bad word, there are worse ones.

34. I do not look beyond myself, I deny myself this relief, I work, I seek values, I sketch morphology, I express myself.

35. viz. Walter Muschg. *Ibid.* p. 276.

36. I consider prayer and humility arrogant and presumptuous. It

presupposes that I am something after all, but just this I doubt. There is only a something which passes through me.

37. viz. Muschg. *Ibid.* p. 276.

38. viz. H. F. Garten: *Modern German Drama*, Methuen, 1959, p. 138.

39. The recrudescence of barbarism in Germany and its temporary victory over reason.

40. viz. Jethro Bithell: *Germany*, Methuen, 1955, p. 343.

41. O, Brethren! Let us look up to heaven
and build in all directions without end!

42. Whosoever asks—answer will only be to him who is capable of love. We know that it is the creative force of Love, and we confess to it. We know that truth, beauty, sovereign humanity on earth are conceivable and obtainable, and we confess to them. We believe in social justice, that is to say: in liberation from the pressure and the compulsion of material distress—and we believe in a new religiousness akin to Man and his spirit. We resist the destruction of the world, we fight for our existence, we want to live, but in a free world worthy of human beings.

43. I possess too much reality.

44. Who became the devil's general on earth and has bombed a clear path for him—he's got to give him quarters in hell, as well.

45. viz. *The Times Literary Supplement*, October 28, 1949.

46. *Ibid.* September 23, 1960.

47. The débâcle of Culture is indeed what the summer of 1914 initiated.

48. There is no "yea" to which a "nay" does not cling.

49. The turn from realism to truth.

50. A life which matters.

51. . . . whose last resort is sexuality and war.

52. Ulrich and Agathe are really attempting of anarchism in love which ends negatively even there. This is the deep relation of the love affair to war.

53. viz. *The Times Literary Supplement*, October 28, 1949.

54. viz. P. B. Salmon, M.A., Ph.D., in *Draussen vor der Tür,* Harrap 1963.

55. An injection of nihilism often effects that one gets courage for a new life out of sheer dread. viz. *Ibid.* p. 39.

56. And then he experiences quite a crazy film.

57. viz. *The Times Literary Supplement*, January 11, 1963.

58. viz. Soergel-Hohoff, *Ibid.* p. 850.

59. Must we not ask ourselves seriously whether the critical reticence or even the merciless rejection does not really rest on misunderstanding? Willy Jäggi in *Der Unbequeme Dürrenmatt,* Basilius Presse, Basle, 1962.

60. viz. *The Times Literary Supplement*, January 11, 1963.

61. Plays without heroes. viz. Soergel-Hohoff, *Ibid.*

Oskar Kokoschka

Oskar Kokoschka

by W. I. LUCAS

Oskar Kokoschka was born on March 1, 1886, in Pöchlarn on the Danube, the son of a goldsmith of Bohemian-Czech origin and a mother from Styria. From 1904 he attended the Vienna School of Arts and Crafts where he came under the influence of Gustav Klimt, the leading Viennese painter at that time, and Sigmund Freud. His paintings were first introduced to the general public at the *Kunstschau* exhibition of 1908. He travelled to Switzerland for the first time in 1909. The years 1910–14 were spent partly in Berlin and partly in Vienna. He contributed most of the illustrations to Herwarth Walden's periodical *Der Sturm*, the mouthpiece of the German Expressionist movement. When war broke out in 1914 he joined the regiment of Dragoons "because (he said) of the fine uniform with the shiny helmet" and was seriously wounded in 1916 on the Eastern front. As soon as he was well enough he went to live in a suburb of Dresden and in 1920 was appointed Professor at the Dresden Academy. He left suddenly without terminating his appointment in order to see Europe—his travels covered France, England, Scotland, Spain, Portugal, Switzerland, Italy, North Africa and the Near East and resulted in his magnificent landscapes and townscapes. In 1934 he went to live in Prague where he met Olda, later to become his partner and wife. He fled from the Nazis in 1938 and spent the war years in England. After the war he returned to Austria and started his summer school of art in Salzburg. Later he made his home in Villeneuve, Switzerland.

THE exhibition of Oskar Kokoschka's works organised by the Arts Council and held at the Tate Gallery in London in the autumn of 1962 made the British aware for the first time of the remarkable range and quality of this artist. It was perhaps insularity that had led to his neglect in this country—the country of his adoption after Hitler and his Nazis had overrun central Europe. In his native Austria and to a lesser extent in Germany his reception was very different : in the years before the First World War he had been subjected to antagonism from art critics, hostility from the kind of society that visits art exhibitions and theatres, and he was at one time even forbidden to teach in any public school in Austria. The Nazis included works of his in the infamous exhibition "Degenerate Art" of 1937 and removed his works from public and private collections whenever they could; his name was on a list of people to be killed if he had been caught when the Nazis entered Prague in 1938. It is true that after the First World War a measure of recognition came to him not only in art circles but in official circles too, so much so that in Dresden he was appointed a teacher at the Art Academy with the title of Professor.

Kokoschka's earliest poem, *Die träumenden Knaben*, was written in Vienna in 1907, and published the following year by the Wiener Werkstätte, the centre of arts and crafts in Vienna in those days. He had been commissioned to write and illustrate a book for children; but Kokoschka produced, in fact, something entirely original and anything but suitable for children. The work consisted of eight or nine lithographs in colour and two illustrations in black and white; the text was printed in the narrow margin left by the illustrations. It was "inspired by a young woman" who "wore a red frock" and came to see the young man in his studio, where "she slept under a veil". Her name was Lilith and she was an art student like himself.[1] The poem is dedicated to Gustav Klimt who was considered at that time to be the leading painter in Vienna. Kokoschka, as this dedication indicates, came under the influence of this artist without becoming a slavish follower. Whilst the work was not received with the hostility that his later works aroused, it was certainly not understood or appreciated at the time of its publication. The art critic of *Deutsche Kunst und Dekoration*[2] wrote: "Kokoschka reminds me of Arthur Rimbaud, who at the age of seventeen wrote puzzling verses. . . . So I thought of Rimbaud, his drunken, unrestrained verses, which have a certain affinity with the colourful drunkenness of Kokoschka's puberty legends." All Kokoschka's works start with a very personal experience that is then transformed by his art into a symbolic presentation of a more general or universal human experience of life. *Die träumenden Knaben* seems almost to symbolise this characteristic of his work by the use of the plural in the title whereas in the poem itself only the first person singular occurs. The poem almost defies close analysis: it is the immature work of a young man who, both in the drawings and in the text, is still uncertain of himself, but in an experimental and, for the period, original manner pours out his soul in a kind of narrative poem of three or four hundred lines. The text can best be described as a remarkably early example of the "stream of consciousness" method of allowing the mind to speak from inside. What we are given here are dreams that pass through the mind of an adolescent during the phase of puberty, lurid visions that come with the awakening sexual urges and the discovery of the physical side of male and female. The reader is presented with all the luxurious, sensuous and sensual imagery, full of vivid colours, that the imagination of the painter can conjure up in words. The world of the subconscious wells up finding expression, not in terms of objective reality, but in the incoherent and illogical flow of the inner life let loose. Objectively this world seems mad—"colourful madness"—it is however the characteristic flow of subjective life at a particular stage in the artist's development towards manhood: impressions, sensations, presentiments and visions that intermingle in a world of reverie. The obsession with sex is thus the theme of this early work. The sultry, exotic atmosphere of this poem has its origins no doubt in the poetry of the German romantics:

rot fischlein / fischlein rot /
stech dich mit dem drei-
schneidigen messer tot
reiß dich mit meinen fingern
entzwei /
daß dem stummen kreisen
ein ende sei /

rot fischlein / fischlein rot /
mein messerlein ist rot /
meine fingerlein sind rot/
in der schale sinkt ein
fischlein tot /(3)

And as in the romantic Märchen the normal laws of time and space do not apply. Modern, however, is the handling of language as if to reinforce the novelty of attempting to convey so dramatically this interior life: as the illustration above shows, capitals are dispensed with, punctuation is replaced by strokes to indicate phrasing, the short rhythmic lines vary in length, the endings of words are frequently transferred to the next line, and the rhyming, where it occurs, is often given to words lacking emphasis. Immature though it may be, there is nevertheless a magic about these lines that stems from youthful exuberance and from a mind that is filled with an astonishing abundance of colourful imagery:

in mir träumt es und meine
träume sind wie der norden /
wo schneeberge uralte märchen verbergen / durch mein
gehirn gehen meine ge-
danken und machen mich
wachsen / wie die steine
wachsen / niemand weiß davon und begreift /(4)

In the year 1907 Kokoschka wrote two plays that created a sensation with the theatre-going public of Vienna when they were produced on the stage. Both—*Hoffnung der Frauen* and *Sphinx und Strohmann*—are only a few hundred lines in length and might be thought of as sketches for larger works rather than complete works in themselves. They would probably escape attention altogether if it were not for their novelty: they have been described as the first Expressionist dramas[5] and as such they point forward to the new type of drama which is associated with the names of Sorge, Hasenclever, and others. (Kokoschka knew the dramatist Hasenclever well and depicts him in several of his paintings; he formed one of the company with whom Kokoschka lived in Dresden during and after the First World War.) The two plays were probably performed for the first time at an open-air theatre in July 1908. Kokoschka relates in his essay *Vom Erleben* how pandemonium broke out during the first performance of *Hoffnung der Frauen* between friends who defended him and spectators who were shocked and hostile, how the fight with sticks and umbrellas almost turned into a tragedy when Bosnian soldiers who, watching from the vantage-point of their barracks overlooking the open-air theatre, misunderstood the quarrel and intervened with real weapons: "der Literaturstreit [wäre] bald in einen blutigen Krieg ausgeartet, wenn nicht Adolf Loos mit einem Häuflein seiner Getreuen mich vor dem Erschlagenwerden gerettet hätte."[6] According to this same account it was the effect of this play that led Kokoschka to be known as the "Bürgerschreck"—the terror of the citizens. The scandal spread the next day to the press and Kokoschka came into disrepute not only with the public of Vienna but with the Austrian authorities too. The plays were, of course, too novel to be understood by a public that was accustomed to its traditional culture. They were taken for "pure farce" and the citizens of Vienna felt "outraged".[7]

The first play, originally entitled *Hoffnung der Frauen,* was written in 1907—written, according to Edith Hoffman (p. 54), on "little tickets handed out to a cast of pupils of a dramatic school". It was first published in 1910 in the periodical *Der Sturm* with the fuller title *Mörder Hoffnung der Frauen* and with four illustrations by the author: a later edition, 1921, was published set to music by the composer Hindemith. This short one-act play is set quite simply in antiquity —"im Altertum"—no further indication of the period is provided. The scene is a tower with a large iron gate and takes place under a night sky. There are two main characters: the man, white in the face, is dressed in blue armour, has a bandage covering a wound in the forehead; the woman is tall, yellow-haired, and wears red clothes. Warriors carrying torches and maidens are part of the background and act as a chorus. These two main characters irresistibly experience the elemental attraction and repulsion, the love-hate complex, of the sexes. After their first encounter the man, with brutal and ruthless cruelty, orders his men to take the woman and burn his sign into her naked flesh with a hot iron. The order is immediately executed. The woman shrieks with pain but reacts by inflicting a wound upon the man with a knife, and puts him in a cage, half dead. However the woman loves the man she has wounded, but as she lies dying, he recovers and is victorious in the end—she succumbs to the wild animal ("das wilde Tier") she tried to tame:

Frau: *immer heftiger, aufschreiend*
Ich will dich nicht leben lassen. Du!
Du schwächst mich—
Ich töte dich—du fesselst mich!
Dich fing ich ein—und du hältst mich!
Laß los von mir—Umklammerst mich—wie mit eisernen Ketten—erdrosselt—los—Hilfe!
Ich verlor den Schlüssel—der dich festhielt[8]

It is significant that, although the play was written in 1907, it was not published until 1910, a year that is frequently given as the point of departure for Expressionism in German literature. It was in that year that Herwarth Walden, with Kokoschka's help, published the first number of his periodical *Der Sturm* with the aim (as the title suggests) of stirring up controversy in the arts and in literature. It was intended to be a radical and progressive periodical and it quickly became the mouthpiece for those writers and artists who were later to be known as Expressionists. Kokoschka's drama was published in number twenty of July 14 with one of the drawings illustrating the drama on the front page of the periodical. This secured a wide circulation for Kokoschka's literary effort and assisted Walden in his urge to propagate a new approach to literature and art. That Kokoschka's play was an example of a new trend in German literature justified its inclusion in the periodical quite independently of his friendly relations with the editor.

The work possesses several characteristics of a typical Expressionist drama. The characters, for example, have no names: they are referred to as "Mann", "Frau", "Krieger", "Mädchen", so that the emphasis is thrown on "man", in general, rather than on individuals distinguished by their dress, gestures or speech peculiarities or their social status. The author no doubt had in mind the example set only a few years before by Strindberg in his *Road to Damascus* (1898–1904) and may well have helped to introduce the practice to Barlach (e.g. *Der tote Tag,* 1912) and Sorge (*Der Bettler,* 1912). The rejection of the prevailing realism in drama is equally seen in the setting : the author seems almost to go out of his way to destroy any attempt that might be made to create the illusion of a familiar world on the stage by giving no more than vague and imprecise details of a setting as remote from the contemporary scene as possible. Whatever may be the defects of this first experiment in dramatic presentation Kokoschka aimed at something deeper than the surface reality of middle-class drama with its petty virtues and vices—he was concerned to present a depth of primitive human experience stripped of convention, class distinction, religious differences or anything else that superficially distinguished one human being from another. To this extent Edith Hoffman is right when she asserts that this work contains "elements of amazing originality, wisdom and greatness",(9) but it needs also to be emphasised that these are *elements* only and that the drama falls far short in achievement. Soergel-Hohoff(10) points out that the syntax reveals that Kokoschka had read Sophocles and Pindar in the original and that his language shows some familiarity with Hölderlin's translations. More significant for the developments to come is the disjointed language, unfinished sentences, and exclamations in place of carefully articulated conversation. But the drama shows the break with tradition most fully in the sheer naked brutality and violence of the passionate outburst between the man and the woman. This must have been a shock to the typical middle-class playgoer of the time and is evidence of the revolutionary frame of mind of the younger generation just before the outbreak of the First World War.

The other drama Kokoschka wrote in 1907, *Sphinx und Strohmann,* appears to have been the result of a bet made with drama students that he could write a play and "the text was mostly composed during rehearsals".(11) It was performed the same year on the stage of the Arts and Crafts School but not published until 1913 in a volume with the title *Dramen und Bilder.* It is a short, fragmentary work that Kokoschka described as a "Curiosum", and must have struck the Viennese audience at the time of its first performance as little more than a crude and grotesque farce like the earlier play. The action, which is very slight, takes place between four characters belonging to a romantic fairy-world of the author's imagination : Herr Firdusi, the man of straw carrying a pig's bladder—possibly a caricature of Kokoschka himself—has been deserted by his wife, Anima : "Ich hatte ein Weib, ich machte einen Gott aus ihr, da verließ sie mein Bett . . . und verschwand mit einem gesunden Muskelmann. Ich habe eine menschliche Seele erschaffen, da verschwand ihr der Boden unter den Beinen. Und meine Schöpfung hängt wie eine Schweinsblase in der Luft."[12] His wife, whom he adored, makes a fool of him : she has turned his head—literally, through 180°, so that in spite of all his efforts, he cannot restore it to its normal position. His hope of recovering her for himself is destroyed when she falls in love with the Rubber Man and when Death—"ein lebender normaler Mensch"[13]—comes to take him. He resigns himself to his fate with the words : "Die menschliche Seele ist wie eine Laterna Magica—früher malte sie den Teufel an die Wand, heute unsere Weiber an die Welt. *(Zittert wie ein galvanisierter Aal, zerschlägt die Schweinsblase.)* Das ist die Seele gewesen. *(ergeben)* O ich will nie wieder keine Märchen mehr glauben, sondern ich will ein bißchen lachen",[14] and at the end he concludes : "Zur Leidenschaft gehört als Filter Geist, sonst überflutet sie Leib und Seele und macht beide unrein. Ich glaube an den Genius der Menschheit, Anima, Amen."[15] This last sentence reveals in the midst of the farcical elements something of Kokoschka's deepest convictions that were to find their expression in his political writings when Europe was later overwhelmed by the evil powers of dictatorship. To add to the effects of comedy, a parrot parodies Anima, and a chorus of dummies, dressed as men with top-hats, holes in place of faces in which heads appear, converse in an animated intellectual jargon. Kokoschka's comedy hardly seems worth attention were it not for the evidence it supplies of ideas that were already forming in his mind and were to be developed later, and of his attachment to the popular theatre that was native to Vienna. Moreover, like the previous play, it was the precursor of another trend in German literature, the theatre of the absurd, for in 1917 the Dadaists staged a performance in Zürich with Hugo Ball and Emmy Hennings in the main roles : "es scheint, daß *Sphinx und Strohmann* in Zürich 1917 sogar als hochaktuelles Beispiel des Dadaismus gefeiert worden ist".[16] Hugo Ball, who in 1916 started the movement he called "Dadaismus", must have been attracted by the primitive expression of human feelings in the play, by the complete disregard of any obvious social conventions, by the grotesqueness of the characters, and by the freedom from any kind of restraint that Kokoschka claimed. Not only the Dadaists and Surrealists acknowledged their indebtedness to Kokoschka, but Thornton Wilder, too, wrote to Hans Maria Wingler[17] that "way back in 1920 and 1921 I read all the plays of Kokoschka I could find".

Kokoschka wrote another short drama in 1911 which was called just *Schauspiel* for want of a better title when it was first published in 1913, but received the title *Der brennende Dornbusch*[18] in the 1917 edition. Again it is a short work of some twenty-five pages in length. It was first performed in the Albert theatre in Dresden in 1917 with Kokoschka himself as the producer. The theme is once again the polarity of the sexes, the attraction and repulsion that belong to the relationship of man to woman, and woman to man: the woman yearns for the man who is to bring the spark of life, as the man searches for and is drawn to the woman; the sweetness of union is followed by the bitterness of separation, love is followed by hate, each drains the strength of the other bringing death, but out of their union there arises new life. The man dies by the hand of the woman, whereas she lives on as mother. Through her suffering, her burning desire that wounds and kills the man, she is enabled to be the life-force. It is a theme that must have had significance for Kokoschka in his personal relationships with a member or members of the opposite sex about the very time when he wrote it; it was also a problem that Strindberg had made familiar in those years before the First World War. Writers on Kokoschka have drawn attention to a parallel treatment of the theme by Paul Claudel in his drama *Partage de Midi,* although whether Kokoschka could have known Claudel's play either in the original or in Franz Blei's translation, *Mittagswende,* published in 1908, is doubtful in spite of some remarkable similarities in the treatment of the theme.

Kokoschka followed the device he had already adopted previously in *Hoffnung der Frauen* of not naming his characters: they are called simply "Mann", "Frau", "Jungfrau", "Mutter und Knabe", "Männer", "Weiber". The list presented in this way reveals his concern not with any particular or personal experience, but with a human problem that is valid at all times and under all circumstances. The highly stylised form of the play must equally be intended to raise this problem of the relationship between man and woman above any extraneous context that might limit, or detract from, its fundamental character. There is indeed "no plot, not even a situation, only a dialogue";[19] and it is, in fact, a play that consists only in part of dialogue—the reader is given a series of *monologues intérieures* spoken alternately by the man and the woman, especially by the latter, in a rhythmical prose that at times becomes rhymed verse. The exclamatory style of the previous works has here given way to an anguished questioning about human relationships that remains unanswered:

"Wär's besser nicht zu sein, als schlecht zu sein?"
"Was ist Erlösen und was Genesen?"
"Warum sind nicht alle Menschen gut?"
"Warum bist du nicht gut—
Mann, der mich mit Wünschen niederrannte.
Ich weiß, du willst sein
mein Freier und Befreier,
Mir Unreinen, Ungekannten—
Und bist mein böser Feind
Und Kerkermeister!"[20]

The drama is raised above the crude violence of Kokoschka's first play by the symbolic use of the ancient myth of the sun and moon to convey the polarity of the man-woman relationship.

In 1917 Kokoschka produced a new and longer version in three acts of *Sphinx and Strawman,* with the title *Hiob*.[21] The publication was accompanied with fourteen lithograph illustrations which Edith Hoffman describes thus: "Over-large heads made the figures top-heavy, while their over-large hands and feet emphasised their expressive gesticulation. These Hiob drawings are very strongly reminiscent of certain Yiddish theatre scenes . . . they have the same grotesque picturesqueness. The same wild gestures, which are as expressive as any words, the same rhythmic movements and the same pathetic humour of people schooled in resignation."[22] In June 1917, Kokoschka produced this play and the two earlier plays *Mörder Hoffnung der Frauen* and *Der brennende Dornbusch* at the Albert Theatre in Dresden. "And here, in order to economise in actors, which were few, and in material, of which there was none, I used for the first time the trick of painting minor parts and props not essential for acting in the background. This trick became the standing novelty for revues on the Continent and in the United States of America for many years."[23] Thus as producer of his own plays Kokoschka was able to initiate a feature that was later to become popular on the stage.

This version of *Sphinx and Strawman* is far more successful than the earlier one. The theme is indeed the same:

"Wie verdrehte mich die Liebe"
"Das Weib hat mir den Kopf verhext . . .
Verdreht".[24]

But in this version Kokoschka has succeeded in capturing something of the rococo charm, the witty playfulness, the fun and rollicking burlesque of the popular theatre of his native Vienna: it is a continuation of a tradition that only Austria had retained unbroken over the centuries. Joseph Sprengler has aptly described its characteristics in these sentences: "Wie die Frau heißt, weiß man eigentlich nicht. Der Mann ruft sie Anima, zum Ende ist sie Eva. Zwischen Anima, der Seele, und Eva, der bittersüßen Verführerin, pendelt das Weib hin und her . . . 'Hiob' ist ein schlummernder Sommernachmittag, vor der lichtprallen Seite des Hauses, auf der Gartenbank, zwischen Schattengrün und Purpurpfirsichen, ein Schläfchen um zwei Uhr, von Schmetterlingen und Hummeln gestört. Ein bißchen Schädeldruck, ein bißchen Verdauungsschwere, ein seelisches Sodbrennen ist auch dabei . . . In Geistigeit, in Visionen aufgelöst, darum ist es Expressionismus. Und einmal ist es sicherlich Dada. . . ."(25) There is too a touch of Shakespearian comedy in this burlesque.

Kokoschka wrote one more drama, *Orpheus und Eurydike*—the only complete work with a recognisably dramatic structure that he really wrote. It is also the most mature of his dramas and less obscure than his earlier works. It also differs from the earlier literary experiments in that its composition was spread over a period of several years instead of being just an improvisation. It owed much to his experiences in the war of 1914 which had a profound effect on Kokoschka. He joined the army in 1915; not long after he was sent to the Eastern front where he was so seriously wounded both in the head and in the lung that he hovered for weeks between life and death; he never recovered sufficiently to take any further active part in the fighting. The nearness of death, the horrors of modern warfare, and the delirious nightmare of those months after he was wounded led to a confused state of mind that yielded only slowly to a saner and more balanced outlook on life. It was during these months and years of uncertainty between 1915 and 1918 that his mind was preoccupied with the drama *Orpheus und Eurydike*. In a letter dated November 9, 1950 to Wingler, Kokoschka wrote that the play had been "gesprochen geflüstert in Ekstase, im Delirium, geweint, gefleht, geheult in Angst und Fieber der Todesnähe"(26)—words that, although written years later, reveal something of the psychological distress that the author suffered during this crisis. It was out of this feverish condition amounting almost to madness that he was able to produce the drama. In 1917 he went to live in a suburb of Dresden with a number of other artists, actors and writers—among them the playwright Walter Hasenclever, the author of *Der Sohn* depicting the conflict between the younger generation and its parents, and of *Antigone*, a protest against war. The delightful surroundings and pleasant company aided not only recovery from his war wounds but stimulated his creative faculty once again, including no doubt the actual writing of the verses of *Orpheus und Eurydike* which he had so far only declaimed to himself. The drama was published by Cassierer in 1919 with other dramas by Kokoschka; and the first performance in public was given in Frankfurt (Main) in 1921. Kokoschka also produced as usual a number of drawings illustrating the theme which were, however, not included in the book edition. In 1921 it was set to music by Ernst Krenek and then produced as an opera in Kassel in 1926. That the worth of the play was hardly recognised by any of the critics at the time of its publication and performance is hardly surprising when so little of his personal experiences was known to the public and when the play seemed so different from the stage-plays that were currently being produced in the German-speaking world.

The development that had taken place is not in the theme so much as in the manner of expressing it. What is presented here is once again Kokoschka's major personal problem, the relationship of the sexes. In this drama he has attempted to come to terms with it by a new and modern treatment of the classical myth of Eurydice and Orpheus. Eurydice, in love with and deeply loved by Orpheus, is seduced by Hades and so becomes the bearer of his child. Orpheus after he has secured the return of Eurydice is unable to restrain his curiosity about her experiences in the home of the dead in spite of warnings by Psyche not to awaken memories in her. He torments her until she reveals her secret and so, aware that by recalling memories of the past he has lost her for ever, he relinquishes her thus forfeiting the happiness that had once been theirs. She returns to Hades, inwardly bound to him by the new life within her—a motif that Kokoschka has added to the ancient myth. The third part of the drama, back in Orpheus's home, also introduces a new element into the love story. Orpheus in his madness gives vent to his disillusionment with what life has brought—nothing but bloodshed and murder. Eurydice reappears to see if she can once more find a way to his heart. But he scorns her:

> "Geh! Geh! Sag ich. Du sollst nichts begehren
> Von Orpheus.
> Ich sage! Noch eine Begierde, was ist das?
> Was für ein Band bindet Mann und Weib zu-
> Sammen.—Unsre eigene Einbildung!"[27]

He tells her he hates her when she pleads with him:

> "Mit teuflischer Freude ich beichte:
> Ich hasse Dich!"[28]

and in his confusion and madness he pours his venom on her, his mother and the whole world. Eurydice, in an effort to stifle his wild fury, takes him by the throat, and throttles him and so frees herself :

> "Du hauchtest die Flamme,
> sie verbrennt Dich. Kentaur!
> Nun—bist Du Asche!
> So im letzten Kampf umarmend,
> Voller Entsetzen,
> für letzten Kuß, aus des Orpheus' erstarrten Kiefern
> lös' ich mich endlich ledig."[29]

Kokoschka poured into the mouth of Orpheus all his own passionate hatred of war—the consequence of what he saw and experienced on the Eastern front. This attitude to war "corresponded with the general change of ideas which in 1918 turned the soldiers of the German army into disgusted rebels".[30] Kokoschka himself later became a pacifist and expressed his convictions in articles and essays of a political nature.

The drama is no doubt intended to present the tragedy of man who draws destruction upon himself. Kokoschka has introduced into the ancient story the idea that regeneration—a familiar theme with the Expressionist dramatists—comes through the union of Hades, the personification of the chthonic element in life, with woman symbolised in Eurydice. The drama thus becomes an apotheosis of woman to a greater extent than in *The Burning Bush*. How far Kokoschka has been successful in transforming the classical myth into a medium for his convictions is a debatable question: it is however his finest attempt to come to terms with modern society and modern life in a literary work but somehow the vision, one feels, is again only partially successful in its actual achievement. The English reader is likely to be repelled by the hysteria, the excess of violence, and the nightmarish visions that predominate. It is, perhaps, significant that Kokoschka gave up drama as a means of communication after writing this play, when he was still little more than thirty years of age.

Kokoschka nevertheless succeeded in writing a work with a dramatic quality about it that he had not been able to achieve in his other plays. It has a clearly defined structure of three acts, a plot and an action that are rounded off. Mixed up with this clearer perception of the essentials of a drama are to be found all the typical excesses of the language of Expressionism, but the play is redeemed by a number of charming touches here and there. Who but Kokoschka would have thought of making Eurydice (in Scene 1) retell the parting from Orpheus in words such as these:

"Der Wagen immer kleiner wurde, ein Punkt zuletzt
Der barg mir ja Dein Angesicht, das mir—nicht—
kleiner ward!"[31]

The second act introduces a mad sailor quite in the style of a Shakesperian clown in a scene that is sultry with the foreboding of catastrophe.

Kokoschka made one more attempt to write a drama, but he got no further than a fragment, of which one act—the fourth—has been published. The rise to power of the National Socialists and the branding of his work as "Degenerate Art" by Hitler, with its threat to his life-work, led him to take a more active interest in politics and to express his opinions in writing. Increasingly he turned back to the ideals of Jan Amos Comenius, the seventeenth-century Czech humanist and pacifist, who advocated that the education of the masses should depend more upon visual experience than upon theoretical knowledge. He had been introduced to Comenius by his father: "The very first book given to me by my father before I could even read, Jan Amos Comenius's *Orbis Pictus*, has never ceased to be useful to me . . . this classic encyclopaedia of humanism . . . ". What this meant to Kokoschka is indicated by another sentence he wrote: "During the Thirty Years War the Czech humanist Jan Amos Comenius, . . . had been the first to try to humanise the warring nations by educating children."[32] One other Czech humanist held his imagination during this period of anxiety, T. G. Masaryk; in 1936 he completed a portrait of Masaryk with, at his side, the figure of Comenius holding up his *Orbis Pictus*. He also expounded his ideas derived from Comenius in an essay entitled *Comenius, the English Revolution and our Present Plight*".[33] This one fragment presents an imaginary meeting and conversation between the painter Rembrandt and Comenius. The main interest of the scene lies not in any historical event that may or may not have taken place, but in the intrusion of political tyranny into the lives of these two freedom-loving humanists. The parallel with Hitler—Germany—and the message for the twentieth century are obvious and are an indication of Kokoschka's feelings about the political developments in central Europe—the area in which he was deeply rooted—that were a complete reversal of everything he clung to. Kokoschka never conformed to or compromised with twentieth-century society, and as the clouds darkened over Europe he tended increasingly to endow his art with a mission. He believed in the rights of the individual and asserted his own independence; he hated regimentation in art as much as in politics and aimed at communicating to others his faith in the freedom of the mind as the heritage of European civilisation.

Kokoschka is only one among a number of artists in this century who have used both painting and literature as media of communication. His gift, however, was essentially visual; he acknowledged this in a broadcast: "I live with my eyes, because seeing is for me the most natural language."[34] After the Second World War he started a summer school at Salzburg which has attracted pupils from all over the world. "It is not an Academy, but a School of Vision . . . they must learn to see;" "in this moonstruck age, who can still see?" are typical remarks he made to a writer in *The Times* (November 2, 1959). One can only repeat, he is essentially a visual artist, and his efforts to write drama have been successful only to a limited degree. His imagination overflows with an abundance of colourful images but he has not always been able to give them adequate form in language, or to make them sufficiently meaningful to his readers. Kokoschka is often effusive, passionate and even hysterical, as many German writers were in the earlier years of this century, but that is not enough to create great literature. Like many of his contemporaries he has been in revolt against the way modern society with its technology has developed. He is aware of human problems and has presented them in his dramas in their most elemental form. His dramas often seem, as a consequence, too far removed from the great political, social and economic issues of the age. And his humanism, in so far as it is expressed in his literary works, is too limited and too nebulous. He is undoubtedly one of the great artists of our time; in literature, however, he can only occupy a humble place among the German "Expressionists"—a label admittedly which he himself would not like to see applied to either his literary or his artistic work.

NOTES AND TRANSLATIONS

1. Edith Hoffman, *Kokoschka, Life and Works,* p. 37, adds that "Lilith was the heroine of all his earliest works, both painted and written."
2. Vol. XXIII, p. 50, quoted by Hoffman, *op. cit* p. 38.
3. Kokoschka, *Schriften,* p. 107—Little red fish, I kill you with the three-edged knife, tear you apart with my fingers, that your mute movement may come to an end. Little red fish, my little knife is red, a little fish sinks dead in the bowl.
4. *Schriften,* p. 112—I dream and my dreams are like the North, where snow-mountains hide age-old tales, my thoughts wander through my brain and make me grow, as the stones grow, no one knows of it and understands.

5. Hoffman, *op cit.*, p. 55; see too *Ency. Brit.*, 14th ed., 1929, p. 475.

6. *Schriften*, p. 51: "the literary quarrel would soon have turned into a bloody war if Adolf Loos with a small band of faithfuls had not saved me from being slain."

7. Hoffman, p. 57.

8. *Schriften*, p. 150—Woman: *more and more violently, shouting.* I will not let you live. You! You make me weak—I kill you—you fetter me! I seize you—and you hold me! Let me go—you clasp me—as with iron chains—strangled—let go—help! I lost the key—that holds you fast.

9. Hoffman, p. 55.

10. Soergel-Hohoff, *Dichtung und Dichter der Zeit*, Düsseldorf, 1963, Vol. II, p. 115.

11. Hoffman, p. 55.

12. *Schriften*, p. 155—I had a wife, I made a god of her, then she left my bed . . . and disappeared with a healthy muscle-man. I have created a human Soul, then the earth disappeared from beneath her. And my creation hovers in the air like a pig's bladder.

13. *Schriften*, p. 154—a living, normal being.

14. *Shriften*, p. 163—The human soul is like a magic lantern—formerly it painted the devil on the wall, today our wives on the world. (*Trembles like a galvanised eel, bursts the pig's bladder.*) That was the soul. (*resigned*) Oh I will never again believe in fairy-tales, instead I want to laugh a little.

15. *Schriften*, p. 167—Passion must be filtered by the spirit, otherwise it floods body and soul polluting both. I believe in the genius of mankind. Anima, Amen.

16. *Schriften*, p. 458, note by the editor Hans Maria Wingler: it seems that *Sphinx and Strawman* was welcomed in Zürich in 1917 as an up-to-date example of Dadaism.

17. *Schriften*, p. 458.

18. *The Burning Bush.*

19. Hoffman, *op. cit.*, p. 106.

20. "Were it better not to be than to be wicked?"—*Schriften*, p. 180;
"What is salvation and what restoration?"—*ibid.*, p. 81;
"Why are not all people good?"—*ibid.*, p. 189;
"Why are you not good—man who overwhelmed me with desires. I know you would be my wooer and liberator, I who am impure and unknown.
And you are my evil enemy and jailer!"—*ibid.*, p. 191f.

21 *Job.*

22. Hoffman, *op cit.*, p. 167f.

23. Quoted by Hoffman, *op. cit.* p. 150.

24. "How has love turned my head"—*Schriften*, p. 205; "The woman has bewitched me . . ."—*ibid.*, p. 214.

25. "We do not know the woman's name. The husband calls her Anima, in the end she is Eve. This woman hovers between Anima, the soul, and Eve, the bitter-sweet temptress. 'Job' is a drowsy summer afternoon, in front of the sunlit side of the house, on the garden-seat, between the

green of the shadows and the purple of the peaches, a nap around two o'clock, disturbed by butterflies and bees. A little pressure on the cranium, a touch of heaviness from indigestion, a heart-burn in the soul are all there too. Dissolved in intellect and visions, it is Expressionism, surely Dada too"—quoted by Wingler in *Schriften* p. 464f, from *Hochland,* 1921/22, p. 676.

26. Spoken, and whispered in an ecstasy, in a delirium, wept over, entreated and sobbed over in the fear and fever of death's nearness"—*Schriften,* p. 467.

27. "Go, go, I say. You shall desire nothing from Orpheus. I tell you—one more desire, what is that? What sort of tie binds man and woman together—Our own imagination!"—*Schriften,* p. 295.

28. "With devilish joy I confess: I hate you"—*Schriften* p. 300.

29. "You breathed the flame, it consumes you. Centaur! Now—you are ash! Thus embracing in the final struggle, filled with horror, for the last kiss from Orpheus's stiff jaws, I free myself at last"—*Schriften,* p. 302.

30. Hoffman, *op cit.* p. 136.

31. "The carriage became smaller and smaller, finally only a point. It hid your face which to me—did not become smaller"—*Schriften,* p. 234.

32. Quoted by Hoffman, *op cit.,* pp. 25n and 24n.

33. Published in the volume *The Teacher of the Nations, Addresses and Essays by President Bene and others,* edited by Joseph Needham, C.U.P., 1942. The Addresses formed part of the celebration in October 1941, in the Senate House of Cambridge University, of the tercentenary of the visit of Comenius to England.

34. See *The Times,* January 26, 1963.

SELECT BIBLIOGRAPHY

Kokoschka's chief literary works have been published in the volume: *Oskar Kokoschka, Schriften* 1907–1955, edited with commentary and bibliographical details by Hans Maria Wingler, 1956, Albert Langen Georg Müller, Munich. It contains short stories and reminiscences, poems, dramas and a selection of essays and letters.

A volume of stories, *Spur im Treibsand,* has been translated under the title *A Sea Ringed with Visions,* London, Thames and Hudson, 1962. Reproductions of Kokoschka's paintings have been published in the volume *Oskar Kokoschka, The Work of the Painter,* London, Faber and Faber, with an introduction and bibliographical material by Hans Maria Wingler. A small selection has also appeared in the "Faber Gallery" with an introduction and notes by Bernhard Borchert.

The one monograph readily available to English readers is by Edith Hoffman, *Kokoschka, Life and Work,* London, Faber and Faber, 1947.

Ernst Barlach

Ernst Barlach

by BRIAN KEITH-SMITH

ANYONE thinking of writing an essay on Ernst Barlach soon realises that there are a number of special problems to be faced which on the one hand draw him on into the core of Barlach's artistry, and on the other hand continually rebuff him. Barlach's facility to express himself in sculpture, woodcuts, lithographs, dramas and prose works shows how closely these creatures of his are bound to their creator. The detailed care of his style in all media bears witness to a continual grappling with problems of communication. The complexity of details of construction and yet overall simplicity of his work shows he perceived different levels of consciousness both in the individual and in the group. The attention paid to light effects, to positioning of his characters, and in particular to subtle descriptions of relationships—whether human or spatial—show his preoccupation with man's need to find the truth, or as he would term this—"It" or the "Other". The almost complete lack of interest in time categories except to deepen man's knowledge of himself perhaps discloses an unhurried patience and spiritual freedom in him—so contrary to much of the superficial evidence of his life. The constant intrusion of a streak of humour seems to underline his individuality—yet his whole condition he so often considers as a state of banishment. And finally his for ever changing points of departure, viewpoints, perspectives and way of looking at things would seem to suggest a dilettante at work—yet Barlach the master can concentrate his imagination into such detailed plastic terms, that his mature works need the minimum of cut and line to bring out their full meaning and power of suggestion. The variety of his works, even though they all bear the signature of his creative spirit, make any attempt at a conclusive essay written from one point of view irrelevant and out of the question. All one can do is to open up vistas which may help to lead to a better understanding of this complex artistic personality, about whom so much has been written in German and so little in English, and whose works—however obscure they may seem to be—never fail to reawaken one's intrigue and enjoyment.

Barlach's early life is narrated in his autobiography, *Ein Selbsterzähltes Leben,* written in 1927. Born in Wedel in 1870, son of a practising family doctor, into a family whose previous generations back to the seventeenth century had been local tailors, doctors or pastors, he drifted into being a sculptor because there was nothing else he particularly wanted to do. In Hamburg, 1889-91, he spent much time sketching passers-by in the street instead of limiting himself to the strict academic training of the Gewerbeschule. Already he was searching for a personal style, already he witnessed the aimless rush of city life. The next four years he was encouraged by his teacher Robert Diez at the Dresdner Akademie to explore his own way, and when his student friend Carl Garbers left for Paris he joined him. Paris for Barlach meant the opportunity to see and sketch a more cosmopolitan society, to visit the Louvre for weeks on end, to be impressed by the timeless monumentality of Egyptian and Korean art, and to indulge in experiments to become a writer. Sketching nude models at the Akademie Julien only resulted for him, as he put it, in:

"ausgezogene Männekens und entfederte Gänslein."(1)

Barlach's works hardly include a single naked body—not only because that would have otherwise been irrelevant to what he has to say through art form, but also because he was primarily an artist of the face and head. Much of his work until about 1906 was directly influenced by, if not a conscious imitation of, the current *art nouveau,* a fashion through which he had to find his own way Yet even at this stage Barlach could laugh at his own limitations and products of Kitsch—for instance in the lines he wrote on a photograph of a ceramic of a self-portrait:

Dieses ist, herrjeh,
Barlachs Selbsporträt!
In Thon gebrannt und dann glasiert
Und mit einem Vers verziert.
Er schüttelt, vor Erwartung stumm,
Seinen Würfelbecher um,
Die Würfel, die beim Wiederrollen
Sein Lebensschicksal entscheiden sollen.
Er würfelt um keinen kleinen Gewinn:
Um ein "Leben" (nach seinem Sinn).(2)

In Hamburg and Altona, Barlach and Garbers worked together and produced a prize-winning design for the Hamburger Rathausmarkt. This was eventually transferred to another architect—the first of many occasions on which Barlach was to be harshly treated. He left for Berlin in 1900 where he lived later on several occasions for a few weeks at a time, and of which his first impressions were to be repeated on every subsequent visit. Life in an industrialised city meant hell for him, and seemed even more so in contrast with the years 1901–04 spent in Wedel. These years, apparently wasted, are related in outline in his novel *Seespeck*; but at this time he learnt to observe and understand human life unblemished by the more flagrant materialism of the modern city, and he learnt to appreciate the quiet harmonies of a natural and agrarian landscape. His year as a teacher at the Fachschule für Keramik at Höhr was upset by suspect heart trouble. In spite of writing a much used textbook, *Figürliches Zeichen,* he was unhappy and unsuccessful. In 1906 while working in Berlin, an illegitimate son Klaus was born, and for three years he conducted long legal wrangles to adopt him, spending all his savings and earnings in the process. Later he was to remark that all his works up to 1906 he could forget with pleasure as lacking in aim and as expressions of "Romantik und Gefühlsschwögerei"(3)—but this was for a very different reason.

For two months in 1906 Barlach went on a trip to Russia to visit relatives working there. His impressions of this visit vary considerably from the ecstatic statements in his *Russisches Tagebuch* in which he says he there discovered his sense of perspective, proportion and form, to denials in later letters of any lasting formative influence from this period on his later work. The visit was a culmination of a search for form almost brought to its end during the unfortunately poorly documented years at Wedel, a search still lacking a final decisive experience to bring full self-assurance to Barlach's artistry. The special conditions in which Russians lived and their way of life made him forcibly realise how closely man and landscape can complement each other. Man set in rather than against nature is the background of most of his works, and Barlach applied this as a most important principle of his artistic activity. The grain of a block of wood, its texture and malleability are all allowed to express their qualities as integral parts of his sculptures. The forces acting in one direction in a soul—fear or elation for instance—are re-expressed in the work of art by a use of shapes and planes to their best advantage; and so we find the covered head and the stooping shoulders of a downtrodden beggar, and the leaping ebullience in all directions at once of the limbs and head of a woman in ecstasy. The central point of gravity or focus of many of Barlach's figures lies outside them—perhaps at a great distance (as with the Stargazer), or sometimes so closely bound up with them (as with the floating Güstrow angel) that "Innen ist wie Außen, Außen wie Innen".(4) Barlach became so sharply aware of this through the Russian people and landscape, that they seemed to him sculptures in themselves. He plunged into this sea of forms, but as he pointed out in a letter to Boris Pines on January 26, 1926, it would be wrong to think that he recognised these forms as specifically Russian:

> Meine innerliche Bereitschaft, meine mir gegebene Verfassung brachte ich mit—denn das Alles war auch in mir und das Alles ist wohl enorm russisch, aber auch enorm deutsch und europäisch und allmenschlich.(5)

Barlach saw after his visit to Russia that man is an imperfect experiment of nature; he took upon himself as an artist man's suffering condition, and by expressing man's dormant possibilities, attempted to redeem him. Suffering now meant for him discord in nature, alive as he was now to man's cosmological rather than social position.

Back in Berlin, Barlach's financial position was solved by the publisher Paul Cassirer who offered to finance his work and buy all his future products. In spite of never knowing when and if Cassirer would close this arrangement, Barlach had cause to be thankful for many years for this help. Without it, he once said, he would have remained a scribbler for the periodical *Simplizissimus*. In 1909 he won a prize for a year's study in Florence, where he appreciated the brightness of the light and the easy-going Italian life, but felt out of place, lonely and ill at ease. He longed to be back in his Northern climate and landscape. In spite of this, the most formative influence he underwent in Italy was the beginning of a life-long friendship with the poet Theodor Däubler—so utterly different, with his Southern temperament, from himself.

> Däubler ist der Bewohner einer anderen Welt, eines anderen Sterns, der aus einem unerfindlichen Grunde hierher zu uns geraten. Hier wird er notwendig zu einem Ungetüm.(6)

He tried to sum up his views on Däubler in *Diaro Däubler* (1912–14), and used this material in the last two chapters of *Seespeck*. Barlach was attracted by Däubler as a Columbus to a new world of the spirit outreaching man's normal limits, as a physical giant, as a world changer, as a man who stood with one foot firmly in myth. Yet he also found in him something of a Hochstapler (fraud) attempting to by-pass the normal categories of experience in trying to reach out to a non-representational use of language. Barlach comments:

> Schließlich soll das menschliche Auge, das Ohr, der Sinn befriedigt werden, angeregt, da kann ich keine Welt, die nicht existiert, formen, da muß ich mich mit verständlichen Zeichen ausdrücken.(7)

Däubler is a Devil leading him away from all that is human; and Däubler is a God making man doubt his position and setting him back on a way towards the true unity of nature, from the centre of which man is shown to be an outcast. As Däubler jolts man out of his egocentricity, so Barlach can see him as a second Christ figure, and Seespeck see him as a mirror to the world. In *Seespeck* Däubler speaks and challenges Barlach's mind :

> "Sie klopfen an die Tür einer Wirklichkeit, aber zum Unterschied von andern Leuten wohne ich nicht innerhalb, sondern außerhalb meiner vier Wände. Ich bin überall zu Hause, alles ist 'Ich'."[(8)]

Däubler teaches Barlach that "being" cannot be characterised, only its locus can be established :

> "Sein ist etwas anderes als Ich-Sein. Das bewußte Ich, Herr Doktor, ist der Klavierspieler, aber das Sein ist die Musik. . . . denn Sie machen die Maske zum Wesen zum Ding an sich und das Wesen zum Nichts am Ding."[(9)]

Barlach settled down in 1910 at Güstrow with his mother and Klaus. Here he wrote the *Güstrower Tagebuch* (1914–17) recording his changing outlook on life and his outer and inner life at the time. At first he looked on war as a blessing to lift man out of his everyday meaningless activity and to inspire him with a supra-personal purpose. But he also saw, especially in the sorrow of women, the cruel side of war, which he crystallises in one of his few important works of the time—the figure of the *Berserker*. He feared the national pride that would follow a German victory, yet could equate the beating of his heart with a national pulse eager to defend the cultural values misunderstood so badly by the Americans and others. Owing to his weak heart he had to remain a non-combatant, but was called up for two months' training as a recruit in December 1915. In almost every entry he registers frustration at not being able to help in the war-effort. He helps to run a Kinderhort (nursery home), and outbursts of anger are tempered by occasional realisations of his good fortune at being away from the trenches so vividly described in letters from his friends. He claims he writes to be able to revoke his feelings later, even to make use of the diary in *Seespeck*; but for weeks on end all the entries start with news headlines, and their tone suggests a child trying to exteriorise himself, to find and formulate his values. Even the "paar Tröpchen Ewigkeit"[(10)] that seep through to him in a Christmas carol service, even the typically Barlachesque pranks of Klaus and the daily reading with him of classic works of literature, even the stubbornness of his ailing mother, do not seem to provide him with a solid trust in his own individuality. He shows a continual need for contact with eternal truths, for his Ich to have:

> stärkstes und höchstes Leben und doch eine Erstarrung.[11]

The war made him more responsive to the call of a level of consciousness free from the demands of the individual ego. How pathetic and how revealing of his struggle is his call into that unexplored region:

> Die Zeit will Form bekommen, also bilde die Zeit! Schaffe Rat, guter Geist, schenk mir in Linien, was ich ahne, sende mir eine Kahn, damit ich auf den Ozean schiffen kann, da ich sehe![12]

In spite of the flagging of his creative energy during the war, Barlach's understanding of his place in nature and his descriptions of nature become more and more emphatic and effective. He experiences a form of return to the first "mystical" experiences of his childhood and approaches these now with a form of active memory described as:

> Beten heißt bei mir, das Wahre, nein, das Unaussprechliche erkennen, nicht betteln, nicht quasseln, nicht beschwatzen—nein, wissen: so ist es also—heilig sein.[13]

(With this in mind we are hardly surprised to find the features of the figure *Der Asket* or *Der Beter* (1925) resemble Barlach's own.) Barlach leads on to attack images of Christ given "modern" qualities such as tidy hair or academic honours, and he admires the Roman Catholic Church for its insistence on keeping man at a respectful distance from God. To feel in complete union with God meant for Barlach death of the individual or the devaluation of God in human terms—a "Vergötterung". Barlach is indeed a seeker after God, but he hesitates to name him, for that would be the first step towards explaining him, to limiting the myth. He seeks continuous dialogue with the Creator, in which "das zarte Versilbern aller Dinge"[14] helps him to pray.

> Da Gott ist, so ist er anders als wir: ohne Erinnern, Wissen Urteilen. Wissen kann ichs nicht, sehen nicht, hören nicht, also nicht glauben letzten Endes. Aber etwas muß ich glauben können, das besteht. Das ist die Lust, der Trieb, das Muß, das Wünschen—da ist Gott.[15]

God's position but not his character can be found and continually recorded. Barlach approaches God humbly and ceaselessly, for he can never say "my God", as he can no more explain his own existence than he can God's. He in fact refers to occasions on which God spurns him, to others on which God goads his desire to enfigure whatever he sees in things.

By 1919 Barlach had become well known in Germany, and he received various commissions to construct war memorials—many of which he carried out, but always with the emphasis on man's suffering through war and the message of peace. He rejected any form of patriotism and strongly resisted attempts by vested interests such as war veteran societies to make him produce works glorifying the patriotic killer instinct. A decade was to follow in which Barlach was more widely honoured than any of his contemporary artists. In 1919 he became a member of the Akademie der Künste in Berlin and was offered a professorship which he turned down. He preferred to bring up Klaus in Güstrow and to work there in the peace of his own studio. In 1920 his mother, after a few days in a rest home for mental defectives, committed suicide by drowning —an event which left a deep scar on his soul for months, even years, to come. In 1924 he won the Kleist prize for *Der Arme Vetter*. In 1925 he became honorary member of the Munich Academy of Arts. In 1933 he received the highest possible award—Ritter der Friedensklasse des Ordens pour le mérite. Even as late as 1936 he was elected honorary member of the Wiener Sezession and of the Viennese academy of plastic arts. His dramas were performed and remained on the theatrical repertoires in at least eight large towns. His sculptures were exhibited at a time when he was producing work after work. These were mainly his most famous and most characteristic figures for the most part in wood, the end products of many preparatory models in plaster and in clay, e.g. *Moses* (1918–19); 1910 *Die verhüllte Bettlerin, Die gemarterte Menschheit;* 1920 *Der Flüchtling, Tanzende Alte, Mutter Erde;* 1921 *Stehende Bäuerin, Lesende Mönche, Der Mann mit dem Mantel;* 1923 *Das Grauen, Weinende Frau, Zwei Schlafende;* 1924 *Der Wartende;* 1925 *Der Asket, Der Träumer;* 1926 *Das Wiedersehen, Die gefesselte Hexe*; 1927 *Güstrower Ehrenmal*; 1928 *Der Geistkämpfer*; and 1930 *Der singende Mann*. These may be called the "typical Barlach" together with most of the important woodcuts, four dramas, the autobiography, and the beginnings of *Der Graf von Ratzeburg*. The story of the gradually encroaching bans on Barlach's works from any public gallery, theatre or church, and the steady whittling down of his security so as to force him to emigrate before he became too awkward a figure for the Nazis to have speaking out against them at the slightest opportunity—for instance in the *Rundfunkrede* of 1932—is one of gathering inhumanity and growing despair. This is best told in the tone and contents of his letters, many of which have already been published, but far more of which are still not available. Individual acts of mockery and sabotage are well known, such as the removal of the *Güstrower Engel,* the defacing and later removal of the *Kieler Geistkämpfer,* the inclusion of his *Das Wiedersehen* in the notorious exhibition "Entartete Kunst" in 1937. The parallel story of Barlach's struggle to express his pity and faith in a better time to come through such works as the *Fries der Lauschenden,* as a memorial to Beethoven, and and the three completed figures of the "Gemeinschaft der Heiligen" *Frau im Wind, Der Bettler* and *Der Sänger* for the St. Katharinenkirche in Lübeck, through the pathos and humanity of the *Magdeburger Ehrenmal* and through the portrayal of suffering in so many figures such as *Das Jahr 1937* is one best left to the figures themselves. These are the works that have attracted so many "Barlach-Verehrer",[16] and it is only in a sense of respectful recognition of masterly genius and talent expressed as a reaction to the brutality of the Third Reich that one can approach them. It would perhaps be wise to apply to them Guido K. Brand's remark in general about Barlach when he said:

> "Nirgends schweigt man so tief, als wenn man von Barlach spricht."[17]

The silence which grew around Barlach during the Thirties was one forced upon him by continual disappointments. There can be little doubt that the frequent bouts of illness that afflicted him during the last four or five years of his life were accentuated by growing fears for the welfare of his friends and family, and more generally for the local and European spirit to which he bore such eloquent witness. Castigated as a Jew by the Nazis, Barlach's works of art were still popular enough with their leaders for him to be allowed to die peacefully in a Rostock clinic in October 1938.

Barlach's woodcuts and illustrations are for many people his most revealing works, for these show both his virtuosity as a craftsman and the difficulties he experienced in adapting himself to enfigure the visions of other geniuses. In the woodcuts especially his individuality is clearly scored, as in these the material he uses becomes a way of recreating himself into plastic form rather than a means of interpreting the world outside him. There are also a number of incomplete models in various materials for most of the major sculptures—most of them exercises in which he worked out proportions for each subject—these too seem to be the remainder as it were of the sum of creative processes being worked out by his imagination. In his plastic art Barlach seeks to encompass and contour the inner essence of a character or event which corresponds to the response of his own imagination. For this reason perhaps, but also because of the weird effects which they produce, the woodcuts to Kleist's *Michael Kohlhaas* and the drawings for a *Nibelungen* cycle are a failure. Barlach's imagination which ironically enough was for ever seeking to escape its own bounds, was incapable of completely identifying itself actively to anyone else's. His plastic art is the expression, sometimes the triumphal lay, sometimes the spectral elegy of the brotherhood that Barlach the artist found between Barlach the man and the real or fictional things in the world about him. Seespeck is carrying out this creative process when Barlach writes of him :

> Was an menschlichen Wesen vorkam, das holte er sich mit den Augen wie mit dem geistigen Fangorgan an seine Seele.(18)

And Barlach writes of himself :

> Ich fange eine Chiffre mit den Augen auf, und sie wird im Dunkeln meines Ich übersetzt und dort verarbeitet.(19)

Barlach's struggle for mastery over his material, so frequently referred to in his letters and other writings is particularly obvious in his woodcuts and drawings. Thus the first set of thirteen lithographs to the essay *Steppenfahrt* never appeared separately, possibly because they lack interesting subject-matter, their main emphasis being on the contourless wavy shaping of figures into the landscape. In the twenty drawings on the theme *Kriegszeit* Barlach never escapes the patriotic purpose for which they were created. The hard restrictions of line found in the first set of woodcuts in 1919 for Reinhard von Walter's poem *Der Kopf* contrast strongly with the flexibility of line arrangement in the *Steppenfahrt* lithographs. Far more effective is the attention to detail and the use of light and shadow brought out as a function for the contrasts of black and white in this medium seen in the twenty woodcuts to *Der Findling* (1921), where grotesque and serious elements are found in the same cutting. Detailed characterisation of separate elements—sometimes particular parts of one body—reveals a growing facility in picking out minor details which yet do not disturb the overall effect of the whole scene. This can be seen as a stage in Barlach's way to his later ability in all his media to portray a doublesidedness in his creatures. *Der Findling* was the last of his own works that Barlach felt the need to illustrate, and it may be found that the later works are more completely pictorial in themselves, or at least that Barlach felt they were. The earlier twenty-seven lithographs to *Der Tote Tag* are an attempt to situate the events of the drama in a mythological setting, which might be said to be underdrawn in the actual play or at least not sufficiently enfigured or explained. This is also the aim of the drawings to *Der Arme Vetter* where the mythological patterns are made clear in both dialogue and drawings. The twenty woodcuts to Goethe's *Walpurgisnacht* reflect Barlach's deep and lasting interest in *Faust*, and it is hardly surprising that they embody his interpretation of the central figures. Faust looks remarkably like a Siegfried or a Hamlet accompanied by a shadowy and equally tormented Mephistopheles. Gretchen represents statuesquely particular lines from the scene. Minor and more gruesome figures allow Barlach to exploit his imagination almost at times to caricature. In 1923 Barlach again turned to Goethe, producing thirty-five drawings to join those of other artists in a volume of illustrations to Goethe's poems. Here Barlach prefers those poems where the demonic or supernatural elements play a leading part, some developing new visions in his mind others eliciting somewhat conventional responses from his imagination. The mysterious power of the woman creating stone from water in *Legende* forcibly links through the drawing Goethe's idea and Barlach's ceaseless preoccupation with the theme of form evolving out of chaos, shape out of shapelessness. On the other hand Barlach has nothing to add with his illustration to *Erlkönig*. *Der Zauberlehrling* becomes a farce and *Die Wandelnde Glocke* an exquisite humorous comment on Goethe's poem. With all the successful drawings Barlach has managed to probe behind the everyday, and has plumbed the depths of myth where individual mask returns to archetypal face, where man is set in space rather than time. This is also seen in the not entirely successful nine woodcuts to Schiller's *Lied an die Freude* (1927), where closed-eyed figures forget their individualities in rapt selfforgetfulness in an individuation into the cosmos about them. The greatest achievement of all Barlach's woodcuts are the seven of *Die Wandlungen Gottes* (1922). The relatively large areas of black and white in the Creator's robes in *Der erste Tag*, framed by receding billows in the dark chaos around his form-giving hands, have all disappeared in *Der siebente Tag* where a tired but pleased Creator views the order and purpose of his creation from a rock seat of the same shaped texture it would seem as the Creator's robes and even the valley below. The Creator's achievement is clear—he has moulded the forces of chaos with his energy into a harmony where creator and creature are one. The other five give proof of Barlach's imaginative powers over perspective, and his visions of God set in the panoramas of horror and peace. In these Barlach all but overcomes with increasing freedom the rectangular limitations of woodcut design.

Barlach's first attempts to write drama date from the years at

Wedel with a fragment that is as yet unpublished. His first completed drama *Der Tote Tag* (1919) was originally called *Blutgeschrei* and deals with the problem of an over-possessive mother whose son waits for the divine horse to carry him away into a separate life of his own. The drama opens out from a family conflict in the naturalist manner into a *Weltanschauungsdrama* whose tension is sprung on the guilt of the son's doubt in the interest of a God-Father. The mother kills the horse, and the son is doomed to stumble blindly through his life—his hope having gone and his day of redemption being dead. Finally the mother and then the son commit suicide.

Der arme Vetter (1918) examines the effect of Hans Iver, whose insight into the true motives in human life has led him to despair and attempted suicide, on other people, especially Frl. Isenbarn. Her fiancé, Siebenmark, a philistine but aware of a purpose behind things and events, remains cut off from all true human contact because of his inability to accept his own and other people's idiosyncracies and faults. Siebenmark's egoism and Iver's humility throw each other into sharp relief, so much so, that the sensitive and innocent Frl. Isenbarn watches herself turn towards Iver, until on his second and successful suicide attempt, she kisses his dead body and leaves her fiancé for ever. Through this act Siebenmark achieves clearer insight into himself and his responsibilities towards others. Barlach also includes a tavern scene in which a grotesque figure of a young man dressed up as Frau Venus represents the unthankful world that the poor cousin Iver has come to redeem. Iver loses faith in the innate goodness of man once again and is obliged to accuse Siebenmark of looking for his own image in his fiancée. In their different ways Iver and Siebenmark are made aware of their inability to accept the independence of a Du figure—for Iver turns Siebenmark into a symbol of all mankind, and Siebenmark can scarcely comprehend Iver's accusations. Only in Frl. Isenbarn does the unasked for presence of God inform her instinct and responses to life.

Die echten Sedemunds (1920) in which a lion—symbol of a corrupt society's conscience—is supposed to have escaped is paralleled in the final chapter of *Seespeck* (*Der Löw ist Los*) where surrealist symbol contains the drama's plot and its hidden meaning. The escaping lion may also be taken as a cipher for young Sedemund cutting loose from the restrictions of family tradition, and more generally as the individual breaking free from the demands of his human condition. Young Sedemund sets out to alter the state of a society based on false values, but is at first also subject to them. He lays bare the dependence of his family on the example of their forebears who could let a wife be driven to suicide and a son of the house be sent to an asylum rather than allow any doubt attach itself to the honour of the family name. Young Sedemund spreads the rumour that a lion has escaped, and this exposes ridiculous human failings in a series of minor episodes. Gradually the major sins of the past are drawn out by fear of the lion's retribution, and it is not until Onkel Waldemar (modelled on Barlach's first drawing teacher in Hamburg?) recognises in young Sedemund the true progressive spirit of the family, that the lion is dead.

The mystery play *Der Findling* (1922) foresees in hideous detail some of the horrors of the Second World War, and seeks a way of hope for a suffering humanity that has cast out its gods and is fleeing continuously from the political upheavals caused by one despot after another. An unwanted adopted child is saved from death by a stone breaker who through his care is eventually accepted as a saviour. After the cannibalism of the first part, the figure of Elise, daughter of Kummer, and ashamed of the despair and bestial conditions of her parents, shines out with full belief in the power of grace even in the midst of misery. Thomas the puppeteer is changed through her example from a good-for-nothing into a Thomas Dogood. Elise, blessed with a faith activating others to seek and cultivate the merciful and hopeful qualities of the human soul, turns the foundling into a saviour figure for them; and at least for Thomas she becomes a new Mary, a new Mother of God. Man is shown to find redemption only by recognising the example of others as an encouragement to overcome the turning towards bestiality of his own self. The first step in this is seen to be to forget one's past by first being ashamed of it, and then by building a hopeful future on a new Ich.

The main underlying theme to *Die Sündflut* (1924) is that of various understandings of and attitudes towards the nature of God. In an important letter to Arthur Kracke referring to this (February 4, 1930) Barlach would seem to give his ultimate answer to this problem:

> Ich ergreife, nein, mich ergreift in besten Stunden die Vorstellung der Entpersönlichung, des Aufgehens im Höheren, ich nenne es das Glück der Selbstüberwindung, in dem das volle Bewußtsein des Ichs enthalten und erhalten bleibt. Unpersönlichkeit, d.h. Unbegrenztheit muß das Wesen dessen sein, den ich nur noch ungern "Gott" nenne.[20]

Forgetting one's past is now seen as not a sufficient basis to overcoming one's self. There must also be a fear of God—and in *Die*

Sündflut Noah is found by an angel to be the only human to still have this. Even after the heaviest tribulations Noah is ready to prepare a sacrifice and recognise his God in the beggar crawling outside his tent. Calan, the rival shepherd, a tempter and embodiment of evil and set actively and proudly against God, brings Noah a beautiful girl Awah as a present to gain his favour. Noah is finally persuaded in spite of Calan's cynicism to go into the hills and build an ark against the coming flood. Awah's statement:

> Die Welt ist winziger als Nichts, und Gott ist Alles—ich sehe nichts als Gott. . . . Gott ist die große Stille, ich höre Gott,[21]

is later modified by Sem, one of Noah's sons, who sees God peeping through chinks from behind everything. This explains for him a God who can allow all his creatures except those in the ark to perish. Noah and his sons prevent Calan from taking over the ark and leave him in chains to face the rising waters, but with a plea to accept God who may then set him free. None of the many interpretations of this play seem entirely satisfactory; for any claim that Noah is not Barlach's ideal man as he turns against his neighbour and therefore becomes the symbol of irresponsibility, does not accord with Barlach's own further comments in the letter already quoted. For by judging Noah by "human" standards we may thereby idealise God in this play into a form of perfect man. Noah is only justified in his action if we accept all human actions as part of God's purpose and forget—as Barlach asks us to do—all categories of good and evil. Calan clearly is through human eyes an evil character if only for his inhuman cruelty—yet we may not interpret his fate as a just reward unless we attribute to Noah the role of God's executioner. Nor is it easy to maintain that Barlach is pointing a moral that God exists as avenger for one man and redeemer for another. Barlach is certainly destroying man as he puts it in this letter "als Ding für sich".[22] Calan after a night out in the storm and mud, and when the rats have gnawed out his once proud eyes, has become to his pleasure and pride "keine Gestalt mehr . . . nur noch Glut und Abgrund in Gott",[23] and yet he sees

> den anderen Gott, von dem es heißen soll, die Welt ist groß, und Gott ist winziger als Nichts—ein Pünktchen, ein Glimmen, und Alles fängt in ihm an, und Alles hört in ihm auf. Er ist ohne Gestalt und Stimme.[24]

Noah still trusts in a God to lead him past the flood and its threat of annihilation. Either could be equally wrong in his certainty, but the play ends with the sound of the approaching flood, and Barlach gives no answer.

Der blaue Boll (1926) tells the story of a man who overcomes the limitations of his self and becomes a higher being. A wealthy landowner by inheritance rather than by choice, Boll has learnt to become overridingly self-confident and stands like a tower overlooking his fellow men. He has theoretically and forcibly overcome the temptations of the flesh, but in a scene set in the church tower, Boll is faced with the temptation of helping Grete who has given birth to three children and who has thus set three souls into the limitations of their human bodies, and who now wants to poison them and set their souls free once more. Boll has repeatedly torn himself to pieces in an effort to overcome the demands of his flesh by denying its power, but his trust in these is brought back when Grete helps him up after a fit of vertigo, and he is humiliated by the old clock maker. Boll agrees to bring the poison for Grete that evening in exchange for her love. For the whole day he is plagued with guilt, but as he will not accept that Boll has to shoulder any responsibility, he goes to fetch the poison. He changes his mind and meets Grete at the rendezvous without the poison. She mocks him and, aided by the devil Elias, leaves him to himself. Herr the stranger and Boll's wife help Boll most towards accepting responsibility for Grete, whose character also evolves after a vision of hell she has in Elias' tavern. Boll's former pride and Grete's former witchlike qualities—both growing out of dissatisfaction with their human lot—have attracted, repulsed and finally destroyed each other against a background of less complex and less extreme characters whose everyday acceptance of their fate serves as a foil and example to Boll and Grete. Boll—formerly so ready to consider suicide rather than accept the conditions of a human society—has overcome his earlier position—

Boll muß? Muß? Also—will ich![25]

Barlach's last two plays *Die gute Zeit* (1929) and the unfinished *Der Graf von Ratzeburg* are martyr dramas that look forward to the theatre of the absurd. Celestine is too close to the "Other" in her vision of the "gute Zeit" that is at variance with Atlas' system of "Absolute Versicherung",[26] and she is crucified as a herald of the time to come, as a proof of the anxiety of the time now. As she puts it:

> Himmel, ja du hast recht, o, wie recht du hast, wir sind eins mit der Zeit, eins mit der guten, eins mit der bösen, und wie wir, so sind die Zeiten und die Zeiten sind wie wir. . . . Alles und Alles ist gut und reine Güte, wenn ich gut bin, und alles ist gut und reine Güte, wenn keine Angst das Böse ruft—nur still, nur still, nur das Böse nicht gerufen, nur nicht ins Böse kommen mit der Angst, die allein das Böse bringt.[27]

Heinrich, Graf von Ratzeburg, overthrown, enslaved, humiliated into a lowly search for God and for his own true self, is eventually murdered ironically for apparently the wrong motives. In his struggles, in his constant preoccupation to keep on the right way, and in the fragmentary record that we have of him, Heinrich embodies perhaps the Pascalian aspect of Barlach's nature. The complex language and plot of this play make any interpretation of it as yet unviable—it may well remain the most puzzling of all Barlach's works.

Barlach's carefully chiselled style and highly poetic language often directly evoke both the ideas and the effects he requires in a particular context; and there are many passages, sentences or phrases into which he compresses a whole variety of stylistic devices, and which only reveal their intricate and sensitively chosen details on closer analysis. Thus the ending to Chapter 2 of *Seespeck* describing the "allerlei Krauses"(28) of Seespeck's dream:

> Bei alledem hatte Seespeck Zeit, aus dem Hinterfenster herauszuschauen auf einen steilen Dorfkirchturm, gegen den sich die niedersteigende Chaussee grade herabrollte und hinter dem rechts und links die Ostsee sich verbreitete. Ganz oben stand eine gnadenlose Sonne der Kirchturm rückte langsam näher, aber Seespeck fiel es nicht ein, darüber nachzudenken, wie man aus der Hintertür eines Omnibusses nach etwas schauen und doch immer näher herankommen kann.(29)

In these two sentences there are frequent changes of perspective. Thus Seespeck, the subject in the third person (we look *at* him) who looks *out* of the rear window of a bus which we learn is moving because the objects which he watches appear to be moving, looks out *at* a church tower, *towards* which the avenue rolls, and *behind* which the Baltic stretches *to* the left and right. We look *up at* the sun, *at* the church slowly appearing to come closer. The church tower becomes in its turn a sort of starting point for further changes in perspective, the avenue and the Baltic only being fixed in relation to it. We note at first that the town is Dorfkirchturm and later just a Kirchturm, as if it is no longer seen within the confines of a village, but as the only object filling the narrow rear window of a bus. The horizontal plane of view in which we have noticed the avenue (clearly setting us at a distance from the church) and the sea behind it on either side of the church, now gives way to a vertical plane of view, the church tower filling it. There is nothing to say if the sun is right overhead the church or just "ganz oben"—the connection with the church is left for us to fill in (just as with Barlach's sculptures where their doublesidedness of character depends on the particular light in which they stand and on the viewpoint of the spectator). Moreover there is looseness of syntactical connection in the last phrase. Is the church coming nearer to the bus, or the bus to the church? Has there in fact been another change of subjects? Are we witnessing a parallel phenomenon to that of seeing wheels apparently change direction when they move fast enough? The final clauses saying that it did not occur to Seespeck to reflect on this optical illusion makes out of this sense of vertigo a form of normal experience. Seespeck's non-observance of this is shown to be abnormal. Barlach has purposely built up the sensations of this developing vertigo as if we were watching through Seespeck's eyes. But Seespeck is never aware of them—he is the passive object of a series of sensations which attain no meaning because he is not actively registering them. The underlying tension of his situation at the time is brought out here by stylistic effect. A still closer analysis shows that the objects of the verbal forms are simply places in a field of perspective, except for "Zeit" which Seespeck has but does not use. Similarily the subjects are merely viewpoints. The verbs are either directional or negative—only one has any permanency "stand". Both this and the non-verbal adjectives refer to sun and tower, and even "steilen" and "gnadenlose" emphasise direction. It is typical that for Barlach sun and church tower seem finally to be the only points of reference around which the rest of the landscape revolves or moves. Seespeck cannot find his own position in relationship to these and remains part of a shifting, uncentred field of perspectives.

Clearly much of the linguistic value of this piece would be lost in translation and one would like to feel that Barlach has succeeded here by the standard he himself set in a letter to his cousin Karl:

> "Ich kämpfte oft tagelang mit einem einzigen Wort, suche nach einem Satz von drei Worten endlos hin und her und muß oft verzichten, weil ich kein Wort mit der nötigen Silbenzahl finde, es gibt das Wort nicht, sollte es aber geben . . . Das Unerhörte kann nur mit unerhörten Worten erzählt werden, aber die unerhörten Worte werden plötzlich zu falschen Worten, denn das Selbstverständliche, das im Unhörbaren liegt und das man zwingen will, damit das Ergebnis befriedigt und hingenommen werden muß, das Selbstverständliche bedingt wieder das schlichteste Wort, die Aufgabe ist: zwingen und nicht bezwungen scheinen."[30]

But when Barlach chooses to introduce elements of playful irony or puns, his style becomes an appeal to the emotions or to a less sophisticated sense of humour than he is sometimes capable of. Barlach's sense of humour is one which does not always have such a direct appeal because it often also gives an extra dimension to what is normally felt to be grim. Thus the humorous treatment of Calan and minor figures in *Der Findling* which turns into the grotesque and at times the loathsome. Sometimes he appears to be using humour as a defence against despair, and he always seems to give it some further function than just being the expression of a writer brimful of play, a natural outburst of spontaneous fun for its own sake. It is a place where he can lose himself, but it is also a place where he never entirely loses sight of man's true condition. Thus the following untranslatable passage from *Güstrower Tagebuch* (August 8, 1915) describing soldiers at Güstrow:

> Da tauchen aus lackiertem Dämmer treumichelhaft gedachte, in der Tat wie zierbengelige, von der dämlichen Backfischleutnants-idealität parfümierte Helden und treten in Beziehung zu irgendwelchen Nino-Nana—oder aber Elfriede-Mimihaften Treugretchen. Die einsame Wacht in finstrer Mitternacht flötet der Stöckelschuhelegantität ein Ständchen.

There is a far more serious problem when Barlach's language trying to express the essence of existence hiding behind the veil of human activity and humanly developed forms and modes of description, chooses to recreate the secret, unknown—perhaps unknowable—essence of things by using a series of abstract phrases, rhyme schemes or alliterative linguistic associations. Barlach's language in such instances fails to become a connecting line from the human world of expression to the essence of existence, and remains a line parallel to it. Thus in *Der Graf von Ratzeburg*:

> Das war die Lust, die lüstern ist nach der letzten Lust, und die letzte Lust ist die Gemeinschaft des Gehorsams mit seinem Widerspruch.[31]

We are left wondering, even in the context, whether the alliterations and plays on words can be any more than a revelation of Barlach's own struggle with a medium whose usefulness he continually questions, and which he sums up in his letters of October 18, 1932 and December 3, 1932 to two priests. To express any absolute concept outside the range of our senses the word, although it is something "was direkt ins Innerste dringt, wo es aus dem Lautersten, der absoluten Wahrheit kommt",[32] is nothing but "ein elender Notbehelf, ein schäbiges Werkzeug".[33] It is because he attempts to use language as a means to express the quality of an event as well as its causes and consequences, that Barlach's style develops at times too much associative meaning. It would be possible to show that all Barlach's creatures contain their own, or rather their creator's interpretation, and are aware of being in a way that reaches out beyond their own limitations as characters. This develops to such a pitch that by the time Barlach writes *Der Graf von Ratzeburg* nearly all concepts are examined, broadened out, and in the process made almost impossible to put successfully on the stage. The concrete explanatory image, powerful in its first direct statement, is examined for its universal quality, and in doing this Barlach at times opens up a level of consciousness, at times even dialogue, below or at least removed from the episodic story of his characters' lives. Thus, to take but one example, Offerus in *Der Graf von Ratzeburg* asks:

> Und ist Warten nicht ein Mantel, durchlöchert mit Gehorsam und von der traurigen Farbe der Untertänigkeit, ohne Ehre und Ansehen zu tragen?[34]

To appreciate the significance of this remark for the characters involved, one is forced to answer yes, to allow some of Offerus' limitations to become one's own. Only then does this visionary language hold the attention, only when we are prepared to overcome all the inherited logical, sensory or spiritual categories and forget ourselves can we follow Barlach's admittedly powerful but also all-demanding use of language. This is why one can only be "Barlach-Verehrer"[16] or accept him as a writer bound down to a personal vision, who can only speak to those who accept his own Weltanschauung. Occasionally, as with Boll, a character is shown as an outsider to this and can develop a personality of his own, but most of Barlach's creatures represent no more than a special stage or feature of a suffering humanity.

Barlach's unfinished Geisterroman *Reise des Humors und des Beobachtungsgeistes* sets an important pattern for much of his later characterisation—especially with Wau and Wahl in *Der gestohlene Mond*. For the dependence of the allegorical Humor on the equally allegorical Beobachtungsgeist not only suggests the interplay of two sides of Barlach's own character as an artist, but is also an early recognition of a basic theme in his work—that an individual is most clearly apprehended through his dialogue with another. The parallel to Jean Paul's Walt and Vult in *Flegeljahre* has often been made—though Barlach's debt to Jean Paul has not yet been fully examined. Written in Paris, this first attempt at a major prose work is buoyant with the humour and scepsis of a young writer experimenting with ideas and devices and pushing them to their extreme. The topsy-turvy world of the Louvre at night when the statues become alive is taken perhaps a little too far to hold the reader's fascination. The allegorical Klub der deutschen Ideen whose members include such as Kunstsinn, Ideale, Pessimismus, Autoritätenglaube,[35] etc. could well be a modern baroque-type conceit, but Barlach becomes intrigued with this, and develops the theme for its own sake. There are signs of a keen sense of fun and an eye for detail, for example in the description of a discarded newspaper on a draughty corner at night:

> Da sie gerade bei einer Querstraße waren, so winkte das Zeitungsblatt dem Winde, ihm über die Straße in den nächsten Rinnstein zu helfen. Denn da war eine Laterne, die sich gern von solchen Geschichten unterhalten ließ, und als (sich) langsam vorwärts wälzte, fuhr es fort, einen Satz Unflat nach dem andern zu berichten. Nun waren sie bei der Laterne angelangt, und alle Lichtstrahlen versammelten sich neugierig um das Zeitungsblatt.[36]

But both the content and the dilettante approach of this work show Barlach at this time to be no more than a Schillerian "Phantast".

Barlach started to write *Seespeck* in January 1913, left it to one side in August 1914, and finally gave it up as a fragment in October 1916. The opening atmosphere is an epic counterpart to that of *Der arme Vetter* showing the environs of Hamburg and the inhabitants of the Lower Elbe. Seespeck is as much Barlach as Werther is Goethe in that the episode and attitudes are those of a recent past psychologically extended into a more universal significance. Yet the carefully constructed literary motivation and psychological interest in Seespeck as an aimless character in the opening scenes breaks down more and more into the realistic chronicle of Barlach-Seespeck in Wedel. The characters become portraits of locals instead of the author's creatures, until Theodor Däubler appears and speaks and becomes the focal point of Barlach's interest. And the last chapter *Der Löw Ist Los* becomes the epic pronouncement of the plot of *Die Echten Sedemunds,* written in a highly imaginative surrealistic language that breaks down conventional plot development in a frenzy of perspective and shifting action. The style and content of the beginning of this work underline Seespeck's lack of a centre of gravity, and by extension Barlach's. Most of the action is told through Seespeck's consciousness and Barlach's imagination. Barlach seems at times to be exploring through Seespeck the possible developments of events that might have taken place—such as the scene with Grete's family at the end of which Seespeck says to himself:

> Eine Schwiegermutter hast du nun, Seespeck, aber keine Braut, das ist dir recht, denn das paßt zu dir.[37]

And there are many passages where Barlach seems to write within a tradition—such as Goethe's or Storm's anthropomorphic use of nature, or Joseph Conrad's descriptions of seafaring families. Much of this novel however seems to be a vessel into which Barlach poured the themes and problems that interested him, for example the effects of light, sufferings as a touchstone for the conscience, beauty as an enfiguration of the Weltseele, the difference of a person seen through the eyes of different people, the similarity in kind of the sinful and the sacred, the prodigal son, the Doppelgängertum of Seespeck's existence, and men caged in their own way of life (Menschentum). *Seespeck* is interesting and artistically valid only in its parts; its rambling diversity of styles deny it as a serious work of art; but through it Barlach can be seen working out a way to mastery over the novel form.

Der gestohlene Mond (April 1936–November 1937) is also considered by some critics as unfinished. As this work includes most of the maturer aspects of his Weltanschauung, it can be seen as Barlach's central work. It is also—notoriously—his most difficult. The two main characters Wau and Wahl are functions for an interplay of self-consciousness in which each reveals the other. Wau, even though not an artist, perhaps stands for Barlach himself, for he is described intimately from within, whereas all the other characters are portrayed from without. The love-hate relationship between Wau and Wahl is developed into the major interest of the work. Wau, being an entirely passive character, wishes to blend himself into an uneventful existence, and so there is no question of this being a Bildungsroman. His experience of the relativity and random encounter with culture in his life leads him to doubt the concept of personality and to have no faith in God. He can see no basis to a better existence and needs to control a Mein-Welt as a "Prüfstein des Anderen".[38] But only a constant preoccupation with death symbolised by the moon can bring him closer to the "Other", for the moon is to earth as death is to life. Wau, to form his character, needs the catalyst Wahl who warns him against subtle speculations with dilettante ideas and word plays in which he has been brought up. At times Barlach as narrator pokes fun at the seriousness of this situation where one man struggles spiritually with the other to avoid being philistine, to achieve a feeling of distance from the demands of the everyday and society. Wahl is selfish—a foil to Wau's lack of belief in any principle. Wahl is an opportunist and parasite feeding off Wau's weakness in needing continual support for his state of being an outsider which he realises after a violent dream. Wau is even haunted by Wahl's features, so demanding does Wahl become. The unsuccessful attempt of Wau's wife Henny to come back to him, makes him realise that his power over himself gradually ebbs away when he thinks back to the past when he gave himself completely to her. The broken record image of the dream and the broken marriage of the present both ironically lead to a fusion of Wau's person, for Wau's present is patterned by incursions from the past. Barlach uses time as formulated in a fragment to *Seespeck*:

> die Zeit ist ein Gummiband und läßt sich unendlich zerren, schließlich aber schnellt sie einmal zusammen, und es ist alles beim alten.[39]

Wau in his cups envies Wahl's certainty that his world of appearances is the true world of reality, and tries to induce a state of intoxication in which he can convince himself of what he knows to be true, resulting in his first "mystical" experience:

> Es war ein Schatten dagestanden, der von ihm selbst ausging, durch die Wolken stieß, den Mond verdeckte, die Sonne trübte und in den Weltenraum unabsehbar heineinragte, ja ihn erfüllte, denn es blieb kein Raum zwischen den Gestalten der Körper und Sterngruppen war, überall waren sie von dem Schatten, der von ihm ausging, verhüllt und in ihm geborgen.[40]

A vision of a giant pulse-beat high over the sun follows and Wau hardly knows if it is an extension of his own. This Märchenwelt in which Barlach's style closely parallels with its long sentences the idea of letting a genie out of a bottle is suddenly punctuated by the direct contact of a living person Friedrich Schult. This is either a Stilbruch or an emphatic assertion that the traditional separation of the imaginary and the everyday is false. Certainly in the chaining together of Wau and Wahl in an ever tightening lock of characters the same device is used to uncover deeper levels of consciousness. In fulfilling each other's existence Barlach can turn the style describing these two from third person narrative to third person conversation to a direct Ich-Du dialogue. The way is open for each to educate the other's spirit, yet planning not to lose face, they prepare for a long spiritual struggle for mastery over the other man. The situation is repeated in the relationship between Wau and Henny, who speaks to him in words reminiscent of the central dramatic idea in Sartre's *Huis Clos*:

> Besinnen wir uns darauf, daß wir nichts für uns sind, immer nur das Gute und Böse für jemand anders, wie er für uns—ach, diese Gegenseitigkeit die uns aufhebt, die uns zu nichts macht . . . und doch . . .[41]

With Wau Barlach allows this to be extended into two voices—Harut and Marut who discuss in his mind the issue of love and hate. A third unidentified voice closes their conversation, proof perhaps that Barlach wishes to allow for the inexplicable intrusion of God, but probably merely a device to close a section neatly. Wau becomes more and more aware of the insidious presence of Wahl in his own mind, but Barlach is careful not to let the novel burst its bounds at any place, and alternately examines Wau at such close quarters that his individuality disappears in the common humanity he has with others, and then steps back and looks at him through the eyes of another and minor character conditioned by accepting the appearance of Wau as his true self. This is perhaps a key to open up a way into the centre of this confused and confusing novel. Once again individual sections stand out for their expressivity, but this time they fit more obviously and intriguingly into the pattern of the whole. Here more perhaps than anywhere else in his works Barlach makes the reader open his eyes in many different ways to look at things, characters and events stereometrically as it were. *Der gestohlene Mond* may be seen as a workshop in which Barlach repeated the many preparatory sketches for his major sculptures in epic form. It reproduces the processes which have to take place before an artist can achieve what Barlach did in his sculptures in particular—the principle of reduction. Seen in this light, it is a tragic statement of the lack of a Du figure in Barlach's own life, perhaps even a surrogate for one.

W. Gielow's bibliography—*Ernst Barlach Literatur-Verzeichnis* (twenty-seven pages) published privately in Munich, 1954, seems now to be unobtainable. The Select Bibliography below can only include a representative list of recent monographs and articles on Barlach together with the main and popular recent editions of his work. The Ernst Barlach Gesellschaft in Hamburg has published restricted annual Barlach rarities and an occasional critical work. Dr. Friedrich Schult now lives in Barlach's Güstrow home and has made it the centre of Barlach scholarship and research, where nearly all of the major manuscripts and some of the sculptures are housed.

Any evaluation of Barlach's position as a twentieth-century artist and writer is bound to evoke a contrary opinion—for not only are his products depersonalised (they are never complete summations of the single moment or of the individual character), but they also display a doublesidedness that is often apparently a paradox in itself. An understanding of this would be essential before one could pass judgement on Barlach's creatures—even to one's own satisfaction. None of them represent complete unity between the self and the other, between the mortal individual with his own characteristics and the undefinable infinity of God. Barlach is at his greatest when he captures in a figure or character the tension between these two poles. The relaxed and carefree in his laughing statues achieve their striking effect because of the presence of lines marking previous grief or stress. The human frame is shown complete in itself but fleeting possessor of a super-human attribute. When this is allowed to fill out the whole of the human frame so that the frame is for gotten—as in the often complicated speech of Boll or the Graf von Ratzeburg for example—Barlach becomes less convincing. It might be shown that where he tries to embrace all the possibilities of one moment, where he is drawn into an ecstatic state which demands full lyrical expression, he fails. Where on the other hand he remains a conscious yet humble craftsman, where he is still alive to the tension involved in dialogue, and when he actively chooses to include this as the main focus of our perspective on to his creatures, he convinces. This is borne out in his use of language—for when his wordplays confirm the double levels of a situation, rather than create them from without, his language vibrates with the pulse of a vital experience. Barlach's humour is never so pungent as when it confirms rather than spotlights. Barlach's characterisation is at its most compelling when it frames a character's limits, and at its worst when it is a hook for endless chains of possible development. Barlach remains an enigma because he himself was constantly and consciously preoccupied with the enigma of human life. To call him a mystic is to misunderstand much of his art and life. To label him an Expressionist is to attribute to him a certainty of attitude that does not belong to an artist whose creatures bear witness to the continuous quest of their creator. Barlach had two outstanding physical features—deep, dark, enquiring eyes, and rugged, supple, tense hands. In these two features with their attributes lay the essentials of his vision and his limitations. His work records their constant interplay, and perhaps only when we can keep that in the forefront of our minds should we begin to evaluate Barlach.

TRANSLATIONS

1. Undressed little men and plucked little geese.
2. This is, dear me, a Barlach self-portrait! Baked in clay and then glazed and embellished with a verse. He shakes, dumb with anticipation his dice-shaker, those dice, which when they roll again shall decide his fate. He's not dicing just for a small win, but for a "life"—as he thinks it.
3. Romanticism and bombast of his feelings.
4. The inner world is as the outer, the outer as the inner.

5. My inner readiness, my own constitution I took with me—for all that was also in me, and all that is indeed terribly Russian, but also terribly German and European and universally human.

6. Däubler is the inhabitant of another world, of another star, who has come to us from an unfathomable distance. Here he necessarily becomes a monster.

7. In the last resort the human eye, ear and senses should be gratified, excited, for I cannot form a world that does not exist, and I must express myself with comprehensible ciphers.

8. You are knocking on a door to reality, but unlike other people I do not live inside but outside my four walls. I am at home everywhere, everything is I.

9. Being is something other than I—being (my existence). The conscious I, Doctor, is the piano player, but being is the music . . . for you make the mask into the essence of the thing: into the thing in itself, and you make the essence into the non-thing.

10. Few drops of eternity.

11. The strongest and highest life and yet a numbness.

12. Time wants to have form, so give shape to time! Dear spirit give me counsel, present to me in lines what I but vaguely feel, send me a boat so that I can push out on to the ocean, that I may see!

13. Prayer does not mean for me being aware of truth—no I mean the inexpressible—neither begging, nor blabbering, nor prattling—no, it means knowing: this is how it is: being holy.

14. The tender silveriness of all things (i.e. their ore-like quality or essence).

15. Because God is, therefore he is different from ourselves and has no memory, knowledge or judgement as we understand them. I can neither know it nor see it, nor hear it, and so in the last resort nor believe it. But I must be able to believe in something, that is tangible. That is desire, compulsion, necessity, whim—for there is God.

16. Barlach worshippers.

17. Never does one remain so deeply silent as when speaking about Barlach.

18. Whatever became apparent to him in human beings, that he grasped to himself with his eyes as he did to his soul with his spiritual catcher.

19. I catch up a cipher with my eyes, and in the darkness of my self it is there translated and worked over.

20. I seize upon, no it seizes me, in my best moments the idea of depersonalisation, of transference to the higher, I call it: the happiness of overcoming the self in which full self-consciousness remains and persists. Impersonality, i.e. illimitability must be the essence of that which I still only hesitatingly call "God".

21. The world is less than nothing, and God is everything—I see nothing but God. . . . God is the great stillness, I hear God.

22. As a thing in himself.

23. No longer a figure and still only a glow and abyss in God.

24. The other God, of whom it is said, the world is great and God is

less than nothing—a little point, a glimmer, and everything begins in him and everything ends in him. He has neither figure nor voice.

25. Boll must? Must? Very well then I shall wish it!

26. Absolute Insurance.

27. Heavens yes how right you are, oh how right you are, we are one with time, one with the good, one with the bad, and just as we so are the times, and times are as we. . . . Everything yes everything is good and pure goodness when I am good, and everything is good and pure goodness when no anxiety is there to call up evil—just be quiet, just be quiet, just don't call up evil, just don't fall into evil through anxiety, which alone brings evil.

28. All sorts of muddled effects.

29. With all this, Seespeck had time to look out of the rear window on to a steep-sloping village church tower, towards which the descending road rolled straight down, and behind which right and left the Baltic spread itself out. Straight above stood a merciless sun, the church tower backed slowly nearer, but it did not occur to Seespeck to reflect as to how one can look at something from out of the rear door of an omnibus and yet be always coming closer.

30. I often fought for days with a single word looking for a sentence of three words endlessly back and forth and often having to give up because I cannot find a word with the neccessary number of syllables, there just is no such word, but there ought to be one. . . . The unheard of can only be narrated with unheard of words, but the unheard words suddenly become false words, for the self-evident that is to be found in the unhearable and that one wants to pull out so that the effect is taken joyfully and completely, the self-evident again demands the simplest word, our task is to compel and not to seem to be compelled.

31. That was enjoyment lurking after the last lust, and the last lust is the community of obedience with its opposite.

32. That reaches right to the innermost where it comes from the purest, the absolute truth.

33. A wretched implement, a rough tool.

34. And is waiting not a cloak holed with obedience and with the drab colour of submission, without bearing honour and standing?

35. Sense for art, ideals, pessimist, belief in authorities.

36. As they were just by a crossing, the paper nodded to the wind to help him over the street into the next gutter. For there was a lamp that liked being entertained by such stories, and as it waltzed slowly forward, it went on giving out one sentence of rubbish after another. Now they had arrived at the lamp, and all the lamp beams gathered round the paper inquisitively.

37. Now Seespeck you have a mother-in-law but no fiancée, and that is just as it should be, for it suits you.

38. Touchstone of the "Other".

39. Time is a rubber band and lets itself be stretched endlessly, but finally it snaps quickly together and everything is back where it all started.

40. There was a shadow that had stood up, eeking out of himself, piercing through the clouds, covering the moon, darkening the sun, towering up as far as the eye could see into space, yes filling space, for there remained no space between the figures of the bodies and star clusters—everywhere they were veiled and hidden by the shadow that went out from him.

41. Let us remember that we are nothing for ourselves, but always only good or evil for someone else, just as they are for us—ah, this opposedness that raises us up, that turns us to nothing . . . and yet. . . .

SELECT BIBLIOGRAPHY

Ernst Barlach. *Das Plastische Werk.* Bearbeitet von Friedrich Schult. Hauswedell Vlg., Hamburg, 1960.

——*Das Graphische Werk.* Bearbeitet von Friedrich Schult. Hauswedell Vlg., Hamburg, 1958.

——*Plastik.* Einführung von Wolf Stubbe. Mit 100 Bildtafeln und Fotos von Friedrich Hewicker. Piper Vlg., Munich, 1959.

——*Zeichnungen,* Einführung von Wolf Stubbe. Mit 100 Bildtafeln und Fotos von Friedrich Hewicker. Piper Vlg., Munich, 1961.

——*Die Wandlungen Gottes. 7 Holzschnitte.* (Nachdruck) Chr. Kaiser Vlg., Munich, 1954.

——*Die Dramen.* In Gemeinschaft mit Friedrich Droß hsg. von Klaus. Lararowicz mit einem Nachwort. Piper Vlg., Munich, 1956.

——*Die Prosa I.* Hsg. von Friedrich Droß und Friedrich Schult. Piper Vlg., Munich, 1958.

——*Die Prosa II.* Hsg. von Friedrich Droß mit einem Nachwort von Walter Muschg. Piper Vlg., Munich, 1959.

——*Spiegel des Unendlichen.* Auswahl aus dem dichterischen Gesamtwerk.

Die Bücher der Neunzehn. Piper Vlg., Munich, 1960. Die *Sündflut* (1959),

——*Zwischen Himmel und Erde* (45 Zeichnungen 1958),

——*Aus seinen Briefen* (1958): Piperbücherei. Piper Vlg., Munich.

——*Der Arme Vetter.* Reclam Vlg., Leipzig, 1959.

——*Der Tote Tag, Der Arme Vetter.* Deutcher Taschenbuch Vlg., Munich (September 1963).

——*Leben und Werk in seinen Briefen.* Mit 25 Bildern. Hsg. von Friedrich Droß. Piper Vlg., Munich, 1952.

——*Frühe und späte Briefe.* Hsg. von Paul Schurek und Hugo Sieker. Classen Vlg., Hamburg, 1962.

Karl Barlach. *Mein Vetter Ernst Barlach.* Heye Vlg., Bremen, 1960.

Karl Dietrich Carls. *Ernst Barlach. Das plastische, graphische und dichterische Werk.* Rembrandt Vlg., Berlin, 1931, 1958.

Helmut Dohle. *Das Problem Barlach. Probleme, Charaktere seiner Dramen.* Czwikltzer Vlg., Cologne, 1957.

Paul Fechter. *Ernst Barlach.* Mohn Vlg., Gütersloh, 1957.

Willi Flemming. *Ernst Barlach. Wesen und Werk.* Dalp Taschenbuch. Francke Vlg., Berne, 1958.
Hans Franck. *Ernst Barlach. Leben und Werk.* Kreuz Vlg., Stuttgart, 1961.
Friedrich Schult. *Barlach im Gespräch.* Aufzeichnungen. Wiesbaden, 1948.
Paul Schurek. *Begegnungen mit Ernst Barlach.* List Bücherei, List Vlg., Munich, 1959.
Heinz Schweizer. *Ernst Barlachs Roman* Der Gestohlene Mond. Francke Vlg., Berne, 1959.
——*Zugang zu Ernst Barlach. Einführung in sein künstlerisches und dichterisches Schaffen.* Beiträge von M. Gosebruch, K. Lazarowicz, H Seiler. Vandenhoeck and Ruprecht Vlg., Göttingen, 1961.
Hanns Braun. *Das Vermächtnis Ernst Barlachs.* Hochland, 1961 (53) (2), pp. 129–39.
Klaus Bremer. *Barlach und die Bühne. Akzente,* 1954, (3), pp. 226–33.
Helmut Krapp. *Der allegorische Dialog. Akzente,* 1954 (3), pp. 210–9.
Karl Markus Michel. *Sprachgewalt oder Gewalt an der Sprach: Der Dramatiker Barlach. Frankfurter Heft,* 1960 (15), pp. 549–53.
Walter Muschg. *Ernst Barlachs Briefe. Die Zerstörung der deutschen Literatur.* List Vlg., Munich, 1961, pp. 66–86.
Hans Schwerte. *Über Barlachs Sprache. Akzente,* 1954 (3), pp. 219–25.
Gottfried Sello. *Ernst Barlach als Illustrator.* Philobiblon, 1960 (4), pp. 199–230 (with 22 illustrations).

Ernst Toller

Ernst Toller

by RICHARD BECKLEY

Ernst Toller was born on December 1, 1893, at Samotschin, near Bromberg, in Eastern Germany, of middle-class Jewish parents. After the usual schooling at the local secondary school he went to the university of Grenoble, where his studies were interrupted by the outbreak of the First World War. He volunteered for the army and saw active service in the infantry, but was discharged in 1916 owing to a nervous breakdown. After the war he spent five years in prison for his part in the Munich revolution following the creation of the Weimar Republic. On Hitler's rise to power in 1933 his books were banned, and he was forced to flee the country. He went first to England, and then to America, where he committed suicide on May 22, 1939.

IN the history of modern German literature Ernst Toller stands out not only on account of his achievements as a creative writer —considerable though these may be—but also by virtue of the fact that his life and work are typical to a remarkable degree of that of so many dramatists of the Expressionist generation. The disastrous course of the First World War with its senseless waste of life and subsequent loss of human values, and the social and economic chaos which followed upon it in Germany as perhaps nowhere else in Europe, are events which find their reflection, direct or indirect, in the work of most Expressionist writers; but for Toller they became the central experience which dictated the course of his life, shaped his attitude to it, and virtually determined its end, while in his creative work he was almost exclusively concerned with the conflicts this experience presented.

His reputation, too, follows a pattern typical of the dramatists of his generation. His early plays were alternately acclaimed and denigrated with the vehemence of an age unsure of its critical standards but conscious of passing through a new and exciting literary phase, while the plays Toller wrote in the late 'twenties and early 'thirties' went almost unnoticed as the development of the political situation in Germany, against which they were intended to be a warning, became the predominant concern of the nation.

In attempting to understand Toller's work as a whole, therefore, and to assess its value as a contribution to literature in the twentieth century, the conditions attending its origins and the public recognition which promoted it are considerations of particular importance. No less important is the question of the extent to which the experience his plays reflect is still significant for us, though this depends not only on whether a succeeding generation produces a writer interested in developing his themes and making them part of the literary tradition, but also on the modifications our own apprehension of life undergoes.

In one respect, at least, Toller had what seems to be almost a prerequisite for the twentieth-century artist—the sense of not belonging, or of standing outside society. His particular sense of loneliness and isolation must be partly attributable to the fact that he was born of Jewish parents in a country and at a time when the prejudice of anti-Semitism was especially virulent. In his autobiography, *Eine Jugend in Deutschland*,[1] which was published in Amsterdam the year Hitler came to power, Toller relates as one of his earliest impressions how at the age of four he was playing outside the house where he lived with a little girl when the girl's nursemaid called her away telling her she was not to mix with Jews. Subsequent experiences of a similar though more serious nature must have made him conscious at all times of his situation in German society and have played an important role in developing his attitude to the problem of allegiances. It is interesting to note that even as a student before the First World War he felt the need to widen his sympathies. This was partly the reason for his decision to study abroad rather than confine himself to German universities.

Yet at the outbreak of war no one could have been more prompt in volunteering to defend his country, which Toller, like most Germans, believed to have been treacherously attacked. After a hazardous journey from Grenoble back to Germany, during which he was twice arrested, he finally reached Munich and enlisted with the artillery in the enthusiastic belief that the arduousness of the ordinary soldier's lot would give him the opportunity he required to prove his loyalty to the Fatherland. In the same frame of mind he transferred a year later to an infantry division and was thrown into the thick of the fighting when he was posted to the machine-gun section at Bois-le-Prêtre. Here it was, however, that he quite unexpectedly underwent that spiritual crisis and change which forms the central experience of his first play. Brought face to face with the nightmare reality of modern warfare and forced to witness human suffering on an unimagined scale his nerves gave way under the strain. Some weeks spent in a Franciscan monastery which the monks had converted into an army hospital re-established the balance of his mind without restoring completely his shattered health, so that in 1916 he was discharged from the army as unfit for active service.

Toller's reaction to the situation of his homeland in 1914 was the first important manifestation of what was to be his life-long concern with all the political and social events of his time which affected the welfare of the community in general. Consequently, although his youthful idealism had been shattered by the experience of war, he could not turn his back on it and attempt to resume a normal civilian life while it continued. He did indeed return to the studies which had been interrupted by the outbreak of hostilities, but he used his opportunities of contact with students of other universities to form a group which aimed, in common with some of Germany's leading intellectuals, at taking some active measure to bring the war to a close and stop further bloodshed as soon as possible.

By itself the group could, of course, do nothing: it had neither the influence nor the power. But Toller found the conference of intellectuals which he attended in 1917 equally powerless. They were too few in number to affect opinion at a level where the important decisions were made, and unwilling to take any other kind of action. Toller gradually realised that the only way to stop the war was to stop the machinery of German economy, to bring the people who worked in the munition factories, and those who produced the food for the nation, out on strike or in demonstration against the war. There was already considerable unrest amongst the industrial workers in various parts of Germany because of the poor wages and the rise in the cost of living, and these conditions were seen to be the result of maintaining a war which was the making of an already unpopular Kaiser. When it came to demonstrations in Munich at the beginning of 1918 Toller threw all his energies into the struggle and brought himself for the first time to the notice of the authorities as a man with ideas and influence to be watched and reckoned with.

Toller's first play, *Die Wandlung*,(2) covers his experiences from the outbreak of war up to this point in his life. He seems to have begun work on it soon after his release from the army, and it would be interesting to know how far he had progressed with it before he himself had lived through the incidents it reflects. *Die Wandlung* is a play of the type which had already become to be known as the *Stationendrama*. As a specific genre it was the creation of the Expressionist generation, who used it to present in a series of stages or tableaux the spiritual progress or conversion of a man to a new ideal type symbolising their aspirations in a society that was felt to have become spiritually sterile and decadent. The great danger for many playwrights attempting this kind of drama lay not only in the frequent vagueness of their ideals but also in the difficulty of conveying visually and in terms of action an essentially inner process. The task demanded the mastery of a new technique which employed the newly-discovered technical resources of the stage, such as spotlighting and the revolving platform, to present the rapidly changing dreamlike quality of inner reality.

In one respect Toller was fortunate. Other dramatists had already experimented with this technique and discovered some of its limitations and possibilities. Toller learnt from their mistakes, and though he must have read more than he actually saw in the theatre his vivid imagination and innate dramatic sense helped him to distinguish the good from the bad.

There is a sureness of conception and an inevitability of dramatic sequence in *Die Wandlung* which is striking even in this period, when dramatists' first plays were frequently their most memorable. It opens on Christmas Eve with the hero Friedrich, himself not a member of the Christian community, standing at an open window watching the Christmas candles burning in the windows of the houses round about. His feeling of loneliness and isolation is particularly strong on an occasion when other people have put aside their differences to celebrate the birth of the preacher of the brotherhood of man. His mother urges him to reserve his sympathies for the traditions and beliefs of his fathers: only these will not fail him; but the image of Ahasuerus, the Jew condemned to wander alone through the ages for his lack of pity and understanding for Christ's sufferings, tortures his mind. When news arrives that the country in which he lives has been suddenly attacked he interprets this as an opportunity to prove his sense of community with his fellowmen.

Toller now presents a series of scenes alternating between nightmare-like exposures of the monstrous reality behind the patriotic façade of war and Friedrich's frantic attempts to maintain his belief in his country's cause as a means of fulfilling his need to belong. On the troop train he meets the ordinary soldiers who see the war in its true colours—a mean struggle for selfish ends. Service at the front reveals to him its degrading brutality, and later on in the military hospital he sees how it perverts men's minds. The doctors rejoice in the opportunities it affords for perfecting artificial limbs for the maimed and mutilated, and a Red Cross nurse, a "Sister of Mercy" is elated at the news that 10,000 of the enemy have been killed in a single battle.

The crisis brought about in Friedrich's mind by the clash between his idealism and the reality of the situation occurs when, invalided out of the army, he tries to express in artistic terms the justification for so much human suffering by sculpting a statue which symbolises the "victory of the fatherland". He is interrupted in his work by two beggars, a crippled ex-soldier and his wife who is riddled with venereal disease contracted from the invading army. The plight of these two figures represents the true extent of the victory of the fatherland in human terms. By presenting a married couple Toller shows how war strikes at the most fundamental and positive expression of man's social instincts. Friedrich sees that the dividing force of war is greater than its uniting force, through which he had hoped to attain his own personal salvation. Overwhelmed with horror he destroys his statue, symbol of his earlier ideal, and goes off in search of a new orientation.

He discovers this by way of a "descent into the depths". As a lodger in the broken homes of the poor, and as a worker in the darkness and din of the factories he gradually comes to realise that he yearns for a wider sense of community which will transcend all national frontiers and religious creeds—the instruments of discord and division in the world—and unite the world's underprivileged millions in the common cause of restoring the dignity of man by peaceful co-existence and equality for all. Toller does not use the word Communism in this play—a word which in any case could not have had the connotations then that it has for us today—but he would not have been uninfluenced by the fact that the founding of the German Communist party was the eventual result of a split in the Socialist party caused by the refusal of certain radicals to vote money for armaments, and that one of the reasons for the Russian revolution was the determination of its leaders to bring the war with Germany to an end as soon as possible.

The idea of class warfare was equally repugnant to Toller. When Friedrich discovers that the active role he is destined to play in his newly found community is to teach the people the way out of their misery he warns them against the speaker who fosters their feelings of hatred and incites them to violence against their employers. Instead, he calls them to a meeting outside the cathedral, symbolic of his peaceful mission, and preaches the salvation of the people through the restoration of their own human dignity. Just as war had crippled, spiritually and physically, the soldiers who were forced to fight it, so in the factories the machines crippled the workers who had to operate them, year in, year out, through most of their waking hours. Their souls had atrophied with the incessant and meaningless motions of their hands and feet on levers and treadles. With Friedrich's public exhortation to a "bloodless revolution" that will change these conditions the play ends.

One of the charges most frequently brought against the Expressionist dramatists was that their situations had no foundation in reality and that their solutions were incapable of practical application. A certain abuse of the Expressionist style and technique, which had to resort to some very bold effects to gain attention in a world of confused and warring ideas, tended to show up any deficiencies in inner content. The dramatists themselves were conscious of these problems, and this consciousness affected their work. Writers like Werfel insisted on presenting the inner regeneration of man uncomplicated by the social and political issues of the day on which Germans were so passionately divided, while Toller was classed with the opposing group of Activists, who saw spiritual reform as primarily a matter of social and political change.

In *Die Wandlung*, however, Toller presents these two elements as inseparably connected. Both are necessary, and neither is possible without the other. From his experience of the social and political situation he distils the conception of a spiritual conflict which is valid both as art and as a comment on the particular problems of the age.

The measure of his achievement may be appreciated if his play is compared with Reinhard Sorge's *Der Bettler*, the theme and form of which influenced Toller considerably. Sorge's hero is a young man aspiring to be a dramatist in a society whose materialist values and narrow sympathies he cannot accept. His search is for an activity that will give meaning to life. His discovery, however, is a re-discovery of the fundamental value of that which already exists. He opposes his father's outmoded attitudes, but builds on the underlying affirmation of life which had activated his ideas when he, too, was young. There is thus no break in continuity between past and present.

In Toller's play the dramatic conflict has been brought into sharper focus by the general situation of war and the hero's belonging to a minority group in the wider community. The gulf which separates Friedrich from society is not so much that which exists between the generations as that between degenerate man and the example of Christ. Friedrich experiences his transfiguration in a dream-sequence which is entitled "Tod und Auferstehung" —the German expression for Christ's passion and ascent into Heaven. The symbolic scenes are, moreover, not solely concerned with Friedrich's own spiritual development. His crisis is linked with that of the rest of humanity by his grotesque visions of the behaviour of a nation caught in a savage conflict, and his own salvation is dependent upon his ability to bring about theirs. Toller's language, too, conveys the greater urgency of an insupportable situation. It is by turns broken, brooding, ejaculatory, or balled into the pounding weight of the slogan and charged with its crude rhythms. The sound of the words becomes part of the action of the play.

A good example is contained in the scene in which the soldiers are transported to the front:

(Vergittertes Holzabteil eines fahrenden Zuges. Ölfunzel tränt flackerndes Licht. Zusammengepfercht hocken schlafende Soldaten. Ein stummer Soldat (Antlitz Friedrichs). Zweiter stummer Soldat mit Totenschädel. Beide schattenhaft wirklich.)

Erster Soldat: Wie lange rattert schon der Zug.
O dieses ewige knirschende Stampfen
Gepeitschter Maschine.
Zweiter Soldat: Wir irren durch endlose Räume.
Tage, Wochen, ich weiss es kaum mehr.
Wollt', ich schlief im Schoss meiner Mutter.
Dritter Soldat: Wollt', das Haus wär zusammengestürzt
Als der Vater die Frau umarmte....
Fünfter Soldat: Unnütze Worte. Lange schon
Klemmt uns verruchter Sarg.
Lange schon modern wir.
Stinkend verfaulendes Menschenfleisch....
Sechster Soldat: Ziellos irren wir, furchtsame Kinder
Preisgegeben sinnloser Willkür
Morden, hungern, vollbringen gewaltige Taten.
Bleiben doch furchtsame Kinder
Schrecküberfallen von lichtloser Nacht...
Erster Soldat: Ewig fahren wir.
Zweiter Soldat: Ewig stampft die Maschine.
Dritter Soldat: Ewig gatten sich Menschen.
Aus gieriger Lust wächst ewig Fluch.
Fünfter Soldat: Ewig verwesen wir.
Sechster Soldat: Ewig Kinder vom Vater geängstigt.
Alle: Ewig fahren wir
Ewig. . . .[3]

The changing patterns of sound and rhythm give a dynamic movement to even the most statically conceived dream-sequences, so that they become a structurally binding, rather than a digressing element in the loose unity characteristic of the *Stationendrama*.

Yet a cruel irony attended this personal triumph of the artist. Before the play could be cast in its final form the situation out of which Friedrich emerges transfigured and victorious had led to events which overwhelmed his author. Toller was arrested for his part in instigating the war-time demonstrations of the workers and forced into uniform again so that he could be court-martialled.

After some weeks spent in an army prison he was saved only by a plea from his mother to the authorities that he was mentally unbalanced. However, Toller resented his mother's intervention and was deeply humiliated by the examination which followed in the army hospital.

When some months later the revolution broke out that led to the end of the war, the collapse of the monarchy, and the establishment of the Weimar Republic Toller entered the thick of the political action and was elected in Munich as representative of one of the revolutionary Soldiers' and Workers' Councils that sprang up all over the country. To him and many other radicals the new government, composed mainly of "majority socialists" who had held office during the war and done so little to oppose the military dictatorship of Ludendorff, was no answer to their demand for a thoroughgoing plan of socialisation on the Russian model that would give to the mass of the people the power of deciding their own fate. In Munich, Berlin and some other cities, the Communist "Spartacist" groups rose in rebellion against the barely created central government and called upon the rest of Germany to do the same. Toller now found himself overtaken by a situation which, in spite of his radical sympathies, he could never have wished for. In fact he saw almost immediately the impossibility of setting up a revolutionary government separate from that of the Weimar Republic with men who had little practical experience of governing, and in the face of opposition from almost the whole of the existing administrative class. Having been entrusted with his office in the Soldiers' and Workers' Councils, however, he did his best to keep order in a city that was now torn with civil strife. But in the final instance he could do little to check the increasing fierceness of the struggle between the two factions. It broke all bounds when the newly formed government, having no army of its own, was forced to enlist the aid of those groups of soldiers who had not yet disbanded to suppress the rising. These groups had been held together or reformed by officers who were resentful of their loss of status in the new republic and were, by nature of their profession anti-Bolshevik. The use of them by a government that claimed to be socialist seemed to the Communists an act of the greatest treachery. As the two forces came to grips both sides resorted to the brutality of reprisals. The shooting of ten hostages by the Communists was countered by an indiscriminate attack on the civilian population by the "white" army. Twenty innocent Catholic journeymen were mistaken for Spartacists and shot before they could speak in their own defence, and a number of the revolutionary leaders were murdered by the soldiers before they could be brought to trial. Toller escaped and went into hiding, but a price was placed on his head, and before order had been completely restored he was discovered and arrested.

It was only through the warning and help of a kindly guard that he, too, lived to face his trial. He and his fellow-revolutionaries went before judges of the old régime who still held office, and the sentences were accordingly harsh, in spite of the plea of the advocate that a government which had itself come into being by means of a revolution could hardly condemn such men, and that the whole of Germany had still been in a state of revolution when this second rising took place. Many prominent men, including Thomas Mann, spoke for Toller's integrity of character and bore witness to his attempts to check the bloodshed in the days of the "Red and White Terror", but he was nevertheless sentenced to five years' imprisonment for treason in the fortress of Niederschönenfeld.

These were the years which, Toller says in his autobiography, changed him from a revolutionary by inclination to a revolutionary out of conviction, and most of the plays for which he is remembered, including *Die Wandlung*, were published from prison. This explains perhaps why *Die Wandlung*, the record of an earlier experience, closes, in spite of its pacifist message, with a call to revolution, albeit a bloodless one. In the early months of his imprisonment, while he was giving the finishing touches to his first play, he did not change his views with regard to the use of violence in bringing about social reform, but he could not ignore the tragic experience of the Munich rising. He saw the conflict between the idealism of the individual leader and the emotional forces which informed the masses struggling for their liberation, and out of the oppressive realisation that bloodshed and injustice are inevitable in times of revolution he conceived his next play, *Masse Mensch*.[(4)]

Unlike *Die Wandlung* it was written at great speed in a short space of time, and is charged with the passionate intensity of an experience still being lived through. It may have been Toller's feeling of the need for enough objectivity to create a work of art out of such recent and harrowing impressions that caused him to concentrate on the external conflict and make the main figure in the events in which he himself was actually involved a woman modelled on the character of a professor's wife who played a leading part in the demonstrations leading to the revolution. Sonia, like Toller, finds herself placed in a position of leadership at the time of the rising, and struggles against the fanatics of the movement to preserve the ideals of the revolution and dissuade the masses from the use of violence. Her isolation is made more acute by the fact that her husband, whom she loves and respects, and to whom she owes obedience, sides with the existing régime and disowns her. When he is captured by the forces of her party, her plea for his life is used by her opponents in the movement to prove that her pacifist attitude throughout was the planned tactic of a traitor intent on undermining the revolution. In her despair at the intolerable tragedy of her situation she accuses God of abandoning blind humanity to its own fate and transfers to him the guilt that men, through no fault of their own, are forced to incur. When subsequently the fortunes of the fight bring the release of her husband and her own arrest, she is visited by a mysterious figure called "The Nameless One" who attempts to convert her to the belief that violence rules over man's destiny by telling her she may escape if she will agree to the killing of her warder. She scorns the temptation, refusing to incur guilt in a situation which allows her to choose. Finally she dismisses the priest who has come to hear her confession, because he represents the belief in original sin, and goes out to face the firing squad without absolution.

Masse Mensch made Toller famous and brought him to the notice of the general public. It presented events in which the whole nation had in some measure been concerned; its theme was highly controversial; and certain scenes, such as that in which the capitalists do a fox-trot round the desks of the stock exchange to celebrate the profits they make out of war, scored a theatrical success which made their attack all the more effective. Moreover, Sonia's proud rejection of the belief in man's need for divine grace accorded with the general revolutionary tone of the play. Its ending was more satisfactory and convincing than that of *Die Wandlung*, where a certain contradiction between mood and message had not been resolved.

A comparison of the references to Christian mythology and the tenets of the faith in *Die Wandlung* and *Masse Mensch* shows that Toller was coming more and more to the realisation that man could look to no one but himself in the working out of his salvation. The inexorably slow passing of his years of confinement and the constant fight with the prison authorities to maintain the few rights to which he was entitled deepened his pessimism and hardened his attitudes. The privations and restrictions of prison life turned the inmates against each other as well as against their guards, and the news that seeped through of political developments in the outside world offered no consolation. Toller seems to have turned in despair from the immediate present, and to have sought relief in a historical subject for his next play.

This did not, of course, represent an escape into the past, but rather provided the dramatist with greater imaginative scope in dealing with the conflicts of his time. Georg Kaiser's *Gas* trilogy, which posed the problem of the survival of human values in a modern industrial age, had just recently made theatrical history. Kaiser had weighed the material benefits of an industrial welfare state against the dangers of a technical advance so rapid that its makers were no longer able to control the forces they had created. The means of prosperity in peace is developed into a deadly instrument of war as conflicts of opinion develop, and power passes into the hands of the unscrupulous. In the end man annihilates himself with poison gas. Kaiser's protagonist advocates the dismantling of the machinery and a return to a peaceful though more modest existence on the land as the only means of avoiding this cataclysm.

Apart from its impossibility, this suggestion must have been distasteful to Toller on the grounds that industrialisation and mechanisation were held by Communists to be indispensable to social progress. His criticism of a reactionary attitude to the coming of the machine-age and its significance for the emancipation of the masses finds expressed in *Die Maschinenstürmer,*[5] which deals with the Luddite riots in Nottingham in the year 1815. Toller's leading figure is a young man called Jimmy Cobbett. Like the figure of Jäger in Gerhart Hauptmann's Naturalist drama *Die Weber,*[6] with which Toller's play has not a little in common, he is a man "from the outside", who has travelled and can see the problem of the weavers with an objectivity which the conditions of their upbringing and environment have denied to them. He has absorbed the ideals and the bitter lessons of the French Revolution.

The weavers are desperate and starving before the arrival of the machines which will throw so many of them out of work, because Napoleon's war-time blockade has brought their trade to a standstill. Nor can they expect sympathy or relief from the government, for, as Toller shows in a prologue, Byron's plea for them in the House of Lords is received with derisive laughter by Castlereagh and the other peers. The retaliatory strike, on which the weavers have decided as a means of hampering the war and obtaining terms for bargaining against the introduction of the machines, has already sown discord in their ranks. Effigies of blacklegs have been strung from gallows and are reviled by the rest of the population. This scene, which begins the action of the play, is most typical of Toller's attitude to the situation. At the risk of sacrificing our sympathy for the weavers he places it in a prominent position to illustrate the mistakenness of the weavers' course of action.

Jimmy remonstrates with them that the success of their plan must depend on the strength of their numbers and the unanimity of their decision. They must be all of one mind, must organise themselves with the weavers of other towns, and they must hold out against hunger and injustice in the meantime. With the power that such organisation will give them they will not only be able to demand reasonable terms from their employers but will also be able to make the machines they fear the means of increased productivity and better standards of living.

Jimmy's arguments against the weavers' reactionary attitude to the machines and his demand for unity and organisation presuppose the social situation in the twentieth century for their fulfilment. They are historically too far in advance of their time. But in setting them back in an age when machines were regarded with superstition and horror as some invention of the Devil, Toller is able to show in a critical light the irrational elements in the misgivings of his contemporaries with regard to the technical advances of their own time. If Toller's play, like Kaiser's, ends tragically, it is not because of man's capacity for wickedness. Although Jimmy's brother, as a tool of the tyrannical factory-owner, brings upon the hero the suspicion and accusations which Sonia has to face on account of her husband in *Masse Mensch*, and although the perpetrator of these accusations is a man who advocates violence, and is jealous of Jimmy's influence with the weavers, it is hate born of hunger, ignorance and inner confusion which rouses the weavers to murder their leader, wreck the machines, and so give the authorities the needed excuse to break their resistance by calling in the army.

In *Die Maschinenstürmer* Toller seems to have set out to illustrate once and for all the practical application of his ideals. Socially as well as spiritually, man cannot stand divided against his fellow man. The use of violence is not only immoral : it positively hinders the process of social emancipation. We must not only believe in the essential goodness of man, but, as one of the characters says at the end of the play, we must *be* good and help each other.

The social scene itself is presented with a harsh realism produced by stark contrasts, yet the historical setting gives to the resulting oversimplification and tendentiousness something of the dimensions of a myth. Byron, the poet-champion of the oppressed, and Castlereagh, the aristocratic ogre, are like the personified forces of good and evil in some primeval conflict. The other characters are grouped on these two sides, and between them and the mass of the weavers stands the mysterious machine, with its potentialities for good or evil, depending on what man can make of them. Toller's treatment of the external world in *Die Maschinenstürmer* might be considered the poetic counterpart to his treatment of the inner world in *Die Wandlung*.

Toller did not produce anything so impressive as *Die Maschinenstürmer* again. It represents the peak of what he was able to work out of his own particular vein, though a later attempt at revolutionary drama which dealt with mutiny in the German Navy at Kiel during the First World War, and to which he gave the title *Feuer aus den Kesseln*,[7] is not without considerable merits as a documentary play.

His last work to be written in prison betrays perhaps not so much the limitations of his art as the dire effects which the tensions produced by his unnatural confinement had on his artistic judgment. Toller was a man with an excess of nervous energy and a feverishly alert mind. He needed both physical liberty and frequent contact and communion with other human beings to maintain his emotional equilibrium and develop his talents. Denied this relief, he was bound at some stage to be turned in on himself and to become absorbed in his private misfortunes. The injustice he and his fellow prisoners suffered at the hands of the authorities, who responded to every complaint or infringement of the regulations with punishments ranging from withdrawal of permission to receive letters to solitary confinement in a darkened cell, made Toller doubly jealous of his rights as a political prisoner and sometimes as petty in his reactions as his guards. Added to this was the strain of emotional and sexual deprivations. In his autobiography, but more frankly in the introduction he wrote for Joseph F. Fishman's *Sex in Prison* (John Lane London, 1935) on "The Sexual Life of Prisoners", he describes both the torments of loneliness and frustration he suffered in this respect and the aberrations which developed amongst his fellow-prisoners in their abnormal situation.

This strain shows through the painful incidents of his play, *Hinkemann*, in which a soldier returns home from war with his genitals shot away, and tries to compensate his faithful wife for the pleasures missing from the marriage bed by providing her with material comforts. These can only be obtained by his taking employment which pays a high salary. The only job available is one of a peculiarly revolting nature : he must bite open the throats of live rats and drink their blood before a fair-ground audience lusting for new sensations! Hinkemann accepts, and reconciles himself to the situation by interpreting it as his chance for an act of self-sacrifice which will reward his wife for her faithfulness. She unfortunately succumbs under the increasing pressure of her husband's self-pity and her own desires to the brutal advances of a seducer, but commits suicide in horror at her own treachery when she learns the secret of her husband's employment and his motives for taking it.

The serious presentation of love relationships in drama has become so fraught with danger since Strindberg discovered the bewildering tangle of ambivalent passion that few playwrights of distinction have attempted the task with any success. Those few who *have* done so have shown a strong disinclination to put the feelings of their characters into words. One calls to mind the silences and laconic utterances of the lovers in Hofmannsthal's *Der Schwierige*(8) and Brecht's *Kaukasische Kreidekreis*(9) or Josephine's frigid responses to Napoleon's frantic attempts to bridge the gap between them in Unruh's *Bonaparte*. In his earlier plays Toller had kept his presentation of personal relationships to a minimum. Friedrich's conversations with Gabriele are confined to the question of allegiances, and Sonia's expression of her feelings for her husband borders on the theoretical. In a later play, called *Die blinde Göttin,*(10) his lovers are separated early in the action by a long prison sentence, after which they do not find their way back to each other.

But the unsatisfactory impression which *Hinkemann* makes may not only lie in a choice of subject-matter unsuited to Toller's talents or the stresses under which it was written. The overcharged action and inflated dialogue could be partly attributed to the fact that the action of the play derives to a considerable extent from Büchner's *Woyzeck*, which had recently been revived in the theatre with great success. In some respects the mood of this play was too near to Toller's own mood. It encouraged tendencies which when given free rein developed into faults. Moreover, the over-emotional tone of so much late Expressionist drama no longer accorded with the disillusion and cynicism of the post-war years. The young Bertolt Brecht's *Trommeln in der Nacht,*(11) with its curt injunction to the audience "Glotzt nicht so romantisch!"(12) was already beginning to set the fashion for a more sober kind of drama.

A comparison of *Woyzeck* and *Hinkemann* suggests however that Toller was not unconscious of the risks he ran in the choice of such a subject. Whereas in Büchner our sympathy is concentrated mainly on the figure of Woyzeck, whose mental torment causes him to murder the unfaithful woman he loves, Toller transfers much of this sympathy to Hinkermann's wife, whose suicide throws a critical light on her wounded husband's self-pity. Hinkemann recognises at the end of the play that his wife's misfortunes were equal to his own and that he had failed in his duty as a member of the stronger sex.

Toller's struggle with the bitterness and despair which threatened his sanity as man and aitrst finds its poetic solution in a collection of verse written some months after *Hinkermann* and entitled *Das Schwalbenbuch.*(13) In the summer of 1922 a pair of swallows had nested in the window of his cell and put up a brave fight against the petty-minded prison authorities, who had pompously announced their presence to be an infringement of the regulations. Toller was touched by the tireless efforts of these birds to build a home for their young, and as nest after nest was officially destroyed, they became for him a symbol of the irrepressible courage and will to be free and happy in a world of legalised tyranny.

The *Schwalbenbuch* does not, as one might expect, present the dramatic conflict between the sure instincts of the animal and man's perversity, although this theme is indeed frequently touched on. It describes instead how the swallows with their simple joy and industry brought life and warmth to Toller's cell and revived in him the belief in those human values which his sense of suffering threatened to destroy. Toller was conscious that his outlook on life was being affected by imprisonment. The opening of his poem has something in common with Rilke's *Panther*; but whereas the panther's vision is blurred by the pent-up force within it, which makes it move restlessly up and down before the bars of the cage, so that it is able to see nothing through them, Toller's vision of loved and familiar things in the outside world is distorted by the iron bars of the prison-window itself :

> Das Stückchen blauer Himmel ist gespiesst von rostigen
> Eisenstäben,
> Die aus dem Gitterloch Deiner Zelle aufbrachen,
> Auf Dich zuwanderten. . . .
> Erst wehrtest Du Dich,
> Aber die Gitterstäbe waren stärker als Du.
> Nun wachsen sie in Deinen Augen,
> Und wohin Du blickst,
> Überall
> Überall siehst Du Gitterstäbe.
> Noch das Kind; das im ach so fernen lupinenblühenden
> Feld spielt,
> Ist gezwängt in die Gitterstäbe Deiner Augen.[14]

The poet longs for something to counteract the effect of this horrible distortion—music, or the reassuring presence of some loved one; but only a miracle could bring them. The miracle then occurs in the unexpected arrival of the swallows, who sing and dance, woo each other, build their nest and produce offspring. Their daily activities open up for the poet visions, untrammelled by prison bars, of a happy and purposeful life in which the true aims of existence are not lost sight of. Drawing the moral for himself and mankind in general Toller closes his poem :

Ich habe gelernt andächtig zu werden vor Eurem unnennbaren Tiersein.
Bevor nicht die Menschen wiederfinden den Grund ihrer Tierheit,
Bevor sie nicht sind
Sind
Wird ihr Kampf nur wert sein
Neuen Kampfes,
Und noch ihre heiligste Wandlung
Wird wert sein neuer Wandlung.[15]

On his release from prison in 1924 Toller again actively participated in combating the reactionary forces in German political life and promoting the efforts of the movement for world peace. He redoubled these efforts in 1933 when Hitler came to power and his books were publicly burnt with those of other "decadent" authors. Although he continued to write plays the work and thought which went into them were naturally affected by the claims on his energies of meetings and congresses, and by his sense of the pressing need for some effective measure to prevent a second war.

The most outstanding product of his pen at this period was his autobiography, in which he hoped, by exposing certain facts concerning political developments in the recent past, to reveal the true nature of the contemporary situation. But his book, which had to be published in Amsterdam, could have had little influence inside Germany. In other works one sees how the years of persecution in prison had affected the clarity of his vision. Experiences gathered in journeys to Russia and America and recorded in *Quer Durch*[16] are marked by his set attitudes. The unfavourable comparison of factory conditions in America with those in Russia rests on the flimsiest of observed facts, and his reaction to what he saw in the slaughterhouses of Chicago—an unedifying sight anywhere, one would imagine—seems to have been conditioned by the gruesome account in Upton Sinclair's *Jungle*, a novel well known in Communist circles. The fact that he is unable to gain access to certain kinds of Russian penitentiaries, whereas in America a tour is arranged for him by a society for prison reform, is passed by almost without comment.

When he arrived in America seeking political asylum shortly before the outbreak of the Second World War he was received enthusiastically as an important refugee and a champion of freedom. His main plays had been translated into English and published collectively as early as 1934, and some of these had received public performances. Translations of some of his prose works, including the autobiography, had followed soon after. When the excitement created by the newspaper reporters had died down he found himself without means of support or any real contacts. No doubt he might have managed as many other refugees did, but he had become accustomed to moving in the limelight of politics and literature, and this was not possible in a foreign country. Moreover, unlike Brecht, who was placed in a similar position, he had passed the peak of his artistic powers, which might otherwise have sustained him. All Toller's plays reflect a fundamentally tragic view of life. The faith and idealism which inform his main characters are maintained by an effort of will in the face of overwhelming odds, and it is not to be wondered at that on May 22, 1939, when the world was on the verge of a second war, he hanged himself in the bedroom of his New York hotel.

The place which Toller's main work occupies in the chronological development of modern German drama is not difficult to define. Growing out of the first phase of Expressionism, which is characterised by a forward-looking youthful idealism and a delight in formal experiment resulting in the creation of the *Stationendrama*, it leads over to the disillusion of the post-war years and the preference for a more regularly constructed type of play better suited to the presentation—in historical guise, for reasons of safety—of the realities of the contemporary political and social scene, with which dramatists were becoming increasingly concerned.

It is not, however, so easy to assess the extent of Toller's influence on later developments in the drama. For instance, the Communist sympathies which Brecht shared with Toller could mislead one into supposing influences where there are none. In the plays of his early period Brecht reacted violently against ideas and beliefs which are the mainspring of Toller's works. *Trommeln in der Nacht* reveals contempt for revolutionary fervour; *Mann ist Mann*(17) is wholly concerned with proving that a harmless man will develop into a bloodthirsty soldier with the most natural aptitude; and *Die Heilige Johanna der Schlachthöfe*(18) sees the refusal to use force in class warfare as tantamount to the betrayal of one's cause.

But perhaps the violence of Brecht's protest is suspect. In his later plays there is much which reminds us specifically of Toller. In *Mutter Courage* we find the exclusive preoccupation with war as a force which disrupts normal life and destroys all human values, but which is nevertheless regarded by the characters as a condition from which they can hope to benefit. In *Der gute Mensch von Sezuan*(19) Shen Te, like Sonia, rejects the belief in man's wickedness on the grounds that it is a result of conditions over which he has no control, while the gods themselves are presented as impotent. In *Das Leben des Galilei* there is a similar attitude to the significance of human discovery and invention for social progress as in *Die Maschinenstürmer*, and a similar awareness of the fact that it can be employed for good or evil. Whether or not Brecht would have produced works such as these, which are now generally considered to rank among the best that European drama has to offer, if another dramatist had not previously wrestled with the problems they treat, is the kind of speculation which he himself often found rewarding.

TRANSLATIONS

1. *Growing up in Germany.*
2. *Transfiguration.*
3. (Cattle-truck of a train in motion. Oil-lamps shed a dim flickering light. Sleeping soldiers huddled together in a squatting position. A silent soldier with Friedrich's features, another with a skull for a head. Both shadowy figures.)

First Soldier: The train goes rattling on and on.
Oh, this eternal grinding and stamping
Of a machine lashed forward.
Second Soldier: We hurtle blindly through endless space.
For days, weeks—I hardly know.
I wish I still slept in my mother's womb.
Third Soldier: I wish the house had collapsed
And crushed my mother and father as they lay together....
Fifth Soldier: Useless to talk. For a long time now
Cramped in a devilish coffin.
We have been mouldering.
Stinking decaying human flesh....
Sixth Soldier: Aimless we wander like frightened children
Victims of senseless tyranny.
We murder, starve, do violent deeds.
But are frightened children still
Fear-seized by the black night....
First Soldier: Endlessly we journey.
Second Soldier: Endlessly the engine pounds.
Third Soldier: Endlessly we pair off and copulate.
Lust breeds an eternal curse.
Fifth Soldier: Endlessly we rot and decay.
Sixth Soldier: Children endlessly fearing the father.
All: Endlessly journeying,
Endlessly....

4. *Masses and Man.*
5. *The Machine-Wreckers.*
6. *The Weavers.*

7. *Draw the Fires!* (It means "Rake out the fires in the ship's boilers.")
8. *The Difficult Man.*
9. *The Caucasian Chalk Circle.*
10. *The Blind Goddess.*
11. *Drums in the Night.*
12. Don't gape so romantically!
13. *The Swallow-Book.*
14. The little patch of blue sky is speared by rusty iron bars,
Which rose up out of your cell-window
And came towards you....
At first you resisted,
But the bars were stronger than you.
Now they grow in your eyes,
And wherever you look—
Everywhere
Everywhere you see iron bars.
Even the child who plays in the, alas! so distantly blooming lupin-field
Is crushed between the iron-bars of your eyes.
15. I have learnt to regard with awe and respect that condition of your animal nature, which cannot be named.
Not until men rediscover the conditions of their own animal existence,
Not until they are themselves
Themselves
Will their struggle be worthy
Of a new struggle,
And even their holiest transformation,
Worthy of a new transformation.
16. Translated in the English version as *Which World Which Way?*
17. Probably an ironic allusion to the *English "A man's a man for all that*".
18. *Saint Joan of the Slaughterhouses.* (The American translation of "Schlachthöfe" by "Stockyards" does not convey the shock-effect of the German title.)
19. *The Good Woman of Sezuan.*

SELECT BIBLIOGRAPHY

Prosa, Briefe, Dramen, Gedichte. Rowohlt Verlag, Hamburg, 1961. (A paperback selection of Toller's plays, poems, prose-works and letters, which includes all the more important works with the exception of the documentary drama *Feuer aus den Kesseln.*)

Plays not included in the above volume.

Der entfesselte Wotan. Eine Komödie. Kiepenheuer Verlag, Potsdam, 1923.

Die Rache des verhöhnten Liebhabers. Ein galantes Puppenspiel in zwei Akten. P. Cassirer, Berlin, 1925.
Tag des Proletariats. Requiem den gemordeten Brüdern. Zwei Sprachchöre. Kiepenheuer Verlag, Berlin, 1926.
Hoppla! Wir leben. Ein Vorspiel und fünf Akte. Kiepenheuer Verlag, Berlin, 1927.
Feuer aus den Kesseln. Historisches Schauspiel. Kiepenheuer Verlag, Berlin, 1930.
Die blinde Göttin. Schauspiel in fünf Akten. Kiepenheuer Verlag, Berlin, 1933.
Pastor Hall. Bruno Henschel Verlag, Berlin, 1947. (Duplicated acting script.)

Verse.

Gedichte der Gefangenen. Kurt Wolff Verlag, Munich, 1921.
Das Schwalbenbuch. Kiepenheuer Verlag, Potsdam, 1924.
Vormorgen, Kiepenheuer Verlag, Potsdam, 1924.
Verbrüderung. (A selection from the above.) Arbeiterjugendverlag, Berlin, 1930.

Prose Works.

Justiz: Erlebnisse. E. Laub'sche Verlagsbuchhandlung GmbH, Berlin, 1927.
Eine Jugend in Deutschland. Querido Verlag, Amsterdam, 1933.
Briefe aus dem Gefängnis. Querido Verlag, Amsterdam, 1935.

English Translations.

Plays

Seven Plays: The Machine-Wreckers, Transfiguration, Masses and Man, Hinkemann, Hoppla! Such is life, The Blind Goddess, Draw the Fires, Mary Baker Eddy (the last in collaboration with Hermann Kesten). John Lane, London, 1935.
Pastor Hall. Drama (trans. Stephen Spender). John Lane London, 1939.

Prose Works.

I was a German (Toller's autobiography). New York, 1934.
Letters from Prison. John Lane, London, 1936.

Works on Toller

F. Droop. *Ernst Toller und seine Bühnenwerke.* Berlin, 1922.
Stefan Grossmann. *Der Hochverräter Ernst Toller.* Rowohlt Verlag, Berlin, 1919.
P. Signer. *Ernst Toller, eine Studie.* Berlin, 1924.
Mathilde Hain. *Studien über das Wesen des frühexpressionistischen Dramas.* Verlag moritz Diesterweg, Frankfurt am Main, 1933.

Franz Werfel

Franz Werfel

by W. H. FOX

Franz Werfel was born on September 10, 1890, son of a well-to-do Prague glove manufacturer. He attended the Stephansgymnasium in Prague and proceeded to a very brief University career, during which he began writing poetry. His first published poem appeared in the Sunday supplement of the Viennese paper *Die Zeit* in 1909. In 1910 he was sent to a Hamburg export firm with a view to his joining the family business later, but again he appears to have neglected his "work" for poetry. His first volume of verse, *Der Weltfreund*, met with immediate success on its publication in 1911. After a year's compulsory military training with a field artillery regiment Werfel was employed as a reader, together with Hasenclever and Kurt Pinthus, by the Leipzig publishing house of Kurt Wolff until the First World War. Then came military service on the Eastern front, but he was transferred in August 1917 to Vienna for propaganda work which involved visits to Switzerland. From 1918 dates his association with Alma Mahler, who was from then on a constant source of inspiration and encouragement for him. Werfel's excursion into the camp of political radicalism during the revolution of 1918 was brief. With homes in Vienna, Breitenstein and Venice during the Twenties and Thirties he travelled widely in Europe and to Egypt and Palestine. Early in 1938 the growing threat of the German annexation of Austria provoked months of bewildering travel and a temporary settling in the South of France until the invasion of 1940. Werfel crossed the Spanish border on foot and eventually in October 1940 sailed to New York. From the end of that year he made his home in Beverley Hills. Work on his last novel and further plans were interrupted by bouts of illness due to heart disease diagnosed in 1943, and to this he succumbed on August 26, 1945 while reading the proofs of a new volume of selected poems.

"HE could not believe that the hairy-chested, unshaven image which stared vacantly out of the mirror was himself. Had not the day been like those he knew so well, blue-skied, with children and nursemaids walking in the town park?"—thus the opening of Werfel's poem *Der dicke Mann im Spiegel*(1) in which he evokes not only the sights and sounds and smells but also the wonderment and fears of childhood. For the reader of the poem, as for the poet, these are vivid, but it is more than mere nostalgia which creates the effect in the six stanzas, for ultimately the continued undimmed existence of these memories and the longing they induce strike terror in the helpless unchildlike mirror image, which can only turn away. Why should such apparently harmless memories inspire terror? Can it be that their very vividness appears so incongruous, so inappropriate when the poet is brought face to face with himself now that childhood is past? Does he feel guilt when he still finds it possible to recall and record such innocence? Self-appraisal and a feeling of detachment are presented in this poem as frightening aspects of maturity. We are not dealing here with the sentimental reminiscences of an old man, for the poem was among those first published in the collection *Der Weltfreund*[(2)] in 1911, when Werfel was only twenty-one, and just beginning a career as poet, dramatist and novelist.

Youthful ecstacy in living and in loving all that experience offers, determines the range of subject-matter and the style of these first poems. He shared with his generation distrust for cultivated form and the consciously "beautiful" word, and gave priority to the urgency and directness of language, even at the expense of euphony. The musicality of this verse seems so often marred by what, traditionally, counted as unpoetic and plebeian: everyday turns of phrase, a litter of journalese and foreign words, and a deliberate sloppiness and tastelessness at odds with the cool control of George or the sophisticated word music of Hofmannsthal. While this application of everyday language is in another tradition initiated by the Naturalist revolt of Arno Holz, Werfel's style involves the subordination of words to the poet's expressive intentions, so that he (as in varying degrees Heym in his mythical visions and Trakl in his elegaic melancholy) wrings new meaning out of unusual, incongruous or even grotesque word clusters. While the influence of Whitman and of the early Rilke can at times be discerned in this youthful rhapsodising, there is much that attracts the description "anti-poetry". But the attitude is not born of neglect nor simply out of a wish to shock. It flows freely from a personality supremely open to the world, marked by an all-embracing, insatiable sympathy, especially for the poor and oppressed, sensitive but not shrinking like the mimosa Rilke, exultantly exposed to life and to the whole cosmos:

> Ich will mich auf den Rasen niedersetzen
> Und mit der Erde in den Abend fahren.
> Oh Erde, Abend, Glück, oh auf der Welt sein![(3)]

In his feelings he could already claim his identity with men:

> Denn ich habe alle Schicksale durchgemacht: Ich weiss
> Das Gefühl von einsamen Harfenistinnen in Kurkapellen,

Das Gefühl von schüchternen Gouvernanten im fremden Familienkreis,
Das Gefühl von Debutanten, die sich zitternd vor den Souffleurkasten stellen.
Ich lebte im Walde, hatte ein Bahnhofsamt,
Sass gebeugt über Kassabüchern und bediente ungeduldige Gäste.
Als Heizer stand ich vor Kesseln, das Antlitz grell überflammt,
Und als Kuli ass ich Abfall und Küchenreste.
So gehöre ich Dir und allen.
Wolle mir, bitte, nicht widerstehn!
Oh, könnte es einmal geschehn,
Dass wir uns, Bruder, in die Arme fallen![4]

The jarring elements of Werfel's revolutionary Expressionist style are analogous to the vision in the fat man's mirror, revealing a disparity between the wish and the reality. In *Der Weltfreund* many would see with W. H. Sokel in his *The Writer in Extremis* a cry "symptomatic of a generation of authors who felt remote from humanity and desperately attempted to bridge the abyss between themselves and 'men' ". This feeling of remoteness in Werfel is something attributable to his love for the world demonstrated in these early poems and well attested throughout his work—a love that in time feels it can never be adequate, such are the demands it makes of itself and of him who bears it.

In *Der Weltfreund* the euphoric state of childlike harmony is disturbed by the developing problem of individuation and by the closely related one of increasing self-awareness:

Nun Du ein Ich mir gabst und mich erschufst
Zur Schwäche-Qual und daseinsdumpfer Engnis
Und zu entwürdigender Selbstkasteiung. . .[5]

The world ceases to be envisaged as the mere reflection of the poet's personality and becomes a complex of relationships, polarities and responsibilities. Existence itself is seen to involve guilt, so the disharmony in the world would seem inherent even in the most intimate of relationships like that between Father and Son:

Wie wir einst in grenzenlosen Lieben
Spässe der Unendlichkeit getrieben
Zu der Seligen Lust,
Uranos erschloss des Atems Bläue,
Und vereint in seliger Kindertreue
Schaukelten wir da durch seine Brust.

Aber weh! Der Äther, ging verloren,
Welt erbraust und Körper ward geboren, . . .[6]

It is this more obviously ethical strain, accompanying the process of disillusion, which characterises the volume *Wir sind*[7] of 1913—a consciousness of personal responsibility for others in their suffering:

Als mich dein Dasein tränenwärts entrückte,
Und ich durch dich ins Unermessne schwärmte,
Erlebten diesen Tag nicht Abgehärmte,
Mühselig Millionen Unterdrückte?

Als mich dein Wandeln an den Tod verzückte,
War Arbeit um uns und die Erde lärmte.
Und Leere gab es, gottlos Unerwärmte,
Es lebten und es starben Niebeglückte!

Da ich von dir geschwellt war zum Entschweben
So viele waren, die im Dumpfen stampften,
An Pulten schrumpften und vor Kesseln dampften.

Ihr Keuchenden auf Strassen und auf Flüssen!
Gibt es ein Gleichgewicht in Welt und Leben,
Wie werd ich diese Schuld bezahlen müssen![8]

This consciousness of guilt lies at the roots of the more reflective melancholy of *Einander*[9] (1915), where Werfel turns to the godhead with longing for redemption—but it is only in and through man that God is realised. Man is still as always the focal point of Werfel's concern:

Adam
Durch tausend abgespannte Stunden
Hab ich zu dir mich hergefunden.
Du wirfst mich fort?

Stimme aus dem Garten
Wir sind, mein Sohn, so sehr verbunden,
Dass du dich triffst mit deinem eigenen Wort.

Adam
Erbarm dich mein!

Stimme aus dem Garten
Erbarm dich mein!

Adam

Mir Abgebückten mit zerrissenen Füssen,
Willst du die Tür des Schlafengehns verschliessen?
Ist Gnade nicht dein Gut, zuhöchst erlaucht?

Stimme aus dem Garten

Ich habe meine Gnade ausgegeben,
Sie waltet unerschöpft in deinem Leben,
Für dich hab ich sie ganz,
Du nie für mich gebraucht.

Adam

So wird dies Altern nimmer enden,
Und keine Heimat macht mich wieder rein?

Stimme aus dem Garten

Bestelle mich mit deinen Händen,
Und Heimat werden wir uns beide sein,
Und kehren ein!

Adam

Weh, dass kein andres Wort mich tröste,
Und dies zurücke mich in Städte stösst!

Stimme aus dem Garten

Kind, wie ich dich mit meinem Blut erlöste,
So wart ich weinend, dass du mich erlöst.[10]

Among the many forms adopted for his lyric verse—song, aria, hymn, ballad, ode and sonnet—one is struck by the occurrence of forms which allow for statement and counter-statement, question and answer, that is dialogue, including even stichomythia, as in the pair of poems which make up *Selbstgespräch*[11], or in the linked pair under the title *Des Turms Auferstehung*[12], or again in the dialogues *Die Prophezeiung an Alexander*[13], *Sarastro*, and *Zwiegespräch*[14] (*Einander*). In a radio talk in 1952 Willy Haas, a lifelong friend of Werfel and the character B.H. of *Der Stern der Ungeborenen*,[15] attributed great importance to the influence of the form of the Italian operatic aria on the young poet, and compared the quartet from *Rigoletto* with poems like *Ein Gesang von Toten* (mit verteilten Rollen zu lesen)[16] and *Gesang der Toten vor neuem Leben*.[17] But the duet form is not just an aspect of Werfel's musicality but the response to an inner need. It reflects the poet's lack of inner harmony, which more and more was demanding dramatic rather than lyrical expression. Thus there is close correspondence between the early dramatic sketches *Der Besuch aus dem Elysium*[18] (written 1910), *Die Versuchung*[19] (written 1912) and *Die Mittagsgöttin*[20] (Autumn 1918) and the poetry as far as the publication of *Der Gerichtstag*.[21] With the "magische Trilogie" *Spiegelmensch*[22] (1919–20), for the first time in a full and original dramatic form, Werfel undertook to follow a path that led from delusion and vanity.

In poems like *Eitelkeit*,[23] and repeatedly in his war poems as in *Gebet um Reinheit*,[24] Werfel used the image of self-encounter and self-contemplation in the mirror to the end of accusing himself of vanity—vanity as a poet. There is indeed, as elsewhere in this early work, an element of the baroque about the argument which presents self-accusation as another, disguised, form of vanity. Can one suggest that the accomplished liar would feel no such pangs of conscience?

In *Spiegelmensch* the hero, Thamal, seeking asylum as a novice in a mysterious oriental monastery, shoots at his reflection in a magic mirror and, in shattering this, releases his alter ego, the Mirrorman of the title, who represents the lower and essentially megalomaniac self:

> Von Stund an ist er entzweit,
> Und muss blutig und mit zerrissenen Händen ringen,
> Zu bezwingen sein Geleit,
> Das ihn schleppt durch Mord und schuld'ge Taten.[25]

There follows a fantastic series of adventures. He murders his father by merely contemplating killing him, seduces and eventually abandons his friend's bride Ampheh. He is set up as the living God for the people of Cholshamba whom he delivers from the tyranny of the snake-demon Ananthas, suffers as a galley-slave after Spiegelmensch has gained in power and influence with every sin Thamal commits. Confronted with his transgressions he willingly pronounces the sentence of death on himself. By taking poison he destroys Spiegelmensch and is aroused, reborn, to a kaleidoscopic vision of a mysterious higher reality through the mirror which now no longer reflects him.

Together with the story *Nicht der Mörder, der Ermordete ist schuldig*[26] (1919) to which it is closely related in its basic theme, *Spiegelmensch* appears to have served Werfel as a form of personal exorcism, which, while it by no means provided even a dramatically satisfying solution to the underlying problem of self-awareness, enabled him in future to debate its jumble of psychological and metaphysical problems in a more readily comprehended and less obsessively subjective way. The trilogy nevertheless shows those characteristics which are seen in all Werfel's writing for the stage. Spectacle, entertainment in the broadest theatrical sense, the intermingling of operatic and pantomime effects, all combine with the expected elements of plot and character and conflict to mark Werfel as a dramatist in the established Austrian tradition of Raimund and Grillparzer, whose *Der Traum, ein Leben* immediately springs to mind in its parallelism to *Spiegelmensch*. It is with *Brand* or *Peer Gynt* and not with the later work of Ibsen or with the Naturalist drama that the play may be compared. And when the Ich-dramas of Expressionism—those of Sorge, Czokor, Johst, Hasenclever, or Kornfeld—are considered, Werfel's drama is seen as one concerned with the inner conflict of the protagonist, not so much with the tragic outward clash of a society and the individual who claims to be its judge and saviour. Werfel continually presented realistically conceived plot and characters in a framework designed to reveal their metaphysical import, thus giving further evidence of the basic duality of his art.

Dramatic structure of the traditional type is abandoned for an organisation which owes much to musical form—which is not so unexpected when one recalls Werfel's early enthusiasm for opera, and his contribution to the Verdi renaissance of the twenties. Thus the musicality of Werfel's plays *Juarez und Maximilian* (1924), *Paulus unter den Juden*(27) (1926), and *Das Reich Gottes in Böhmen*(28) (1930), where, as A. D. Klarmann has described, "it permeates even into the innermost structure of his work, in the duets of the contrasting couples which complement each other to form a new unity, which, however, has always been theirs and was only temporarily separated, like two voices, that going their way mingle with each other in a higher harmony". Thus also in *Jacobowsky und der Oberst*(29) (1944), the last of his plays, written after his escape from invaded France in 1940.

Unconventionality in dramatic form is matched in Werfel by frequent avoidance of the usual nomenclature, e.g. *Romantisches Drama*, *Ein Gespräch*, *Ein Zauberspiel*, *Magische Trilogie*, "*Bocksgesang*"(30) (a deliberately meaningful mistranslation of the Greek "tragoedia"), *Dramatische Historie*, *Dramatische Legende*. *Jacobowsky und der Oberst* he described as *Komödie einer Tragödie*!

In their flight before the rapidly advancing German forces, a Polish Jew, Jacobowsky, and Stjerbinsky, an anti-Semitic Polish colonel, with the former's servant and later a French girl, Marianne, undergo adventures which, while they are plausible and in fact based on the accounts of refugees like Werfel himself, combine to appear as fantastic and fairy-tale-like as those of Thamal are nightmarish. This atmosphere is created by the comic way in which Jacobowsky and his companions repeatedly, by luck and his quick-wittedness, escape from the dangers, which more often than not are due to their own absurd behaviour. The comic element is in equal measure dependent on the incongruity of their behaviour and attitude in the tragic circumstances of the fall of France. This European tragedy itself gains in poignancy when seen as the background for actions and characters whose interplay can cause such laughter, and at the same time be seen as laughable by Jacobowsky himself, the truly tragi-comic figure of the piece.

In the first act Jacobowsky and the Polish cavalry officer, who under normal circumstances would never have spoken to each other, are thrown together in Paris by fate—in particular by the fact that the Jewish refugee has secured a car and the Polish officer can drive. Stjerbinsky however is concerned not only to reach a rendezvous near Bayonne and deliver his secret documents to England but also to honour a promise to visit his beloved Marianne in Brittany. In the second act their long and mad detour exposes them to the danger of capture and almost certain death—and this is the constant risk incurred by the romantic adventuring of the officer who clings to his code of honour and gallantry, even to the extent of serenading Marianne in the middle of an air-raid or challenging Jacobowsky to a duel. After the adventures of the second act the third is played out against a background of well-nigh absolute hopelessness. The harbour café in St. Jean de Luz is like some limbo for the luckless souls who can now only wait to fall into the hands of the Gestapo, still feared despite their burlesque portrayal in Act II. Jacobowsky is the one who can still wrest humour from the situation while Stjerbinsky appears only incidentally funny in his inability to adapt himself. It is the adaptability of the Jew which sets him apart from the Roman Catholic. It allows him continually to find some possible consolation in every circumstance, and this adaptability is a measure of his ability to see himself and his situation objectively. The threatening tragedy is averted only by the intrusion of a deus ex machina in the person of an English naval officer. The ill-assorted pair are rescued at the last possible moment, and it is at this point that Stjerbinsky allows the slightest of cracks in his prejudice and shows a grudging respect for his companion, although their differences persist:

Oberst Stjerbinsky (schlägt Jacobowsky auf die Schulter): Freuen Sie sich nicht zu sehr, Jacobowsky.... Unser Duell ist nur aufgeschoben....

Jacobowsky: Unser Duell ist ewig, Stjerbinsky....[31]

Their association runs parallel to that of the two characters in Act II who appear on a tandem and introduce themselves as The Wandering Jew and Saint Francis. Jacobowsky's first comment in the episode is an oblique comment on his own situation; the answer indicates Werfel's conception of its implications:

Jacobowsky: Ich sehe zwei Gegensätze, die ganz gut miteinander auskommen!

Der Ewige Jude: Oh, wir sind ein Herz und eine Seele! Lassen Sie Gegensätze nur alt genug werden, dann finden sie sich wie die Parellelen im Unendlichen.[32]

Here as in the many other works where the problem of Jewishness is debated, whether specifically or incidentally, Werfel reveals the inner tension which resulted from his own Jewish origins and his feeling for Austria. In the English foreword to the collection of stories in the volume *Twilight of a World* (1937) he revealed a nostalgic and almost reactionary love for the old Austria which seemed to provide for the peaceful co-existence of so many nationalities and creeds. He nevertheless dealt with Jewishness not only in terms of history or topicality in works like *Paulus unter den Juden*, *Höret die Stimme*,[33] *Der Weg der Verheissung*[34] and the unfinished novel *Cella*, but also in terms of his own continual search for the cause and justification of the separateness of his kind. He turned again and again to the conception of Israel as the chosen people and found that metaphysically it has been allocated a special role until the end of time. A role which is subject to both divine grace and a divine curse. Through its suffering, persecution and destruction the Jewish race is seen as bearing witness to Christ, the unacknowledged Messiah. Thus the Church and Israel need each other, as the characters Saul Minjonman and F.W. put it in *Stern der Ungeborenen*:

> "Die Kirche wird solange leben, wie wir leben, um zu zeugen für Abraham, Isaak und Jakob, die den wahren Gott zuerst erkannten...."
>
> "Die Kirche meint, Israel werde solange leben, wie sie lebt, also bis zum Ende der Dinge, um für den Messias zu zeugen...."
>
> "...Unendliche Strecken sind gleichlang, und wir können's ruhig abwarten, wer für wen zeugen wird...."[35]

In 1922 Rudolf Kayser found the specifically Jewish element in Werfel's work in his longing to overcome duality within the individual (in *Juden in der deutschen Literatur*, ed. Krojanker). The problem for Werfel resulted from a native sensitivity augmented by the nagging introspection of the self-conscious poet. The poet in turn projected his inner doubts into the world about him, so that he saw in abstract intellectualism and individualism those things which separated man from man, and man from God. Metaphysically Werfel regarded the problem as a result of man's Lucifer-like defection from divine origins, and in the society of his day found evidence for this in the modern nationalistic state with its cult of self-assertion. In his early work the longed for unity was that of the condition of childhood celebrated in his verse; later it was found in the ever-repeated relationship of parent and child.

In both *Nicht der Mörder*... and *Spiegelmensch* the hero is afforded insight into "the mystery of unity and blood", the mystery of love and hate between succeeding generations and between man and God. The two motifs of father and son and of the maternal female figure of *Die Mittagsgöttin* are further developed and continue to play a basic role in the prose works. There follows a corresponding loss of extremism, violence and extravagance of style in the novels which Werfel wrote from the mid-twenties until the end of his life, and a more positive accent is put on the theme of integration.

In his first major novel, *Verdi* (published in 1924) Werfel is basically concerned with the integration of the artist in the community. With a facile command of realistic detail and character delineation he depicts the Verdi of 1882 in his unproductive stage between the composition of his *Requiem* and that of *Otello* bitterly suffering his silence in Venice and eclipsed by the ascendant Wagner. This "Roman der Oper"[36] is antithetical in its structure, setting Verdi, opera and Italy against Wagner, Musikdrama and Germany, and examining their respective effects on the Senator, Verdi's friend, and his son, Italo. Here Werfel's sympathies are with the father figure and with Verdi, who retires behind his work. The Romantic Wagner is shown as dependent on the enthusiasms of his youthful supporters and on the force of the personality he projects through his work. Annemarie von Puttkamer points out the relevance of the implied social criticism in this novel to the events which accompanied its writing—the rise of Fascism in Italy, a new and terrible aspect of the Romanticism which in Werfel's view Wagner represented. As a Künstlerroman[37] *Verdi* demonstrates the need for the artist to wait patiently and humbly, without asserting himself, for that combination of outward circumstances which will allow his recognition and the release of his creative ability once more.

It has been held against Werfel that he consciously sought to integrate himself by popularising his art, gaining a mass audience and making his spiritual anchorage "a happy and profitable blend of commercialism and Judaeo-Christian sentiments" (Sokel). The evidence for this commercialism is no doubt sought in the occasional topicality in these prose works, in their emotional sweep and in their style which betrays an almost journalistic freeness and facility. There is a principle at work here, however, which is ultimately the same as that in his drama with its exploitation of theatrical effect, which while it may veil the more profound issues does not invalidate them. Popularity does not necessarily imply that a work is aesthetically suspect. Nor do paperback editions and a sentimentalising Hollywood film adaptation of a novel like *Das Lied von Bernadette*(38) make the author a charlatan. In novel, drama and in verse Werfel continued with that conviction, urgency and human warmth which characterised his earliest work and earned him recognition.

Within the loose framework of what seems part chronicle, part "Entwicklungsroman"(39) and part "Schlüsselroman"(40) *Barbara, oder die Frömmigkeit*(41) (1929) has as its central experience, like so many contemporary novels, the First World War. The personal history it recounts however covers the childhood and youth of its hero, Ferdinand R., *and* the revolution which immediately followed the war. Here the implications of the conflict between the individual and the political and military and revolutionary powers he is helpless to resist go far beyond those of the many stories of the time about the blood and mire of trench warfare. It is an impersonal power which is portrayed and to which the orphaned boy is subjected as a military cadet and in the army. Similarly in the revolution he sees it exploiting and consuming without mercy, a whole population. The tools of this power are represented not by any enemy soldier but by the figures of Steidler, a fellow cadet and later a staff captain in the army, and by Elkan, the alien, cold-blooded revolutionary. Both have in common an inhuman and machine-like disregard for human life, and it is through Steidler that Ferdinand is brought to demonstrate a simple and unassuming humanity in the action which provides the axis for the whole novel. In 'Richtgang',(42) the thirteenth chapter of the second of four parts, Ferdinand halts the execution of three alleged but innocent deserters and allows the men to escape. The hero is presented as relying always, even unconsciously, on the comfort and guidance of the old woman, Barbara, who since his childhood has been the source of that completely free and selfless love which is the pure expression of motherliness.

The piety of the title is a naive, uncalculating and almost undemonstrative relationship with God which corresponds to the feeling of safety and repose which Barbara in turn inspires in the child

Ferdinand. It is to him that she bequeaths her life's savings, not to her relatives. Such is the love he feels for her that he consigns this symbol of her devotion to the sea, where it is beyond risk of losing that spiritual value it holds for him. Ten years later Werfel was to write a novel which, for all its dissimilarities, was essentially a variation on this theme in *Der veruntreute Himmel*[43] (1939). Here the old cook Teta scrapes and saves in order to pay for the education of her nephew Mojmir, who figures in her calculations as the future priest to intercede for her soul. When he betrays her trust it is the willing sacrifice she makes and the pains she suffers on a pilgrimage to Rome which bring promise of the salvation she seeks.

In *Der veruntreute Himmel* the story is played out against the background of the threatening Anschluss of 1938, while in *Barbara* it is the 1918 revolution, and the collapse of the Austro-Hungarian Empire which are brought into the foreground. We notice here a change of emphasis, signalled at the outset by the transformation of the clash between Ferdinand and his father. The latter is understanding and not tyrannical, and in a similar way the figure of Barbara is intended to represent what was good in the old Austria, and what was lost with it when opportunism and the misuse of power led to the inhumanities of the revolution.

The third essential character in this novel is the Jew, Alfred Engländer, Ferdinand's pathetically funny and awkward friend, physically repulsive, passionate in his intellectualism and religious ideals, tragic in his longing for the reconcilation of Christian and Jew and for that of himself with his father. In him, and indeed in other characters like the coffee-house messiahs and the journalist of this novel, one can see not only Werfel's associates but also facets of his own character as he envisaged himself in those years of what he now saw to be misguided idealism, violence and literary extravagance. These characters are developments of those many tempting and dangerous potentialities he for ever perceived in himself. In the figure of Barbara he paid homage to the steadying influence of his own nursemaid, the Babi of his youthful poems.

In similar vein the novel *Die Geschwister von Neapel*[44] published two years later demonstrates the working out of similar themes on more than one level. There is a further development of the parent and child relationship, in which the father, Domenico Pascarella, with sacrifice and suffering wins back the love and respect of his children. A love story, the only one of any account in Werfel's novels, takes on a deliberately conventionalised operatic form, which is set against the political developments of contemporary Italy, as had been the case indirectly in *Verdi*. On yet another plane the portrayal of the youthful poet Placido is the means whereby Werfel continued his own self-examination.

With *Die vierzig Tage des Musa Dagh*[45] (1933) and *Höret die Stimme* (1937) Werfel shifted his attention, directed by personal observation and concern and by political developments, to larger social units—the persecuted religious communities of the Armenians during the First World War and the Jews in the story of Jeremiah. In both the scope of the subject matter allowed for the panoramic sweep and detailed character observation which he had begun to develop in the earlier novels, but the central problems still asserted themselves despite the mass of realistic detail demanded in the chronicles.

Der veruntreute Himmel and *Das Lied von Bernadette* continued the theme of religious devotion, and in the latter brought further comment on the scepticism and materialism of a self-satisfied scientific age as it gathered momentum in mid-nineteenth century. Werfel delights in showing how the representatives of authority and state, science and intellect were powerless to defeat the miracle of Lourdes and the unworthy vessel of divine grace, Bernadette Soubirous. Of the many symbolically charged figures in the novel in addition to Bernadette herself, the aristocratic nun Vauzous, her teacher as child and novice, and the poet Lafite, command most attention. Bernadette serves as the mirror for the "lady", the apparition. Divine and poetic inspiration are all but one here in the descriptions Werfel finds for the devotions and lonely suffering of Bernadette. Sister Vauzous must also suffer much mental and spiritual anguish for her hatred, envy and doubts. In the end Lafite too falls on his knees at the shrine after years of feeling privileged to dissociate himself from the spectacle of life and rejoice in his detachment.

Werfel's last novel *Stern der Ungeborenen* (1946), finished only a short time before his death and written in the knowledge that this was at hand assumes the aspect of a grand finale. Ostensibly a Utopian venture with many of the appurtenances of a science fiction extravaganza, projected into the far distant world 100,000 years from now, the novel also recaptures much of Werfel's own story, including for example in a disguised form conversations between the author and his friend Willy Haas, which date from their boyhood together in Prague. Through the exercise of an alien will the author finds himself resurrected in this distant "astromental age" in order to judge it by our relatively prehistoric standards, and sub specie aeternitatis.

A playful fancy is indulged in the depiction of the topography of this strangely monotonous earth, on which Man has secured for himself a complete and uniform welfare state, which provides all his needs. He enjoys remarkable longevity and has all his mortal fears of suffering, violence and even death calmed. But they are only calmed—for these men, for all their hairless physical beauty and technical super-sophistication, are no wit different from Man today. What has happened here is that Werfel, like so many Utopian writers, has taken modern tendencies in technical development and in human aspiration to a point where he attains a more fundamental judgment of man and his condition.

But it is not merely a grand tour that F.W., as he calls himself, has in this "astromental" world of technical perfection, where one moves one's destination rather than oneself. Despite the security that intellect has created, there remains the threat of the "jungle". This is the term used for the surviving patches of original earthly vegetation which flourish on, cultivated and inhabited by a naïve pastoral folk. As in Hesse's *Glasperlenspiel* the duality of intellect and nature, which these parallel forms of life suggest, constitutes a danger for mankind.

The essential insecurity of the astromental culture is demonstrated as lying in its uniform and unoriginal qualities, and thus in the monotony which provokes even some of the younger generation to side with the "jungle" people when war comes. Simple, organic life re-asserts itself with the weapons against which the new culture has no defence—depression, melancholy and disappointment.

For Werfel the assured unchangeability of man's basic nature involves the survival of the Church, that is of the Roman Catholic Church. The Pope, now known as the "Grossbischof", continues to rule over the one organised religion of the time, and his words towards the end of the work sum up Werfel's judgment of what is in one sense the logical conclusion of the civilisation he witnessed in California at the end of his life. The "astromental" culture avoids the real issues, while :

> "Die alten Zivilisationen, von denen Sie sprachen, mein Sohn . . . haben wenigstens das Leiden und den Tod auf sich genommen und damit dem Fluch des Erzengels Rechnung getragen."(46)

In these last three works the wheel Werfel began to turn in his youth came full circle. The suffering he so longed to alleviate in those early poems found a positive significance. In the Jew, Saul Minjonman, of this future age we also find another projection of himself, unable to become a Catholic, as we have already seen. Even as he embraces a Romantic primitiveness, metaphysics and Catholic permanence, Werfel could not help questioning them at the same time, knowing full well that he had himself been conditioned and moulded by the scientific attitude he so often repudiated. Werfel's Romantic outlook differs essentially from that he criticised so vehemently in *Verdi.* It is graced by a sincere ethical strain, tempered by an awareness of the dangers of a poet's pride, and lent human warmth and sympathy in its avoidance of moralising.

The poem which Werfel was correcting in proof when he died was one first written in the early twenties. In many ways it sums up so much of his own character as a man and poet. His spirit and bravoura, the exaggeration of his gestures and the excited sweep of his emotions are mirrored here with a gently ironic humour:

Der Dirigent

Er reicht den Violinen eine Blume
Und ladet sie mit Schelmenblick zum Tanz.
Verzweifelt bettelt er das Blech um Glanz,
Und streut den Flöten kindlich manche Krume.

Tief beugt das Knie er vor dem Heiligtume
Des Pianissimos, der Klangmonstranz.
Doch zausen Stürme seinen Schwalbenschwanz,
Wenn er das Tutti aufpeitscht, sich zum Ruhme.

Mit Fäusten hält er fest den Schlussakkord,
Dann staunt er, hiflos eingepflanzt am Ort,
Dem ausgekommenen Klang nach wie ein Clown.

Zuletzt, dass er den Beifall, dankend, rüge,
Zeigt er belästigte Erlöserzüge,
Und zwingt uns, ihm noch Grössres zuzutraun.[47]

The image of the writer as a clown, as an entertainer, and even as a deceiver, is one frequently used by German authors since the late nineteenth century. It figures in the work of many, from Wedekind and Rilke to Thomas Mann, and represents that concern with self-awareness and self-expression which is the central problem in Werfel's work. The balance between the poet as entertainer and the poet as a man with a mission is a precarious one, and a slip either way threatens the "metaphysical ambiguity" which for Werfel constituted the value of a work of art. He conceived his mission to be one of singing the glories of divine mystery and of the sanctity of man. For all the extravagance and violence of much of his earlier work this positive intention persists throughout all his work, and sets him apart from those of his time in whom pessimism and nihilism are so often seen as virtues. It is an element which cannot be ignored in judging him.

TRANSLATIONS

1. The fat man in the mirror.
2. The friend of the world.
3. Upon the twilight grass I will sit down,
 And with the earth into the evening ride.
 Oh Earth, oh Evening, Joy! Oh in the world to be!

(from the translation by Edith Abercrombie Snow in *Franz Werfel. Poems*, Princeton, 1945, p. 9).

4. For I have endured all fates: I know the feeling of lonely women harpists in spa orchestras, the feeling of shy governesses in strange families, the feeling of debutants trembling as they take their place before the prompter's box.

I lived in the woods, held a post on the railway, sat crouched over account books and served impatient guests. As a stoker I stood in front of boilers, the glare of the flames in my face, and as a coolie I lived on slops and kitchen scraps.

Thus I belong to You and to all. Please, do not resist me! Oh, if only it could sometime happen, my brother, that we could fall into each other's arms!

5. But now You gave me an I, and created and consigned me to the pangs of weakness and the stifling constriction of existence and to profaning self-castigation.

6. As once in boundless love we cavorted in infinity to the delight of the blessed, Uranus unlocked the blueness of his breath, and, one in blessed childlike fidelity, we hovered there in his breast.

Ah woe! The ether was dissipated. Roaring, a world took form and body was born. . . .

7. We are.

8. While by your being I was charmed to tears,
 And I through you in space soared far away,
 Did not unhappy people live that day,
 Millions oppressed and wretched all their years?

 As your sweet ways enraptured me to death,
 The earth was noisy, workers round us trod,
 And there were wastes, and folk unwarmed of God.
 Men lived and died unblest to their last breath.
 As you inspired me till my senses whirled,
 There were so many who in darkness fretted,
 Crouched over desks and before boilers sweated.

 I hear on street and stream their gasping yet!
 If there's a balance in this life and world,
 In what way will I have to pay this debt?

(Snow, *op. cit.*, p. 17)

9. To one another.

10. *Adam:* I have found my way to you through a thousand hours of languor. And now you cast me out?

Voice from the garden: My son, we are so closely joined, that these your own words have bearing on your own self too.

Adam: Have pity on me!

Voice from the garden: Have pity on me!

Adam: Will you close the door of slumber to me, bent low, with feet all torn? It not supremely noble grace the wealth you hold?

Voice from the garden: I have expended my grace, it reigns unspent in your life, I have used it wholly for you while you have used none for me.

Adam: Will this ageing never end then? And no home ever make me pure again?

Voice from the garden: Bespeak me with your hands, and we shall both be each other's home, and shall enter in!

Adam: Alas. There is no other word to comfort me, and this word thrusts me back into the towns!

Voice from the garden: My child, as I redeemed you with my blood, so do I weep and wait for my redemption through you.

11. Conversation with myself.
12. The raising of the tower.
13. The prophecy to Alexander.
14. Duologue.
15. Star of the Unborn.
16. A song of the dead (to be read by separate voices).
17. Song of the dead before new life.
18. The visit from Elysium.
19. The temptation.
20. The Goddess of midday.
21. The day of judgment.
22. Mirrorman.
23. Vanity.
24. Prayer for purity.
25. From that hour on he's split in two, and must with hands torn wrestle bloodily to subdue his escort, who will drag him through murder and guilty deeds.
26. Not the murderer, his victim is the guilty one.
27. Paul among the Jews.
28. The Kingdom of God in Bohemia.
29. Jacobowsky and the Colonel.
30. Goat song.
31. *Colonel Stjerbinsky* (slaps Jacobowsky on the shoulder): Don't be too happy about it, Jacobowsky.... We have only postponed our duel....

Jacobowsky: Our duel goes on for ever Stjerbinsky....

32. *Jacobowsky*: I see two opposites who are getting on quite well together!

The Wandering Jew: Oh, we're one heart and soul! Just let opposites grow old enough together, and they'll meet in infinity like parallel lines.

33. Hearken unto the voice.

34. The promised road. (Translated under the title "The Eternal Road".)

35. The Church will live as long as we live, to bear witness for Abraham, Isaac and Jacob, who were the first to acknowledge the true God....

The Church thinks that Israel will live as long as she endures, to the end of time, in order to bear witness for the Messiah....

...Infinite distances are all equal, and we can just wait to see who bears witness for whom....

36. Novel of the opera.

37. Novel about an artist.

38. The Song of Bernadette.

39. Novel about (the hero's) development (to maturity).

40. Roman à clef.

41. Barbara, or piety (published in translation under the title *Hidden Child* in England, and as *The Pure in Heart* in the U.S.).

42. The way to the place of execution.

43. Embezzled Heaven.

44. The Family of Naples (translated under the title *The Pascarella Family*).

45. The forty days of Musa Dagh.

46. The old civilisations of which you spoke, my son... at least took suffering and death upon themselves and thus reckoned in terms which acknowledged the curse of the Archangel.

47. The Conductor

He hands the violins a flower and with a roguish glance invites them to the dance. Despairingly he begs the brass for brilliance, and, childlike, scatters many a crumb to the flutes. He bends his knee low before the sanctuary of the pianissimo, the monstrance of sound. But storms tousle his swallow tails, when, to his own glory, he whips up the tutti. With fists clenched tight he holds the final chord. And then he stands helplessly rooted to the spot, staring like a clown in his amazement at the resultant sound. Finally, to reprove the applause as he acknowledges it, he shows the harassed features of a saviour, and forces us to expect even greater things from him.

BIBLIOGRAPHY

The *Gesammelte Werke* (1948–) edited by Professor Adolf D. Klarmann are being published by the S. Fischer Verlag, Frankfurt. Where a volume is not yet available in this edition the publisher and date of first publication are recorded below.

Der Weltfreund. Erste Gedichte. Leipzig: K. Wolff, 1911.
Wir Sind. Neue Gedichte. Leipzig: K. Wolff, 1913
Einander. Oden, Lieder, Gestalten. Leipzig, 1915.

Der Gerichtstag. In 5 Büchern. Leipzig: K. Wolff, 1919.
Beschwörungen. München: K. Wolff, 1923.
Verdi, Roman der Oper. G.W., 1949.
Der Abituriententag. Die Geschichte einer Jugendschuld. Wien: Zsolnay, 1928.
Barbara; oder Die Frömmigkeit. G.W., 1953.
Die Geschwister von Neapel. Wein: Zsolnay, 1931.
Die vierzig Tage des Musa Dagh. Wein: Zsolnay, 1933.
Schlaf und Erwachen, Neue Gedichte. Wien: Zsolnay, 1935.
Höret die Stimme. G.W., 1956.
Der veruntreute Himmel. Die Geschichte einer Magd. G.W., 1951.
Gedichte aus dreissig Jahren. Stockholm: Bermann-Fischer, 1939.
Das Lied von Bernadette. Stockholm: Bermann-Fischer, 1941.
Stern der Ungeborenen. Ein Reiseroman. G.W., 1949.
Zwischen oben und unten. Stockholm: Bermann-Fischer, 1946.
Erzählungen aus zwei Welten. (Bde. I-III) G.W., 1948–54.
Gedichte aus dem Jahren 1908–45. 1953.
Dramen. (2 Bde.) G.W., 1959.

Werfel also translated and adopted the libretti of Verdi's operas Simone Boccanegra and La Forza del Destino (1929 and 1926), and edited Verdi's letters (1926) in collaboration with Richard Specht. Werfel's essays and miscellaneous prose writings have yet to appear in the Gesammelte Werke. Apart from excerpts which have appeared in Alma Mahler-Werfel's autobiography *And the Bridge is Love* (London: Hutchinson, 1958) and in articles by Professor Klarmann, the Diaries and Notebooks remain unpublished.

There is no full biographical study of Werfel to date. A certain amount of detail is available in his wife's autobiography mentioned above and in the following critical works:

Richard Specht. *Franz Werfel. Versuch einer Zeitspiegelung.* Berlin, 1926.
Marysia Turrian. *Dostojewskij und Franz Werfel. Vom östlichen zum westlichen Denken.* (Sprache und Dichtung, Heft 73). Bern, 1950.
Annemarie von Puttkamer. *Franz Werfel. Wort und Antwort.* Würzburg, 1952.
Ernst Keller. *Franz Werfel. Sein Bild des Menschen. Aarau,* 1958.
Lore B. Foltin (ed.). *Franz Werfel. 1890–1945.* Pittsburgh, 1961.

There are also sections devoted to Werfel in the following:

Fritz Martini. *Was war Expressionismus?* Urach, 1948.
H. Friedmann and O. Mann (ed.). *Deutsche Literatur im zwanzigsten Jahrhundert.* Heidelberg, 1955.
H. Friedmann and O. Mann (ed.). *Expressionismus.* Heidelberg, 1956.
Wilhelm Grenzmann. *Dichtung und Glaube.* (2 Auflage). Bonn, 1952.
Walter H. Sokel. *The Writer in Extremis.* Stanford, 1959.

Gottfried Benn

Gottfried Benn

by IAN HILTON

Gottfried Benn was born on May 2, 1886, in Mansfield, Westprignitz, the son of a Lutheran pastor and a Swiss-French mother. His early upbringing was in this Lutheran environment. Relations with his father, whom he greatly respected, later became strained over the agonising death from cancer of his mother. He had been sent to the University of Marburg to study theology and philology, but his heart was more in medicine and soon he went to a Berlin academy to train as a military doctor. In 1912 Benn left the army and went into private practice in Berlin, and very shortly there appeared his first collection of verse (*Morgue*), quickly followed by other collections of verse (*Söhne*, 1913, and *Fleisch*, 1917) and prose (*Gehirne*, 1916).

By this time, of course, the storm of the First World War was over Europe. Benn saw war as biologically inevitable and certainly not as a splendid opportunity for high-minded adventure as did, for example, Rupert Brooke and his "swimmers into cleanness leaping". After this war, in which he served as a doctor, Benn returned to Berlin and his practice—and also his literary activities, though there was a break in these in the 20's. In 1932 Benn was admitted to the Prussian Academy of Arts and the following year, at a time of "crisis and dismay", to use Auden's words, when many literary figures were emigrating, flirted with National Socialism for a short period before disillusion set in. However, Benn was soon in trouble, and in 1934 he writes to Ina Seidel that he is living with silent lips. One year later he rejoins the army, which action he describes as "the aristocratic form of emigration". In 1938 Benn was excluded from the "Reichsschrifttumskammer" as an "entarteter Asphaltliterat".

Following the Second World War, in which he again served, Benn returned to Berlin to practice medicine. Because of his attitude in the Thirties, however, he was looked upon initially with suspicion from all sides. Nevertheless in 1948 Benn experienced a remarkable come-back on the literary scene with the revival of old works and the publication of new ones like the verse *Statische Gedichte* and the prose *Der Ptolemäer* and *Drei alte Männer*, and achieved a hitherto unenjoyed fame, which has lasted beyond his death in 1956 at the age of seventy. Benn's literary prowess was officially recognised by the award of the Büchner-Preis in Darmstadt in 1951.

Aber man fühlte immer deutlicher die Unmöglichkeit einer Menschheit, die sich ganz und gar abhängig gemacht hatte von ihrer eigenen Schöpfung, von ihrer Wissenschaft, von Technik, Statistik, Handel und Industrie, von einer erstarrten Gemeinschaftsordnung, bourgeoisen und konventionellen Bräuchen. Diese Erkenntnis bedeutet zugleich den Beginn des Kampfes gegen die Zeit und ihre Realität.[1]

IT was against this background of the gradual loss of old traditional values with the vast scientific and technological advancements, of the impending doom in the shape of the First World War looming on the horizon, of the steady rise of an atheistic materialism, that Gottfried Benn first came into the public eye in 1912 with the publication of his verse collection, entitled *Morgue* (not an uncommon subject at this time: one recalls, for example, Heym's poem with this title). Two of the poems in this cycle (amongst others) are included in Pinthus' collection of Expressionist verse, significantly under the section called "Sturz und Schrei". For in this time of crisis facing European man Benn utters a cry of bitterness as his trust in reality is shattered by his medical experiences. Well could A. R. Meyer, the publisher of the short cycle, say of it: "Wohl nie in Deutschland hat die Presse in so expressiver, explodierender Weise auf Lyrik reagiert, wie damals bei Benn",[2] for the poet here is consciously and deliberately setting forth to shock the reader out of a state of apathy, as with, for example, his description of a cancer ward and decaying bodies in *Mann und Frau gehn durch die Krebsbaracke*[3] (the command in the second strophe: "Komm, hebe ruhig diese Decke auf", and in the third: "Komm, sieh auf diese Narbe an die Brust", is a clear call to man to face up to, and not shrink from, the realism of decay and death!), or of vermin in the body of a drowned suicide in *Schöne Jugend* (one is reminded again of Heym's poem *Ophelia*: "Im Haar ein Nest von jungen Wasserratten").[4] Here the usual lyrical world is not evoked; all feelings which may have been excited by the title of the poem are immediately deflated and shattered on reading the content. This is clearly indicated still further in the poem *Kleine Aster*[5]:

Ein ersoffener Bierfahrer wurde auf dem Tische gestemmt.
Irgendeiner hatte ihm eine dunkelhellila Aster
zwischen die Zähne geklemmt.
Als ich von der Brust aus
unter der Haut
mit einem langen Messer
Zunge und Gaumen herausschnitt,
muss ich sie angestossen haben, denn sie glitt
in das nebenliegende Gehirn.
Ich packte sie ihm in die Brusthöhle
zwischen die Holzwolle,

als man zunähte.
Trinke dich satt in deiner Vase!
Ruhe sanft,
kleine Aster!

Here the corpse becomes, in fact, the symbol for Nature, which for Benn has no beauty. Science and technology have denaturalised the world and Benn makes no attempt, as Carossa, for example, did, to recapture the old spirit. Moreover, Benn demonstrates that death is horrible and unavoidable, that it is simply the end. Death has no meaning for life, it is not the start of a new life. Life on this earth is not a preparation for life beyond. The poet entertains no ideas of transcendental values as do the religious writers. To illustrate the futility of it all, Benn would merely maintain that "das Leben war ein tödliches Gesetz und ein unbekanntes".[6]

The doctor element in Benn comes out very strongly in these poems—but not in the way that it appears in the writings of a somewhat older fellow doctor and poet, Carossa. The latter is concerned with the human being as such, and in his poems shows himself to have the interest of the individual at heart in his facing of the crisis. His poems are meant to act as a tonic for the reader. But Benn is no healer, rather the clinical dissector of life, merely presenting the factual side of sickness, decay and the futility of life, with no thought of human compassion. Like his prose character, Dr. Rönne, he is not concerned with individual patients but only patients as a whole. And in these early poems the cold matters of fact are matched by the cold, impersonal style of presentation, an objectivity achieved as much as anything by the syntax of prose logic; a matter of factness, "Neue Sachlichkeit".

This cold matter-of-factness of approach in *Morgue* should not, however, lead one to miss the point that behind it all there is a vitalism in Benn's thinking at this time, which further manifests itself in his second and third collections of verse, *Söhne* (1913) and *Fleisch* (1917). Once again cynical realism is to be found as in *Wir gerieten in ein Mohnfeld* (from *Söhne*), where the language is coarsely colloquial:

......
Du zerspritzt nur den Dreck deiner Pfütze
und trittst einen Wurmhügel nieder, wenn
du uns zertrittst,
wir sind und wollen nichts sein als Dreck.
Man hat uns belogen und betrogen
mit Gotteskindschaft, Sinn und Zweck
......[7]

Another poem from the same cycle, however, introduces the reader to an entirely new facet of Benn's make-up and attitude to the real world. In *Untergrundbahn*, for example, Benn creates his own form of reality by descending into the unconscious (Jungian influences are evident here) and into the timeless : Consider the last strophe :

> So losgelöst. So müde. Ich will wandern.
> Blutlos die Wege. Lieder aus den Gärten.
> Schatten und Sintflut. Fernes Glück : ein Sterben
> hin in des Meeres erlösend tiefes Blau.(8)

"A languid dying down into ocean's deep redeeming blue"—the ocean, symbol of depth, the unconscious. "Water is darker than earth", one reads in *Roman des Phänotyp.* It is no chance that the sea is a recurring motif in Benn's work, water—this elemental symbol—as the antithesis of substance-lacking daily life. "Eternally the sea calls", runs the last line of *Gesänge II* (from Fleisch). In *Gesänge I* this regression, as being the only way from the fate of nihilism, finds expression in the longing for the primal source of life (see also the prose writing *Urgesicht*) :

> O dass wir unsere Ururahnen wären.
> Ein Klümpchen Schleim in einem warmen Moor.
> Leben und Tod, Befruchten und Gebären
> glitte aus unseren stummen Säften vor.
>
> Ein Algenblatt oder ein Dünenhügel,
> vom Wind Geformtes und nach unten schwer.
> Schon ein Libellenkopf, ein Möwenflügel
> wäre zu weit und litte schon zu sehr.(9)

This urge for the archaic world and myth is because, Benn feels, one can look back with surety on this "Urwelt" as evidence of something real and positive, at a time when everything is so negative around him, when there exists such a lack of continuity of life due to the loss of communication.

Such a loneliness and isolation of the individual as expressed in verse is likewise portrayed in his prose. *Gehirne*, his first attempt in this field written 1915–16 in the period of Benn's military experiences in Brussels, is a short story collection of an autobiographical nature recording the loss and destruction of "reality" as experienced by the central character, a Dr. Rönne.

> Dr. Rönne—"der keine Wirklichkeit ertragen konnte, aber auch keine mehr erfassen, der nur das rhythmische Sichöffnen und Sichverschliessen des Ichs und der Persönlichkeit kannte, das

fortwährend Gebrochene des inneren Seins und der, vor das Erlebnis von der tiefen, schrankenlosen mythenalten Fremdheit zwischen dem Menschen und der Welt gestellt, unbedingt der Mythe und ihren Bildern glaubte".[10]

For "nichts war wirklich. War er wirklich? Nein; nur alles möglich, das war er".[11] Rönne's problems over emotion, action and social contact were those confronting Benn himself. "Conversationally I am no matador", he records. Rönne has a desire to contact man, envying the ordinary man his ability to communicate even on trivialities, and going to great lengths to get included into the social circle, as the episode over lunch reveals. After listening to a discussion, he eventually plucks up enough courage to pose a question: "Vor dem Nichts stand er; ... ob Antwort käme? ... Und nun war kein Zweifel mehr: einige nickten kauend". The result is electrifying. "Jubel in ihm, Triumphgesänge ... Einreihung geschah, Bewertung trat ein."[12] Contact has been made if only temporarily. Yet at the same time Benn, despite envying the ordinary man's ability to communicate, despises the philistinism of it all: "Der Mitmensch, der Mittelmensch, das klein Format, das Stehaufmännchen des Behagens, der Barrabasschreier, der bon und propre leben will ..."[13]; or again, talking of the Expressionist generation in 1933, he describes it as "rein und arm, nie am bürgerlichen Erfolgen beteiligt, am Ruhm, am Fett des schlürfenden Gesindes".[14] This scorn is basically resulting from what Benn describes as "eine gehirnliche Schwere innerer und äusserer Art".[15] The problem is one of excessive cerebralism. For theoretical mentality cannot attain spontaneous communication, and thus philistinism is almost unattainable. Rönne, with his disintegrated personality, with his hatred of the "Self" ("Individualität ist nur belanglos"), has to query every fresh experience he undergoes. It is a mechanical process which leads to reverie and isolation (as for example in the barber's shop episode in *Die Eroberung*). *Die Eroberung*, in fact, describes Rönne setting out to conquer a city in an attempt to find a new relation to man and the world around. He utters a cry from the heart. "Liebe Stadt, lass dich doch besetzen! Beheimate mich! Nimm mich auf in die Gemeinschaft!"[16] Rönne is "der unbehauste Mensch", the city becomes the object of longing, the symbol of the concrete and static (not necessarily the symbol of evil and destruction as found in many writers of the day). It will be remembered that Benn lived in and loved Berlin, and the city for him is like the "Hütte", which Goethe's Storm and Stress poetic hero seeks as a place of refuge and security.

But hypothesis is no substitute for the loss of reality. Reason is useless, Benn argues, for it only leads to a "dead terrain" and banalisation of the world. Consequently he longs for primal vision as a radical reaction to cerebralism, seeking contact with a deeper layer of life. The struggle for reality becomes in effect that between the outer world of consciousness and the inner world of the unconscious. And in this struggle the dream becomes a means of communication. For although a dream may be an illogical sequence (but: "nur das Sinnlose ist Realität", writes Benn elsewhere), it provides a form of security and at the same time a freedom from frustration and the fulfilment of erotic desires (all in all Benn shows himself to be aware of Freud's interpretation of dreams). Thus Rönne dreams up communication with Edmée in *Der Geburtstag*. (Woman in Benn's work, incidentally, acts as the possibility of escape, indispensable to the poet, though she never really acts as the agent of a mission, providing spiritual support in the way that women characters do in the work of Gertrud von le Fort, for example.) *La vida es sueño* holds good for Calderon; for Benn the same is true, allowing him to face the present and the future. Thus his character Diesterweg remarks: "Ich trage sie im Traum, die Welt". Significantly Rönne in one episode enters a cinema with its world of make-believe for the same purpose. Indulging in thought fantasy, as he so happily does, Benn often dreams of the whole "Ligurian complex". The South acts as a narcotic, enabling him to combat the "Wirklichkeitsverlust". The dream is a trance of forgetting and longing. The South offers him bliss, colour and excitement; the warmth of the sun, the scent of flowers, the blue of the sea—ethereal blue providing, as it were, a form of transcendence of harsh reality on the one hand, and on the other an affirmation of life. This "southern complex" is a continually recurrent theme in Benn's work; one need but think of the well-known poems *Palau* or *D-Zug*, or in prose of the Rönne stories. In an oft-quoted example from *Der Geburtstag*, for example, Rönne notices a glass sign with the inscription "Maita Cigarettes" illuminated by a sun ray: "Und nun vollzog sich über Maita-Malta-Strände-leuchtend-Fähre-Hafen-Muschelfresser-Verkommenheiten-der helle klingende Ton einer leisen Zersplitterung, und Rönne schwankte in einem Glück".(17) He (and Benn) like adverts, for they too conjure up a world within themselves and act as a magic formula: as Emil in *Die Stimme hinter dem Vorhang* declares: "Aber erst die Annoncen! . . . Wir sind überhaupt nicht mehr vorhanden, aber die Annoncen sind gebildet".(18)

Dreams may give Rönne confidence, but happiness is only fleeting and the tensions of the mind are relieved but momentarily. This southern complex is a substitute reality, it is not reality. "Wo war sein

Süden hin? Der Efeufelsen? Der Eukalyptos, wo am Meer? Ponente, Küste des Niedergangs, silberblaue die Woge her!"[19] Is it all a romantic delusion, or is there behind it all an indication of a quest for order and a meaning in life? Rönne, however, is forced back to the harshness of real life, and with this comes the admittance of defeat. For example, he finally decides against going on a trip to Antwerp:

> "Eine Wolkenbruch von Hemmungen und Schwäche brach auf ihn nieder. Denn wo waren Garantien, dass er überhaupt etwas von der Reise erzählen könnte, mitbringen, verlebendigen, dass etwas in ihn träte im Sinne des Erlebnisses?"[20]

What would be the point, he wonders, it would all be so senseless. In the end the doctor sinks back into apathy, unable or unwilling to do anything constructive about anything because of his disintegrated personality.

But there is an interesting contrast to be made between the Dr. Rönne of the short stories and the Dr. Rönne of the dramatic sketches. Where there is but longing on the part of the hero of the "Novellen", this was *preceded* by a form of action in the earlier written *Ithaka* (1914). Here Rönne is Assistant to the Professor of Pathology. He is opposed to the banalisation of life by reason and thus is opposed to the professor, who symbolises intellectual stuffiness: "Ich war logisch bis zum Kotbrechen. Und als sich der Nebel verzogen hatte, was war dann alles? Worte und das Gehirn. Worte und das Gehirn. Immer und immer nichts als dies furchtbare, dies ewige Gehirn".[21] Rönne is won over to action by the student Lutz (symbolising the person seeking wider horizons—"kommen Sie nun nicht mit dem Kausaltrieb") and kills the professor. Significantly the scene concludes with the cry of the student: "... ja, Seele! Seele! Wir wollen den Traum. Wir wollen den Rausch. Wir rufen Dionysos und Ithaka!"[27] The fear of progressive cerebration is very great and is one which besets Benn's heroes. Pameelen in *Der Vermessungsdirigent* bemoans "oh, dies Verwelken der Welt in meinem Hirn", or again: "Ich bin der neue Mann, das heisst eigentlich der Urmann ... das Gehirntier, das logische Wüstenphänomen, die mathematische Lilie, Programm: Entgeschlechtigung des Gedächtnisses oder Verhirnung des Geschlechts".[23] The murder of the professor in *Ithaka* is seen as a way to regeneration from this progressive cerebration. But this more "positive" approach as hinted at in *Ithaka* is far from maintained in Benn's immediately subsequent writings, as has been seen. Indeed, what one finds really is a gradual change from vitalism to an intellectual abstraction.

About 1921 Benn stopped writing for a time and never underwent a regeneration in the way that other Expressionist writers achieved. The influence of Nietzsche and his "God is dead" cry has far too strong a hold over him. "For my generation he was the earthquake of the epoch", Benn writes. By this time too, of course, Spengler's philosophy of life as expressed in his *Untergang des Abendlandes* has made itself felt on Benn. It was only to be expected, therefore, that Benn's own attitude to history, his relation to God and to Nature should be tinged by and reflect Nietzschean and Spenglerian thought.

With regard to his attitude to God, Benn, though coming from a Christian cultural background and heritage, has no wish to remain within its sphere of influence. Benn does not deny God, only refutes Him. In the moment of decision for or against God and the Church, a decision which faces all men at one time or another, Benn chooses against, considering religion as an illusion. He feels no lead has been given to man by God, and though he has indeed a sense of God, he does not accept God's presence. As he says himself in *Erwiderung an Alexander Lernet-Holenia*, he has not been granted the gift of faith. He is unable to just accept and believe, he has to question everything because of his scientific-medical upbringing, and doubts for him are greater than faith. He does not like "Gott", but "die Götter", the "Götter" of myth and the ancient world. This is a form of regression again. He feels, however, that a distant relationship with God is preferable to one of too great an expectation and dependence on God, and this is really why he finds prayer and humility rather arrogant and presumptuous (an opinion expressed in *Doppelleben*). The real question to be posed, Benn considers, is *why* does one seek God in the first instance?

As for Nature, an imitation of nature is not to be found in Benn's writings. His view of nature is compatible with his view of God. Nature is not seen as something behind which the hand of God is evident, as happens in the case of Eichendorff's poetry, for example. Stifter's *Das sanfte Gesetz* does not apply in Benn's works. There is no peaceful harmony as an image of human life. True, nature is sometimes seen as an idyll in Benn's regression to the "southern complex", but more likely is nature to act as something chaotic, since Benn views the world as anti-natural. For Benn, nature is not "zweckmässig und mechanisch" but "willkürlich, spontan und schöpferisch", an attitude revealing at one and the same time an anti-Darwinism and the Nietzschean philosophy of the irrational in nature.

Benn's view of history is likewise not inconsistent with his view of life. He cannot believe in the traditional concepts of history. Certainly the theological concept of history as employed by Bergengruen and again by Gertrud von le Fort finds no place in Benn's way of thinking. History has no social significance either. Rather does Benn view it as a series or chain of senseless unmotivated catastrophes. History must not be systemised, it must remain acausal: "typischer historischer Prozess: unmotiviert und sinnlos".(24) Being antithetical to rational behaviour, it must not be measured as a process of development.

Since there exists no metaphysical horizon in life and since the mystery of creation is rationalised and intellectualised, man becomes the centre of the universe. God is no longer the "Krone der Schöpfung", but man is. "Der Mensch wurde die Krone der Schöpfung und der Affe sein Lieblingstier" (in *Nach dem Nihilismus*) is echoed by the verse, "Die Krone der Schöpfung, das Schwein, der Mensch" (*Der Arzt II*). Man is disappearing as a spiritual entity: "Es ist kein Irrtum, anzunehmen, der Mensch habe noch einen Inhalt oder müsse einen haben. Der Mensch hat Nahrungssorgen, Familiensorgen, Fortkommensorgen, Ehrgeiz, Neurosen, aber das ist kein Inhalt im metaphysischen Sinne mehr".(25) There occurs the loss of individuality, the disintegration of the personality, and man's horizons become ever more limited. Life comes to have no sense, "denn das Leben ist nicht unseres, sondern das Laster eines Gottes, der verborgen bleibt".(26)

All in all, therefore, no development in the form of regeneration or integration takes place in Benn at this time as it does in other Expressionist writers who seek new values or the retention of the old ones with a desperate optimism, writers like Becher, who turns to Marxism, and Werfel and Barlach, who turn to religion. But Benn makes no concessions, no compromises. Like Heym did up to his premature death, Benn continues in his key of stubborn gloom and despondency. As to the function of the poet, Benn can not share the view of Becher, who maintained that art should be enrolled in the service of politics. Nor could he accept Werfel's assertion that one would believe in and serve God because it meant a return to reality, since God was no abstraction—Benn's denial was a most emphatic one at a time when the Catholic literary resurgence was making itself especially felt over the whole of Europe, and when Claudel's influence in Germany was by no means inconsiderable. Nor could he agree with Wilfred Owen's view that "all a poet could do was to warn. That is why the true poet must always be truthful", for Benn was sceptical over the idea of truth. As he saw it, art was not concerned with truth, only with expression.

And so with the overall picture in Germany after the First World War being one of gloom as a result of the economic distresses and political upheavals, Benn retains a cynical approach to life which is manifest in his verse collection *Spaltung*, published in 1925. The vision of disintegration which is presented in such poems as *Chaos* and *Schutt*, and the tensions of the mind that this causes, are only to be relieved by dreams of the south in a poem like *Palau*, of mythical consciousness that is the recollection and expression of really lived fates (one recalls the application of mythical consciousness in this connection in Broch's *Tod des Vergils, int. al.*). But any idea of revolt that here finds expression is tending to become one of an increasingly abstract tone. What Benn is maintaining really is an intellectual isolation; an isolation and uncommittedness that he follows likewise after the Second World War.

By the time of the first years of peace following that war, Benn could truthfully be said to belong to the older generation of writers. A new generation was emerging in Germany, but any supposed distance or lack of sympathy between it and Benn was immediately dispelled with the latter's rediscovery in 1948, after an unhappy period of reorientation. Rapidly he achieved a popularity hitherto not enjoyed and soon outstripped in favour of his fellow ageing writers in Germany, who had remained "accepted" writers but not widely read ones. The reason for this unexpectedly successful "comeback" (Benn's own term) was that this young generation was readily able to identify its own predicament (as summed up by Borchert's words: "Wir sind die Generation ohne Bindung und ohne Tiefe. Unsere Tiefe ist Abgrund"[27]) with that of Benn, who steadily continued his aesthetic nihilism and was unable to share T. S. Eliot's concern that "without Christianity as a background there would be no meaning of intellectual life at all". It was the age of anxiety and it was not without point that Benn should write the foreword to the German translation of Auden's *Age of Anxiety*. Benn's writings of this post-war era, *Statische Gedichte, Der Ptolemäer* and *Drei alte Männer* are all literary evidence of the spiritual situation at the mid-century.

A phrase from the last of the above titles, namely: "Leben ist nichts, Sein ist alles", serves for the understanding of the meaning of the 1948 collection of verse with the title *Statische Gedichte*. These poems represent something permanent against the decline and fall of man. Each poem is static because it appears as a complete image or work of art, static because, although it may well be stylistically dynamic, it has a form which is objective and is to be contrasted with the senseless process of perpetual change in life. This basic hatred of change and its futility has caused Benn to seek something which is lasting. Thus he seeks "Sein" (the static), not "Werden" (the process of change). Hence his love of the archaic world, his longing to return to the amoeba (as in the poem

Verlorenes Ich: though in one poem at least, *September,* the absurdity of life has led Benn to a new reality where he can express himself and nature without a sense of longing, romantic delusion and sentimentality). Hence his love of the sea and of darkness. Benn likes the city because it is real and concrete, something he can cling to in the transience of life. Thus can one begin to understand phrases which abound in Benn's writing like: "Kunst ist statisch" and "Kunst ist Sein im Strom des Vergehens".

Der Ptolemäer (1949) presents the thoughts of a beauty-specialist in Berlin looking at life in 1947. The Ptolemean does his work satisfactorily without ever really taking part in it (in this way he resembles Rönne who deals only with patients, never interesting himself with one patient as an individual). His work, in fact, symbolises the empty luxury of life. The scientific discoveries from Kepler and Galileo on are dismissed and life is considered to hold for the future nothing but banality. One is reminded of a few lines taken from *Fragmente,* a poem dating from about 1950:

> . . . .
> Ausdruckskrisen und Anfälle von Erotik:
> das ist der Mensch von heute,
> das Innere ein Vakuum,
> die Kontinuität der Persönlichkeit
> wird gewahrt von der Anzügen,
> die bei gutem Stoff zehn Jahre halten. [28]

Man is a vacuum without illusion. "... Lebenseinheit, Harmonie—das lehnte ich ab. Wir alle leben etwas anderes, als wir sind",[29] is echoed more fully in *Drei alte Männer*: "Wir lebten etwas anderes, als wir waren, wir schrieben etwas anderes, als wir dachten, wir dachten etwas anderes, als wir erwarteten und was übrigbleibt, ist etwas anderes, als wir vorhatten".[30] No chance of a synthesis or compromise is offered by the author, as is further indicated by his assertion that the coming century would produce but two types—criminals and monks, the active and the passive; "diejenigen, die handelten und hochwollten, und diejenigen, die schweigend die Verwandlung erwarteten—: Verbrecher und Mönche, etwas anderes würde es nicht mehr geben . . . "[31] Significantly he prefers the "Schwarze Kutten". Only the artist can get the better of things: "Der Künstler ist der einzige, der mit den Dingen fertig wird, der über sie entscheidet."[32] He is to be equated with the glassblower, since to him is given the power and ability to instil the breath of life into something. In this work the difference of approach in Benn's thinking is clearly to be observed. The loss of reality with which the hero is faced is no longer met with scorn as earlier in *Weinhaus Wolf* (written in 1937, though not appearing until the time of *Der Ptolemäer*), for example, but with an indifference. The former urge to be irresponsible now gives way before the constructive mind, through which cerebral man may act.

In *Drei alte Männer* (1949) the note is one of stoical acceptance of the worst. Once again there can be little thought of a compromise:

Der junge Mann: "Wer Strophen liebt, der liebt Kata-strophen auch; wer für Statuen ist, muss auch für Trümmer sein."

Der Andere: "Sie meinen Polarität? Ach, synthetisieren Sie doch nicht! Verweilen Sie vor dem Unvereinbaren, halten Sie durch usque ad finem. Ihr Leben in seinen Abwegigkeiten, Irrtümern, Zerknitterungen, Halbheiten—das tragen Sie Ihrer letzten Stunde zu und ich bin sicher, sie wird es hinnehmen und Sie nicht verweisen. . . ."[33]

But in the conversations of the men the former note of belligerence is missing. The tone is rather a more positive one: "... und wenn die Nacht kommt, werden wir sie ertragen".[34]

Stoic acceptance of the worst is also the formula in *Die Stimme hinter dem Vorhang,* published in 1952, where the picture of empty transcendence is presented. God has left man in the lurch the moment he seeks a meaning to life—hence the symbolism of the title of the work. The advice offered to man is "im Dunkel leben, im Dunkel tun, was wir können". This work can be seen as another example of the interesting development in Benn's thinking since the Twenties, as an advance on the mere longings of Rönne and the formula as then presented—namely: "Wie soll man da leben? Man soll ja auch nicht". In both formulas the verb "to live" appears, expressing the concept of an active process, but whereas in the Twenties the idea was that one was not really able to live, now three decades later there is the more positive exhortation to live, even if it be in the dark. True, the individual is left very much to himself to interpret matters as best he can. The onus is indeed on man to do what he can in the dark, but the point is that, as long as he *acknowledges* that he is in effect living in a world of which he is not actually part, living a life which has really no external absolute point of reference, man can survive.

But any "message" that one thinks to find here in the work is certainly not directed at man in general. Benn is the isolated artist who is writing for himself, expressing his own thoughts and sentiments, addressing no one or nothing other than his own mind. His poetic loneliness, the "Kommunikationslosigkeit" finds particularly effective expression in the poem *Ein Wort* (cf. also the poem *Schöpfung*):

> Ein Wort, ein Satz—: Aus Chiffren steigen
> erkanntes Leben, jäher Sinn,
> die Sonne steht, die Sphären schweigen
> und alles ballt sich zu ihm hin.
>
> Ein Wort—ein Glanz, ein Flug, ein Feuer,
> ein Flammenwurf, ein Sternenstrich—
> und wieder Dunkel, ungeheuer,
> im leeren Raum um Welt und Ich.[35]

Benn's art is his personal answer to the loss of communication with the substance. He denies the necessity of viewing and interpreting art politically and socially (in *Heinrich Mann zum sechzigsten Geburtstag*) and defends his isolation and loneliness when the Austrian Lernet-Holenia points an accusing finger at Benn as to why the latter does not speak to the nation (in *Erwiderung an Alexander Lernet-Holenia*). "Kunstwerke sind phänomenal, historisch unwirksam, praktisch folgenlos. Das ist ihre Grösse" is echoed elsewhere by Benn with "Kunst aber ist ein isoliertes Phänomen".[36] A work of art has a beauty and this beauty is the answer to the decay of the day. Like G. Eich, Benn could say that he wrote poetry to find his bearings in reality. He becomes the champion of "Artistik". Rephrasing the expression to the effect that "art is the last metaphysical activity within European nihilism", Benn writes in *Probleme der Lyrik* (1951):

> Artistik ist der Versuch der Kunst, innerhalb des allgemeinen Verfalls der Inhalte sich selber als Inhalt zu erleben und aus diesem Erlebnis einen neuen Stil zu bilden, es ist der Versuch, gegen den allgemeinen Nihilismus der Werte eine neue Transzendenz zu setzen: die Transzendenz der schöpferischen Lust.[37]

As already indicated, Benn commenced his literary activities as an Expressionist and critics have been wont to declare that he remained an Expressionist throughout his career. This is important in the sense that Expressionism started off after all as a movement of style rather than of content ("Stil trägt in sich selbst den Beweis der Existenz",[38] writes Benn) and throughout Benn has been solely concerned with the method of expression—"die Ausdruckswelt". As for Baudelaire, so too for Benn does art act as a counter to the world around, not just as an idealisation or imitation of it. Benn is not interested in presenting in his work pure description of milieu, for example, or psychological problems. He has no wish to express the obvious. And so Benn's prose is not merely a logical sequence of words in the generally accepted fashion, but becomes, as it were, a series of newspaper headlines (significantly Benn had a life-long love of newspapers and journalism), to correspond to the accelerated tempo of life. There is a condensation of language to the bare essentials (one of his verse collections is entitled *Destillationen*), which creates an air of allusiveness as part of the technique of implication and demands from the reader both the power of concentration and interpretation to appreciate the tremendous thought associations (which have a special beauty in their richness) implied in just one word (for example, the thought process involved in Maita-Malta and the Mediterranean in the Rönne-story, or in the concepts evoked in a line from the poem *D-Zug*: "Darin ist Süden, Hirt und Meer"). Then again, on the other hand, this reduction of language may be taken by Benn to the point of sheer nonsense, where the understandability of it corresponds to Benn's view of the senselessness of modern life, as illustrated perhaps in *Karandasch*, itself a word without sense, being made up from an advert for fountain pens from "caran d'ache".

For Benn the individual word is the key to inspiration and the world of expression, the basis of his style, and one is reminded of Mallarmé's "parole essentielle". "Das Wort", writes Benn, "enthielt keine Zeit und ich liebte es, in Worten zu formulieren".(39) Thus he works outside of time, in a timelessness which is in contrast to the limitations of time in the world around. In an evocative sequence of (significantly technical) images Benn likens the poet to a lighthouse beam and to a radar pulse, and he further stresses the importance of "Flimmerhaare"—each in its own way, the lighthouse beam, the radar pulse, the feeler, is a highly sensitive piece of apparatus enabling the poet to select the right word carefully at the correct moment. And so in Benn's work as in that of Eliot key words appear strategically like symbols around which everything revolves. As for symbols, J. Lehmann has declared that we cannot escape them, and the modern age has been described as one in search of, and in need of, symbols as a saving myth. But since art is no longer seen as a means of communication between public and artist in Benn's case, he, like many others, tends to move towards the more private and unintelligible symbol in contrast, say, to the committed religious writer, who must rather employ well chosen common symbols taken from the Bible and the liturgy of the Church so as to allow the reader a degree of identification. Benn, for his part, likes building up his own language and mental associations which produces a stream of consciousness, a private little world, for, it would seem, he has no wish to be *too* readily understood. But not all Benn's symbols are incomprehensible and one thinks easily, for example, of his use of blue—"das Südwort schlechthin, der Exponent des 'ligurischen Komplexes' ". He loves images which appeal to the sense of smell and sight—the scent of fragrant flowers in *Palau* contrasts sharply with the putrefaction of decaying corpses in *Krebsbaracke*; the blue of the Mediterranean warmth and sunshine with the black of the unconscious and the archaic world. The image in fact has no decorative function, it becomes the end in itself.

The matter of key words existing in Benn's work corresponds to his interesting innovations in style as seen, for example, in the novel form. The novel for Benn is not one logical sequence of events and thoughts, as normally encountered, but is seen as something fragmentary. Thus the *Roman des Phänotyp* would seem to comprise an alogical grouping of diverse sections with such headings as "Der Stundengott", "Gestützt auf Pascal", "Stadtpark", "Geographische Details", etc. The process involved Benn describes in *Absolute Prosa*: he calls the "novel" a "sequence of factually and psychologically disconnected parts" and it is built up "in the shape of an orange", by which he means that the individual segments have a separate being as they stand side by side, yet at the same time they all tend to the centre, to the "existential" ("existential—that is the deathblow for the novel", writes Benn). Why, Benn argues, "Gedanken in jemanden hineinkneten, in eine Figur, in Gestalten, wenn es Gestalten nicht mehr gibt? Personen, Namen, Beziehungen erfinden, wenn sie gerade unerheblich werden?"[40] And so, since there are no real characters, there is not much action as such either in the prose or in the dramatic sketches. The characters in these works, characters like Rönne and Pameelen, are not really convincing people of flesh and blood who "develop". Rather are they to be considered as types, mouthpieces for Benn himself. This then is carried to the extent, for example, of the three voices of the old men in *Drei alte Männer* really serving one voice—that of the author. Here all conventional connections are destroyed and the work becomes a monologue corresponding to Benn in his isolation. It is no chance, incidentally, that Benn should readily turn to the essay form in the way and to the extent that he does, for although the essay may be written more with an audience in mind, yet is it closely bound to the personality of the essayist himself and so comes near to the monologue.

But behind all this innovation of form and experimentation in language that one encounters in Benn's work, the note of deliberateness is to be observed throughout. Benn does not approach the task in hand in a slipshod manner, for, as H. E. Holthusen, himself a poet, maintains, the poet of today is a technician and Benn for his part asserts that a poem arises of itself but very rarely. A poem he argues, is made, it is a technical construction, and to illustrate this he points to his own poem *Welle der Nacht,* the second strophe of which was composed many years after the first. In other words, the whole process becomes an intellectual problem. Benn's mastery of this is evident from a survey of his literary production. Style and language match the mood of the content throughout. Thus the impersonal "neue Sachlichkeit" approach blends well with the cold dissection of life in *Krebsbaracke* or *Kleine Aster*; his pulsating vitalism breaks through vividly in a poem like *Nachtcafe*, where the staccato rhythm in the often asyntactical verses is provocatively fascinating. When Benn wishes to turn from the urge to be irrational, when he wishes to impose some sort of self-discipline and limitation on the dissonance of life (which is so frequently echoed in his work by the combination of the beautiful and the ugly, the shattering of a mood by a cynicism and an irony which is Heine-esque in its bitterness), he writes a poem like *Palau*, a poem which conjures up the exotic to be sure, yet also exerts a soothing effect, a mood of peace reflected in the employment of a regular rhyming pattern (which stands in marked contrast to the pattern as found in *Nachtcafe*, for example). Again, the longing for order in life in *Gesänge* is complemented by Benn's application of a regular rhyme and metrical pattern. Then in the later poetry, beside the sober neo-classical style of poems like *Ach das Erhabene* and *Auferlegt,* which matches the poet's quest for a meaning to life, and where few modernist features are observable, stand poems in loose free-verse, poems like *Fragmente* which may imitate the manner but certainly lack the passion of the early poetry in their vision of life's dissonance and discontinuity. The same diversity of approach is likewise evident in Benn's prose which overall can be seen as a kaleidoscope of countless allusions and streams of consciousness and intellectual dissertations with learned references; a so-called montage-art of visionary and cerebral sequences in a prose ranging from journalistic jargon and slang (as in *Karandasch*) to lyrical dynamism (as in *Der Geburtstag* and some paragraphs from *Lotosland* in *Der Ptolemäer* int. al., which are to be contrasted with a poem like *Spät,* for example, which reads as prose) and finally to a scientific and technical language.

Undeniably Benn is a complex character to understand because of paradoxes inherent in his nature and his work. He is a creative artist and a theoretical programmatic writer, but it is far more rewarding to read his imaginative works than his critical writings. For Benn is an erratic thinker.[41] He is the artist who demands the retention of his independence, yet at the same time wishes for a measure of identification with and acceptance by his fellow beings (the joy at his acceptance into the Prussian Academy of Arts in the Thirties is a measure of this wish). It is Thomas Mann's Künstler-Bürger problem all over again. But whereas in the course of time Mann's artist-figure becomes fully integrated into society, in Benn's case this final stage remains unachieved because of his hatred of synthesis. He is the person who, while supposedly seeking the complete loss of "Self", is wholly preoccupied with his personal position. Significantly his "autobiography" is entitled *Double Life*; he is W. H. Auden's "Double Man".

And this stark dichotomy appears throughout Benn's work, in the way that the brain and intellect is suddenly countered by flights of fancy to the South, or myth is treated in scientific terms; in the contrast of the concepts of time and timelessness, the conscious and the unconscious; in the individual words: Schutt, Chaos, Trümmer, Hirn, Geist, as against Süden, Meer, Rausch, Traum, Leben. It is also reflected in the titles of critical works on Gottfried Benn: M. Hamburger's essay in *Reason and Energy*, E. Lohner's *Passion und intellekt*.

With art as his credo, can Benn be accused of living in an ivory tower? Is it really an avoidance of reality when he turns so readily to primal vision? The very fact that he reverts to the past is in itself an acknowledgement of his awareness of the present, and this in its way can be equated with, for example, Bergengruen's and more especially Gertrud von le Fort's use of history which is certainly not an escape from the threatened values of the day, but rather a conscious counter to, and mirroring of, the present. Benn has been much criticised for a philosophy of negation, but, as he himself points out, it all depends what one does with one's nihilism. Benn believes in the world of expression which he describes as one standing "zwischen der geschichtlichen und der nihilistischen" and maintains that "ein moderner Mann denkt nicht nihilistisch; er bringt Ordnung in seine Gedanken und schafft sich eine Grundlage für seine Existenz".[42] This in itself has a somewhat positive ring, and certainly in his prose works of the mid-century period Benn's attitude to life was a stoical acceptance of the worst—and the very act of acceptance is something positive. In any case, apart from all this, Benn is being positive in actually creating a work of art, for he is thereby creating something out of nothing. And this is achieved with a language which, far from debasing (of which Benn has not infrequently been charged in the past), actually enriches the German tongue in a way—even with his startling neologisms, his journalese and scientific terminology. For what Benn is really doing is to legitimately apply modern techniques to deal with present-day situations and problems (and this in itself is another answer to the charge that Benn is shunning reality and the present). And the answer is a markedly modern language and style. Benn, therefore, is to be seen as an exciting innovator whose prose (as well as his verse, for which he is at present better known) will stand the test of time. It is always important and necessary to keep distinct ethical and aesthetic standards in any appreciation. Unfortunately as far as an appreciation of Benn is concerned, this has not been done every time. T. S. Eliot has declared that poetry must not be a substitute for religion and philosophy: but one must also accept at face value a sentence which Benn once wrote; to the effect that "das Moralische und Religiöse zu erleben, habe ich keine Organe". For Benn one could well adapt words which Eliot again once delivered apropos Rilke and Nietzsche: "He is lonely, driven by inner compulsion to shun all binding human relationship so as to be able to transmute his personal and private agonies into something rich and strange, something universal and impersonal."

NOTES AND TRANSLATIONS

1. K. Pinthus: *Menschheitsdämmerung*. Berlin, 1919. Page X. "But one felt ever more clearly the impossibility of a mankind which had made itself entirely dependent upon its own Creation, on science, technology, statistics, trade and industry, on a benumbed communal order, bourgeois and conventional customs. This knowledge signifies the commencement of the struggle against the time and its reality."

2. "Probably never in Germany had the press reacted to lyric verse in such an expressive and explosive manner as at that time in the case of Benn."

3. *Man and Woman go through the cancer ward.* "Come, quietly lift up this coverlet"; "Come, now look at the scars upon this breast." (Translations of Benn's own writings are where possible those found in *Primal Vision;* see bibliography.)

4. Benn's poem, *Lovely Childhood.* Heym: *Ophelia,* "in her hair a nest of young water-rats".

5. *Little Aster*: "A downed truck-driver was propped on the slab.
Someone had stuck a lavender aster
between his teeth.
As I cut out the tongue and the palate,
through the chest
under the skin

with the long knife,
I must have touched the flower, for it slid
into the brain lying next.
I packed it into the cavity of the chest
among the excelsior
as it was sewn up.
Drink yourself full in your vase!
Rest softly,
little aster!"

6. *Primal Vision*: Collected Works, Vol. 2, page 118. "Life was a fatal law and an unknown one."

7. *We came upon a minefield*: "You squirt only the slime of your pool and tread down a worm cast when you trample us, we are and we want to be nothing other than dirt. We have been lied to and deceived by ideas of God, by sense and purpose."

8. *Subway train*: "So lax, adrift. So tired. I long to wander.
The ways all bloodless. Songs that blow from gardens.
Shadows and Flood. Far joys: a languid dying
down into ocean's deep redeeming blue."

9. *Songs*: "O that we were our primal ancestors.
A little clump of slime in a warm bog.
Then life and death, then pregnancy and birth
From our dumb lymph would issue forth that quag.

A leaf of alga or a simple dune,
Windshaped yet weighted by its rooted clutch.
A gull's wing, the head of a dragonfly
Were too remote and would endure too much.—"

10. *The Way of an Intellectualist*: *Coll. Works,* Vol. 4, page 30. "Dr. Rönne—the man who could bear no reality, nor grasp any; who knew only the rhythmic opening and closing of the ego and the personality, the continual disruption of inner existence; and who, confronted with the experience of the deep, unbounded, mythically ancient strangeness between man and the world, believed completely in the myth and its images."

11. *The Birthday*: Vol 2, page 56. "For nothing had reality. Did he have reality? No; all he had was every possibility."

12. *The Journey*: Vol 2, pages 30–31. "Facing him was the void. Would there be an answer? . . . And now it was evident: some of them nodded, chewing . . . Jubilation in him, chants of triumph . . . Acceptance followed, evaluation took place."

13. *The Modern I*: Vol. 1, page 17, "The fellow creature, the middle man, the tiny form, the little supporter of comfort and ease, the Barrabas crier, who wants to live bon et propre."

14. Vol. 1, page 256. "Pure and poor, never having had a share in bourgeois successes, in the fame, in the fat of the tippling servant."

15. "A cerebral obstruction of an inner and outer nature."

16. Vol. 2, page 23. "Dear town, take possession of me! House me! Take me into the community!"

17. Vol. 2, page 50. "And now—via Maita-Malta-beaches-shiny-ferry port-mussel-eating-corruptions there ensued a bright, ringing, gentle splintering sound, and Rönne swayed with happiness."

18. Vol. 2, page 430. "But first the adverts. . . . We are no longer actual at all, but the adverts are carefully formed."

19. Vol. 2, page 57. "Where had his South gone? The ivied rock? The eucalyptus, where by the sea? Ponente, coast of decline—where the silver-blue wave?"

20. Vol. 2, page 28. "A rainstorm of inhibitions and weakness burst upon him. For where was assurance that he would be able to tell, bring back, enliven anything about the trip at all, that he would receive anything in the sense of experience?"

21. Vol. 2, page 298. "I was logical to choking point. And when the fog had lifted, what was everything then? Words and the brain. Words and the brain. All the time only this terrible, this eternal brain."

22. Vol. 2, page 303. "Yes, o soul! o soul! We long for the dream. We want intoxication. We call on Dionysos and Ithaca!"

23. Vol. 2, page 334. "Oh this fading of the world in my brain." "I am the new man, that really means the primal man . . . the cerebral animal, the logical desert phenomenon, the mathematical lily; programme: degendering of memory, or cerebration of the race."

24. "Typical historical process; unmotivated and senseless."

25. Vol. 1, page 492. *Nietzsche—Fifty years later.* (One of the many signs of Benn's indebtedness to Nietzsche. Other notable influences on Benn include that of Heinrich Mann "who created us all".) "It is no error to accept the fact that man still has a meaning, or must have one. Man has struggles for existence, family worries, concerns over success, ambition, neuroses, but all that is not meaning in the metaphysical sense."

26. Vol 2, page 78. "For life is not ours, but the vice of a God who remains hidden."

27. "We are the generation without ties, and without depth. Our depth is the abyss."

28. . . . . .

Crises of expression and bouts of eroticism,
That is man of today,
His inwardness a vacuum;
The survival of personality
Is preserved by the clothing
Which, where material is good, may last ten years.

29. Vol 2, page 212. ". . . harmonius life, harmony—that I declined. We all live something other than we are."

30. Vol 2, page 391. "We lived something other than we were, we wrote something other than we thought, we thought something other than we expected, and what remains is something other than we intended."

31. Vol 2, page 223. "Those who acted and were covetous, and those who silently awaited the transformation: criminals and monks, there would not be any other kind."

32. Vol. 2, page 233. "The artist is the only person who can get the better of things, who decides over them."

33. Vol. 2, page 411. The young man: Whoever loves strophes, also loves cata-strophes. Whoever is in favour of statues, must also be for ruins.

The Other: You mean polarity? Ah, don't make syntheses! Stop before the incompatible, hold firm usque ad finem. Bear your life with its deviations, errors, its disintegration, its incompleteness right up to your last hour and I am sure it will put up with it and not censure you. . . ."

34. Vol 2, page 412. " . . . and when the night comes, we will bear it."

35. A word, a phrase—: from cyphers rise
Life recognised, a sudden sense,
The sun stands still, mute are the skies,
And all compacts it, stark and dense.

A word—a gleam, a flight, a spark,
A thrust of flames, a stellar trace—
And then again—immense, the dark.
Round world and I in empty space.

36. "Works of art are phenomenal, historically ineffective, without practical consequence. This is just their greatness." "Art, however, is an isolated phenomenon." Vol. 1, page 47.

37. Vol. 1, page 500. " 'Artistics' is the attempt of art to live itself as meaning within the general decline of meaning and from this experience form a new style, it is the attempt to place a new transcendence against the general nihilism of values: the transcendence of creative desire."

38. "Style bears in itself the proof of existence."

39. "The word contained no sense of time and I loved to formulate in words."

40. Vol. 2, page 154. "Mould thoughts into someone, into a figure, in forms when there are no longer any forms? Invent persons, names, associations, when they are becoming in fact unimportant?"

41. Erratic to the point of admitting considerable inconsistencies to his train of thought and reasoning, and also into his work. One has only to think of, amongst other examples, Benn's ambivalent position over history.

42. Vo.l 2, page 399. "A modern man does not think nihilistically; he brings order to his thoughts and creates for himself a basis for his existence."

BIBLIOGRAPHY

Gottfried Benn. *Gesammelte Werke in vier Bänden,* ed. Dieter Wellershoff. Limes Verlag, Wiesbaden, 1959.

Gottfried Benn. *Ausgewählte Briefe,* mit einem Nachwort von Max Rychner. Limes Verlag, Wiesbaden, 1957.

Gottfried Benn. *Primal Vision.* Selected writings of Gottfried Benn, ed. E. B. Ashton. London, 1961.

E. Buddeberg. *Gottfried Benn.* Metzler Verlag, Stuttgart, 1961.
M. Hamburger. *Gottfried Benn* (in *Reason and Energy.* London, 1957)
W. Lennig. *Gottfried Benn* in Selbstzeugnissen und Bilddokumenten. Rowohlt, 1962.
E. Lohner. *Passion und Intelleckt.* Die Lyrik Gottfried Benns. Luchterhand Verlag, Neuwied, 1961.
E. Nef. *Das Werk Gottfried Benns.* Arche Verlag, Zürich, 1958.
D. Wellershoff. *Gottfried Benn. Phänotyp dieser Stunde*, Köln, 1958.
F. W. Wodtke. *Gottfried Benn.* Metzler Verlag, Stuttgart, 1962.

Fritz von Unruh

Fritz von Unruh

by W. F. MAINLAND

Born in Koblenz, May 10 1885, the son of Lieutenant-General Karl von Unruh, Fritz von Unruh was educated at Plön with a view to a career in the Army. He became an officer in the Imperial Guard but relinquished his commission in order to pursue his chosen career as a writer. On the outbreak of war in 1914 he joined the Uhlans and was wounded in the fighting on the Western Front. He devoted himself to the cause of peace and made, in addition to his writings, many impassioned speeches. As a supporter of the ideals of a republican Germany he came into conflict with the National Socialists and had to seek refuge in Switzerland and France. Interned in the early stages of the war, 1939–45, he made his escape to Spain and eventually to America. There, befriended by Albert Einstein, he eked out an existence, partly by painting, partly by writing. Invited back to Germany in post-war years, he found some restitution after the disregard of the National Socialist régime. He has divided his time between a small estate inherited from his mother and a modest establishment in Long Island. His old age saddened by the materialistic trend of our time, in 1962 he had to suffer the loss by fire of his house and possessions in the United States.

> Meine Familie, meine Vorfahren sie alle haben dieser Welt der Realität jahrhundertelang gedient . . . dieser Realität "Staat" . . . Was bin ich da? Doch auch nur ein Glied in der Kette. Also was will ich eigentlich?(1)

> Wer bin denn ich,
> dass ich mich aus dem ew'gen Kräftekreis
> ablösen könnte? jemals meine Hand
> erheben dürfte wider jenes Ur,
> durch das ich wurde?(2)

THESE two brief passages, the first from a speech delivered by Fritz von Unruh in 1947, the second from Hans Franck's play *Klaus Michel* (1925) may serve to remind us of the beginning of an epoch. Their common theme seems now outdated: it is the serious heart-searching of the individual about his right to abandon the station in life in which his birth has placed him. But it also involves the question of responsibility to society, a question which has changed only in form, but not in intensity. In Franck's play, after a farmer's son has left the land and risen to fame as a surgeon, the claim of tradition is reaffirmed in the next generation. On the battlefield the surgeon sacrifices his life to save his son, who, when the war is over, goes back to the ancestral home and turns farmer. War, and the training for it, evoked a different kind of answer in Fritz von Unruh. His family, which can be traced back to the time of Charlemagne, had long maintained its renown in the military annals of Germany. Both Hans Franck and von Unruh believed that the world must change. But whereas Franck wrote in *Mein Kriegs Buch* (1916):

> Und dennoch, lasst uns glauben, dass die Bahn
> den Völkern vorbestimmt ist wie den Welten
> . . . . dass längst der Wille ihres HERRN
> den Völkern vorbestimmt die Todesnot,
> damit uns neue Völkersterne werden(3)

von Unruh proclaimed the responsibility of the individual to bring about the change in the structure of world society. The persistent message of his writings and his speeches is "Du fang an!"(4) In Franck's prologue (written in 1914) we read:

> Wenn nicht der Krieg auf Erden wär,
> Man müsste Gott drum bitten!(5)

Von Unruh, addressing an audience of 20,000 in the Berlin Sportpalast in January 1932, uttered the challenge which had become articulate in the carnage of Verdun:

> Vor—gegen die Laien und Opportunisten!
> Vor—gegen die Wetterfahnen in den Ministerien und Schulen! Vor gegen die Vereisung und Vergreisung!
> Vor—gegen den Tod!(6)

There is obviously a substantial conflict of temperament between two such writers; the difference is clearly marked in Franck's criticism of von Unruh in an article on Expressionism in *Die Literatur* (Jahrg. xxvii, 1925, pp. 513–18). Von Unruh is praised as a genuine poet and dramatist. But he suffers, Franck says, from a hypertrophy of the heart, which constantly endangers the message which his will seeks to proclaim: "neben meisterlichen Wortprägungen und hinreissenden Rhythmen Abstruses, Bombastisches, Hohles, Leeres, Lächerliches in Hülle und Fülle. Und zum Führertum fehlt dem Nichts-als-Herzmenschen nahezu alles. Wie will überzeitlichen Zielen zuführen, was selber hilflos und heillos in der Zeit verstrickt ist?"(7) To the conflicting nature of the two men, to the critical and tragic contrast of ideology in which their generation shared, the word "Führertum" gives the unhappy clue. The measure of what their conflict represented in the vacillating and fateful decade which surrounds Adolf Hitler's rise to power can be seen clearly and simply in two volumes of Soergel's *Dichtung und Dichter der Zeit.* In the 1927 volume there are scattered references to both authors, and twenty consecutive pages devoted to von Unruh; in 1934, when the work had the added title *Dichter aus deutschem Volkstum,* Hans Franck has twenty consecutive pages, and von Unruh is mentioned, among other names, in the Introduction. Now at any rate, less than twenty years after the end of World War II, a general study of Fritz von Unruh can scarcely fail to revolve round the theme of his alienation from what was in Hitler's time emotionally defined as "deutsches Volkstum". It is this theme which has shaped the mode and tenor of his works for nearly half a century. When the publicists of National Socialism were venturing into the open with their first manifestos, they found in him an articulate adversary ready to rebut their modish vocabulary. Their followers in the late 'forties and 'fifties, planning and contriving in a welter of equally pernicious neologisms from all sides, encountered in the speeches and novels of this man old enough to have been the fellow cadet of the Crown Prince Wilhelm an opposition to the origins of their theories and practices just as determined as it had been in the days before the First World War when he chose to renounce his career in the Imperial German Army. But by this time his opposition was much better informed by isolated suffering and by observation of vast evils which he had only in part foreseen.

Fritz von Unruh's work may be seen as a continuous development from the pattern of an early conversion. Again and again he reveals aspects of his own story. A fascinating and revealing study can be made of his frequent play upon his own name and other names. He appears unmistakably as Ulan in *Opfergang* and *Vor der Entscheidung,* as Uhle in *Phaea* and the novels *Der nie verlor* and *Der Sohn des Generals.* Possibly the very early mutation of his family name, originally Ohnrug (=ohne Rüge)(8) tempted him into other variations, even to associate his name with Till Eulenspiegel in *Sohn des Generals* (where perhaps the mere motif of the aeroplane may owe a little to Gerhart Hauptmann's epic). Our repeated encounters with von Unruh in his stories and plays, his own compulsive efforts to define and redefine his relations to the political and social demands tempt us to look for some occasion which may have started this long process, and to find, if we can, the key to what I have called his conversion. Von Unruh himself recounts what may seem to be the occasion in the text of his speech *Friede auf Erden.* On a May morning he was at rifle-practice as a young cadet. "Die kleinen Vögel sangen, Gräser und Büsche blühten—und verströmten den süssen Duft jener anderen Welt, für die wohl Schubert seine Lieder komponierte . . . Plötzlich rief mich der diensthabende Offizier vor die Scheibe! Ich nahm die befohlene Schießstellung ein. Mit einmal bemerkte ich, wie eine der Jasminblüten am Strauch neben mir, windbewegt, den Lauf meines Gewehrs mit lauter feinen, gelben Blütenpollen überstäubte. . . ."[9] As he sighted the target, the pasteboard figure with the blue uniform and the painted pink features and the black spot to represent the heart became, in his imagination, a living figure. The barrel of his rifle trembled. The officer, impatient, shouted commands. "This was the moment in which all the unrest of my soul began!" This unrest, the harrowing awareness of incongruity between Christian worship of God and the soldier's training to kill men made in the image of God, filled him, as he said, with shame. Doubts about the ethics of the soldier's profession found expression in his writing. Official displeasure was inevitable, and although his play *Offiziere,* eagerly taken up by Max Reinhardt, was not anti-militarist, it was decisive, in spite of the offer of mediation by the Empress, in the matter of his resignation. But then, with the outbreak of war in the autumn of 1914, came another severe test. His brothers were on their way to their units, and, disregarding his mother's entreaties, he enlisted. How severe the test was may be judged not by the mood of 1939 so well as by the memory of the days twenty-five years before, when poets wrote:

> Deutschland muss leben,
> Und wenn wir sterben müssen[10]
> (Heinr. Lersch)

and

> Joyful hear the rolling drums,
> Joyful hear the trumpets call,
> Then let Memory tell thy heart:
> "England! what thou wert, thou art!"
> (Henry Newbolt)

Von Unruh speaks of the almost religious exaltation of resisting the war-fever, and then of his "defeat": ". . . die Niederlage meines Gewissens, als ich mich dann plötzlich als Freiwilliger in einem Ulanenregiment meldete",[11] of a renewed sense of shame when it was publicly acclaimed that this well known young poet of noble lineage had joined the Ulans. It was known that his *Offiziere* had been followed by another more outspoken drama, *Prinz Louis Ferdinand,* which, set in the Napoleonic time, was recognised by the authorities as an unseasonable warning against military ambition and banned from production on all the stages of the Reich.

These events in his personal life and in his career as a poet can be seen in retrospect as necessary stages towards the great resolve which he made in a time of crisis in the war and in a moment of extreme danger to himself. Wounded at Verdun, stripped and left to die, he watched the first rays of the morning sun spreading over the battlefield. "In dieser Sekunde kam etwas ganz Neues in mich. Ein neuer Mut! Ich begriff, dass die uralte, sogenannte 'Feigheit' im Kriege der Anfang eines neuen Mutes zum Leben war! und dass der uralte, sogenannte 'Mut' zu sterben im Krieg . . . in Wirklichkeit nur Feigheit war, vor der eigentlichen Sendung und Aufgabe des Lebens!"(12) This may be a simple, healthy, and common assertion of stubborn human nature in the face of danger. But it is the quality of this particular experience, its setting in von Unruh's life, and its effect that concerns us now. Its outward effect was soon to be the formation of the "Soldaten des Friedens";(13) for after Verdun, at von Unruh's instigation, many of his comrades took the oath with him to turn away from the heroics of death and to affirm the values of life. Later it was to lead to von Unruh's "eiserne Front"(14) against the renewed pseudo-pathos and the hysteria of the Hitler régime. The experience itself is probably the occasion we have been looking for in order to try to understand this courageous, sensitive, skilful, intense, uncompromising, and sometimes brutal fighter for peace.

Recalling the grains of pollen on the rifle on that early May morning, and thinking again of the rays of the rising sun falling aslant a scene of untidy death, we find a slender clue to the sensory nature of Unruh's experience. And this, we know, we must pursue. After many years he gives the hint of explanation which we have surmised. From the few but insistent references in von Unruh's works to Angelus Silesius we may have been impelled to think of the visual inspiration of somewhat earlier German mysticism—the gleam of light on a pewter plate which illumined the spiritual path of Jakob Böhme. For a moment we may think of Stanley Spencer's vigils in Salonika in the First Word War in which that constant vision of the Resurrection which was to inspire so much of his later work possessed his mind. But we know that these are only hints to put us on the path of our quest. Then, in the fourth scene of von Unruh's drama *Wilhelmus* of 1953 we find Alexander Farnese taunting William of Orange: "Oranien, Sie haben Ihre Begeisterung nur aus Büchern! Sie haben zuviel in den Büchern des Erasmus von Rotterdam gebüffelt. . . ."(15) And William calmly replies: "Nein! Herzog Farnese. Nicht aus Büchern—sondern mitten im Kriege erwachte diese Freiheit in mir! . . . Der Jammer unschuldiger Menschen weckte mich—wie einst den Saulus auf der

Strasse nach Damaskus das weisse Licht!"[16] In the tenth chapter of the Acts of the Apostles we may find the exalted prototype of the irascible missionary who discovered the misguidance of his early days and, losing nothing of his rebellious zeal, turned in vigour to the works of sympathy and brotherhood. For a time at the cadet school in Plön von Unruh had accepted the heritage of his male ancestors and a pattern of patriotism which should lead him, untroubled by doubts, to the destruction of his country's enemies and to the sweet and decorous pagan death *pro patria*. Then he found his "furor anti-teutonicus", the zeal which was to make him question again and again the might and the right of the Prussian state and its ideal of duty. Henceforth his message was to be "Geh in dich!"[17]

We cannot hope to piece together the family story of the convert Paul; we know a little more of the early environment of this militant twentieth-century German disciple of peace and goodwill. The religious inspiration in von Unruh's work and his early awareness of a conflict between doctrine and the ethics and practice of secular life can be appreciated when we recall his parents' insistence upon religious instruction. It may well be that both his insight and his preoccupation with spiritual problems were intensified by the complex nature of this instruction: his father, a Protestant, directed that his sons should be brought up as Protestants, while the daughters were brought up in the Catholic faith of their mother. But von Unruh's discontent with the shallow expediences of national life and with the materialist bias of the time seems to have been a development of something already apparent in his father. When the young cadet was censured by his superiors for being so fanciful as to say that a landscape was beautiful, or if, at the rifle-butts on that May morning his thoughts strayed to Schubert, the impulse was the same as that which made his father, who accepted the austerity and discipline of army life, seek solace and freedom in music. Not infrequently in the poet's reminiscences and later fictions the recognisable figure of the "officer with the cello" reminds us of the pattern of his early experience. There was nothing wayward or even untraditional in such devotion to music: Frederick II had had his concerts at Sans Souci. But when the cadet who bore the name of that admired shaper of Prussian destinies allowed the arts to intrude and usurp, the risk was considerable.

From an early age von Unruh showed himself to be "musisch". He wrote poetry and he painted. If the Empress had had her way, he would have been sent to a college of art. But the elder von Unruh refused to accept her bounteous offer; nothing was to disrupt his plans for the boy's military career. Years later, in America, von Unruh, partly from necessity, resumed his painting. The few reproductions of pictures from this time which are commonly accessible show an aptitude for bold expression; figures such as the *Liftboy* and *Homeless* (probably a self-portrait) are social comment. Internal and external contours are firm, but in difficult passages where the trained artist learns to cope with form or to flaunt technical convention in a knowledgeable way, von Unruh makes the amateur's mistakes. Evidence of composition is slender. Von Unruh's *métier* is words.

The two decades in the middle of which he was born produced many writers who were goaded into action by the inadequacy of traditional word-patterns. What they did may now be seen as the second stage in a stylistic revolution started by men born in the 'sixties. These "naturalists", fired with social indignation and a kind of scientific zeal, had tried to represent in recognisable detail an environment and a mode of living which, they believed, must be radically changed. They eagerly exploited the resources of nouns and adjectives. The younger writers, such as Reinhard Sorge, Walter Hasenclever, Georg Kaiser, Ernst Toller, went more intensely to work, trying to get near "the palpable essence of things" (Bithell). As the work of some of the older writers consisted in the recording of impressions, the younger men's utterances of ecstasy or of suffering became known as "expressionism". There is in their style an obvious and forceful concentration of effort, a condensation of syntax, an appreciation of the supposed dynamic of the verb. Their awareness of organic, elemental forces in human life, revived by militant mood and conflict in the years 1912–18, and brought poignantly to the surface in those years by the disturbing terms of new psychologies—creative evolution, psycho-pathology of everyday life—suggests correspondence between Expressionism and the Storm and Stress of the 1770's and 1780's. But whereas nowadays, as we read Lenz and Klinger, and the early plays of Goethe and of Schiller, we may carry out the old and comfortable school exercise of "analysis of character", we find we have to apply other criteria to *Gas*, *Koralle*, *Masse Mensch*, *Ein Geschlecht*. For here we find ourselves listening to representative voices; we see not characters, but figures, and these figures could well wear masks and still declaim with full force, unrecognised as individuals, the discordant song of their sufferings.

> "No matter where I look, I see the hands of fathers stroking in pride the creatures of their libido. Dull-witted on well-trodden ways they pass by all the questions which clamour for an answer,

timid and anxious, hoping for new courage in their children, that these shall find solutions they themselves evade. But if the primal urge must pass in sloth through millennia of generations chewing like brute oxen the cud of hope, I will not join their game of blind-man's buff."

Thus is the loathing of paternity expressed by the eldest son in *Ein Geschlecht.* To the mother, who has said her heart is not of stone, he answers: "Weakness in you, when fat worms crawl and in the eyes of offspring as in filth newts and the midnight mushroom with roots of corruption have their home. Mothers! Wives: in that humid place under your heart it is the grave you carry, and what you bear forth is death, and naught but death." Out of this frenzy of negation in its graveyard setting, where one soldier son incurs the death penalty for cowardice and another shares with his sister incestuous love, there emerges the mother who was to be in Unruh's later work the ideal and ineffective opponent of a community bred to kill, and the son who was to find at least the individuation of a name in *Platz.* But *Ein Geschlecht*, of set purpose, lacks individuation; its arguments, its conflicts, its recriminations represent the plight of families in which war has laid bare the longing, the lust, and the loathing which civilisation uneasily conceals, In such a play we may not look for dramatic action in the traditional sense of Shakespearian drama. Rather perhaps it is to be thought of in association with Attic tragedy. This found passing comment in the review by Müller-Guttenbrunn in the *Wiener Abendzeitung* (September 16, 1918): "Sie" (the mother) "gebärdet sich als antike Himmelsstürmerin und redet Flammen".(18) "Ein dunkler, philosophischer Hymnus im Namen aller Mütter an das Schicksal, der eine verwegene Auflehnung gegen alle überlieferte Ordnung ist und die Umgestaltung des Vaterlandes in ein phantastisches Mütterreich fordert"(19) was, in his opinion, no fit material for the stage—"diese Welt des schönen Scheins".(20) Not quite so conservative or so morally weighted is the comment of a more renowned critic some eight years later. Julius Bab (*Chronik des deutschen Dramas* V, 1926, pp. 33–4). *Platz* and its predecessor *Ein Geschlecht* are quoted by Bab as "Variation des politischen Oratorienstils";(21) he refers almost immediately before to Reinhard Goering's *Seeschlacht.* Sporadic evidence of "edle Gesamtgesinnung"(22) and "echtes, menschliches Gefühl"(23) does not, in his opinion, counterbalance the vagueness and confusion, the lack of substance in von Unruh's style. He describes the effect on audiences, other than those of the Frankfurt-Darmstadt region, where the enthusiasm of Gustav Hartung helped, in brilliant productions, to establish an Unruh tradition: "beim prasselnden Lärm dieser ewig aufgeregten Worte vergeht ihnen Hören und Sehen. Der Katarakt durcheinander tosender Bilder reisst sie ins Bodenlose".(24)

In the play *Stürme,* the 1913 version of which was revised for production in 1922, Bab finds the same "Wortgewässer"(25) and beneath it merely a "banale Geschichte von einem edlen jungen Fürsten, mit Weltverbesserungsplänen".(26) This static definition of the theme gives no hint of the powerful forces in and around the young prince, the dynamic exposition of which may recall the dramatic style of Leisewitz (1752–1806). From the moment of the burial of his father, surrounded by clerics and courtiers and the old General, representative of the military caste, the prince assumes power in an arrogant proclamation:

> Was kümmert mich der Bischof! Was das Schicksal!
> Ich bin mein Schicksal! Ich mein Schicksalsspruch!(27)

Smarting under the recollection of his own sufferings just as much as under the general tyranny of an old, harsh, law-bound system, he has to find his way, through licence and sin, to admission of his faults, to renunciation of power, of life itself, and the proclamation of a new system of living, a new law. His will is to hand over control to those who have shown love and constancy:

> Nur sie—
> Denn ich zerbrach mein Herz—sind wert, das Zepter
> Zum Kreis zu biegen, das der Pole Eis
> Auftaut vom Mittelpunkt!(28)

Defeat, the inevitable defeat of the idealist as seen by von Unruh, and shown in the pattern of his own life—is foreshadowed in the last words of the Bishop:

> Gestählter als Ignatius kehr ich wieder...(29)

Stürme is a work heavy with rhetoric; but there is great variety in its structure. Interspersed passages of prose give the impression of a Shakespearian pattern which has undergone the distortions of the "Sturm und Drang":(30) the porter and his wife Lieschen utter naïve words of homely wisdom; there is the heavily matter-of-fact prose of the General. At the end of Act II there is significant and allusive comment on tradition, place-seeking, the emptiness of honours, the passing of the generations; the Kammerherr, tearing off his cloak, throws it at his father and dashes out to throw open the prisons: "Wehe!" cries the father (the Marschall) "zieht denn eine andere Zeit herauf? Laufen wir Alten noch weiter... Tun dies und das... und über uns fort braust das Neue? Wir verstehen es nicht! Ist es da? Wir erleben es nicht? . . . Grässlich! Wehe, wer heute Vater ist! Wehe, wer an der Wende der Zeiten zeugt!"[31]

Such declamation may weary us today because we feel that we are familiar with the general tone of it. It may even ring dolefully in the ears of some young readers of the 1960's as a modulation of Meister Anton's plaint in Hebbel's excessively widely read *Maria Magdalene*: "Ich verstehe die Welt nicht mehr!"[32] (1844). The necessity in literary study (as historical enterprise) of trying to see more clearly the imaginative and the critical works of the past in their sections and their sequence, may find interesting illustration when a thorough study of Fritz von Unruh's work is undertaken. Critics who were watching him in his early days were alert to fluctuations in the strident cry of the so-called New Europe. But even while they were still permitted in the inter-war years to talk about him, their approval, sometimes their enthusiasm, was undermined by prevalent awareness of what is often called his excessive "Pathos". In the years following World War II when thousands were busy trying to forget that they had ever used such words as "Aufnordung", "Gleichschaltung", "arteigen", "volksfremd", it was found that a sizeable queue of German authors had formed for rehabilitation, or even for discovery by their compatriots. "Als in Deutschland der grausige Spuk vorüber, als der vom Hitler-Deutschland in alle Welt getragene Krieg zu Ende war—gab es dann für Fritz von Unruh eine Art von Wiedergutmachung?"[33] asks Friedrich Rasche. Von Unruh was invited back to Germany to make speeches, to receive the Wilhelm Raabe prize in Brunswick, the Goethe prize in Frankfurt. This was some little recompense. But was it recognition of his significance as an author? I think the way to recognition of von Unruh is a long one, and most of it still lies ahead of us. There will be varying assessments, and he may never again be regarded as a great writer in the same way as he was in the late 'twenties. But this is not of immediate relevance. What must concern us, as an early step on the way, is what we can detect as certain intrinsic qualities of his work. When the whole task is undertaken, it will probably be found that it entails, to a remarkable extent, a close study of his critics. For so much of the work of von Unruh in its propositions and in the intricacies of its motifs, is a sustained attack upon his adversaries. He has anticipated attack, and things which have been said against him he has used repeatedly in subsequent works in order to press home a new offensive.

Repetition with variation and much elaboration is a dominant, sometimes distressing characteristic of his writing. In the last decade and a half he has been largely lost from view in the glare of publicity accorded to his contemporary Kafka and to the dramatist Bert

Brecht who was thirteen years younger. This may be a merited obscurity; it is much too early to say. What I think we must admit is that von Unruh has, with some obstinacy, contributed to the neglect of what he has had to say by saying it too often. As an old soldier, a courageous veteran of many defeats, he has written his memoirs in many forms—plays, novels, speeches. To the outside world, listening with a mixture of respect and misgiving and shame to accounts of battles long ago, it may have seemed that he was fighting the same battles over again. To von Unruh, I think, it has been an expanding campaign. Thirteen when Bismarck died, in his early thirties inspired by the vision at Verdun, at forty-seven pleading vigorously for support for the Weimar republic against the threat of dictatorship, escaping from an internment camp in France, enduring the fatigues of the fugitive, he entered upon his fifties as a not altogether desirable alien in the United States. In his seventies, with his treasured convictions, the assurance of his vision, and the harrowing knowledge that he had uttered true prophecy, he had to witness in contemporary events the re-enactment of men's tyranny, their defection, their hatred and suspicion, their refusal to accept responsibility. The adversary had spread his dominion. The ageing eyes of the poet saw him in different periods, in different uniforms, as clearly as the young poet who had conceived the dialogue between the volunteer and the Ulan in *Vor der Entscheidung*:

> Die Kerle müsst' ein grosser Künstler packen :
> Die bärtgen Köpfe mit dem hellen Blick,
> Dem Eisengang and breiten Männernacken.
>
> . . . .

Ulan:

> Unmöglich scheint mir's, daß in Blut und Waffen
> Ein Volk sich seinen reinsten Kelch erringt :
> Viel hohe Geister haben noch zu schaffen,
> Eh' Seelenkraft in uns das Tier bezwingt.[34]

A scene in *Bismarck* (n.d. publ. for the first time in Fr. v. Unruh, *Dramen*, Nürnberg 1960) seems to parody the situation in the third act of Schiller's *Don Carlos*. To Onog, historian and private tutor to a princess in St. Petersburg, Bismarck (at that time, 1859, Prussian Ambassador) offers the post of secretary.

Onog: Mir, einem Rebellen?
Bismarck: Jawohl, Ihm. Aber selbstredend : Ohne alle seine brausenden neuen Menschheitsideen.[35]

As the democrat, Onog, veteran of the 1848 barricades, speaks of Kant's *Vom ewigen Frieden*—

Bismarck: Ewiger Frieden? Das ist, wie mein Freund Moltke sagt, nur ein Traum. Und nicht einmal ein schöner.

Onog: Der schönste, den je ein Menschentraum geträumt hat. Mein Deutschland geeint, nicht durch Kasernengewalt, sondern durch seinen eigenen geistigen Entschluß zur Menschenwürde, mit der Friedenshand, ausgestreckt zu allen Völkern... Herr Gesandter, es war der Traum unserer Väter.

Bismarck: Nicht von meinem alten Herrn... (Deutet auf seinen Ordensstern) Aber dieses Abzeichen schützt mich vor solchen Träumereien.[36]

This is the theme—the rejection of peace—taken up again in von Unruh's vehement story of the Hitler régime, *Der nie verlor*, in which the hatred of the dictatorship is reinforced by the scorn of the military caste, to which by birth von Unruh belongs, for the pompous demagogue corporal (the satire was already apparent in *Bonaparte*, 1927). I quote from the American translation (*The End is not yet*, 1947):

> He could never have swollen into such a world-wide black plague all by himself! You parents, who let your children play at war in the streets like savages, with toy revolvers in their belts! *You* have made him great . . . and you girls too, who float around the city streets picking up soldiers on leave, crazy about a uniform —you have made him great. . . .

In this "panorama of our apocalyptic age" as Unruh himself called his novel, there are jottings in a note-book "stained with blood and soil":

> An odd fact. Belligerents exchange characteristics. And so we shall presumably find the goose-step and the drum-majors of the German army (it is defeated) turning up again in Russia in the Red Army. Or the Prussian military state will be destroyed, only to live again in Washington.

The name of the man who turns the pages of the note-book is Uhle. As the adversary is presented in varied guise, so does von Unruh himself, as we have seen before, reappear under a variety of names, always recognisable, sometimes sharing his character with other figures, such as Dietrich and the Unknown Soldier. For an understanding of the metamorphoses in his works, these re-appearances would have to be carefully studied, and, together with them, perhaps more carefully still, certain accompanying figures which have sometimes kindred names with one another. For example the Irene-Iris variation would have to be traced. This would soon involve the pursuit of a number of motifs, such as the throwing away and retrieving of the Iron Cross. A foil to von Unruh as author appears as Krah for example in *Zero* and *Phaea.* There are motifs not associated with specific characters or figures, but of great significance in trying to determine von Unruh's habits of thought. Such is the "Peitsche" in *Heinrich aus Andernach,* in *Stürme* and else where.

One alluring, perhaps genuine example of recurrent pattern with a number of motifs which was to emerge again after a number of years in an entirely different setting may be traced if we revert for a moment to the play *Stürme.*

Fürst: Doch wer befreit mich aus dem Zuchtgefängnis
Von Ja und Nein? . . . Was willst du in den Gittern?
Du Märchenvogel? . . . Flattere doch davon.
. . . .
Iris: Dein Blick wird plötzlich wie ein Grabgewölbe,
Du könntest mich ermorden, glaube ich,
Wenn deine Väter riefen : "Tue es!"
(Sie beginnt langsam zu tanzen)
Fürst: Was drehst du dich wie eine Seifenblase
Goldsprühend, zitternd mir vom Munde fort?
Iris: So tanzt ich einst aus dem Bann der Gruft
Von Michelangelos Kapelle! Lache!
Ich schwebte hin, mich spiegelnd in den Fliesen,
Bis die gewölbte Kuppel über mir
Zu kreisen anfing. . . .
. . . .
Ach! Ein befreites Lachen klang wie jezt
Als Grabgeläut für alles, was nicht Leben!
(Sie ist ihm an die Brust geflogen)
Fürst: Geliebte! Die behelmten Wände, Waffen,
Der hohle Pomp der väterlichen Zeit
Hängt mir, ein Spinngewebe, da, vorm Licht
Aus deinem Blut. . . .
Iris: Nimm seinen Inhalt hin!
(Umarmung. Graf Stefan ist vorgetreten)

From the sultry, Salome climate of this dialogue we come eight years later to the film-set of the Photographisch-Akustische-Experimental-Aktiengesellschaft, a name reduced (by analogy with Ufa) to form the comedy title with its deceptively classical flavour : *Phaea.* Adam Uhle the writer is with Toni, a dance hostess :

Uhle: . . . Dabei hieß es doch einmal, im Anfang war das . . . ja—im Anfang. Aber vielleicht sind wir eben am Ende. Um Gottes willen, kommen uns denn nur tote Worte?

Toni: Aber gesund sind Sie doch? Sie sollten tanzen. Ich tanze egal weg. Schon mit drei Jahren hab ich mich immer so vorm Spiegel gedreht (sie tut es) immer so rum . . . stundenlang.

Uhle (ausbrechend)*:* Sie leben ja!

Toni: Merken Sie das erst jetzt?

Uhle: Sie sind, ich meine, so wirklich, so—

Krah (stürzt freudig aufgeregt herein)*:* Toni! Er hat dich vorno— (stutzt plötzlich . . .) Ist sie nicht eine Prinzessin? Oje, oje, spinnt sich da was an? Adam! Ist mein Freund Adam, ich bin mit ihm zur Schule gegangen . . . Kunstgeschichte.(38)

Freddy Krah, the other author, delighted that Toni may become a film-star, dances with her as Adam goes out. Toni, gazing after Adam, says suddenly: Freddy, ich mach dir 'n Vorschlag, heirat mich.

Krah: Heiraten? Um Gotteswillen! Warum denn?

Toni: Hab Lust drauf. Du nicht?

Krah: Heiraten? Ich? Im Gehirn erotische Belastungen? Oje, oje, nein Toni.(39)

In *Stürme* it is Count Stefan, the husband of Iris, who surprises her and the Prince:

Fürst: Ich liebe sie . . .! —Und suchst du Waffen? Unten
Beim Kruzifix, vergilbtem Ehrenkodex
Will ich dir Rede stehn.

Stefan: Mein Freund, bin ich ein Tier, daß du so sprichst?
Sind wir nicht Menschen? Liebe, weltvergessende,
nimm mich auf in deinen Hauch . . . Bruder, Schwester
. . . eure Herzen klopfen zart an meine Seele . . .
Wo sind wir? Freund, ist das Wirklichkeit?(40)

At first sight it may seem incongruous, distasteful, to set these two scenes side by side. The substance they share is either embarrassing or tragic—the interruption of a love-scene. Yet, looked at more closely, they have more than this in common. There is the changing of partners, the dance, the mirror motif, the emancipation from the emptiness of environment—in *Stürme* the heritage of outworn tradition, in *Phaea* the hollow make-believe of the cinema-set. The trios in both have a glimpse of what is called reality—in the "Schauspiel" by a controlled pathos, in the comedy by the swift deflection of pathos.

These are matters which could not be slowly and consistently followed by the critics. When I saw *Phaea* in Berlin in 1930, the majority of the audience was probably unaware, as I was, that this was to be the last Reinhardt production of a play by von Unruh.

We had already entered upon the decade which was once again to repress the utterances of the poet, and to curtail free investigation by the critics. So the critics lost ground, and could not see, or at least could not freely comment upon a very interesting development in von Unruh, for which they shared, with him, some responsibility. He had begun to answer them in a complicated way by parodying himself. Even in *Phaea* he saw himself as others saw him. With sharp self-irony he made Uhle, the target of attack, lose control of his sentences, meandering uneasily through unfinished clauses, losing contact with those to whom he was talking, and seeming thus to justify the early complaints of some critics that by excess of feeling he had obscured the meaning of his message. How much of this was fully under his conscious control it is hard to say. Years earlier, with the accelerated, unwitting impetus of the forceful character, he had blundered and caused offence. Out of a good-will mission to France and England after the First World War there emerged a travelogue, *Flügel der Nike*. It is a book of uneven quality, with much sentimental enthusiasm and a medley of impressions:

> An der Mühle, der alten von Granchester.... Ich benetze die Stirn mit dem kühlen Naß, an dessen Bett Lord Byron gesungen —auch Tennyson—wo sich Shelley mit Keats Empörung trank gegen den Obergott Zeus.—In dem Wind, der die silbernen Weiden bewegt, Shakespeare, ahn ich auch Dich....[41]

Of D. H. Lawrence von Unruh writes:

> In dem englischen Mittland war seine Geburt, sein Vater ein Säufer, seine Mutter das Licht.... Romantisch schrieb er *Songs* (sic) *and Lovers*, herrliche Lieder aus den Zweifeln der Liebe.[42]

The book found high praise in Alfons Paquet's review (*Die Literatur*, xxvii, p. 397): "dieses Kämpfen für eine Harmonie, die höher ist als die kühle Vernünftigkeit des Pazifismus, höher als das narzissische Fürsichsein der Literaten um ihrer selbst willen. . . ." But some of his comments on the social life of Paris, where he had found a warm welcome, caused offence. Otto Grautoff (*Die Literatur*, xxvii, p. 750) mentions complaints about von Unruh's "injures brutales qui se mêlent assez souvent aux effusions humanitaires ... accusations les plus impertinentes". It would seem that the visit to Paris at all events did nothing to help the cause of Franco-German understanding.

It may be supposed that as circumstance and the foundering of his hopes increased his tendency to fanaticism, von Unruh's intense observation of himself in relation to opposing forces ensure-

at times a startling and effective clarity of utterance. At other times they led to that sort of behaviour, social and literary, which produces in the disconcerted onlooker the impression of the grotesque. When such a man as von Unruh is stung to reproof by apathy, by the destruction of his cherished values, by the failure of means of mass-communication to do anything but foster cheap sentiment, greed, or hate, the texture of his response will be uneven, and his style will jar even upon those who are deeply in agreement with him. Out of a visit to Germany at a time when the term "Wirtschaftswunder"(43) was more widely current than it is now, he produced the novel *Der Sohn des Generals*. On the back of the title-page we read: "Die Charaktere dieses Romans sind symbolisch".(44) It may be that his encounters in post-war Germany assumed symbolic significance, but probably not all readers would agree that he has contrived a convincing symbolism in this work which again bears the mark of the von Unruh autobiographical exposition. Uhle, this time Kaspar Friedrich, is once more in contact with the film world. On the plane he meets "Mister Christlieb Lincoln Schleich" whom he had formerly known as Ivan Schleich. Schleich asks him:

> Darf man fragen, was wollen *Sie* in Preußisch-Berlin?

He answers:

> Ich soll heute abend im Hebbel-Theater eine Rede über die Brüderlichkeit halten.
> —Über die Brüderlichkeit?—verschluckte sich Schleich vor Lachen am Rauch seiner Zigarre. —Aber Männeken, es gibt doch gar keine Brüderlichkeit!
> —Deshalb soll ich sie ja beschwören!(45)

His wordly-wise acquaintance advises him:

> Hüten Sie sich, pathetisch zu werden! Vor dem Pathos, da läuft heut jeder so weit er kann davon! Seit dem Geschreie der "geliebten Führer". . .
> —Was hatte das mit Pathos zu tun? Herr Schleich—Pathos, das kommt von dem Griechenwort πατειν—erleiden! Wo aber ist die Tragödie des Zusammenbruchs aller Werte je in solch pathetischem Sinne erlitten worden? Wo? Wo?(46)

This excited delivery, with its applied pedantry (perhaps again in self-satire) is not so much argument as the wearing-down technique of verbal assault. In such an encounter von Unruh is impelled to pronounce his views on courage and cowardice in relation to good and evil: "Gut heisse ich den Mut zur Erkenntnis. Zur

Selbsterkenntnis. Böse heisse ich die Feigheit vor der Erkenntnis! Vor der Selbsterkenntnis".[47]

"Know thyself". This has been the supreme imperative in Fritz von Unruh's life. What do we know of his knowledge of himself as an artist? One of the most penetrating things he has to say about his art as a writer is to be found in the dialogue immediately preceding the lines quoted from *Phaea*. Toni, on the film-set, suddenly notices that Uhle has five shadows. She, he says, has many more. Then he asks: What about the word? "Das wirft eben keine Schatten, und deshalb gilt's auch nicht mehr". (Was von Unruh thinking of the *déraciné* Chamisso, and his Peter Schlemihl?) The transition to the text of Genesis is swiftly made: "Als Gott sprach, es werde Licht, da hat ein Wort noch Schatten geworfen".

Toni: 'n Wort? Aber Herr Uhle, wie soll denn 'n Wort Schatten werfen?

Uhle: Ich bitte Sie, ein Wort! Das war doch bisher etwas Lebendiges! Natürlich zwischen all diesen Lampen, Kulissen, Bäumen, überhaupt in dieser ganzen Pappennatur—das Wort läßt sich eben nicht photographieren ...[48]

As the practised cry of the heroine is heard from another set, Uhle says:

Mich sollte man schreien lassen.

Toni: Sie sind aber ulkig.[49]

He begins to talk about his loneliness, at his desk, with his pen and paper, and asks, was she ever alone?

Toni: Ich glaub, ich bin das erste Mal allein—Das heißt mit Ihnen. —(sie lacht) Und noch dazu im Walde. (singend) Im Wald und auf der Heide—

Uhle: Wald? (lacht verrückt auf) Ja, so plastisch. (Er springt auf und fährt mit der Faust in den hohlen Stamm) Ich meine—wahrscheinlich ist auch das Wort von der einen Seite hohl. Sonst wär's ja nicht möglich ... überhaupt, wenn's noch lebendig wäre, nicht wahr, zum Beispiel, wie Sie, dann würde es sich behaupten, wehren und keiner dürfte es streichen. Aber es hat keinen Schatten. Dabei hieß es doch einmal, im Anfang war das ... ja —im Anfang. . . .[50]

So for a moment, within the protective framework of comedy, von Unruh, looking at himself, sees that his material—the word—is not material, that *his* words fall and leave no trace. He had used so many, with an intricacy of invention in pattern and rhythm, and was still to use many more. It may be a misfortune that the incentive of his time which has driven him to write and speak, has charged his mind so much with political, social, moral purpose, that he has become excessively aware of failure.

We cannot know whether, if von Unruh were to have enjoyed that harmony in life which he has, almost feverishly, sought, his stubborn and vigorous talent would have turned to a freer and more gracious play with words, or whether, through lack of opposition, it would have deserted him. We only know that through the tenseness of his early verse drama a wonderful, rich new music emerges, that some of his prose narratives, such as the *Opfergang* of 1916 and *Fürchte Nichts* of 1952, show a continued mastery of clear, terse syntax, and that in certain of his satirical plays (*Bonaparte*, *Bismarck*) and especially in the comedy *Phaea* and the historical comedy-fantasy *Duell an der Havel*, he creates subtle situations and devises dialogue with a clear perception of the social environment of words. These are evidence that the artist is at work, that his mind is not for ever preoccupied with ideas, that though he is possessed of a mission to mankind, he observes and creates, moving with apparent freedom within the discipline of his art.

TRANSLATIONS

1. My family, my ancestors have served this world of reality for centuries... this reality which is called the "State"... And what am I? Surely only a link in a chain. So what do I want?

2. And who am I that I should have the power to separate myself from this eternal cycle of forces? ever to raise my hand against that origin to which I owe my being?

3. Yet let us believe that for the nations as for all the worlds the path is foreordained... that the will of the Lord has decreed the death pangs for His nations that new nations may arise as new stars.

4. It is for you to make the beginning.

5. If there were no war on earth we should have to ask God for it.

6. On, on against the laymen and the opportunists! On, on against the weather-cocks in the ministries and the schools! On, on against the cold restraint of custom and of age. On, on against death!

7. Side by side with masterly new phrasing and exhilarating rhythms there is an abundance of abstruse, bombastic, hollow, empty and ludicrous things. The man who is nothing but heart lacks almost everything that would befit him for leadership. How is anybody who is helplessly, irredeemably enmeshed in his own time to lead onwards to those goals which are free of the trammels of time?

8. Blameless.

9. The little birds were singing, grasses and bushes were all abloom spreading the sweet scent of that other world for which Schubert com-

posed his songs. . . . Suddenly the officer on duty ordered me to the range. I took up the required position. All at once I noticed that one of the jasmin-blossoms beside me, stirred by the breeze, had scattered fine yellow grains of pollen on the barrel of my rifle. . . .

10. Germany must live, though we may have to die.

11. The defeat of my conscience when I suddenly enlisted as a volunteer in a regiment of Uhlans.

12. In that moment something came to me that was quite new. A new kind of courage! I knew that the old so-called cowardice in war was the beginning of a new courage to face life! and that the old so-called courage to face death in war . . . was really only cowardice before the real task and mission of life!

13. Soldiers of peace.

14. Iron front.

15. Orange, your enthusiasm comes from books! You have been grinding away too much at Erasmus of Rotterdam's books!

16. No! Duke Farnese. Not books—it was in the middle of the war that this freedom awoke in me! . . . The misery of innocent men stirred me—just as in the olden days Saul was awakened by the white light on the road to Damascus!

17. Look into thyself.

18. She behaves like a heroine of antiquity rebelling against heaven and uttering words of flame.

19. An obscure philosophical hymn to fate in the name of all mothers, which is an audacious revolt against all traditional order and demands the transformation of the "Vaterland" into a fantastic matriarchy.

20. This world of fair semblance.

21. A variety of the oratorio style with political content.

22. A general nobility of sentiment.

23. Genuine human feeling.

24. Under the ceaseless hail of emotionally charged words they lose their sense of sight and hearing. On a cataract of turbulent images they are swept into a bottomless chasm.

25. Deluge of words.

26. A banal story of a noble-minded young prince with plans for the improvement of the world.

27. What care I for the bishop! or for Fate! I am my fate, my own decree of fate.

28. Only they—not I, for it was I who broke my heart—only they are worthy to bend the sceptre into a circle which from its centre shall melt the polar ice.

29. I will return, stronger than Loyola in resolve.

30. Storm and Stress.

31. Are we at the beginning of a new epoch? Are we, the old, still going on, doing this thing and that . . . while over our heads the new age is roaring past? We cannot understand it! Are the new things here and are we insensate to them. . . .? It is horrible! Woe to him who today is a father! Woe to him who has begotten children at the turn of the times!

32. I can't understand the world any more.

33. When the horrid nightmare was over, and the war which Hitler's Germany had carried to the four corners of the world was at an end, was there any kind of reparation for Fr. v. Unruh?

34. There should be some great artist to catch the likeness of these fellows: hirsute heads and the brightness of their eyes, their iron tread, their broad and manly shoulders.

. . . . . .

It seems impossible to me that a nation should find its purest prize in the midst of blood and weapons: many men of noble mind have yet to work before the strength of the spirit vanquish the beast in us.

35. *Onog:* Me, a rebel?

Bismarck: Yes, you. But mind of course—without any of your hot-headed humanitarian ideas.

36. *Bismarck:* Everlasting peace? As my friend Moltke says, that is only a dream. And not even a nice dream.

Onog: The finest dream that ever came into human dreams. My Germany united, not by the power of prison warders but by its own spiritual resolve to establish the dignity of man, with the hand of peace proffered to all the nations ... Mr. Ambassador, it was the dream of our fathers.

Bismarck: Not my old man's dream ... (pointing to the Star of the Order on his breast) This badge will protect me against all visionary nonsense of that sort.

37. *Prince:* Who is to set me free from the prison house of Yes and No?... What are you doing behind the bars, you bird of fairy-land?... Fly away.

Iris: There is the look of the grave in your eyes; I believe you could murder me if your ancestors were to cry: Kill her! (she begins to dance slowly).

Prince: Why do you turn trembling away from my lips, like a soap-bubble with a glitter of gold?

Iris: So I danced once out of the spell of the tomb of Michel-angelo's chapel! Laugh! I soared away, mirroring myself in the stones, until the arched vault above me started to revolve... Laughter rang out free as now it does, sounding the dirge for all that is not life . . . ! (leaping into his arms)

Prince: Beloved! The armour on the walls, the hollow pomp of centuries hangs around me like a cobweb in the light that shines from your blood ...

Iris: Take the gift that it holds . . . !(they embrace. Count Stefan has stepped forward)

38. *Uhle:* It was said at one time: in the beginning was... H'm ... in the beginning. Perhaps we are at the end. For Heaven's sake, is it only dead words that come to us?

Toni: But you're fit, aren't you? You should dance. I go on dancing regardless. When I was only three I used to spin round and round in front of the mirror (dances)... for hours on end.

Uhle (excitedly): You're alive!
Toni: Is this the first time you've noticed it?
Uhle: But I mean, you're so real, so—
Krah (rushing in delightedly): Toni! He's put you on—(stops suddenly)... Isn't she just like a princess? Oh dear, oh dear! Have I interrupted something? Why Adam! It's my old friend Adam. Used to go to school with him... History of art.

39. Freddy, I've got an idea. Marry me.
Khar: Marry you? For goodness' sake, why ever should I?
Toni: 'Cos I'd like you to. Wouldn't you?
Krah: Me? Marry? And load my brain with a lot of erotic encumbrances? Not on your life Toni.

40. *Prince:* I love her . . . ! Now you look for weapons? Down by the crucifix, by the code of honour, yellow with age, I will meet you.
Stefan: My friend, am I but a beast of the field that you should speak to me thus? Are we not men? Oh love, that dost forget the world, raise me that I may feel thy breath upon me... Brother, sister... your hearts beat gently at my soul.... Where are we? My friends, is this then reality?

41. By the mill, the old mill of Granchester... I moisten my temples from the cool stream by which Byron sang—Tennyson too—where Shelley and Keats pledged rebellion against Zeus, chief of all the gods.—In the breeze which stirs the silvery willows, Shakespeare, I sense thy presence too. . . .

42. In the English midlands he was born, his father a drunkard, his mother the light . . . Romantically he wrote *Songs* (sic) *and Lovers,* magnificent songs, conjured from love's doubting.

43. The economic miracle.

44. The characters of this novel are symbolic.

45. May one ask what you propose to do in Prussian Berlin?
I'm to give a talk this evening in the Hebbel Theatre about brotherhood.
Brotherhood?—Schleich burst out laughing, choking with the smoke from his cigar.—But my dear chap. There's no such thing as brotherhood.
That's why I must call it into being.

46. But mind! Don't try any pathos! As soon as anybody comes up with the pathos stuff these days, they all take to their heels. After all the carry-on about our beloved leaders.
—What had that to do with pathos? Pathos, Mr. Schleich, comes from the Greek word to suffer. Where has the tragic collapse of all values ever been suffered in such a truly pathetic sense? Tell me, where, where?

47. For me good is the courage to know—to know yourself. Evil is cowardice in the face of knowledge. Cowardice which makes you flinch at the thought of knowing yourself.

48. It just doesn't throw any shadows at all. So it's no longer any use.
When God said Let there be Light, a word cast a shadow.

Toni: A word? But Mr. Uhle. How can a word cast shadows?

Uhle: Yes, a word! It used to be something living. Of course among all these floods and flats and cut-out trees, the whole plywood landscape—the word can't be photographed.

49. *Uhle:* They ought to let *me* cry out.

Toni: Aren't you funny.

50. *Toni:* Do you know, I think it's the first time I've been alone. Of course I mean, with you. And in a forest too. In the forest and on the moors (sings)...

Uhle: Forest? (laughs wildly) Yes. It's so plastic. (jumps up and bashes the hollow tree-trunk with his fist) What I mean is in all probability the word is hollow on one side. Otherwise it wouldn't be possible . . . and after all, if it were still alive, don't you think, sort of like you as it were, then it would assert itself, and be on the defensive, and nobody could touch it. But then, it just hasn't got any shadow. It was said at one time: in the beginning was the . . . H'm, in the beginning. . . .

SELECTION OF WORKS

(*dr.* = drama; *com.* = comedy; *n.* = novel; *sp.* = text of speech)

Jürgen Wullenweber. dr. 1910.
Offiziere. dr. 1911.
Louis Ferdinand Prinz von Preussen. dr. 1913.
Vor der Entscheidung, dr. 1914.
Opfergang. n. 1916.
Ein Geschlecht. dr. 1916.
Platz. dr. 1920.
Rosengarten. dr. 1921.
Stirb und Werde! sp. 1922.
Stürme. dr. 1922.
Reden. collection of speeches, 1924.
Flügel der Nike. travelogue. 1925.
Heinrich aus Andernach. dr. 1925.
Bonaparte. dr. 1927.
Phaea. com. 1930.
Zero. com. 1932.
Politeia. Speeches. 1933.
Gandha, com. 1935.
Europa erwache! sp. (Switzerland) 1936
Charlotte Corday. dr. 1936.
Hauptmann Werner, dr. 1936.
Miss Rollschuh, com. 1941.
Der nie verlor. n. 1942.
Der Befreiungsminister. com. 1948.

Die Heilige. n. 1952.
Fürchtet Nichts. n. 1952.
Wilhelmus. dr. 1953.
Brüderlichkeit. sp. 1954.
Duell an der Havel. com. 1954.
17 Juni. dr. 1954.
Schiller-Rede. sp. 1955.
Bismarck. com. 1955.
Der Sohn des Generals, n. 1957.

Lion Feuchtwanger

Lion Feuchtwanger

by W. E. YUILL

Lion Feuchtwanger was born in Munich in 1884, the son of a Jewish manufacturer of strict orthodox views. After studying German literature, philosophy and history at the universities of Munich and Berlin he graduated in 1907 with a doctoral thesis on Heinrich Heine's *Rabbi von Bacharach*. Feuchtwanger's interests were from the very beginning in literature and the theatre: he founded a short-lived literary periodical, *Der Spiegel*, and became theatrical critic for *Die Schaubühne*. In 1912 he married Martha Löffler. At the outbreak of war in 1914 Feuchtwanger was in Tunis and was interned by the French authorities. He quickly escaped and made his way to Germany, where he enlisted in the army, only to be discharged after six months on account of poor eyesight. He devoted himself once more to literature and, after the war, became a close friend of Bertolt Brecht, with whom he collaborated in several works. After the phenomenal success of *Jud Süß* he moved to Berlin. At the time of Hitler's accession to power, Feuchtwanger was on a lecture tour in the United States, and thus escaped certain arrest. His villa in the Grunewald and all his other possessions in Germany were confiscated, however, and he was deprived of his German citizenship and even of the doctor's degree which he had gained in a perfectly regular academic manner. From 1933 until 1940 Feuchtwanger lived in the South of France and played a leading part in organising émigré resistance to Hitler. In connection with the publication of the periodical *Das Wort* he visited Moscow in 1937 and published an enthusiastic account of the Soviet Union. When the German armies invaded France in 1940 Feuchtwanger was interned by the French for the second time in his life and was fortunate to escape through Spain and Portugal to the United States. He made his new home in California and spent the remainder of his life there. In 1953 he was awarded a *Nationalpreis* for literature by the government of the German Democratic Republic and on the occasion of his seventieth birthday the Humboldt University in East Berlin conferred an honorary degree upon him. Feuchtwanger died on December 21, 1958, in Pacific Palisades, California.

> Ich für mein Teil habe mich, seitdem ich schrieb, bemüht, historische Romane für die Vernunft zu schreiben, gegen Dummheit und Gewalt, gegen das, was Marx das Verinken in die Geschichtslosigkeit nennt.
>
> —L. Feuchtwanger.

I

FOR a writer like Heinrich Mann, whose work exudes the atmosphere of a contemporary age, the historical novel became a form of expression only when circumstances drove him from the German scene; for Feuchtwanger, who shared the opinions of Mann and hence his exile, history was the chosen element. Throughout his career he seeks the long perspectives of history and the pattern of progress and relapse as a means of interpreting the present and predicting the future. It may be that his Jewish race and upbringing give him a particular sense of tradition; certainly he uses historical themes to illustrate the problems of his race and personality. Historical settings enable him, too, to look upon ideas and emotions with a degree of objectivity. For Feuchtwanger, the historian is the sage : he may be observed in the background of many of the novels —Johannes von Viktrin in *Die hässliche Herzogin,* Siegbert Geyer in *Erfolg,* Musa and Don Rodrigue in *Spanische Ballade*—while in the Josephus trilogy it is the historian who is the hero. Even when he is dealing with contemporary themes Feuchtwanger adopts the manner of the historian, seeking not particular truth but typical truth; he depicts "not *real,* but *historical* people". By infusing topical notions and feeling into accounts of the past, on the one hand, and be describing contemporary events ostensibly with the detachment of the historian, on the other, Feuchtwanger tries to break down the barrier between past and present, to convey truths that are independent of historical context. Such truths are important because they help in the prediction of the future, and this is where the historical writer becomes a politician.

> Wir wollen doch nicht nur das Heute beschreiben und das bisschen Gestern, says Musa in *Spanische Ballade,* wir trachten doch, den Sinn der Ereignisse festzuhalten, wir wollen die Richtung der Geschehnisse erkennen und in die Zukunft weisen als wahre Kundschafter Gottes.[(2)]

It was some time before Feuchtwanger's bent for the historical novel emerged, for it was not until after the First World War that he turned to the genre that was to make his reputation. His earliest work was written for the theatre and, like that of Heinrich Mann, was marked by the aestheticism and over-sophisticated psychology of the day. Even in a somewhat enervating atmosphere, however, the young man's sympathies were liberal, and they rapidly became radical after the outbreak of the war. Looking back on his youth Feuchtwanger remarks:

> Der Krieg hat mir das Geschmäcklerische weggeschliffen, mich von der Überschätzung des Ästhetisch-Formalen, der Nuance zum Wesenhaften geführt.(3)

Feuchtwanger never shared the war-hysteria of many intellectuals and as early as February 1915 he published a bitter *Lied der Gefallenen* which, with its threatening refrain reminds one of Heine's *Die Weber*:

> Es dorrt die Haut von unsrer Stirn.
> Es nagt der Wurm in unserm Hirn.
> Das Fleisch verwest zu Ackergrund.
> Stein stopft und Erde unsern Mund.
> Wir warten.
>
> Das Fleisch verwest, es dorrt das Bein.
> Doch eine Frage schläft nicht ein.
> Doch eine Frage wird nicht stumm
> Und wird nicht satt: Warum? Warum?
> Wir warten.(4)

A protest again jingoism and war is implicit in Feuchtwanger's adaptation of Aeschylus' *Persians* and in the drama *Die Kriegsgefangenen,* which describes the tragic love of a French prisoner of war and a German girl. In two other dramas written during the war years, *Warren Hastings* and *Jud Süss,* a more profound and characteristic theme begins to emerge, a theme which in one form or another features in nearly all of the author's works: this is the conflict of "Macht und Geist", of authority and free intellect. In these two plays the conflict is seen under the particular aspect of the active and the contemplative life, the restless, thrusting, questing ethos of the West in conflict with the tranquil, passive wisdom of the East; a conflict epitomised in the philosophies of Nietzsche and Buddha. Some years later Feuchtwanger summed up this dominant theme as follows:

> Wenn ich aber, 42-jährig, auf dem Scheitel meines Lebens betrachte, was ich bisher gemacht habe, versuchend ein Gemeinsames zu finden, eine Linie, die meine Bücher an mich, an mein Leben und aneinander bindet, einen Generalnenner; dann glaube ich, trotz aller scheinbaren Differenz doch immer nur *ein* Buch geschrieben zu haben: das Buch von dem Menschen, gestellt zwischen Tun und Nichttun, zwischen Macht und Erkenntnis.(5)

A modification of this theme, the gulf between insight and action, idea and deed, morality and expediency, is illustrated in *Thomas Wendt*. This is a work which reflects the collapse of the revolutionary régime in Germany in 1918, and which in its form—"dramatic novel"—marks Feuchtwanger's transition to the epic genre. The eponymous hero, an idealistic Socialist, shrinks from the drastic measures which are essential to consolidate the revolution; he is plagued by scruples and cannot accept the advice of a friend who tells him: "You will always be forced to hit men when you aim at ideas. You must be unjust, Thomas Wendt, for the sake of justice." Crushed by the weight of responsibility, Wendt resigns and the presidency of the republic is assumed by the rakish profiteer Gustav Lebrecht Schulz with the laconic words: "Revolution: different flags, same thing. Politics: question of secondary importance, the economy is everything." Feuchtwanger, like Heinrich Mann, had few illusions about the democratic nature of the republican régime.

II

The first of Feuchtwanger's historical novels, *Die hässliche Herzogin*, makes a somewhat tentative impression. There is little sense of the personal involvement and topicality that are later so characteristic, while the style is terse and cramped in the manner of the day. Two things seem to have attracted the author to the figure of Margarete Maultasch, the "ugly duchess" who struggled among rival princes to maintain her position in the strategic territory of the Tyrol during the first half of the fourteenth century: the personal problem of a temperamental woman totally devoid of physical charm, and the social and economic transition from the age of feudalism to that of bourgeois capitalism. The two themes are linked in the rivalry of Margarete and the beautiful Agnes von Flavon. Agnes embodies the glamour of chivalrous culture—as well as its irresponsibility, arrogance and sloth; she is acclaimed by the populace who see in her a Sunday's child, the "Goldmarie" of the fairy-tale as opposed to Margarete, the ill-favoured and ill-starred "Pechmarie". But Margarete compensates for ugliness by a penetrating intelligence and an appetite for power. She sees herself as the herald of a new age which is less glamorous but more practical and more prosperous than the dying feudal era:

> Ihre Hässlichkeit war Geschenk, der Wegweiser, mit dem Gott ihr den rechten Weg zeigte. Rittertum, Abenteuer, das war bunter Schaum und Schein. Ihr Amt war, in die Zukunft zu bauen. Städte, Handel und Handwerk, gute Strassen, Ordnung und

Gesetz. Ihr Amt waren nicht Feste und Fahrten und Liebe; ihr Amt war nüchterne, ruhvolle Politik.[6]

Margarete is attracted both by natural sympathy and economic interest to that group of outcasts whose activities foster the new age—the Jews. She compares herself with their representative, Mendel Hirsch: "He was ugly and an outsider. He was reserved and crusty. She was Maultasch, he was the Jew." When the Jews' commercial rivals, the Florentine bankers, represented by the sinister Messer Artese, engineer a pogrom, Margarete's progressive policies are confounded, but that is not all: she suffers a grievous personal blow.

Die hässliche Herzogin is, on the whole, a gripping story, but the account it gives of the fourteenth-century mind is perhaps not very plausible. It leans, too, towards the sensational and a scene which opens as follows smacks altogether too much of Hollywood:

> "Ich mache kein Geschäft mehr mit den Habsburgen!" rief heftig mit seiner harten Offiziersstimme Herzog Stephan von Niederbayern und warf den Metallhandschuh klirrend auf den Tisch.[7]

The predicament of the Jews in European society is peripheral in *Die hässliche Herzogin,* although even there it probably has some relevance to the growing anti-Semitism of post-war Germany. It is the central theme of *Jud Süss,* which, with its three million copies, its innumerable translations and its film versions, established an international reputation for the author. As is shown by his drama on the subject Feuchtwanger had become interested as early as 1918 in the figure of Josef Süss Oppenheimer, who enjoyed a brief and baneful career as financial adviser to the Duke of Württemberg between 1733 and 1737. He was intrigued by the paradoxical fact that Süss—in almost every regard an unscrupulous rogue—declined to save himself from impeachment by abjuring his Jewish faith:

> . . . ich sah . . . plötzlich den Weg und das Bild des Mannes, Zentrum und Gleichnis seines Lebens, wrote Feuchtwanger. Nicht dass er einem Bekenntnis treu blieb, in das er, vermutlich übrigens nur halb, hineingeboren war, zog mich an und erhellte mir sein Schicksal. Sondern es war dies, dass ich sah, wie er sich fallen liess. Ich begriff sein Glück und seinen Sturz in einem.[8]

In the novel Feuchtwanger is able to develop the complex character and situation of the Jewish financier in much more detail than in the original dramatic version. Josef Süss Oppenheimer represents a new generation of Jews, determined to exploit the power which has been put into Jewish hands by the development of a money economy. Unlike the elderly banker Isaak Landauer he is not content to remain in the background, savouring the secret of his power; he revels in his financial virtuosity and flaunts his wealth defiantly in the faces of the Gentiles. His employer, the licentious and brutal Duke Karl Alexander, despises him but cannot dispense with him: Süss panders to the Duke's sexual appetites, surrenders his own mistresses and abets the ruler in his attempt to overthrow the Protestant religion and the rudimentary democracy of Württemberg. There is another side to Süss's character, however: his autocratic ways and his lusts may link him to the Duke, but his Jewish breeding, his sense of suffering and of life's vanity link him to the Rabbi Gabriel, an ascetic and mystic, "who simply by his presence tarnished his colourful view of the world, turned reality into a phantom, made his clear, round figures ambiguous, erased them". Again and again, at the height of his power, Süss has a vision of himself joined in a phantom dance with the Duke and Rabbi Gabriel:

> Er dehnte sich und badete in der Macht. Aber manchmal war es ihm, als sei es nicht er, von dem der ganze, glänzende Wirbel ausgehe. Dann hob er wohl die Schultern, überfrostet, wie in Abwehr. Jäh schnürte ihn eine unheimliche Gebundenheit. Die Dinge um ihn verfahlten; er sah sich schreiten in einer stummen, schattenhaften Quadrille, Rabbi Gabriel hielt seine rechte, der Herzog seine linke Hand. . . . (9)

Even when Süss discovers that his true father was a Gentile, and a nobleman, he clings to the faith in which he was brought up: his Jewishness is a mark of humiliation, but it is also a mark of distinction, a source of pride:

> Jude sein, das heisst verachtet, verfolgt, erniedrigt sein, aber auch einmalig sein, immer bewusst, aller Augen auf sich zu haben, immer gezwungen, gespannt, gerafft zu sein, alle Sinne lebendig und auf der Hut.(10)

The better of the two souls is symbolised in Süss's daughter Naemi, a girl of great beauty and purity, whom he conceals from the Duke's lewd gaze. The secret is betrayed by an outraged father whose daughter Süss has procured for the Duke, the girl is discovered in a secluded Oriental villa in the Black Forest and dies in escaping from the Duke—a motif remarkably similar to that of C. F. Meyer's *Der Heilige* as well as to the story of *Rigoletto*. Süss conceals his hatred from the Duke, but betrays the plans for a

Roman Catholic putsch and triumphs over the monarch as the latter expires from an apoplectic stroke. Once revenge is achieved, however, triumph fades, and the ascetic passivity of Rabbi Gabriel becomes dominant in Süss. In this change of character, Feuchtwanger demonstrates the contrast of man of action and thinker, of agent and patient. This is an ambivalence characteristic of the Jewish character and explained by Feuchtwanger in terms of history and geographical situation. It is in Canaan that the ethos of the West collides with that of the East and of the South:

> Vom Abendland her schlägt eine wilde, ewige Welle nach dem Lande Kanaan: Durst nach Leben, nach Persönlichkeit, Wille zum Tun, zur Lust, zur Macht. Raffen, an sich reissen, Wissen, Lust, Besitz, mehr Lust, mehr Besitz, leben, kämpfen, tun. So klingt es vom Westen her. Aber im Süden unter spitzen Bergen liegen in Gold und Gewürz tote Könige, der Vernichtung herrisch ihren Leib versagend; in die Wüste gesetzt, in kolossalischen Alleen höhnen ihre Bilder den Tod. Und eine wilde, ewige Welle schlägt von Mittag her nach dem Lande Kanaan: wüstenheisses Haften am Sein, schwelende Begier, nicht die Form und Bildung, nicht den Körper zu verlieren, nicht zu vergehen. Aber von Ost her klingt sanfte Wiesheit: Schlafen ist besser als wachen, tot sein besser als lebendig sein. Nicht widerstreben, einströmen ins Nichts, nicht tun, verzichten.[11]

The sons of Zion go out into the West, they covet, they strive and acquire wealth, "but in spite of everything they are not at home in the world of deeds, they are at home on the bridge between action and renunciation. And they are always turning back, looking back to Zion. Often, indeed, in the fulfilment of victory, in the awareness of defeat, in the midst of their headlong course they stop, seized by a strange thrill, they hear amid a thousand sounds a gentle voice with a dying fall: do not wish, do not act, renounce the self."

In obedience to this nihilistic impulse Süss allows himself to be made a scapegoat for the abortive putsch. With a readiness bordering on the voluptuous he surrenders to humiliation and ill-treatment. Like Edward II in the version of Marlowe's play prepared about this time by Bertolt Brecht and Feuchtwanger, he seems to embrace his suffering, to say:

> Lobet
> Mangel, lobet Misshandlung, lobet
> Die Finsternis.[12]

Süss goes gladly to his death on a monstrous gallows, atoning for his crimes and triumphing morally over his enemies, who have condemned him under an archaic law.

Jud Süss is an advance on *Die hässliche Herzogin* not only in the subtlety of its psychology and the depth of feeling which informs it but also in its re-creation of an historical episode. This may be simply because the eighteenth century is that much nearer to us in its mode of thought. Certainly Feuchtwanger demonstrates his ability to handle a complicated intrigue and to make plausible the characters and motives of those involved in it. The picture he paints is lurid, but hardly more so than the recorded facts seem to justify. The style of the work is more flexible than that of *Die hässliche Herzogin;* it ranges from the breathless and lapidary sentences of the latter to solemn Biblical periods and passages of involved reflection. Every now and then the focus lengthens, the writer turns, from the stuffy atmosphere of council-room or bed-chamber to a panorama of Württemberg, from the analysis of passion to topographical description and factual accounts of the economic and political systems of Germany in the eighteenth century.

The success of *Jud Süss,* which represents a climax in Feuchtwanger's career, has tended to overshadow his other works of the period. Although these are of lesser intrinsic interest than the historical novels they are worth noting as representing another facet of the author's talent. While in the main stream of his work Feuchtwanger was reconstructing and interpreting the past and incidentally expressing an individual philosophy, he was also writing in a satirical vein about contemporary society. The coolness and intellectuality of his approach in these minor works makes a strange contrast with the predominant sultriness of his historical novels, and in fact the satirical was a vein which seems to have petered out fairly rapidly. Its prominence at this time is perhaps a consequence of Feuchtwanger's friendship with Brecht. Both men seem to have been fascinated and repelled by the image of American capitalism and the Transatlantic influences in Germany. This preoccupation may be seen in such plays as Brecht's *Joe Fleischhacker, Die heilige Johanna der Schlachthöfe* and *Happy End,* and Feuchtwanger uses much the same dramatic idiom in *Die Petroleum-Inseln* and the comedy *Wird Hill amnestiert?,* in which the allegedly class-ridden justice of the United States is attacked. The satirical note also sounds in Feuchtwanger's lyric of the period. *PEP, J. L. Wetcheeks amerikanisches Liederbuch,* which purports to be a translation from American, mocks the vulgarity and philistinism of B. W. Smith, the type of the American businessman, who discovers to his disgust that his money will not buy intangibles—the beauties of nature or the things of the mind:

Da sass er jetzt mit 26 Naturzähnen und sechsen von Golde,
ein erstklassiger Bursche, mit Bankkonto, eine Pracht,
und konnte nicht kriegen, was er doch bezahlen wollte.
Wozu also hatte er die vielen harten Dollars gemacht?[13]

Feuchtwanger is attacking not only the American tycoon but also the Americanised European who has sold his cultural heritage for a million dollars. Such a "homo americanisatus" is Filippo Novella, the hero of the comedy *Der Amerikaner oder die entzauberte Stadt*. Novella returns, a millionaire, to his native town in the South of Italy and sets about "modernising" it ruthlessly and to the ruin of all its native traditions.

III

Feuchtwanger is not a particularly gifted satirist, and this note soon fades from his work. The pattern of parallel development—historical study on the one hand, study of contemporary society on the other—remains, however, and becomes, in fact, more marked in the central phase of his career, the years from 1930 to 1942. This phase is dominated by the two trilogies. *Der Wartesaal* (*Erfolg, Die Geschwister Oppenheim*, later *Oppermann*, and *Exil*) and *Josephus* (*Der jüdische Krieg, Die Söhne* and *Der Tag wird kommen*). The *Wartesaal-Trilogie*, more diffuse and loosely articulated than the other, describes the genesis of the Nazi movement and traces the typical fate of a number of Jewish families. The Josephus trilogy is dominated by the figure of the Jewish historian Flavius Josephus (born A.D. 37) and deals with the ambiguous situation of the Jew in Western civilisation—an elaboration of the *Jud Süss* theme, in fact.

Feuchtwanger formulates the aim of the *Wartesaal-Trilogie* in these words:

> Inhalt des Roman-Zyklus sind die Geschehnisse in Deutschland zwischen den Kriegen von 1914 und 1939, das heisst, der Wiedereinbruch der Barbarei in Deutschland und ihr zeitweiliger Sieg über die Vernunft. Zweck der Trilogie ist, diese schlimme Zeit des Wartens und Übergangs, die dunkelste, welche Deutschland seit dem Dreissigjährigen Krieg erlebt hat, für die Späteren lebendig zu machen. Denn es wird diesen Späteren unverständlich sein, wie wir ein solches Leben ertragen konnten, sie werden nicht begreifen, warum wir so lange zuwarteten, ehe wir die einzig vernünftige Schlussfolgerung zogen, die nämlich, der Herrschaft der Gewalt und des Widersinns unsererseits mittels Gewalt ein Ende zu setzen und an ihrer Statt eine vernünftige Ordnung herzustellen.[14]

Erfolg is a lightly camouflaged account of events in Bavaria between the years 1921 and 1924. It is a work of great complexity, a veritable kaleidoscope of personalities and parties. In the midst of this turmoil Feuchtwanger lays bare what he believes to be the roots of Nazism: a reactionary administrative machine, a greedy and demoralised middle class, a few fanatical demagogues exploiting the masses and used in their turn by cool-headed industrial and agrarian magnates. All this is a familiar story, but it took no small degree of perspicacity—and of courage—to tell it in 1929.

The novel has no single hero: Martin Krüger, the director of the State art gallery whose conviction on a trumped-up charge of perjury provides the initial impulse for the narrative, is simply a victim, a passive, unpolitical pawn. Around him revolve a number of principal characters, sometimes symbolic, sometimes thinly disguised historical personalities. Ranged against Krüger are the brutal and arrogant Minister of Justice, Klenk, with his judicial apparatus, the Minister of Culture, Flaucher, and the *éminence grise*, Dr. Bichler. On his side are his mistress, Johanna Krain, emancipated, enlightened and loyal, Dr. Siegbert Geyer, his defending counsel, and Jacques Tüverlin, a Swiss writer, liberal and rational in his outlook. Tüverlin, in particular, stands as the intellectual in opposition to the authoritarian Klenk: it is once more the characteristic conflict of "Macht und Geist". On Krüger's side, too, is the Marxist Kaspar Pröckl, mechanic by trade, poet by inclination—and reliably reported to be a portrait of Bertolt Brecht. In the figures of Tüverlin and Pröckl Feuchtwanger pursues a debate which increasingly concerned him and many of his contemporaries during the 1920's—the problem of commitment and the justification of violence and revolution. Pröckl denounces Tüverlin's urbanity and "objectivity":

> Der Ingenieur Pröckl verlangte von Tüverlin gebieterisch, dass er aktivistische, politische, revolutionäre Literatur mache oder keine . . . Dokumente der Zeit machen müsse der Schriftsteller. Das sei seine Funktion. Sonst sei seine Existenz ohne Sinn.[15]

Tüverlin, however, places his trust in the power of reason and rejects the Marxist doctrine of armed revolution: in a conversation with the sardonic Klenk he confesses, "I believe in sound words on paper rather than in machine-guns." Even in *Erfolg*, it is clear that Feuchtwanger had grave doubts about the optimistically idealistic position represented by Tüverlin, and he openly abandons it before his trilogy is completed.

Around the central characters of *Erfolg* there is a whole throng of secondary figures, some purely episodic, others reappearing in a thematic way, but all of them sketched firmly and clearly, even where, in pursuit of typical truth, the writer alters particular features. There is no mistaking the prototype of the hysterical rabble-rouser Rupert Kutzner, with his lank hair, small moustache and wild eyes.

The narrative chapters of the work are interspersed with blocks of statistics; it is in the laconic comments accompanying these data that a satirical vein may still be observed. "The materially under-privileged", writes Feuchtwanger in mock-historical style, "were mostly organised in the parties of the Left, the mentally under-privileged in those of the Right." Or: "In those years one of the most popular methods of refuting one's political adversary was to murder him. In Germany it was principally the adherents of the Right-wing parties who, being unequal to the leaders of the Left in the use of intellectual weapons, made use of this method."

Apart from the satirical intent, it is by such arrays of statistics and by the reporting of historical events like the murder of Kurt Eisner that Feuchtwanger seeks to achieve the effect of an historical account, to place a distance between the reader and events which were practically contemporary, as well as to fulfil his obligation to future generations. One might almost speak here—in view of Feuchtwanger's association with Brecht—of an alienation effect applied to the novel. One of the consequences of this technique here is a striking contrast between the detachment of the statistical sections and the descriptions of the pullulating life of Munich beer-cellars, the emotionally charged atmosphere of the courts or the grey squalor of a prison-cell.

The other two volumes of the trilogy show an increasing concentration as well as a manifest autobiographical bias. *Die Geschwister Oppermann* describes the fate of a Jewish family in the weeks before and after Hitler's accession to power. The sufferings of these distinguished people—a writer, a doctor, two businessmen—and their dependants are described with compassion, but seen nevertheless as a consequence of their disdainful indifference to politics: they have tried to preserve the intellectual and contemplative life in circumstances which call for determined action. Ultimately they are brought to realise that the intellectuals' abdication of responsibility leaves power automatically in the hands of brutal men of action. This is clearest in the figure of the writer, Gustav Oppermann, who—no doubt like Feuchtwanger himself—comes to realise the futility of the aesthetic attitude in these circumstances:

> Hätte er sich mit Politik befasst, mit Nationalökonomie, mit irgend etwas im Geschäft, alles wäre sinnvoller gewesen als das, was er getrieben hat.[16]

Gustav, who has escaped to Switzerland, is so appalled by what he hears of Nazi barbarism that he returns to Germany in a forlorn attempt to remonstrate against the brutalities of the régime. His death in a concentration camp is both a protest and an atonement. The development from the view of Jacques Tüverlin in *Erfolg* represented in the action—ineffectual as it is—of Gustav Oppermann, no doubt indicates a further movement in Feuchtwanger's own mind towards the idea of commitment, a movement away from the ideal of contemplation. With Oppermann, too, another notion is introduced—the artist's solidarity with the masses. Gustav is convinced of the fundamental integrity of the people:

> . . . nicht das Volk habe die Untaten begangen, he maintains. Es sei ein grossartiges Zeugnis für die Gutartigkeit des Volkes, dass es, von der Regierung vierzehn Jahre hindurch zu Pogromen gegen Sozialismus und Juden aufgeputscht, sich so wichtig gehalten habe. Nicht das Volk sei barbarisch, die Regierung sei es, das neue Reich, seine Beamten und seine Landsknechte.[17]

Exil concerns itself even more intensively with the dilemma of the artist in times of political repression. The central character, in this case a musician, Sepp Trautwein, is required to take over the editorship of a newspaper for German emigrants in Paris when the original editor is abducted by Nazi agents. Trautwein sees his involvement in politics as an unpleasant temporary necessity, as the price he must pay for the freedom to practise his art in the future. The campaign for the release of his friend Friedrich Benjamin involves Trautwein with a representative array of Nazi fanatics and hangers-on—the unscrupulous ambassador, von Gehrke, the time-serving journalist Wiesener and the brutal party envoy Konrad Heydebregg. Trautwein suffers privation and personal tragedy before his cause is won and Benjamin is freed. But even although he feels he has earned his discharge—"He can make music with a clear conscience . . . he has done his bit"—his view of art has undergone a radical change in the sense that he now looks upon his music as a weapon: the "Wartesaal-Symphonie" on which he embarks is an indictment of the reign of unreason. The relevance to Feuchtwanger's own development is clear. There is perhaps an element of personal confession, too, in the reservations which Trautwein has about the Socialist doctrine: it is left to a younger generation—his son Hanns, and Tüverlin, who reappears here—to embrace with heart and mind the notion of proletarian revolution. The note of melancholy and resignation with which Trautwein yields to his son's argument may indicate the persistence of a dilemma in Feuchtwanger's mind, even after the rational decision has been made. :

> Mit deinem wichtigsten Prinzip, Hanns, hast leider du recht und ich unrecht. Es ist leider ein Schmarrn, wenn man behauptet, Geist ohne Gewalt könne sich durchsetzen. Eine gerechte Ordnung auf der Welt lässt sich ohne Gewalt nicht herstellen . . . Ich habe begriffen, dass eure Grundprinzipien richtig sind : aber ich hab' es eben nur begriffen, mein Hirn sieht es ein, aber mein Gefühl geht nicht mit, mein Herz sagt nicht ja. Ich fühle mich nicht heimisch in deiner Welt, in der alles Vernunft und Mathematik ist. Ich möchte in ihr nicht leben. Mir scheint, es haben in ihr die Massen zu viel zu sagen und der einzelne zu wenig. Ich hänge an meiner altmodischen Freiheit . . . Ich müsste lauter liebe Gewohnheiten aufgeben, ohne die ich mir mein Leben überhaupt nicht vorstellen kann . . . Das Alte ist noch nicht tot, und das Neue ist noch nicht lebendig, es ist eine scheussliche Übergangszeit, es ist halt wirklich ein jämmerlicher Wartesaal.[18]

With this confession the notion of the "waiting-room" acquires a wider significance than it had for the first parts of the trilogy. The inmates of the "waiting-room" are not simply waiting for the collapse of the Hitler régime; they are waiting for the advent of an entire new social order. The ambivalent situation of the artist and intellectual, bound to the past and dedicated to the future, is summed up in the epilogue to the trilogy :

> Wie wir hilflos bemüht waren, das Alte festzuhalten, während wir uns nach dem Neuen sehnten, wie wir das Neue fürchteten, während wir doch erkannten, dass es das Bessere sei, wie wir schwankten und hofften und bangten : das seltsame Lebensgefühl, das die Berührung und die Trennung dieser beiden Pole entstehen liess, dieses einmalige Lebensgefühl unserer Übergangszeiten festzuhalten, darauf kam es mir an.[19]

The problem of the artistic individual's dedication to the mass movement of Socialism continues to echo through the works of Feuchtwanger's later life. This is the problem of Beaumarchais, of Goya, and of the intellectual, Fernand de Girardin, in *Narrenweisheit*. The latter, at least, solves the problem by a kind of *salto mortale*, by a plunge into the anonymity of "the people", and in this solution there is perhaps something of Süss's voluptuous surrender of the will, the compulsive longing for oblivion and death.

The Josephus trilogy, the other great branch of Feuchtwanger's work in this period, has the organic unity of the hero's life. Not that it is a simple biography: Flavius Josephus is a symbolic figure who embodies in his character and fate conflicts and contradictions that not only concern Feuchtwanger personally but are also typical of his race. Like Süss, Josephus is a Jew in a Gentile environment, he is both thinker and man of action, soldier and historian; he is torn between ideals of Jewish nationalism and cosmopolitanism, acting now by reason, now by feeling—"this Joseph, however, was rational and emotional at one and the same time, a rare mixture". He expresses in his person the archetypal situations of Hebrew legend:

> Seltsam, wie sich in seinem eigenen Leben die Sagen und Geschichten seines Volkes spiegeln . . . Abraham, der die Hagar austreibt, Josef, der des Pharao Günstling wird, Juda Makkabi, der das Volk in den Krieg führt, Hiob, der alles verliert, und wieder Abraham, der seinen Sohn opfert: wahrhaftig, ihm schien auferlegt, die Geschichten und Situationen der Bibel auf eine bittere, sonderbar verzerrte Art neu zu erleben.[20]

After the collapse of the Jewish rebellion against the Romans, Josephus, who has played a leading part on the Jewish side, throws in his lot with Vespasian, the Roman general and later Emperor, in the conviction that it is his mission to wed "Macht und Geist", the power and efficiency of the Roman Empire and the spirituality of Judaism:

> Ja, Rom, das ist die Ordnung, die sinnlose Macht, Judäa, das ist Gott, das ist die Verwirklichung Gottes, das ist die Sinngebung der Macht. Eines kann ohne das andere nicht leben, eines ergänzt das andere. In ihm aber, in Josef, strömen sie in einander, Rom und Judäa, Macht und Geist. Er ist dazu ausersehen, sie zu versöhnen.[21]

It is in this spirit that Josephus, torn by a divided allegiance, forces himself to witness the destruction of Jerusalem, and it is in this spirit that he composes his *Psalm des Weltbürgers*:

> Lobet Gott und verschwendet euch über die Länder.
> Lobet Gott und vergeudet euch über die Meere.
> Ein Knecht ist, wer sich festbindet an ein einziges Land.
> Nicht Zion heisst das Reich, das ich euch gelobte,
> Sein Name heisst: Erdkreis.[22]

Jerusalem, the vessel of Jewish religion, must be shattered so that the precious spirit may flow over the whole earth. Joseph's hopes are raised by the accession of the Emperor Titus, who is fascinated by the East as symbolised in the Jewish queen Berenike: Joseph and Titus are to be the first men of a new age, the first cosmopolitans. The plan fails, however, and Joseph's efforts to reconcile the two cultures bring him only the hatred of his fellow countrymen and the contempt of the Romans—and always there is the cause of Jewish nationalism, the inbred exclusiveness of his race tugging at his heart-strings. In a moment of despair he longs to be freed from these conflicting claims and from his mission :

> Warum, wenn ich Josef ben Matthias bin, muss ich dazu
> Noch Römer sein oder Jude oder beides zugleich?
> Ich will ich sein, Josef will ich sein,
> So wie ich kroch aus meiner Mutter Leib,
> Und nicht gestellt zwischen Völker
> Und gezwungen, zu sagen : von diesen bin ich oder von jenen.[23]

It is the problem of those who stand "between the races", but whereas for Heinrich and Thomas Mann this was a highly individual problem, for Feuchtwanger, and for almost every Jew, it is a problem weighted by a heavy ballast of tradition and a crushing history of conflict and calamity.

Joseph loses his sons, either by death or by defection to an alien culture, he loses the woman he loves, even his literary work brings him little credit among his people, for his account of the Jewish past and the Jewish war is seen as romanticised and idealistic. The peasant leader of the revolt, Johann von Gischala, and the bitter rationalist, Justus von Tiberias, to whom Joseph is bound in a love-hate relationship, decry his account of the causes of the war: "In those days it wasn't a matter of Jehovah or of Jupiter. It was a matter of the price of oil, wine, corn and figs." In his cosmopolitan ideas Josephus is far ahead of his time, in his view of history he belongs to a past age.

Under the dictatorship of Domitian Josephus finally sees his hopes of a union of cultures die. He reverts to the proud nationalism of his youth, has the courage to assert his race and his faith. When he returns to Judea, however, it is to find himself regarded by the nationalists as a dilettante, a traitor even—like Gustav Oppermann he has sought refuge in contemplation, in literary expression :

> Sie haben die Arbeit, sowie sie anfing, Mühe und Mut zu verlangen, hingeschmissen, the peasant leader Akawja tells him. Sie haben sich in die Literatur verdrückt und kosmopolitisches Geschwätz gemacht. Das hat Sie auf die Dauer gelangweilt, und Sie sind zurück in den Kampf gegangen. Dann wurde es dort wieder mulmig, und Sie sind von neuem verduftet, zurück in Ihr bequemes und unverbindliches Geschreibe. Ein Mann aus dem Volke wie ich heisst das Verrat.[24]

The increasing role of the proletariat and its elevation to the arbiter of political wisdom is a theme which emerges most clearly in the novel *Narrenweisheit*. In *Josephus* it is coupled with the quasi-tragic failure of the intellectual : Joseph's life flickers out in the unrest of a new rebellion without his accomplishing either the reconciliation of Rome and Judea or the liberation of the Jews. His appeal to reason is doomed to failure :

> Vernunft hat er verkünden wollen, das Reich der Vernunft, des Messias. Solch ein Prophetentum . . . das ist zu teuer. Wer da den Propheten macht, hat das mit zu vielen Entbehrungen zu bezahlen. . . . Wer sich zur Vernunft bekennt, muss leiden.[25]

Josephus, as Feuchtwanger represents him, was a man in advance of his age—and in advance of ours. The story of his life is the most problematic of Feuchtwanger's works; there is a sense of perplexity about it which raises it artistically above works like *Waffen für Amerika* and *Narrenweisheit* which are more doctrinaire in their approach.

These two great trilogies, the two main lines of Feuchtwanger's work, are brought together by the author's universalising tendency : on the one hand he seeks to give historical perspective to contemporary events; on the other, he describes the Roman Empire in the terms of a modern dictatorship, taking characteristically modern account of economic factors. This is the kind of stereoscopic technique used by Brecht in *Die Geschäfte des Herrn Julius Caesar* and in his play *Arturo Ui,* and by Heinrich Mann in his novel *Henri IV*. There are two lesser works which spring like offshoots, as it were, from the two main branches of Feuchtwanger's work, and one of which illustrates the stereoscopic technique particularly clearly. *Der falsche Nero* elaborates an episode which is barely mentioned in *Die Söhne*. Varro, a magnate with great estates in the Roman province of Syria, sets up, for reasons of personal animosity to the Governor, a pretender to the Imperial dignity in the person of a potter, Terence, who has acted as Nero's "double" during the latter's lifetime. Before the false Nero has run his course there has been a reign of terror reflecting in its details and the personalities of the leaders the history of Nazism. Terence develops into a pathological maniac, intermittently convinced of his actual identity as the god Nero. He is flanked by a brutal soldier, Trebon, who has an unmistakable resemblance to Göring, and by a malicious psychopath, Knops, who has the cunning of a Goebbels. The seizure of power is engineered by the flooding of the town of Apamea and the subsequent trial of the Christian leader, John of Patmos : the parallel to the burning of the Reichstag and the trial of Dimitroff is clear.

Even successive purges cannot keep the abominable triumvirate in power; Varro escapes to the East, but Terence and his henchmen end on the cross.

Die Brüder Lautensack might well be an episode from the *Wartesaal-Trilogie*. It has in common with *Der falsche Nero* the concern with the manic aspects of dictatorship, and it is in fact based upon the story of one of Hitler's astrologers, Jan Hanussen. The brothers Oskar and Hannsjörg Lautensack flourish in the early days of the régime: Oskar's clairvoyant gifts so impress the Führer that an Academy of the Occult Sciences is planned under his direction. However, Oskar's vanity, his moral weakness—and a remnant of integrity—bring about his fall, whereas his brother, a former pimp, adjusts himself to the world of terror and survives. It was Feuchtwanger's aim in the novel to explore the occult background to Nazism and to show the sordidly irrational appeal it made to the masses, but he himself confesses that the argument of the book is not wholly convincing.

IV

The completion of the two trilogies, and of the shorter novels which are appendages to them, more or less marks the close of a phase in Feuchtwanger's work. From 1945 until 1952 his attention turns from Germany and the ancient world to France and to Spain. Here, too, the parallelism of his approach is in a sense sustained; on the one hand, historical novels—*Waffen für Amerika, Goya* and *Narrenweisheit*—on the other, topical works—*Simone,* a novel about a latter-day Saint Joan, perhaps better known in the theatrical version by Brecht, and *Der Teufel in Frankreich,* an account of Feuchtwanger's personal experiences in a French internment camp. In this phase, however, the centre of gravity has moved to the historical novel. The central event is the French Revolution, and the three novels form a kind of trilogy: *Waffen für Amerika* sees the American War of Independence as a prologue to the French Revolution; *Narrenweisheit* describes the Revolution and the Terror; *Goya* involves the repercussions of the Revolution in Spain.

Feuchtwanger's account of the genesis of *Waffen für Amerika* illustrates his persistent concern with historical parallels:

> Seit Jahrzehnten hatte mich die merkwürdige Erscheinung beschäftigt, dass so verschiedene Menschen wie Beaumarchais, Benjamin Franklin, Lafayette, Voltaire, Ludwig der Sechzehnte und Marie Antoinette, ein jeder aus sehr anderen Gründen, zusammen helfen mussten, die Revolution in Amerika zum Erfolg zu führen und durch sie auch die in Frankreich. Als das Amerika

> Roosevelts in den Krieg gegen den europäischen Faschismus eingriff und den Kampf der Sowjetunion gegen Hitler unterstützte, wurden mir die Geschehnisse im Frankreich des ausgehenden 18. Jahrhunderts leuchtend klar, und sie erleuchteten mir die politischen Geschehnisse der eigenen Zeit. So ermutigt, wagte ich mich an den Roman "Die Füchse im Weinberg" (original title of *Waffen für Amerika*). Ich hoffte gestalten zu können, was so viele verschiedene Menschen und Gruppen antrieb, mit oder ohne und sogar gegen ihren Willen in der Richtung des Fortschritts zu wirken.[26]

The novel, in spite of its length and its multitude of characters is much more concentrated in its action than either of the trilogies which preceded it. The action takes place in the years 1777 and 1778 and is centred in the court of Versailles and the city of Paris. There are two main incidents : the granting of a loan by the French monarchy to the American insurgents, with the attendant intrigues, and the public performance of Beaumarchais' subversive comedy, *The Marriage of Figaro*. Both these events represent an undermining of the French absolute monarchy, but Louis XVI is forced to sanction them in spite of his awareness that "the waters of revolution will rise and rinse the oil from the heads of the Lord's anointed". He is driven to assist the American rebels as a blow against the old enemy, England; decadent aristocrats, intent, like the bourgeois audience in Heinrich Mann's *Im Schlaraffenland,* on the morbid thrill of seeing their own vices on the stage, force the king to permit the public performance of *Figaro*. In each case indulgence towards his beloved queen gives the final impulse to concessions which, for all his simplicity, the monarch knows to be fatal. History is stronger than he is, in spite of his absolute power :

> Er war ein absoluter Monarch, der König von Frankreich, keinem Parlament verantwortlich, er konnte tun, was er wollte, und musste tun, was er nicht wollte. Das, was man gemeinhin Weltgeschichte nannte, war stärker als er und zwang ihn. Und es stak also Sinn in der Weltgeschichte und trieb die Menschen, sich in einer bestimmten Richtung zu bewegen, ob sie wollten oder nicht.[27]

Feuchtwanger's conception of history has changed somewhat since the days of *Die hässliche Herzogin* and *Jud Süss* : no longer does he see the destiny of society as dependent upon human vices and virtues, upon the whim of colourful individuals. Men are driven by forces over which they have no control; this deterministic view tends to erode the impression of human greatness and implied tragedy that is discernible in figures like Josephus, and to that extent it is not an aesthetic advance. There are striking characters in *Waffen für Amerika,* resolute men and fascinating women, but the real "hero" of the novel is an abstraction : "that invisible guide of history, which, discovered in the eighteenth century, was clearly recognised, described and praised in the nineteenth, only to be bitterly abjured and maligned in the twentieth : progress."

From *Narrenweisheit* it is clear that "progress" now means unequivocally the Marxist doctrine of dictatorship of the proletariat. Here, the individual is eclipsed, absorbed into the mass. The novel opens with the last phase of Rousseau's life, showing the greatness and the wretchedness of a pathological genius, it concludes with the triumphal entry of his body into the Panthéon; the hero, however, is not Rousseau himself, but a young aristocratic disciple, Fernand de Girardin, the son of the philosopher's patron. Impelled by idealistic zeal, Fernand fights in the American War of Independence and returns to participate in the French Revolution. His sincere efforts to assimilate himself to the people are looked at askance by the plebeian friend of his boyhood, Martin Catrou, who claims that only those who have been hallowed by their proletarian birth can understand the gospel of the prophet Jean-Jacques. Inevitably, with the overthrow of the moderate party, Fernand finds himself unjustly denounced and imprisoned. In spite of his technical innocence, he comes to accept his fate and views his impending execution with equanimity : his crime has been condescension towards the people :

> Wir haben es gut gemeint, wir Gebildeten, gewiss, Fernand reflects, wir waren herablassend, wir haben dem Volk die Schulter geklopft, wir haben uns nie bemüht, die Sprache des Volkes zu lernen. . . . Und nun hat uns das Volk auf den Düngerhaufen geworfen. Mit Recht. Denn unsere kunstvolle Klugheit hat versagt. Und wer die Revolution durchgeführt und Geschichte gemacht hat, das war die plumpe, primitive Weisheit des Volkes.[28]

Having uttered his "mea culpa" and acquired true "revolutionary humility", Girardin has earned his release and may join the vast crowd which acclaims the state funeral of Rousseau :

> Er war kein Fremder mehr, er war eins mit denen, die da sangen. Was ihn umgab, drang in ihn ein, er wurde zu einem lebendigen Teil aller, wurde mehr als er selber, wurde Volk.[29]

It is strange that this mystic sense of solidarity with the "people" should not apparently remind Feuchtwanger of certain aspects of

Nazi philosophy, and that he should take identification with a class to be superior to identification with a race: it is perhaps best seen in the light of a subconscious longing for oblivion, or possibly of a Jewish preoccupation with sacrifice. The voluntary humiliation of Girardin is all too reminiscent of the brain-washed hero of Kleist's *Prinz Friedrich von Homburg* or of the confessions of deposed Communist leaders. Feuchtwanger seems to be betraying here not only his own career and calling but also his guiding principle of reason. It is a matter of regret that he seems to have overcome, temporarily at least, the misgivings of Sepp Trautwein in *Exil.*

The novel of Goya elaborates the dilemma of Trautwein, of Tüverlin and Gustav Oppermann; the issue is problematic, and it is only after an inner struggle of great bitterness that Goya develops political consciousness. Born into a monolithic and autocratic state where even the masses are reactionary in their sympathies, the artist feels himself drawn on to the side of progress, infected by the liberal ideas filtering into Spain from the new French Republic. He is torn by the conflict

> Zwischen altem Brauch und neuem,
> Zwischen Fühlen und Verstehen . . . (30)

as Feuchtwanger puts it in one of the balladesque trochaic verses which form the climax to each section of the narrative. He is held back on the path of progress not only by fear of the Inquisition, but also by emotional attachment to the glittering corruption of the old régime, symbolised in the person of Cayetana, Duchess of Alba, "lust, lure and lie incarnate". Emotional suffering, the affliction of deafness, and political enlightenment turn Goya from a subservient court painter and coldly brilliant technician into a bitter social satirist. The splendid colour of his commissioned portraits—"bright as a monkey's bottom", he calls them contemptuously—in which the satire is unconscious, gives way to the grotesque monochrome savagery of his Capricho engravings. The king, and even his astute consort, are tricked into giving their patronage to these scurrilous cartoons—like Louis XVI they cannot help fostering forces which undermine the throne. Their court, like that of Louis, consists of the dull and the effete, and of those who are moved by a decadent wish to degrade themselves socially and morally. In the subversive comedy of Beaumarchais and the satirical drawings of Goya, Feuchtwanger sees the way in which the power of the intellect can be brought to bear against authority: it is the way of art. The mind need not abdicate in the face of force, it can still attack under the cloak of art:

> Künstlerische Begabung, mit politischer Leidenschaft vereint, könnte das Höchste erzielen, was der Mensch zu erreichen vermag.[31]

The portrait of the artist in *Goya* is perhaps the best feature of the novel : the painter is a man outwardly coarse, sullen and sturdy, inwardly hypersensitive, plagued by moods of despair verging on madness and by a host of melancholy phantoms : a peasant and a visionary. There are many familiar figures and patterns in the work : Cayetana, the imperious *femme fatale* on the model of Marie Auguste in *Jud Süss,* Lucia in *Josephus,* Marie Antoinette in *Waffen für Amerika,* stands in opposition to the queen Maria Luisa, who has "made herself intelligent because she was ugly" as Agnes von Flaven stood opposed to Margarete Maultasch. Goya, like Josephus and Fernand Girardin has a crude familiar in his assistant Agustin, who personifies his conscience and with whom he lives in affection and hatred subtly mixed.

V

Although not the last of Feuchtwanger's novels, *Waffen für Amerika, Goya* and *Narrenweisheit* are in the nature of a political testament. The two works of his final period revert to less specifically doctrinaire problems and to more personal preoccupations; in particular they show the obsession with sacrifice which lies behind so many of his novels. It is possibly significant that these last two novels leave the field of recorded history for that of legend. *Spanische Ballade* takes up the story of the Castilian king Alfonso who became enamoured of Rachel the Jewess, the story which provided the theme for Grillparzer's play, *Die Jüdin von Toledo.* Rachel's influence, like that of Esther on Ahasuerus, is a shield to her people, but it is more : it helps the advance of reason, peace and prosperity through the agency of her father Jehuda, the Jewish merchant who is summoned by Alfonso to repair the finances of his state. Jehuda is in fact the central figure of the novel and he combines in character and situation the features of Süss and Josephus. Like the former, he rises to power and influence in a Gentile state; like the latter he dreams of wedding the wisdom of the East to the energy of the West. Although he lacks the malevolence of Süss he thrives on a sense of power that offends his orthodox brethren. The God whom Jehuda serves is not only Jehovah but also reason, his enemy is the fanaticism and the bloodthirsty atavism personified in Bertran de Born. So devoted is Jehuda to his ideal of progress that, like Jephthah, he is prepared to sacrifice his daughter to it. In this novel again, as in *Die hässliche Herzogin,* Feuchtwanger tries to depict an age of transition in which the knight is giving way to the artisan, fanaticism to reason. As the wise Muslim, Musa, says :

> In diesem Jahrhundert kommt es weniger auf die Ritter an als auf die Wissenden und auf die Sachverständigen, auf Baumeister und Waffenschmiede und Ingenieure und Kunstfertige aller Art und gelernte Landwirte.(32)

Jehuda is centuries ahead of his time; in the king's entourage only the mild Don Rodrigue understands and sympathises with his aims. When the war-party murder Rachel and Jehuda the spell is broken, Alfonso reverts to his military role, and the dream of peace, prosperity and reason vanishes from Spain for centuries.

In the last of his novels, *Jefta und seine Tochter,* Feuchtwanger finds his way back to the primitive beginnings of his race, to the story of the judge in Israel who, by the sacrifice of his daughter, saved his people. It is perhaps significant for the recurrence of the sacrifice motif in his works when Feuchtwanger tells us that this episode from the Book of Judges had fascinated him ever since his childhood. It is here, probably, rather than in the more rational attempt to represent the "changing inner landscape" of Jephthah, that the real inspiration of the work lies. *Jefta* is Feuchtwanger's ultimate, and perhaps his most difficult, exercise in historical empathy, an attempt to evoke in a legendary theme the sense of circumstance and of progression that raises historian and reader out of the limitations of the present and thus helps them to understand their own age. What the author says of this novel might stand as a motto for all his endeavours in this field :

> Der historische Roman ist der legitime Nachfahr des grossen Epos. Er befreit denjenigen, der ehrlich daran arbeitet, aus seiner statischen Nur-Gegenwart. Hebt ihn über sich hinaus, gibt ihm Spürung des unendlichen Werdens, lehrt ihn die eigene Zeit als ein Dynamisches verstehen.(33)

It is this constant endeavour to comprehend and to communicate, to make the reader understand human nature and the progress of the human race which most impresses us when we look back on the long catalogue of Feuchtwanger's published works. It is certain that he has his weaknesses both as a writer and as a thinker. His voice is often too strident, although much can be excused a man of his race and political sentiment in the circumstances of the last forty years. His view of past ages is often naïve and tendentious, his devotion to reason is undermined at times by a kind of temperamental nihilism. There is in much of his work a strong suggestion of sadism—lurid scenes of torture and death abound: the execution of Süss, the crucifixions in *Josephus* and *Der falsche Nero,* the garotting of the bandit in *Goya.* There is, too, an intermittent salaciousness, a fondness for erotic scenes that is disturbing. These features, together with a general leaning towards the sensational and a style that is sometimes prolix and undistinguished, may debar him from the company of the greatest German writers of today. In spite of such defects, however, Feuchtwanger has considerable qualities as a novelist: vivid imagination, very considerable erudition and a sense of literary form. But perhaps what is most attractive about his work at its best is the impression of a vehement temperament—the strong emotional impulse behind the philosophy of reasonableness. It is this which will make at least some of his novels retain their attraction, for, as Josephus says: "The living Word is born wherever feeling and knowledge come together."

TRANSLATIONS

1. Ever since I began writing I have endeavoured, for my part, to write historical novels in support of reason and against stupidity and violence, against what Marx calls submersion in historical ignorance.

2. What we are trying to describe is not merely today and a little bit of yesterday; we are seeking to determine the meaning of what happens, we are trying to discover the direction of events and to point to the future as true explorers of God.

3. The war stripped me of preciosity, it led me away from an excessive admiration of the aesthetic and the formal, from a concern with shades of meaning to the essence of things.

4. The skin shrivels from our brow.
The worm gnaws at our brains.
Our flesh rots away and forms the humus.
Our mouths are sealed with stones and soil.
We're waiting.

Our flesh decays, our bones grow dry.
But still one question slumbers not.
And still one question holds not still
And never tires: Oh, why? Oh, why?
We're waiting.

5. When, at the age of forty-two and at the water-shed of my life, I look back on what I have done so far, trying to find a common factor, a line which links my books to me, to my life and to each other, a lowest common denominator: then it seems to me, in spite of all apparent differences, that I have written only *one* book over and over again—the story of man placed between action and inaction, between power and knowledge.

6. Her ugliness was a gift, the sign-post by which God showed her the right way. Chivalry, adventure—all this was glittering froth and show. Her function was to build for the future. Cities, commerce, crafts, good roads, law and order. Her function was not feasts and errantry and love: her function was sober, coolheaded policy.

7. "I'll do no more business with the Habsburgs," Duke Stephan of Lower Bavaria cried indignantly in his hard parade-ground voice as he hurled his gauntlet on to the table with a metallic crash.

8. All at once I perceived the path and the image of this man, the very centre and the parable of his life. Not that he remained true to a certain religious faith—which, incidentally, he probably inherited from one of his parents only—this was not what fascinated me and cast light on his destiny. It was the fact that I perceived how he allowed himself to fall. I comprehended his success and his fall at one and the same time.

9. He stretched his limbs luxuriously in the sense of power, he bathed in it. But occasionally it seemed to him as if the whole glittering carnival did not emanate from him. Then he would raise his shoulders and shiver, as though he were warding off something. He was all at once conscious of an uncanny constriction. Things around him faded; he saw himself pacing through a dumb and shadowy quadrille, with Rabbi Gabriel holding his right hand, the Duke his left . . .

10. To be a Jew meant being despised, persecuted, humiliated; but it also meant being unique, eternally conscious of oneself, the cynosure of all eyes, constantly forced to be tense, keyed up, with every sense alive and on the alert.

11. From the West an eternal tempestuous tidal-wave bears down upon the land of Canaan: thirst for life, for personality, the will to action, lust and power. Grasp, seize—knowledge, lust, possessions, more lust, more possessions, live, struggle, act. This is the refrain from the West. But in the South, beneath the pointed pyramids, dead kings lie amidst gold and spices, autocratically withholding their bodies from corruption; set in the waste-lands, in colossal avenues, their images scorn death. And an eternal tempestuous tidal-wave bears down from the South on the land of Canaan: a torrid, barren craving for existence, a smouldering desire not to forfeit form and shape, not to surrender the body, not to pass away. But from the East comes the refrain of gentle wisdom: to sleep is better than to wake, to be dead is better than to be alive. Do not resist, dissolve into the void, do not act, renounce.

12. Praise
privation, praise ill-treatment, praise
the darkness.

13. So there he sat with twenty-six authentic teeth and six of gold,
a first-rate guy with dough in the bank, a joy to behold,
and what he was willing to pay for he couldn't buy,
so why had he made those hard, hard dollars, why?

14. The content of the cycle is the events in Germany between the wars of 1914 and 1939, that is, the recrudescence of barbarism in Germany and its temporary victory over reason. The purpose of the trilogy is to make

comprehensible to posterity these hard times of waiting and transition, the darkest that Germany has experienced since the Thirty Years War. For later generations will not understand how we were able to tolerate a life like this, they will not see why we went on waiting for so long before we drew the only rational conclusion, namely to put an end to the dominion of violence and unreason by means of violence on our part, and to erect in its place a rational order.

15. Pröckl demanded categorically that Tüverlin should go in for committed, political, revolutionary writing, or else none at all ... he should produce documents of contemporary life. That was his function. His existence made no sense otherwise.

16. If he had gone in for politics, economics or something in the business line—anything would have made more sense than what he actually had done.

17. It was not the people who committed the atrocities. It was a great tribute to the inherent soundness of the people at large that, although incited by their government for fourteen long years to carry out pogroms of Jews and Socialists, they had nevertheless clung to their self-respect. It was not the ordinary people who were barbaric, it was the government, the new Reich, its civil servants and its brutal soldiery.

18. As far as your main principle goes, Hanns, you are right, unfortunately. To suggest that the mind can realise its will without recourse to force—it's just tripe. Without force a just order cannot be established in the world. I have come to grasp that your basic principles are true; but I merely understand it, my brain comprehends it, but my feelings do not concur, my heart does not assent. I do not feel at home in your world, where everything is reason and mathematics. I would rather not live in it. It seems to me that the masses have too great a say, and the individual too little. I cling to my old-fashioned freedom ... I would have to give up a lot of habits that I am attached to, habits without which I cannot picture my life at all.... The old order is not yet dead and the new has not been born yet, it is a terrible time of transition, it's really a wretched waiting-room, in fact.

19. How we were helplessly concerned to cling to the old order, even while we longed for the new, how we dreaded the new, even while we realised that it was a better order, how we wavered and hoped and feared: the strange sensation that was generated by the coming together and the separation of these two poles—to set down this unique sensation of our era of change was what I was trying to do.

20. Strange, how in his own life the legends and stories of his race were mirrored ... Abraham driving out Hagar, Joseph becoming the favourite of Pharaoh, Judas Maccabeus leading his people into battle, Job, who lost all he had, and Abraham again, sacrificing his son: indeed, it seemed to be his fate to re-live in a bitter, strangely distorted fashion the stories and the situations of the Bible.

21. Yes, Rome is order, unreasoning power, Judah is God, the realisation of God, power endowed with meaning. One cannot live without the other. In him, however, in Josephus, they are mingled, Rome and Judah, power and spirit. He is destined to reconcile them.

22. Praise God and scatter yourselves over the lands.
Praise God and lavish yourselves over the oceans.
He is a bondsman who binds himself to a single country.
The kingdom I promised you is not called Zion,
Its name is called: the globe.

23. Why, if I am Joseph ben Matthias, must I also be
A Roman or a Jew, or both together?
I will be I, Joseph will be I,
As I crawled from my mother's womb,
And not set between the peoples
And constrained to say: I am of these, or of those.

24. As soon as the job began to need hard work and guts you chucked it up. You took refuge in writing and in cosmopolitan chit-chat. In the end you got bored with that as well, and you went back to the fight. Then things got a bit too hot for you again, and you made yourself scarce, went back to your cosy, wishy-washy scribbling. A man of the people like me calls that treachery.

25. He had sought to proclaim reason, the empire of reason, of the Messiah. Prophecy of that sort is too dearly bought. The man sets himself up as the prophet has to pay for it with many afflictions. . . . Whoever puts his trust in reason is bound to suffer for it.

26. For decades I have been intrigued by the remarkable fact that such diverse individuals as Benjamin Franklin, Lafayette, Voltaire, Louis XVI and Marie Antoinette had to co-operate—each for very different reasons—so that the revolution in America, and hence in France, might achieve success. When the United States under Roosevelt intervened in the war against European fascism and supported the struggle of the Soviet Union against Hitler, the events in France during the latter part of the eighteenth century became crystal clear to me, and, conversely, these events cast light on the political happenings of my own time. Thus encouraged, I set to work on the novel, *Foxes in the Vineyard*. I hoped that I could give shape to the things that induced so many different individuals and groups to work in the direction of progress—voluntarily, involuntarily, or even against their will.

27. He was an absolute monarch, King of France, responsible to no parliament; he could do whatever he wished, and was bound to do things that he did not wish to do. That thing commonly called "history" was stronger than he was and drove him on. And thus there was sense in history and men were constrained to move in a certain direction, whether they wished it or not.

28. As cultured people we meant well, we were condescending, we patted the common people on the shoulder, and never troubled to learn their language. . . . And now the people have thrown us on the dung-heap. Quite rightly. For our subtle cleverness has failed. And what carried through the revolution and made history was the clumsy, primitive wisdom of the common people.

29. He was no longer alien, he was one with those who were singing. He was not only surrounded, he was imbued by them, he became a living part of them all, he became more than himself, he became the people.

30. Between the old ways and the new,
Between feeling and understanding...

31. Artistic talent, wedded to political passion, could achieve the highest that it was given to man to achieve.

32. In this century the people who mattered were not knights so much as knowledgeable men and experts, architects and smiths and engineers and skilled workers of every description and trained farmers.

33. The historical novel is the legitimate descendant of the great epic. It liberates the writer who works at it honestly from his static and exclusive present. It raises him above himself, gives him a sense of eternal evolution, teaches him to understand his own age as something dynamic.

BIBLIOGRAPHY

WORKS

There is no definitive complete edition of Feuchtwanger's works: most of the novels are available, however, in editions published by Aufbau-Verlag, Berlin and Rowohlt-Verlag, Hamburg. These are marked A or R in the following chronological list. Aufbau-Verlag also publish a volume of dramas, one of short stories, one of essays and one of memoirs.

1903 *Die Einsamen. Zwei Skizzen* (short stories).
1905–6 *Joel*; *König Saul*; *Das Weib des Urias*; *Der arme Heinrich*; *Donna Bianca—Die Braut von Korinth* (dramas).
1907 *Der Fetisch* (drama).
1910 *Der tönerne Gott* (novel).
1915 *Julia Farnese* (drama).
1916 *Vasantasena* (from the Indian); *Warren Hastings, Gouverneur von Indien* (adapted in collaboration with Bertolt Brecht in 1925 as *Kalkutta, 4. Mai*) (dramas).
1917 *Der König und die Tänzerin* (from the Indian); *Die Perser* (from Aeschylus) (dramas).
1918 *Jud Süß*; *Die Kriegsgefangenen*; *Friede* (from Aristophanes, *Acharnians* and *Eirene*); *Appius und Virginia* (from John Webster) (dramas).
1920 *Thomas Wendt* (dramatic novel).
1921 *Der Amerikaner oder die entzauberte Stadt* (drama).
1923 *Der holländische Kaufmann; Der Frauenverkäufer* (from Calderon) (dramas); *Die häßliche Herzogin* (novel: A, R).
1924 *Leben Eduards des Zweiten von England* (from Marlowe in collaboration with Bertolt Brecht) (drama).
1925 *Jud Süß* (novel: A, R).
1927 *Die Petroleum-Inseln*; *Wird Hill amnestiert*? (dramas).
1928 *PEP, J. L. Wetcheeks amerikanisches Liederbuch* (lyric).
1929 *Erfolg* (novel: A, R).
1932 *Der jüdische Krieg* (novel: A, R).

1933 *Die Geschwister Oppermann* (novel: A).
1934 *Marianne in Indien und sieben andere Erzählungen* (short stories).
1935 *Die Söhne* (novel: A, R).
1936 *Der falsche Nero* (novel: A, R).
1937 *Moskau 1937* (travel and politics).
1940 *Exil* (novel: A).
1942 *Der Tag wird kommen* (also as *Das gelobte Land*. Novel: A, R).
Unholdes Frankreich (memoirs).
1943 *Die Brüder Lautensack* (novel: A).
1945 *Simone* (novel: A).
1946 *Venedig (Texas) und 14 andere Erzählungen* (short stories).
1947–8 *Die Füchse im Weinberg* (also as *Waffen für Amerika*. Novel: A, R).
1948 *Wahn oder der Teufel in Boston* (drama).
1949 *Odysseus und die Schweine* (short stories: A).
1951 *Goya oder der arge Weg der Erkenntnis* (novel: A, R).
1952 *Narrenweisheit oder Tod und Verklärung des Jean-Jacques Rousseau* (novel: A, R).
1955 *Die Jüdin von Toledo* (also as *Spanische Ballade*. Novel: A, R).
1956 *Die Witwe Capet* (drama); *Centum Opuscula* (essays).
1957 *Jefta und seine Tochter* (novel: A, R).
1961 *Das Haus der Desdemona* (essays. A).

SECONDARY LITERATURE

V. Wittner: *Lion Feuchtwanger*, Schweizer Annalen 3 (1946–7).
L. Feuchtwanger zum 70. Geburtstag. Worte seiner Freunde. Berlin, 1954, 163 pp. (contains a full bibliography).
W. Jahn: *Die Geschichtsauffassung Lion Feuchtwangers in seiner Josephus-Trilogie*, Rudolstadt, Greifenverlag, 1959, 93 pp.
Lion Feuchtwanger (Schriftsteller der Gegenwart No. 2), Volkseigener Verlag Volk und Wissen, Berlin, 3rd ed. 1959, 132 pp.

Carl Zuckmayer

Carl Zuckmayer

by SHEILA ROOKE

Carl Zuckmayer was born on November 27, 1896 at Nackenheim in Rheinhessen. He left school to volunteer for the army in 1914 and spent most of the war years on the Western Front. He was awarded the Iron Cross First Class. At the end of the war he studied law in Heidelberg, but abandoned his studies for the theatre in Berlin and Kiel, taking work of every kind when necessary and travelling widely in Germany and Scandinavia. Shortly before the Second World War he settled in Henndorf, in Austria, but was obliged to emigrate to America when the Nazis came to power. He spent the war years farming in Vermont and took American citizenship. Since the war he has lived in Switzerland. In 1952 he received the Goethe Prize of the city of Frankfurt and was awarded an honorary degree of Doctor of Literature by Dartmouth College, U.S.A. in 1956. In 1957 an honorary degree of Doctor of Philosophy was conferred on him by the University of Bonn.

> "Talbauern empören sich wider das Bergjoch. Ein Scheusal mit einer Peitsche. Fliehende Gattin. Ein Schmied. Verschollene Tochter, Brückenmann, Bauerngott. Buhlerei. Arbeit. Irrsinn. Liebesschmerz. Gewalt. Gewaltlosigkeit. Ich will die Zusammenhänge dieses Dramas gern erklären, sobald ein Andrer sagt, was vorgeht. Schwer ist nur zu sagen was vorgeht, weil alles vorgeht. . . ."(1)

THUS, in brilliant parody of the excesses of Expressionistic telegram-style and with an apt summary of the incredibly tortuous plot, Alfred Kerr's dismissal of Carl Zuckmayer's earliest courtship of dramatic fame in *Kreuzweg* (1920). The play was, of course, a failure and deserved to be, as the author himself readily admitted. The numerous characters were wooden and lifeless, speaking in strained outbursts of lyrical rhetoric with two separate actions concurrently and separately vying for supremacy, both petering out in the exhaustion which inevitably follows any orgy. It is not surprising, therefore, that when five years later, *Der fröhliche Weinberg* was received with such overwhelming acclaim, Zuckmayer had not only "arrived" but was neatly labelled and pigeonholed as a successful exponent of an entirely different genre —the "Volksstück". This uproarious comedy of his native Rhein-Hessen heralded two other "Heimatsstücke" which followed in quick succession—*Schinderhannes* (1927) and *Katharina Knie* (1928) and also *Ein Bauer aus dem Taunus* which was first published in a small collection of stories in 1927. These early works set in that part of Germany with which the author was most familiar, are vital, realistic and often humorous portrayals of the simple people of the Rhineland and have a warm and immediate appeal. Although Zuckmayer only depicted this area as the background for two other works—*Der Schelm von Bergen* (1934) and his most recent novel *Die Fastnachsbeichte* (1959)—he developed an undoubted gift of portraying simple, unspoiled people, no matter where their roots. He reflected the social extremes of Berlin, where he himself settled and struggled and starved in the process of finding a living as a playwright in the twenties and thirties, in *Der Hauptmann von Köpenick* (1930) and in the two stories *Eine Weihnachtsgeschichte* (1931) and *Die Affenhochzeit* (1932); his various visits to Scandinavia for odd jobs set the background for another short story, *Geschichte einer Entenjagd* (first published in 1927) and the play *Bellman* (1938) later published under the title *Ulla Winblad* (1952). With the exception of *Des Teufels General* (1946), these pre-war works are nostalgically judged by many to be Zuckmayer's best. The post-war works, it is often maintained, are less successful because they are "intellectual". Zuckmayer's forte, they continue, is farce, working-class humour, peasants and things of the soil; as long as he makes these the mainstay of his writings he is successful, when he departs from them he cannot hope but fail. I should like to return to this view later, but wish first to examine the pre-war writings in order to see where their real strength lies.

Zuckmayer's affinity with unsophisticated people, in particular those who live close to the soil cannot be disputed. But it is not insignificant that he was the son of comparatively wealthy middle-class parents and grew up in a Catholic atmosphere, although admittedly, a free and easy one. His parents were keenly disappointed when his first marriage ended in divorce after only six months and his father was convinced that his second son would achieve nothing with his life, particularly after leaving Heidelberg without a degree and the utter failure of *Kreuzweg*. Such a shattering failure seems to have shown Zuckmayer that it was inexpedient as well as artistically abortive merely to imitate current conventions in the theatre. From then on he set out to go his own way. In Kiel, the citadel of the former German Navy, he adapted an old Roman comedy, *The Eunuch* of Terence (1923) and filled it with satire and political allusions. A phallic symbol was shown, as in the Roman theatre, to indicate the erotic content of the play and the language faithfully adhered to the theme. There was an uproar following the performance. The next day the theatre was closed by the police and Zuckmayer was dismissed, as he himself has it in his autobiography, *Second Wind* (1940), on grounds of "complete artistic incapacity". The fight against smug, self-satisfied bourgeois society was on. His successful works do not again outrage bourgeois opinion and morality so crudely, but beneath the developing artistry, beneath the good yarn, the boisterous farce and the colourful pageantry, it is not difficult to detect the rebel thumbing his nose at authority. Criticism of accepted attitudes towards sexual relationships and marital bonds are clearly the focal points in *Ein Bauer aus dem Taunus*, *Geschichte einer Entenjagd* and *Der fröhliche Weinberg*. In the two stories an optimistic variant of the triangular situation is envisaged. The hero of *Ein Bauer aus dem Taunus*, Seuffert, a soldier invalided out of the First World War before its end, suddenly has an irresistible urge to revisit a Russian woman with whom he had lived for a time whilst he was stationed in the Balkans. He sets out in the middle of the night, leaving his wife, whom he loves and who is pregnant, and after incredible hardships reaches the Balkan town to find the Russian woman dead. Her little son, who is also his, is still alive and together they travel slowly back to the Taunus. There is no sense of guilt on the part of Seuffert, nor resentment on the part of his wife, who receives her husband and his son with open arms. Stress is laid on the essentially harmonious quality of human relations presented in this story and also in *Geschichte einer Entenjagd*—where a temporary "ménage à trois" is formed—as being of more importance than rigid codes of behaviour which are man-made and have no pattern in non-human Nature. The close affinity of sexual intercourse with the fertility of the soil is captured in the imagery employed.

> "Das Weib, dessen Namen er kaum mehr aussprechen konnte, und das Weib in der Heimat, Anna Barbara, das auf ihn wartete jetzt, all das war eines für ihn, wie die Äcker, die er hier oder dort gepflügt hatte. Und das Kind, das damals schrie und das Kind das die im Taunus von ihm trug, beides brannte in ihm und liess ihn nicht los und musste zusammenkommen."(2)

In the concluding lines of the work as Seuffert arrives home, the sexual imagery is again unmistakable.

> "Die Obstblüte war längst vorüber, die Kirschbäume hatten machtig angesetzt, und die Beerenbüsche standen alle in starken Fruchtbarkeit".(3)

In neither story is there, in point of fact, a problem. All the sexual relationships are approved and accepted by the people concerned.

And although one may be sceptical of the naïvety of the author, one can see the rightness and the plain common-sense of his argument, which is also the basis of Gunderloch's seemingly fantastic and improper condition of marriage for his daughter, Klärchen, in *Der fröhliche Weinberg*. As Gunderloch himself explains, his own marriage was not successful in producing any offspring and so he was obliged to turn to a barge-girl in order to beget a child. Klärchen has now become engaged to a pedantic and mercenary "Korpsstudent" whose virility is doubted by Gunderloch. As he graphically explains:

> "Ich weiss, was ich will! Ich pfeif auf die öffentliche Meinung! Ich hab mei Sach beisamme, ich kann mir's leiste! Was wolle denn die Leut? Wenn se Wein kaufe, wird e Prob gemacht, sonst kann ich ja Firnessig für Messwein verkloppe! Wenn einer e Sau kauft, muss er wisse, dass se ferkelt. Dafür gibt's die öffentliche Deckung von Gemeindewegen. Wenn aber einer heirat, wo das beiderseitige Leib—un Seeleheil damit verbunde is, da soll er Blindekuh spielen, he?"[4]

And his sensible, if unconventional condition is justified. Klärchen's engagement to Knuzius, which came about largely because of his importuning and desire for her father's wealth, is terminated when she meets Jochen Most, a massive sailor whose virility is in no doubt at all.

Gunderloch's "Ich pfeif auf die öffentliche Meinung!" applies equally in the social sphere to Bückler in *Schinderhannes* and Wilhelm Voigt in *Der Hauptmann von Köpenick*. Both are outcasts from society and take the law into their own hands. Whilst Bückler would have been a rebel in any surroundings from sheer force of personality, as Zuckmayer clearly states:

> "Der Schinderhannes war keineswegs das, was man heute unter einem Revolutionär versteht. Er war ein Rebell. . . . Er rebellierte nicht aus 'erkannten Mangelns', sondern aus der Fülle der Natur."[5]

His situation is aggravated by the social injustice of the society in which he lives, thereby enabling him to become a legendary figure of romantic lawlessness. Voigt, on the other hand, only rebels against society when he has tried all other means within his power to obtain work. Whereas Bückler is the eternal spiv

> "Das wär mir neu, dass ma durch die Arbeit zu was kommt!"[6]

Voigt wants nothing more than a permit from the pass-office to enable him to work as a shoemaker, for which he is skilled.

Oberwachtmeister: Quasselns nich, Sie haben wohl auch Luft im Kopp, was? Was wollense denn hier in Potsdam?
Voigt: Arbeeten will ick.
Oberwachtmeister: Das kann jeder sagen.

. . . .

Voigt: Ick muss doch arbeeten. Von wat sollt ick denn leben?
Oberwachtmeister: Das ist Ihre Sache. Sehense zu, dass Sie'n ordentlicher Mensch werden. Wenn einer arbeiten *will*, denn kriegt er auch Arbeit.
Voigt: (schüttelt den Kopf) Nee, nee, det is nu'n Karussell, det is nu ne Kaffeemühle. Wenn ick nich jemeldet bin, krieg ick keene Arbeet, und wenn ick keene Arbeet habe, da darf ick mir nich melden. Denn will ick wieder raus. Denn jebense mir'n Pass mit'n Grenzvisum, det ick rieber kann.
Oberwachtmeister: Dafür sind wir hier nicht zuständig(7)

Neither Bückler nor Voigt has the desire or the ability to act as reformer in his society. But they both represent the determination of the individual to wrest from society what has been denied him by force of station or circumstance and yet which is accepted by others as their unquestionable right. Bückler, like Bellman, is an "epic" figure in the Eulenspiegel and Robin Hood tradition, robbing the rich mainly to feed himself and his followers on one bank of the Rhine during the Napoleonic Wars and selling his loot on the other. He takes the law into his own hands because this is the only way to execute a minimum of justice. The justice is arbitrary, but is necessitated by the corruption of the existing political system, whereby the princes, merchants and clergy get richer and vie with the French forces of occupation on the left bank of the Rhine in crushing the poorer members of society. The majority complain but submit; Bückler finds society and the law unjust to his kind and so becomes his own law-maker.

Voigt becomes an outcast as the result of an initial deviation from the law, namely falsification of a form at the post-office. The severity of the sentence—fifteen years in prison—is beyond credence. When the sentence is over, he goes abroad to Bucharest, but is so homesick that he returns under a false name, at the discovery of which he is again given a prison sentence in Plötzensee. At the beginning of Zuckmayer's play, Voigt has just been released and is trying unsuccessfully to get a pass. The vicious circle of "No pass, no job; no job, no pass" leads him to break into the police station to steal a pass in order to go abroad again. He is caught and sentenced to a further ten years' imprisonment, this time in Moabit. Thus his initial indiscretion, born of poverty, has made of him a jail-bird and an outcast. Voigt is, however, a social outcast in another sense—only to be fully understood in the Wilhelminian era—he has not served in the army. This has played a not inconsiderable role in his failure to get a job and a pass on leaving prison. One has the impression that his past record might well have been overlooked at the police station and at the various places of employment he visited, if only he could have answered in the affirmative to the inevitable question "Hamse gedient?" Faced therefore with the utter hopelessness of the perpetual down-and-out (like those from all parts of Germany so clearly depicted in the scene "Herberge zur Heimat"), Voigt decides to make a last desperate effort to conquer both the Prussian military machine and petty officialdom, by masquerading as a captain and forcing the mayor of Köpenick to relegate to him the section dealing with passes. The vast hoax fails for Voigt personally, because in his excitement at the undertaking, which he carries out impeccably, he overlooks the fact that the townhall of Köpenick does not possess a pass section. Circumstances therefore require his capitulation. Similarly, Bückler, having pitched the united force of the French army and the German princes against him for his lawlessness, is sentenced to death, and executed. Ultimately neither man has gained anything for himself through his rebellion, and society remains, for the time being at any rate, unaffected by their actions. But they are magnificent figures, towering above the pettiness and intrigue that surrounds them and confident in their own indomitable spirit for survival.

In his longest and best prose-work *Die Magdalena von Bozen* (1936), reminiscent in many ways of Mann's *Zauberberg*, Zuckmayer achieves the culmination of his sexual and social protests. Two separate worlds, that of the aristocratic intelligentsia of the castle in the mountains of Bozen, and that of the unsophisticated peasants in the valley, are fused for a short period in the actions of the hero, Thomas, who stays with his friends at the castle and falls in love with Mena, the waitress at the inn below. The affair is short-lived, but the bitter-sweet experience is regretted by neither of the lovers and in its passionate enrichment, it stands in sharp contrast to the barrenness of the artistocratic brother and sister, Firmin and Magdalena. Both are incapable of happy sexual relations—Magdalena is in love only with dark, chthonic elements and so breaks off her engagement to a young Italian; Firmin is married, but shuns both his wife and children. His barrenness of spirit is also reflected in his inability, as a poet, to complete a single work of art. The destructive forces within the brother and sister bring about their deaths in the rarefied air of the mountains; whereas Thomas, after the refreshment of his relationship with Mena, is inspired with new vigour for his painting. Mena's eventual pregnancy, symbolises here, as in *Ein Bauer aus dem Taunus*, *Schinderhannes* and *Der Schelm von Bergen*, the fruition of a happy, harmonious contact.

Firmin's tragedy is that his intellect has forced his *eros*, his natural, warm productive self, into submission—a fact of which he is uneasily aware in the course of an argument with his sister's fiancé, Mario.

> " '*Ordnung* und *Formung* . . . sind völlig verschiedene Disziplinen Die ordnenden Mächte, die heute in Kampf und Umschichtung begriffen sind, treten nach andren Gesetzen an als die formenden, denen der Menschengeist alle Zeit verpflichtet ist. Formung—ich könnte auch sagen—Wachstum oder Selbstgestaltung—steht jenseits des Organisierbaren. Dort, wo die Organisation aufhört, beginnt erst das Organische.' "(8)

This view is not, of course novel in any way. Society has a habit of becoming fossilised and only its own members can force it to move and breathe again. Firmin fails because he isolates himself from society. Unlike him, Voigt is aware of this danger and in the brilliant diatribe between him and his well-meaning brother-in-law, all the young Zuckmayer's anti-conventional and anti-authoritarian spleen is given full expression.

Hoprecht: 'n Mensch biste überhaupt nur, wenn du dich, in ne menschliche Ordnung stellst! Leben tut auch ne Wanze!

Voigt: Richtig! Die lebt, Friedrich! Und weisste, warum se lebt? Erst kommt de Wanze, und dann de Wanzenordnung! Erst der Mensch, Friedrich! Und dann de Menschenordnung!

Hoprecht: Du willst dich nich unterordnen, das isses! Wer'n Mensch sein will—der muss sich unterordnen, verstanden?

Voigt: Unterordnen jewiss! Aber unter wat drunter? Det will ick janz jenau wissen! Denn muss de Ordnung richtig sein, Friedrich, det isse nicht!(9)

Der Hauptmann von Köpenick is a comedy of the first rank, but it is easy to see how intrinsically tragic is the material. This is the great gift that Zuckmayer brings to his pre-war works: the ability to conceive basically serious themes in terms of comedy and satire, and to avoid all suspicion of being tendentious. More than this, his heroes are big men, anxious to sweep away the petty controls and taboos that prevent the fulfilment of the ego. Some of them like Voigt and Seuffert are gentle creatures, motivated by an instinctive sense, born of impulse or personal need. Even the extrovert Gunderloch and Bückler are not entirely anarchistic. Bückler is ultimately prepared to try to submit to society and Gunderloch does not advocate the overthrow of marital ties as such; what both unequivocally demand is that the regulations and conventions governing personal and social behaviour should be in a state of flux.

It is customary to regard the artistically unproductive war years of 1939–45 as a turning-point in Zuckmayer's works. In many ways this is reasonable, since all the works that follow the war years are more obviously and self-consciously problematic than the earlier ones. Particularly significant is the fact that the four most famous dramas of the post-war period all treat problems experienced by contemporary Germans and which result directly out of the Second World War. Moreover, we are aware now of the gradual introduction of the guilty hero, already hinted at in *Die Magdalena von Bozen* and in a less successful novel, *Herr über Leben und Tod* (1938).

Des Teufels General, begun in exile in America, but first performed in 1946, is generally acknowledged to be Zuckmayer's greatest work. It will almost certainly go down in history as the most powerful play about the Nazi régime to be written by a German so soon after the end of the war. The fact that its author was an émigré makes its verisimilitude with life under the Third Reich the more striking. It is also noteworthy that the statistics of the Deutscher Bühnenverein indicate that *Des Teufels General*, together with Borchert's *Draussen vor der Tür* were the two plays most performed in the immediate German post-war theatre. *Des Teufels General* was performed 3,238 times in the course of the years 1947–50.

Harras, in *Des Teufels General*, is the last of the Gunderloch, Bückler, Voigt line. He, like his predecessors, is a character of great stature, based like the others on a factual personality with an almost legendary reputation, who dominates events throughout. Like Bückler and Voigt, Harras brooks no interference in the expression of his personality; he is a pilot intoxicated with his profession and utterly incapable of turning his hand to anything else. His ambition inevitably leads him to serve the Nazi régime, although he does so unwillingly and with undisguised contempt for their ideology. He is conceived with great sympathy and we react accordingly. He is an attractive personality, warm-hearted and yet with a scouring wit.

Otto (etwas unsicher): Heil Hi—Guten Abend, Herr Präsident. Heil Hitler, Herr Doktor.

Harras: Sagen Sie ruhig: Guten Adolf, das trifft jeden Geschmack. (Zu den andern) Die Herrn haben sich wohl schon miteinander

> bekannt gemacht—soweit sie nicht verwandt sind? Das ist Kulturleiter Dr. Schmidt-Lausitz vom Propapopogandamysterium, ich kann das Wort nie richtig aussprechen, mein alter Afrika-komplex. Schmidt-Lausitz, zum Unterschied von Schmidt-Lützelsdorff, Schmidt-Pforzheim, Schmidt-Sodbrennen und anderen Herrn ohne besondere Kennzeichen.(10)

He helps Jews to escape the Nazi concentration camps and he signs a paper exonerating his mechanics from sabotage, because he admires their courage, even though he knows that they are in fact guilty. He, like Bückler and Voigt, is true to himself to the very end; having chosen his path, he accepts the consequences of his choice. He has temporarily thought of flight either with his newly found love, Diddo, or to his chief engineer's Resistance group in Switzerland, but these he soon recognises as deflections.

> "Wer auf Erden des Teufels General wurde und ihm die Bahn gebombt hat—der muss ihm auch Quartier in der Hölle machen."(11)

He takes out a faulty aircraft and crashes to his death. The irony of the play's concluding lines spoken by his arch-enemy from the Gestapo is unmistakable.

> "Hauptquartier? Reibungslos abgewickelt. General Harras soeben in Erfüllung seiner Pflicht tödlich verunglückt. Beim Ausprobieren einer Kampfmaschine. Jawohl. Staatsbegräbnis."(12)

Where Harras parts company with Bückler and Voigt, however, is in his acknowledgement of the guilt, which his self-orientated career must bring with it. He has no desire to make excuses for himself,

> "Entschuldigung—gibt es keine. Das heisst—wenn ich mir eine schreiben lassen wollte, für den Oberlehrer (weist mit der Zigarre zum Himmel)—dann wäre es—wegen meiner Mutter. Aber sonst —ich bin ganz kalt in die Sache hineingestiegen, und ohne Illusionen."(13)

and despises those of others.

> "Es rettet ja jeder etwas, heutzutage, was er nicht beweisen kann. Die Religion, die Kultur, die Demokratie, das Abendland —wohin man rotzt, ein Kreuzzug. Wenn ich nur einen treffen würde, der zugibt, dass er nichts als seine Haut retten will. Das möcht ich auch sehr gern. Aber nicht mittels Dämmerschopfen. Sollte ich ein Ideal haben, so ist es ein ganz bescheidenes geworden; mich nicht selber anspucken zu müssen. Nicht mal bei Gegenwind."(14)

Harras' tragic situation lies in the realisation that by the end of the play, this simple ideal no longer applies. He passes his own sentence on even his good actions—kindnesses to individual Jews—which he had allowed to serve as a panacea to his conscience.

> "Jetzt wollen wir mal in den Spiegel gucken und über uns selbst gerührt sein. Was wir für edle Menschen sind. So schaun wir aus. Jeder hat seine Gewissensjuden, oder mehrere damit er nachts schlafen kann. Aber damit kauft man sich nicht frei. Das ist Selbsttrug. An dem, was tausend anderen geschieht, die wir nicht kennen und denen wir nicht helfen, sind wir deshalb doch schuldig. Schuldig und verdammt, in alle Ewigkeit. Das Gemeine zulassen ist schlimmer als es tun."[15]

Completely overshadowed by Harras until the last scenes of Act III, is a minor character, Oderbruch, the chief engineer, who perpetrates sabotage as a Resistance activity. There seems little doubt that it was not Zuckmayer's intention to give him any more significance other than that of a last link in the chain of events leading up to Harras' suicide. He did not, however, reckon with the press. There were many reviews of the play—the majority favourable. Some criticism was levelled at Harras—there was the fear that the German public would equate him with all generals and thus exculpate them too easily from their responsibility—but the main flood of criticism was directed at Oderbruch. He was felt to be too nebulous, too slight a character to compete with Harras for our sympathy, but most of all he was condemned, not for being a member of a Resistance group, but for the methods of sabotage in materials and lives which he and his fellows employed to achieve their ends as opponents of the Third Reich. The Catholic periodical *Hochland* disowns him (he is described as a Catholic in the play) and most other reviewers consider that his action merely replaces one fanaticism with another. Such unexpected criticism of a minor character seems to have put Zuckmayer in something of a dilemma. Initially he vehemently supported Oderbruch. In *Die Welt* (February 28, 1948) he writes:

> "Wir können und dürfen doch nicht aus Angst vor einer Dolchstosslegende nun die Leute, die in dieser Zeit die wirklichen Helden Deutschlands waren, die Träger des Widerstandes... totschweigen. Genau das Gegenteil ist nötig, man muss diesen Menschen ein Denkmal setzen, zu dem Oderbruch überhaupt nur eine schwache Skizze ist, und muss sie zu den Idealgestalten einer neuen deutschen Generation machen, auf die sie mit Recht stolz sein darf. . . ."[16]

And yet, within a matter of days, his attitude noticeably changes. In the *Schwäbische Landeszeitung* (March 2, 1948) he claims:

> "Ich selbst stimme mit Oderbruch ja gar nicht überein. Denn vom ethisch-politischen reicht das Problem tief in ein religiöses hinein: Es geht um die Heiligkeit des Lebens, an die ich unbedingt glaube."(17)

Why Zuckmayer changed his attitude to Oderbruch is uncertain. One reason may have been the shock of such adverse press criticism or he may have felt that his own lack of accurate knowledge of the various German Resistance groups at the time of drafting the play (1942) had handicapped him and allowed him to offend his public out of ignorance. In his speech in memory of the Socialist Carlo Mierendorff given in America in 1944, he indicated clearly that he had no first-hand knowledge of groups such as the Left-wing "Rote Kapelle" or the other numerous organisations, from the pacifists led by Moltke and his Kreisau circle, to the group within the Army which planned the abortive bomb-plot on Hitler's life in 1944.

> "Politische Arbeit war ihm (Carlo Mierendorff) im heutigen Deutschland versagt, denn jenes 'Underground' von dem die Zeitungen reden, das gibt es nur in Hollywood. Der Untergrund des wirklichen Deutschland ist tiefer. Dort ist die Seele, das Herz, der Gedanke unter Grund gegangen und wie, wann, in welcher Form sie wieder zutage treten, weiss keiner von uns."(18)

The work starts epically, showing us Harras in varying moods, backgrounds and situations, and it is not until the end of Act II that he assumes an active role, when events move with startling rapidity. Oderbruch assumes an enigmatic quality by being spoken of, like Wallenstein, long before he makes an entrance. The dialogue is scintillating, witty and for the most part pithy, with the notable and deliberate exception of Harras' anti-"Blut und Boden" speech to the young airman, Hartmann. The character-drawing is masterly, with the possible exception of the somewhat shadowy Oderbruch. This minor defect is rectified in the film version, completed in 1954. The press heaved a sigh of relief and Zuckmayer appeared to be delighted with the alterations. As early as April 4, 1950 he wrote in the *Abendzeitung*:

> "Ich habe mich bemüht, das Problem Oderbruch auf eine unmissverständliche Formel zu bringen. Für den Oderbruch des Schauspieles gab es aus dramatischen Gründen keine Entwicklungsmöglichkeiten. Der Film gibt uns, da er ja eher episch abrollt als dramatisch vorandrängt, Gelegenheit, die Gestalt des

Oderbruch und seine Handlungsweise so anzulegen, dass keine Missverständnisse entstehen."[19]

These attempts at avoiding misunderstanding are highly significant. Oderbruch now works as a single individual and does not belong to any form of organised resistance. Instead of tampering with the aircraft so that they crash and his own comrades are killed, he is made to notice a fault in the steering construction which he fails to report. The planes could thus be rejected but no lives lost. Nearly all his pronouncements have lessened in impact. For example, it is Harras, not Oderbruch in the film who states the lack of any real motive for Oderbruch's actions, other than a feeling of shame, and Oderbruch's impassioned argument for the necessity of the defeat of Germany for her spiritual salvation, is weakened to the somewhat dubious viewpoint that Germany seems certain to lose the war. An examination of an important section of dialogue from the play and of its film variant should suffice to illustrate the extent of the alterations made to Oderbruch's character. In Act III of the play we find:

Harras: Und warum trefft ihr uns—aus dem Dunkel, aus dem Hinterhalt? Warum trefft ihr uns—anstatt des Feindes?
Oderbruch: Ihr seid seine Waffe. Die Waffe, mit der er siegen kann. Und wenn er siegt, Harras—wenn Deutschland in diesem Krieg siegt—dann ist Deutschland verloren. Dann ist die Welt verloren.
Harras: Haben Sie bedacht, was Niederlage heisst? Fremdherrschaft? Neue Gewalt? Und neue Unterjochung?
Oderbruch: Es gibt keine Unterjochung, die nicht Befreiung wäre —für unser Volk.
Harras: Ist denn kein andrer Weg—um Deutschland zu befreien?
Oderbruch: Wissen Sie einen andern Weg?
Harras: Wenn ich ihn wüsste—dann wüssten ihn Millionen.
Oderbruch: Das war die Antwort. Es ist kein anderer Weg. Wir brauchen die Niederlage. Wir dürsten nach Untergang. Wir müssen dazu helfen—mit eigner Hand. Nur dann können wir, gereinigt, auferstehn.[20]

In the film-script this is softened to:

Oderbruch macht eine Bewegung. Er ist für einen Augenblick unsicher. Mit einer beginnenden Erregung sagt er, immer versuchend, sich zu beherrschen:

Dieser Krieg ist nicht mehr zu gewinnen. Das wissen jetzt langsam auch die, die ihm zugestimmt haben. Das ahnen sogar die, die ihn gebettelt haben. Jetzt kommt Amerika. Du warst drüben. Du weisst, was die amerikanische Rüstung aufbringen wird. Jeder Tag, den dieser Wahnsinn früher zu Ende ist—

Er bricht verzweifelt ab:

Ach, wozu lässt Du mich das alles aussprechen?

. . . . . .

Ich weiss natürlich, dass ich so gut wie nichts ausrichte. Was kann ein Einzelner tun? Es ist sogar die Frage, ob man etwas tun soll.

Fast hilflos bricht er ab:

Ich wollte nicht Mord mit Mord bekämpfen.[21]

Whatever the reasons therefore for these alterations, they mark the beginning of a new and cautious Zuckmayer, imbued with a feeling of social responsibility. From Oderbruch onwards this earnest school of heroes follow their impulses initially as much as Bückler and Harras, but come to the ultimate realisation that this is a selfish and sinful path. Individuality must be sacrificed to the public good. Even after Oderbruch's enforced metamorphosis, his position is not without ambiguity, and it is not until the next play, *Gesang im Feuerofen* (1950), that Zuckmayer resolves the problem. It is an interesting play, enacted on two levels—one cosmic, the other earthly. It is based on two extracts from the *Basler National-Zeitung* (October 8, 1948), one telling of the execution of a former member of the Maquis who had betrayed his comrades to the Nazis, causing them to be burnt alive in a derelict castle, and another, seemingly with no connection, describing how forty-four whales came ashore at Florida and resisting all efforts to return them to the water, eventually died on land. The first report needs no comment, as it is around this incident that the action takes place and the traitor,

Louis Creveaux, is judged guilty by heaven and earth alike. The second report is used apocalyptically, as an indication that an unparalleled act of savagery is at hand, similar to one that would bring about the end of the world. As one of the German soldiers in the army of occupation says:

> "Das ist nur einmal in tausend Jahr. Da tauchen grosse Scharen aus dem Meer, man könnte auf ihren Rücken durch die Wellen gehn, und lassen sich auf den Sand spülen, um zu sterben. Das ist die Zeit, wo der Luzifer auf die Erde kommt, und keiner mehr weiss, was gut oder schlecht ist. Was im Wasser lebt, will aufs Land, und was in der Luft atmet, will ins Feuer, und die Erde nimmt die Toten nicht mehr auf, sie legen nackt ohne Gräber. Aber denn ist die Heimkehr ganz nahe."[22]

The play suffers to some extent from being enacted on two levels. It is not that the blending of the cosmic and the earthly is not a valid device, but a certain lip-service to an out-of-date Expressionism is noticeable in the introduction of the figures Vater Wind, Mutter Frost and Bruder Nebel. Louis Creveaux's crime against humanity and the earth itself is sufficiently clear without the use of anthropomorphism. Neither do confused biblical references elucidate matters. Louis Creveaux, the bastard son of a dypsomaniac Frenchwoman and a German soldier of the First World War, also fails to convince us as a symbol of international hatred, for he is so uncompromisingly evil and sub-human that he lacks credibility.

One of the high-lights of the play, however, is the dialectical dispute between two young Resistance workers, Marcel, a Communist, and Francis, a Catholic priest. Their differences are ones of method.

Francis: Du weisst, Marcel, dass ich zu euch halte. Und dass ich die äusseren Folgen nicht fürchte. Aber da sind andere Dinge—die fürchte ich.

Marcel: Wovon sprichst du jetzt?

Francis: Von den Waffen. Ihr habt hier eine Zuflucht gefunden, das ist in Ordnung, was mich anlangt. Aber es werden hier Waffen versteckt, von vielen Händen, und wer das Versteck weiss, kann sie benutzen. Das ist nicht in Ordnung.

Marcel: Francis, du bist kein Narr, obwohl du dich manchmal so stellst. Sollen wir mit Dessertgabeln kämpfen? Sollen wir Schneebällen schmeissen und Kirschkerne spucken, wenn es losgeht?

Francis: Es mag ein Kampf bevorstehen, den die Waffe entscheidet. So weit sind wir noch nicht. Ich bin für den Widerstand—aber ich bin nicht für Meuchelmord.

. . . .

Marcel: Es sind rohe Zeiten, Kaplan. Mit zarten Händen kann man sie nicht verändern.
Francis: Aber mit reinen Händen! Sonst verändert man nichts. —Man zählt von alters her die Völker nicht nach Fäusten, sondern nach Seelen.
Marcel: Der Gegner zählt nach Panzern, Gewehren und Handgranaten. Und nach Leichen waggonweise.
Francis: Drum wird er verlieren. Wer an Mengen glaubt, erliegt dem Gesetz der Menge.[23]

As given here both views are acceptable, but also incompatible and so it comes as something of a shock to hear Marcel's words in Act III to his men as the flames close round them.

"Kamaraden, wir sind ausersehen, für unsre Sache zu sterben. Jetzt kommt es nur noch drauf an, wie wir es bestehn. Wer es nicht tapfer tut, der war nie wert, gelebt zu haben. Jeder hat freie Wahl. Ich will denen da draussen nicht in die Bahn laufen, wie ein schussbares Wild. Und wer ihnen lebend in die Hände fiele, der wüsste nicht ob er stark bleiben kann, beim Verhör. Wenn wir das Ende hier erwarten, fallen wir unbesiegt. Feuer und Rauch tun rasche Arbeit, und unsre letzte Waffe sei unsre glühende Asche auf ihr Haupt."[24]

Here, of course, is the solution of the Oderbruch problem. Resistance, or opposition to authority of any kind, is allowable only if one does not cause harm to others in any way. It must, therefore, be passive. In the light of this play, the altered dedication to *Des Teufels General* also becomes meaningful :

"Den ersten Entwurf zu diesem Stück widmete ich im Jahre 1942 DEM UNBEKANNTEN KÄMPFER. Jetzt widme ich es dem Andenken meiner von Deutschlands Henkern aufgehängten Freunde THEODOR HAUBACH, WILHELM LEUSCHNER, GRAF HELMUTH VON MOLTKE."[25]

All the three men mentioned were supporters of passive resistance to Hitler.

One feels that *Hochland* must have been placated to at least some degree by this play. Francis, as the representative of Catholicism, is surely a most acceptable replacement for Oderbruch.

The question of increased adherence to Catholic orthodoxy in the more recent works of Zuckmayer is an interesting one and forms a parallel with his increasingly conservative social views. Protestants have never come off very well in his work—they either do not figure at all or are treated deprecatingly, like the hot-Gospeller, Nathaniel, in *Ein Sommer in Österreich* (1937). In *Der fröhliche Weinberg* Catholicism has mainly only linguistic interest, in that its beliefs and doctrines are crudely reflected in colourful oaths and expletives; whilst in *Schinderhannes* there is a barely disguised antagonism to the Church. By the post-war period, there is a more affectionate feeling towards it as expressed in the story *Der Seelenbräu* (1945), coupled with a nostalgia for the Salzburg area where Zuckmayer had lived happily until the "Anschluss". Although Catholicism as such is not stressed in *Gesang im Feuerofen*, it is not insignificant that the chief protagonist is a Catholic priest who advocates an attitude to life and its problems which is approved by the author. It is only a stone's throw away from the dominant role played by the Catholic Church in Zuckmayer's latest novel, *Die Fastnachtsbeichte* (1959)—a "whodunnit" of complicated and intricate proportions. All the mistakes and sins culminating in the murder of one of the characters result from sexual experiences, and this statement by Viola, erstwhile mistress of the murdered man, indicates a striking departure from the attitude to erotic relationships in the earlier works.

> "Denn ich liebte ihn—ich liebt ihn tödlich, mörderisch—ich wusste nichts von der Liebe, jetzt weiss ich, sie ist eine furchtbare, eine unbarmherzige Gewalt."[26]

It is true that one couple retain something of the idyllic passion that forms the "raison d'être" of *Ein Bauer aus dem Taunus* and *Die Magdalena von Bozen*. The slow-witted brother of the murdered man and the tart with the heart of gold are allowed to love, for by doing so they do not affect the lives or happiness of anyone else. But they do not convince us. In the lives of all the other characters love, unless accompanied by a sense of responsibility, is shown to be a dangerous and disastrous phenomenon. One by one all the characters who have deviated from the Catholic norm, confess their crimes to the priest, Henrici, and are shown how best to make atonement. The title of the novel reveals the importance of the sacrament of penance and the work opens and concludes with a confession. Even the agnostic nobleman, Panezza, virtually makes a confession, the only difference being that he does not go to church to do so, nor use the accepted formula.

This device had already been used in the play *Das kalte Licht* (1955). Here it bears no outward relation to sacramental confession, for the priest-figure is exemplified in a member of the British Civil Service, Northon, and the penitent is a naturalised German scientist, Wolters. Wolters, who has betrayed information relating to the manufacture of the atomic bomb to Russia, is based on the character of Klaus Fuchs and it is obviously the author's intention that he should be a continuation of the Oderbruch-Marcel "Problematik". In his *Nachwort zum kalten Licht*, Zuckmayer states that the initial impetus for the play was the Fuchs case, but that this merely served as a point of departure and that the play was not conceived as a documentary. His theme is "nicht die Spaltung des Atoms, sondern die Krise des Vertrauens" or as he says elsewhere in the *Nachwort*, "Verwirrung des Menschen in unserer Zeit". But for all that, Wolters' circumstances approximate so closely to those of Fuchs, even in minute details, that we cannot help but make comparisons. And whereas Fuchs is a man of definite views whose case is a clear one of ideological betrayal—like Oderbruch and potentially, Marcel—Wolters is a confused, immature case for a psychiatrist. It is this fact which makes nonsense of the "conversion" of Wolters by Northon. For in his protracted interrogation, Northon assumes that he is dealing with a character of the Fuchs mentality—that is to say, a purely ideological betrayer. Wolters is far from being so clear-cut, however. Not only is he swayed by ideological arguments, but also by bitterness at the British policy of deporting Nazis and non-Nazi aliens alike to Canada, only to be recalled when they can be of use to the war-effort, as in his own case. To some extent this factor is not entirely absent from Fuchs' motives, although it is merely a contributory not a primary factor in his case. Wolters' motives become less convincing, however, when they include a superior of such outstanding wickedness that he is utterly beyond credibility and when a love affair between the superior's wife and Wolters develops, the bounds of the ludicrous have been not only reached but overstepped. For Wolters' dilemma is that of a man continually vacillating between proselytism and apostasy. He is a member of the Communist Party in Germany. When he flees to Britain, he does not make any contact with the Party and desires British citizenship. He continues to be apolitical and pro-British until his disillusionment at his deportation to Canada and only then does the Communist Buschmann, who has pestered him since his arrival in Britain, have any success with him. By the time the climacteric has been reached in his relationship with Hjördis, he has been delivering information to the Russians for some time, and yet we are given to understand that if she had not demanded an explanation of whom he was meeting at Santa Fé and had not broken off their relationship, he might have put an end to his spying activities. Consequently, after so many comings and goings, we are not really surprised when Northon manages to extract a confession from him. And, of course, a conversion from such a confused personality as Wolters, is itself worthless. He might easily recant tomorrow. One is left with the uncomfortable feeling, that Northon is introduced not to lift the weight of guilt from Wolters' shoulders, but to serve as a mouthpiece for the author's own theories. Northon is referred to in the *Nachwort* as an "intakt Gebliebener" and his arguments follow exactly the same line as those of Francis, who "convinces" Marcel, and the German press and public who were largely instrumental in the reshaping of the Oderbruch of the film. The question of guilt and conversion is clearly defined in the *Nachwort*.

> "Der Mensch tritt hier, wie in der antiken Tragödie, aus seinen natürlichen und sittlichen Grenzen heraus, greift ins Weltschicksal ein. An diesem Übertritt wird er schuldig, an dieser Schuld muss er scheitern. Die Erkenntnis der Schuld, durch die dramatische Gegenüberstellung mit einem in seinen menschlichen Grenzen intakt Gebliebenen, ist die Wurzel einer möglichen Entsühnung."(27)

These "conversions" are in fact the main weaknesses of the post-war works, not the fact that they have largely departed from the cheerful, bawdy atmosphere of the "Volksstück", nor that they are more serious and problematic in content. The charge that Zuckmayer is ill at ease with an intellectual atmosphere seems to have no foundation, for we are surely not to believe that a serious consideration of the divided loyalties involved in resistance and treason is so intellectual as to be beyond the ability of so versatile a writer as Zuckmayer. As I have tried to show, the main defect in his major post-war works is the tendency to force a character to fit into a fixed compartment which meets with the author's approval—in this case, the subordination of the individual and his ego to the requirements of society. This is not to say, of course, that Zuckmayer does not have the right to his own philosophy, but only that it would be more convincing dramatically if his protagonist did not automatically err, and then be convinced by a second protagonist. Much of the greatness and grandeur of *Des Teufels General* is due to the defiance of Harras and his unswerving devotion to his own ideal. Death is the only dignified and characteristic solution. In this the work becomes a tragedy in the fullest sense. This aspect could, one feels, be developed. For the serious post-war works have in many ways the material of tragedy and might well be more suited to such a treatment rather than the much less compelling one of sin and atonement. One critic (Peter Weiser, *Frankfurter Allgemeine Zeitung*, October 18, 1961), saw possibilities of Greek tragedy in Zuckmayer's latest play to date, *Die Uhr schlägt eins* (1961), where the guilt of one generation is visited mercilessly on the next. The play, indeed, might be more effective as a trilogy, for the variety of themes which it treats are too many for one action—the German conscience over the Jews, murder, gang-warfare, the Berlin East-West question, Nazis in the Bundesrepublik, the Korean War, euthanasia—all these are layered one upon the other all in the space of nine "Bilder". The dying hero, Gerhard, gives us indeed promise of the possibility of further heroes of the Schinderhannes, Harras type. He receives enlightenment, but from his own experience, not as a result of dialectic. His concluding words could apply to any of Zuckmayer's truly great and uncompromising heroes.

> "Wenn einer sagt, die Eltern sind schuld, der belügt sich. Wir sind nicht Herr unsrer Geburt. Wir sind nicht Herr unsrer Geschicke. Aber der Mensch ist Herr seiner Seele."(28)

It is difficult to know where to place Zuckmayer in the literature of the twentieth century. He cannot claim to be an innovator like Brecht, nor does he subscribe to the views of any particular groups of writers such as the "Young Angries", the Existentialists, or those who feel that the Theatre of the Absurd offers the only true reality in a chaotic world. His conservatism has its drawbacks, as I have tried to indicate. Both *Galilei Galileo* and *Die Physiker* are more powerful plays about the role of the scientist in society than *Das kalte Licht*, for instance. But, nevertheless, because he is uncommitted as a writer, he is able to offer us a very great variety of dramatic techniques and themes: Expressionism, Naturalism and mysticism, the indeterminate past, historical and contemporary figures, dramatic and epic theatre, comedy and tragedy. Perhaps his greatest contribution to this century is his complete and utter love of fatherland in its truest sense. He is the most German of German writers and it is for this reason that he has so often been his country's harshest critic. Despite its comedy, the social criticism inherent in *Der Hauptmann von Köpenick* cannot be denied, and no more agonised indictment of his beloved country's error could be found than in *Des Teufels General.* He leaves us in no doubt that Voigt and Gunderloch are better patriots than the Wilhelminian State and Knuzius, in spite of the latter's militaristic bombast, and it is clearly a matter of extreme pathos to him when a man ceases to believe that he has any roots at all, as in the case of Wolters.

In the Introduction to volume 4 of her social and political treatise, *Der Verrat im 20. Jahrhundert*, Margret Boveri pays this tribute to Zuckmayer:

> "Das schönste *pro domo* unserer Tage, das ich kenne, ist die Auseinandersetzung des Emigranten und Dichters Carl Zuckmayer mit seiner deutschen Heimat. Es gehört, ebenso wie Zuckmayers im Krieg gehaltenen Gedächtnisrede auf den Angehörigen des Kreisauer Kreises Carlo Mierendorff, wie *Des Teufels General* und *Das kalte Licht* zu meinem Themenkreis. Die beiden Theaterstücke behandeln den Verrat

in bezug auf die totalitären Ideologien. Das Prosastück *Pro Domo* und die Gedächtnisrede sind Beispiele für die positive Seite des Themas: die Frage, wie ein Mensch es vermag, in der Verratssituation, in die er gestellt war, die Treue zu halten nicht so sehr dem Vaterland, nicht der Nation, nicht einer bestimmten politischen Idee seines Landes, sondern dem Bild, das er von diesem Land und von den Freunden in diesem Land in seinem Herzen trug."(29)

It is a tribute of which Zuckmayer can be justly proud.

TRANSLATIONS

1. Peasants from the valley rebel against the tyranny of the Bergjoch overlord. A horrible episode with a whip. Fleeing wife. A smith. Missing daughter. Statue on the bridge. Rural prophet. Lechery. Toil. Madness. Pangs of love. Force. Impotence. I will gladly explain the structure of this drama if someone else will tell me what it is all about. Is only difficult to say what is happening because everything is happening.

2. They were all one to him, the woman whose name he could now barely pronounce and the woman back home, Anna Barbara, who was waiting for him; like the fields he had ploughed here and there. And the child, which was crying there and the child which the woman in the Taunus was carrying for him, both burnt within him and would not let him be and had to be brought together.

3. The fruit-blossom was long past, a good crop had set in on the cherry-trees and the currant bushes stood heavy with fruit.

4. I know what I want! I don't give a damn for public opinion! I've got my affairs sorted out, so I can afford to! What do people expect anyway? When they buy wine, they have it tested first, otherwise I can flog them stale vinegar instead of communion wine! When a man buys a sow he wants to know that she'll farrow. For this reason the parish arranges the mating to be done in public. But if a man enters matrimony where the health of body and soul is an important factor to both parties, he's expected to play blind man's buff, is he?

5. Schinderhannes was in no way what one understands today to be a revolutionary. He was a rebel. . . . He rebelled not from "a recognised need", but from an excess of high spirits.

6. That's news to me, that one gets anywhere by working!

7. O: Don't talk rubbish. You haven't got much up top have you? What do you want in Potsdam anyway?

V: I want work.

O: Anyone can say that.

V: But I must find work. What else should I live for?

O: That's your worry. Mind you behave like a decent man. When a man *wants* work, then he gets it.

V: (shaking his head) No, no. It's like a roundabout, like a mill that grinds you to powder. If I don't report at the police station, I won't get any work, and if I don't have work then I can't report. So I'd rather get out. So give me a pass with a visa and then I can cross the frontier.

O: We're not authorised to do that.

8. *Organising* and *forming* are completely different disciplines. The organising powers of today, which are occupied with violence and social revolution, follow different laws from those which form and to which the human spirit has a duty at all times. Forming—I could just as well use the terms growth or self-moulding—is situated beyond what can be organised. Only where organisation finishes does the organic begin to exist.

9. H: You're not a human being unless you become part of an organised human society! After all, a bug lives!

V: That's it! It lives, Friedrich! And do you know why it lives? The bug comes first and then the organised bug-society! Human beings come first and then we can have organised human society!

H: You won't discipline yourself to anything, that's your trouble! If you want to be a human being you've got to discipline yourself, understand?

V: Discipline myself—all right! But to what? That's what I want to know! In that case the discipline's got to be a just one, Friedrich, and it isn't!—

10. O: (somewhat confused) Heil Hi— Good evening, President, Heil Hitler, Doctor.

H: Just say Good Adolf—that'll suit everybody's taste. (To the others) I take it you gentlemen have been introduced to each other—those of you who are not related? This is our Director of Culture. Dr. Schmidt-Lausitz from the Impropaganda Mystery—I can never pronounce the words—a hangover from my fighting days in Africa. Schmidt-Lausitz, not to be confused with Schmidt-Lützelsdorff, Schmidt-Pforzheim, Schmidt-Belcher and other gentlemen with no special marks of distinction.

11. The man who has become the Devil's general on earth and has bombed a clear path for him—he's got to give him quarters in hell, as well.

12. Headquarters? Everything gone according to plan. General Harras killed in the course of carrying out his duty. Whilst testing a fighter. Yes, indeed. State funeral.

13. There is no excuse. At least if I want to write one for the boss (points upwards with his cigar)—then I could say it was on account of my mother. But otherwise—I went into the business with my eyes open and with no illusions.

14. Everybody these days is saving something that he can't demonstrate. Religion, culture, democracy, western civilisation—wherever you spit there's a crusade. If I could just meet one man who admits that he only wants to save his skin. That's what I'd like to do, too. But not between beers. If I've ever had an ideal it's been a very modest one; not to have to spit at myself. Not even when the wind changes.

15. Well, now's the time to look at ourselves in the mirror and be filled with emotion. At what noble men we are. That's how we look at any rate. We've all got a Jew or two we can sooth our consciences with so that

we can sleep at nights. But you can't buy yourself off that way. That's just self-deception. We're guilty of all that happens to the thousands of others whom we don't know and whom we don't help. Guilty and condemned for all eternity. It's worse to ignore an evil than to perpetrate it.

16. We cannot and must not hush up the deeds of the members of the Resistance, those men who were at that time the real heroes of Germany, from fear of another legend about a "stab in the back". We need to do just the opposite; we must set up a monument to these men, of whom Oderbruch is only a faint shadow, and must make them into the ideal of a new generation of Germans who have every right to be proud of them.

17. I myself am not in agreement with Oderbruch. For this problem extends from an ethical and political view to the heart of a religious one. It is concerned with the sanctity of life, in which I categorically believe.

18. He (Carlo Mierendorff) was denied the chance of political activity in the Germany of today, for this Underground movement which you can read about in the papers only exists in Hollywood. The real Underground movement in Germany goes much deeper. There the heart and the soul and the mind have gone under ground and none of us knows how or when or in what guise they will see the light of day again.

19. I have tried to reduce the problem of Oderbruch to a formula devoid of ambiguity. For the Oderbruch of the play there was little possibility of development owing to dramatic requirements. The film, since it develops in epic rather than dramatic fashion, gives us the opportunity to depict the character of Oderbruch and his actions in such a way that misunderstanding cannot occur.

20. H: And why do you attack us—out of the darkness and behind our backs? Why do you attack us—and not the enemy?

O: You are the enemy's weapon. The weapon which will make him victorious. And if he wins, Harras—if Germany wins this war—then Germany is doomed. Then the whole world is doomed.

H: Have you considered what defeat means? Foreign rulers? New force? And new bondage?

O: There is no bondage that would not be liberation for our people.

H: Is there no other way—to liberate Germany?

O: Do you know of any?

H: If I knew it—then millions would.

O: There is your answer. There is no other way. We need defeat. We long for destruction. We must help bring it about—with our own hands. Only after purification can we hope for resurrection.

21. We can't hope to win this war now. Even those who consented to it have slowly realised this. Even those who begged for it have an inkling of this truth. Now America is joining in. You were in the States. You know what American mobilisation can do. Every day which can bring this madness nearer to its end.... (He breaks off in despair) Oh, why do you let me say all this? I know, of course, that I can do practically nothing. What can a man working alone do? There's even the question of whether one ought to do anything.... (Almost helplessly he breaks off) I didn't want to substitute murder for murder.

22. This only happens once in a thousand years. Then great schools of them come up from the sea—you could ride through the waves on their backs—and then they get washed up on to the sand and die. This marks the time when Lucifer comes to the world and no one knows any longer what's good and what's bad. The creatures from the sea want to come on land and those in the air want to go into the fire and the earth will not take in her dead—they just lie about naked and unburied. But this means that our homecoming isn't far off.

23. F: Marcel, you know that I am one of you. And that I'm not afraid of the obvious consequences. But there are other things—which I am afraid of.

M: What are you referring to?

F: The weapons. You've made a hide-out for yourselves here and that's all right as far as I'm concerned. But the weapons are hidden here by many hands, and anyone who knows where the hide-out is can use them. That's not all right.

M: Francis, you aren't a fool, even though you do pretend to be at times. Are we to fight with dessert forks? Are we to throw snowballs and spit cherry stones when the carve-up begins?

F: There may be a struggle which will be decided by the weapons we use. We don't know yet. I'm in favour of resistance, but not of murder.

M: We live in harsh times, father. They won't be changed by soft hands.

F: But by clean hands! Otherwise one never changes anything.—It is customary to count the nations not by their fists but by their souls.

M: The enemy counts by tanks, guns and hand-grenades. And by corpses, by the cartload.

F: That's why he'll lose. If you put your faith in crowds, you will be subjected to the laws of the crowd.

24. Comrades, we have chosen to die for our cause. Now it is only a question of how we do it. The man who doesn't die bravely was never worthy of having lived. You all have a free choice. I don't want to rush out into the path of those men out there, like a hunted deer. And if you fall into their hands alive, you don't know if you could stand firm at your trial. If we wait here for our end to come we shall fall as conquerors. Fire and smoke will do their work quickly and our final weapon will be our glowing ashes heaped on to their heads.

25. In 1942 I dedicated the first draft of my play TO THE UNKNOWN WARRIOR. Now I dedicate it to the memory of my friends who were hanged by Germany's executioners—THEODOR HAUBACH, WILHELM LEUSCHNER, COUNT HELMUTH VON MOLTKE.

26. For I loved him—I loved him frenziedly, insanely.—I knew nothing of love, but now I know that it is a terrible and pitiless force.

27. In this context as in ancient tragedy, man steps outside his natural and moral boundaries and intervenes in the fate of the universe. By this transgression he incurs guilt and by this guilt he is destroyed. The acknowledgement of guilt, by means of an encounter with one who has remained intact within his human limits, is the source of a possible redemption.

28. If we say that our parents are to blame we deceive ourselves. We do not control the circumstances of our birth. We do not control our fate. But man is master of his own soul.

29. The finest *pro domo* of our times with which I am acquainted is one where the emigrant and poet Carl Zuckmayer comes to terms with his German background. It has a place in my thesis, as have also Zuckmayer's wartime speech in commemoration of a member of the Kreisau circle, Carlo Mierendorff; as have *Des Teufels General* and *Das kalte Licht*. The two plays are concerned with treason in the sphere of totalitarian ideologies. The prose work *Pro Domo* and the commemorative speech are examples of the positive aspect of this theme. The question here is how a man placed in a position where treason is possible, may keep faith, not so much with his fatherland, nor his nationality, nor with any particular political idea for which his country stands, but rather with the image of this country and of his friends which he has carried with him in his heart.

BIBLIOGRAPHY

The latest edition of Zuckmayer's *Gesammelte Werke*, in four volumes, was published by S. Fischer Verlag, Frankfurt, 1960. Some prose and autobiographical works are not included in it and these are obtainable in single editions as follows:

Ein Sommer in Österreich, short story. Vienna, Bermann-Fischer Verlag, 1937.
Pro Domo, essay. Stockholm, Bermann-Fischer Verlag, 1938.
Second Wind, autobiography. Tr. Elizabeth Reynolds Hapgood. London, Harrap, and New York, Doubleday, Doran, 1940.
Carlo Mierendorff, Porträt eines deutschen Sozialisten, speech. New York, published privately, 1944.
Die Brüder Grimm, essay. Frankfurt, Suhrkamp Verlag, 1948.
Die langen Wege, speech on receiving Goethe prize. Frankfurt, Fischer Verlag, 1952.
Herbert Engelmann, completion of Gerhart Hauptmann's play. Munich, Beck, 1952.
Ein Weg zu Schiller, essay for Schiller bicentenary. Frankfurt, Fischer Verlag, 1959.
Die Uhr schlägt eins, drama. Frankfurt, Fischer Verlag, 1961.
Ein voller Erdentag, speech for Gerhart Hauptmann centenary. Frankfurt, Fischer Verlag, 1962.

Little has so far appeared in the way of secondary material on Zuckmayer. There is a useful Festschrift *Fülle der Zeit*, Frankfurt, Fischer Verlag, 1956, containing articles by Luise Rinser, Gertrud von le Fort, Johannes Urdizil and Alexander Lernet-Hloenia and also some unpublished material of Zuckmayer's.

There are two good assessments of his work. One by Ingeborg Engelsing-Malek: *"Amor Fati" in Zuckmayers Dramen,* Konstanz, Rosgarten Verlag, 1960, deals with a specific theme in Zuckmayer's dramatic work and the second by W. Adling: *Die Entwicklung des Dramatikers Carl Zuckmayers,* Leipzig, 1956, was originally a dissertation, but has recently been published. It is a very sound appraisal of Zuckmayer's dramatic (and other) works, although sometimes the scholarship takes second place to Marxist dialectic. An unpublished dissertation, W. Teelen: *Die Gestaltungsgesetze im Bühnenwerk Carl Zuckmayers,* Marburg, 1952, is also of interest. There is a useful general chapter on Zuckmayer in H. Garten: *Modern German Drama,* London, Methuen, 1959, and several articles—O. Basil: *Der österreichische Autor und sein Werk: Umriss von Carl Zuckmayer,* which contains some unpublished material and is to be found in *Wort in der Zeit,* Hft. 6, 1960, Jg. VI; H. Glade: *Carl Zuckmayer's theory of aesthetics, Monatshefte,* 1960; G. Guder, *Carl Zuckmayer's post-war dramas, Modern Languages,* Vol. XXXV, No. 2. 1954; I. Loram: *The resistance movement in the recent German drama, German Quarterly,* 33, 1960; M. B. Peppard: *Cold Light in a divided world, Monatshefte,* 49, 1957; M. B. Peppard: *Moment of moral decision. Carl Zuckmayer's latest plays, Monatshefte,* 4, 1952.

Zuckmayer's latest novel, *Die Fastnachtsbeichte* (Carnival Confession) has been translated by John and Necke Mander, London, Methuen, 1961.

There are school editions, with useful introductions and notes, of four works by Zuckmayer: *Der Seelenbräu,* ed. A. R. Robinson, London, Harrap, 1960; *Das kalte Licht,* ed. F. C. Ryder, London, Methuen, 1960; *Der Hauptmann von Köpenick,* ed. H. F. Garten, London, Methuen, 1961 and *Des Teufels General,* ed. C. B. Johnson, London, Harrap, 1962.

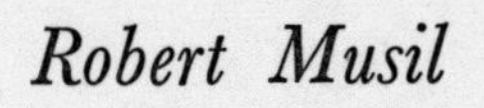
Robert Musil

Robert Musil

by YVONNE ISITT

On November 6, 1880, Robert Musil was born in Klagenfurt, Austria, to a railway engineer, Alfred, and his wife Hermine. His upbringing as an only child was the lonelier because his parents' marriage proved to be the strangely unhappy relationship of two incompatible people who could nevertheless not become entirely loveless.

Two years later the family moved to Steyr, and even from this early period of his life, Musil retained memories of people and events which he later used in his writing. The year 1891 was spent in Brno (then Brünn), where his father became professor of engineering at the Technical University. The following year Musil was sent to the military academy in Eisenstadt and in 1894 to that in Mährisch-Weisskirchen, where he stayed until 1897. Although he loathed the life in both of them, he continued the training for an army officer for a further three months in Vienna, before rejecting it finally as a choice of career, in favour of studying engineering. He studied at Brno from 1898–1901, at the end of which time he qualified, and worked for a year as an assistant at the Technical University in Stuttgart—only to change his mind again. Consequently, he studied philosophy and experimental psychology in Berlin from 1904–1908, ultimately gaining his doctorate with a dissertation on Ernst Mach.

The year 1911 saw his marriage to Martha Marcovaldi, née Heimann, and his appointment, which lasted until 1914, at the library of the Technical University in Vienna. After this, for a matter of months only, he became an editor of *Die Neue Rundschau* in Berlin, whither the intellectual pursuits of that city had attracted him. During the war he served as an officer in the Austrian army, and was decorated for editing a military newspaper, as well as for bravery. During a post-war period in Vienna, from 1919–22, he was employed by the government in the Ministry for Foreign Affairs, and the Ministry for Military Affairs, and worked for a time in 1921 as a critic for the *Prager Presse*.

Thereafter he became a free-lance author, attempting to live on his limited, private means. Friends who were aware of his increasing financial difficulties, founded a society to help in 1934, but this necessarily collapsed four years later, when Musil left Vienna to spend the rest of his life in voluntary exile in Switzerland. He died in Geneva on April 15, 1942, after a period which had been troubled and poor. Hopes of finishing *The Man Without Qualities*, and of seeing it published, had been apparently annihilated by the hand of circumstance. Musil left the novel as the monumental and complex fragment of his literary creation.

THERE was an imminent duality about Robert Musil. It ranged about his career as a spirit of indecision, filtered through his mind as an agonisingly keen awareness of the irony of human existence, and revealed itself in his work as a constant ambivalence. It was distilled finally into the positive thought of a "morality of possibilities", the product of Ulrich,* the man without developed "qualities"† only because his vast potential was coupled with a fundamental and prohibitive integrity. His was a make-up, shared by Musil himself, which dictated that any quality propagated independently and for its own sake, detached itself at once from an ultimate cause, became a cause in itself, and was at once useless. "Ich bin auf das Äusserste vielseitig ungebildet"(1) was how Musil once described himself. Ulrich might have said the same thing. Their common creed forbade them to become talented, for consciously to develop a talent involved the decision to act, which in turn involved the deception of a shift of emphasis from all things generally, to one thing particularly. The only honest way to live was in unceasing recognition of an infinity of possibility, void of a finite scale of judgment, refusing to admit right and wrong as absolutes.

Many critics have called Musil most things, but few, until comparatively recently, a good author. His concern for the abysmal dichotomy of his own and all life, and his constant endeavour to force this recognition into a pattern by which he, and man, could live, hoodwinked numbers of them. They called him psychologist, pervert, "educational Philistine". A few, more far-sighted, saw something more; Thomas Mann was one, and Hugo von Hoffmannsthal was another. It was the latter who praised "Grigia", one of the three stories in *Drei Frauen* (1924), although he criticised

* Hero of *Der Mann ohne Eigenschaften*. It is not easy to discuss this novel at present, since the only available edition (cf. bibliography) has been fiercely attacked by Ernst Kaiser and Eithne Wilkins on the grounds that it is not a fair representation of what Musil wrote, and of what he finally intended to include in the published work. Their accusations are based on ten years' research with the MSS, which must give them considerable substance, although they seem to have been delivered in an unwarrantedly harsh tone. At any rate, they make it impossible for us to steer, for the moment, anything but an obstacle course, along which no comment may be made without the reservation that we are necessarily working from the only available edition.

† It is a matter of speculation whether "qualities" is the best way of translating *Eigenschaften*, as Kaiser and Wilkins have chosen to do. In some ways it is certainly misleading for the English reader, since Ulrich is honest, sincere, capable—and these are qualities. On the other hand he remains too functional ever to possess the *characteristics* of a real person; he is a man without character.

its lack of construction, but it was in reaction to this same work that a leading Braunschweig newspaper wrongly asserted "Man kann nicht sagen, dass auch Musil. . . . Suchender um die Synthese von Geist und Gefühl ist."[2] We may not like hitting this long nail, which must surely stretch back to the very dawn of philosophy when man began to be aware of himself, squarely on its rather common head, but once we have established firmly its basic position, we are free to enjoy and admire the individuality of Musil's construction.

This was the aim which was central to Musil's work and thought. He sought tirelessly to forge a link between the two realities of the human mind, which, as he experienced it, was divided against itself; the reality of the understanding, and a strange, "other" reality of the senses. That is why he has so often been called a psychologist, because he was concerned with the vaguaries of thought and feeling, locked apart without mutual means of communication. His own thought on the subject often descended like a depth-charge into the realm of human experience, but wrangling with the problems of motivation and behaviour at this level was a task which admitted only sparse results. One day, for example, Musil sat down to begin writing something under contract, which he anticipated would take him some six weeks, but which he finished only after two years of what he described as "verzweifelte Arbeit".[3] The result was the two Novellen published as *Vereinigungen* (1911). With his mind focused simultaneously on the twin poles of a dual reality, his literature could do little else but attempt to establish a bond between them.

Törless enters the battle as Musil's first and youngest hero (*Die Verwirrungen des Zöglings Törless* 1906). Like Ulrich, he reflects many of Musil's own traits, but at a much earlier age. For Törless is at school. He arrives there as a boy, and at first experiences a huge emptiness inside him which he can analyse as loneliness. He writes home with fervour, stretching out to a childhood which has suddenly forsaken him, ". . .; und er lebte nur in diesen Briefen".[4] Törless is standing at the point where two worlds meet, the world of the child and the world of the adult. And this is where Musil's ambivalence begins. Törless reflects the crushing irony of a young mind which finds suddenly it can no longer live by sensing, but which has not yet grasped that it must understand. He is unconsciously beginning to intercept the images which invade his mind with a growing critical capacity. If Freud had already published at this time, Musil would have had a store of relevant vocabulary on which to draw (although it is far more likely that he would have elected to fight his own battle!), for in Freudian terms Törless was leaving the world of conceptual reality, and entering that of perceptual reality. But Freud was not to publish for several more years, and the ironic experience of Törless is depicted in searching terms with a poignancy that a static vocabulary could never have achieved. Although the style of *Törless* has been claimed as the first example of Expressionism in German literature, and the apparent theme, homosexuality in a military academy, would seem to be pretty revolutionary, the ironic experience of the boy, which is revealed at a much deeper level, harks back as far as the Romantics. During 1905, the Romantic writers and philosophers had provided Musil with a reflection of the problems in which he himself was currently immersed. It is not without significance, for example, that Musil wrote in a diary for this year, "Ich lese jetzt Novalis, Heinrich von Ofterdingen".(5) Nor is this likely to be merely a stray jotting, for the diaries of this particular year are among the most important Musil wrote. His first entry for the year is to the effect that he is beginning to write a diary "...; ganz gegen meine sonstige Gewohnheit, aber aus klargesehenem Bedürfnis".(6) He goes on to explain his purpose, "Es soll nach vier Jahren der Zersplitterung mir Gelegenheit geben, jene Linie geistiger Entwicklung wiederzufinden, die ich für die meine halte".(7) Musil is here beginning the search destined to last his life-time. The diary of this year was begun with the special intention of its being used as a battle-field to sort out the contradictions of his ideas. Although his entries therefore, are unlikely to have been cursory, it would be exaggerated to assert a direct influence on *Törless* by a source as far removed as *Heinrich*. The interest lies in the fact that Musil's choice of literature at this time was often Romantic, and that his own thought seems to have seized upon the tenets of Romantic thought in a vicarious process of self-explanation; Heinrich and Törless stand at the same crossroads of boyhood and manhood, although well over a century separates them. But time cannot transmute experience, and Törless finds himself encountering in his own setting, much that Heinrich had encountered. Their mental experiences are often broadly comparable.

> "Ich weiss nicht, aber mich dünkt, ich sähe zwei Wege, um zur Wissenschaft der menschlichen Geschichte zu gelangen. Der eine, mühsam und unabsehlich, der Weg der Erfahrung, der andre, fast *ein* Sprung nur, der Weg der inneren Betrachtung".(8)

Heinrich's description has the coherence of a character created within an established literary order, in this case Romanticism, and reflects the objective clarity of the author's knowledge that there will be a resolution, the mythical "Erfüllung". Törless, by comparison, is incoherent. He stands well outside the safety of such an order, and his expression is stunted because he is a directly subjective upshot of an author who is searching just as frenziedly as he. He cannot know that the mythical resolution will be attempted by Ulrich in years to come. For the moment he is forced by his schoolmasters to deny his two realities, and to crush them into an ill-fitting unity in which he himself privately refuses to believe.

> "Ich weiss: die Dinge sind die Dinge und werden es wohl immer bleiben; und ich werde sie wohl bald so, bald so ansehen. Bald mit den Augen des Verstandes, bald mit den anderen. . . ."(9)

It is a mathematics lesson which furnishes Törless with an epitomising experience of something which, on the other hand, increases his awareness of the ironic circumstance to an almost unbearable degree, whilst on the other, it fills him with an exhilarating sense of wonder. He senses an unrelenting paradox, linked in an uncanny and almost unbelievable manner, with a tremendous facility of movement. The experience is shared with the theorist of the Romantics, Friedrich Schlegel, who advocated that irony was not only "Die Form des Paradoxen", but also an "ewige Agilität". Törless sensed the same paradox and concurrent agility through learning about imaginary numbers, in that, although they did not really exist, for practical purposes one could assume that they did exist, and furthermore, use this assumption as the factual basis for calculations which would otherwise be impossible. For Törless this meant access to a world without substance which nevertheless enjoyed a paradoxical existence by virtue of a workable, and thus legitimate assumption. He comprehends intuitively, by means of what he describes as a ". . . Brücke, von der nur Anfangs und Endpfeiler vorhanden sind",(10) a new world of a *different* reality, which he cannot reject because of its functional purpose in everyday life. He concludes, "Aber diese beiden hängen miteinander durch etwas zusammen, das es gar nicht gibt",(11) and the realisation makes him feel giddy. Like Ulrich, he cannot merely accept a thesis which works on a basis of "given that". For between the unprovable world of man's subjective experience and the provable world of man's objective cognisance is a chasm, as unappointable in space as T. S. Eliot's *Shadow* in *The Hollow Men* is elusive in time. Ulrich, for all his scientific ability, knows that even were he to calculate the amount of greenness in a whole lawn of grass, down to the exactest possible measurement, there would still remain an unbridgeable rift between this scientific reality, and the natural, untouched, experienced reality "... dass, grünes Gras eben grasgrün ist".(12) Something uncanny stands between them.

Musil's preoccupation with the ironic circumstance has its roots however, in something much firmer than a passing, youthful interest in Romantic problems, for this was but a brief reflection of an inborn condition. It is nurtured to a far greater extent by Musil's Austrian blood and founded on the Janus-headed literary tradition of Austria, of which the greatest dramatic exponent was Franz Grillparzer. It would be wrong to suggest that Musil drew his inspiration from the Viennese theatrical tradition, for he was not primarily a dramatist, nor was he au fait with this, or any other particular aspect of his national culture. But he shared the "double-vision" which resulted from the awareness of a deep dichotomy. It is the prevailing attitude to life presented by Austrian literature; the interplay of the magical and the real world in the *Zauberstück*, the interaction of magic and morality in the *Geisterstück*, the combination of spontaneity and rehearsed composition, of farce and pathos, so typical of Nestroy and Raimund, the incongruity of man as Franz Grillparzer sees him, guiltless in his original estate, but degraded and dislocated by the world at large, and, from one of Musil's contemporaries, the complete dissociation of Hofmannsthal's Maria/Mariquita. Because he was primarily an analyst, Musil transposed this inconclusive state of mind, which most Austrians had chosen to present within the momentarily total, but thereafter irretrievable, world of a drama, into the medium of the novel, where it could be scrutinised and examined. This is true even of his two dramas, for they take no advantage of the fully-emancipated, horizontal representation of life which the stage can command, but remain rather within safer, novellistic bounds, where the characters can retreat at will into the vertical world of their own subjectivity. Thus the need for action is superfluous, since progress through the plot is made possible only by the clash and reaction of inner events which subordinate outward circumstance to themselves. In *Die Schwärmer* (1920) the characters are ranged in two parallel lines, so to speak, which represent duelling attitudes to life. People are "so nahe . . . wie die Seiten eines Kartenblattes"[(13)]—but the thickness of the playing card, the chasm which denies communication between them, remains. The bridge still has no central supports. Thomas and Maria stand in opposition to Anselm and Regine. Thomas is a scientist and experimenter, cool and rational, as opposed to Anselm, who is a failure in life and ruled by his emotions. Maria is feminine, heavy and majestic, quite the opposite from the childlike, imaginative, but somewhat evil Regine. Musil uses the apparently trite "change partners" theme to indicate a possible synthesis at a deeply emotional level. The opposites attract and spiritual links appear to be forming; but the end is inconclusive and the process provides at most a momentary breathing-space in the constantly evolving fate of man's ironic duality—"es (ist) immer das gleiche Spielkarten, nur anders gemischt und ausgespielt".[14]

A first hint of the moveable moral scale of right and wrong, which is to be the guiding light of Ulrich's ethical philosophy, appears in this play as the characters seek to integrate themselves. But it has not yet been objectivised by Ulrich, and appears here still in its subjective form as a moral code graded by emotional intensity. An emotion so intense that it no longer answers to the circumstance which gave rise to it, but becomes autonomous, is the only force Musil is able to designate at this stage of his development, to attempt to form an honest and uncultivated link between the divided spheres of his experience of reality. In moods of intense anger or fear, the distinctions of personality are fused together in subjection to one overall cause, and only the emotion engendered continues to exist as a united, autonomous force. The distinctions of body and soul disappear for Thomas in his paroxysm of fury and disgust at the attraction he sees between Maria and Anselm, and which he expresses through a series of powerful, biological images.

> "Blut durchqualmt euch den Kopf! Das noch nicht vereinigte Mark steht in der Tiefsee der Körper wie Korallenwald! Vorstellungen rinnen hindurch wie die wandernden Wiesen blumenhäufiger Fischscharen! Du und Ich pressen sich geheimnisvoll vergrössert aus dem Kugelglas der Augen! und das Herz rauscht dazu!"[15]

An expression of tremendous sensuous potency is released through a flood of lyrical language—a poetic device which in itself indicates the fusion of physical and emotional aspects into the one intensity of the situation. The same fusion is evident in Anselm's "suicide", which is faked with the involvement of such emotional expenditure that it is indistinguishable from a real one. The incident gives Thomas his first impression of a scale of judgment extending in both directions into an infinity which by definition can know no absolutes. He is beginning to understand what it means to live with such intensity; later he may even understand Regine's cryptic pronouncement that all such people, she calls them "dreamers" (Träumer, the word has an unusual significance for Musil) share in a certain condition of creation and carry "den feurigen Tropfen" of creation in some degree within them. In other parts of his work Musil refers to this creative seed as "den Feuerkern",[16] and later on it is to take on a specific meaning for him. For the moment, it probably means that spark which engenders autonomy of emotion; which sets off the process of blurring the contours between mental and physical experience. But it cannot remove the barrier altogether to create a final synthesis in which the spheres are totally and reciprocally balanced. The nearest state to this perfection it can achieve is one in which physical form has no immediate implication of distinction, so that people may be identified by a property as wispy as a "Seelengeruch"—an indefinable, intangible, but individual scent of the soul: but even then there must come the final rub. Thomas, describing himself and Anselm in the third person says "Nichts unterscheidet sie vor sich selbst, als ein papierdünnes Gefühl, von geschlossenem Leib und das Hämmern des Bluts dahinter".(17) The barrier, albeit as thin as paper, still denies them complete integration of experience.

Vinzenz (*"Vinzenz und die Freundin bedeutender Männer"* 1924) is a grotesque extension of Thomas. Thomas only senses the unity which intense emotion can provide, Vinzenz has converted the feeling into an intimate and useful part of his knowledge. This is betrayed by the farcical scepticism with which his view of life is coloured, and which allows him to distort the infinite moral code which Thomas senses, into the sheer expediency of living a lie. Inspired perhaps by Anselm's "suicide", he advises Bärli, who intends to shoot Alpha and then himself, to use blank shots, for this will enable him to experience the murder and suicide he plans, without the inconvenience of police enquiries and hearses which would naturally ensue for others if the act were really to be committed! The suggestion is ludicrous because the play is a farce and because the author has not yet reached the stage where he feels that his infinite moral code can sincerely be implemented within society. This is to be Ulrich's task. Vinzenz' interests do not yet lie with mankind, but very much with himself, and he adopts the code of living a lie because it is useful to him personally. The device he uses for coercing reality into his own framework of expediency is language. He describes himself, when Bärli questions him about his profession, as "ein Wortemacher"—a maker of words. For Vinzenz, words have the power to seal over the crevices and divergencies which normally appear between experiences to rend them apart and to cause disunity in life. By believing in a concept which he expresses as "Kolibri", Vinzenz can allow the sheer power of words to reunite the disunity. If words are dissociated from their traditional meaning, they impute a meaning which heralds a totally new attitude to reality, just as Alpha, who summonses her five admirers at three o'clock in the morning to celebrate her Namenstag, flaunts tradition and has the effect on them which Bärli describes as looking through one's legs at life, so that "everything looks quite different and new". The name Kolibri, which (as W. Braun has pointed out) really means a tropical humming-bird, conjures up for Vinzenz a purely verbal concept of "roasted words", of "hot-coloured words which fly about in the flaming sun of primeval forests". The term is his manifestation of "der feurige Tropfen"; it no longer has any immediate reference to a bird, but, enjoying the freedom of a bird, it represents a primeval creativeness which words can possess if man will forbid himself to look beyond them, but will believe in them undeterredly at their face value. Alpha has this ability, which is why she cannot only make the world look "new and different", but also live a lie to the extent of disbelieving what to other people are obvious facts. She refuses to recognise as such, the mourning dress which she is wearing for Bärli, whom she believes to be dead, but on learning that he is still alive, she proclaims it to be a wedding dress instead, which she is wearing for Vinzenz. By any normal standards this is merely ridiculous, but for Alpha, the fact of pronouncing the words in which her fantasy sincerely wishes to believe, makes them true. In the same way, Bärli's blank shots, which Vinzenz calls "Kolibrischüsse", are real simply because he shot them with the same intensity of emotion as he would have felt for real shots. The whole episode sports the final, overlying texture of reality when Alpha reacts to the extent of thinking she had died as a result of them!

The process of allowing words to create their own reality has been well described (again by W. Braun) as "metaphorical living". It is based on deception; but not on malicious deception with an evil intent, but rather on a desire to improve on reality by means of a deceptive imagination. Vinzenz lies only in order to make his experience homogeneous. That is why he is able to refer afterwards to the whole situation, based entirely on his fabrications as it was, as a "reunion with his own soul". Ulrich's new morality is indeed shining through this double-edged situation in which Vinzenz finds himself, for, precisely by being a liar and a swindler according to the common code, he is being intensely true to himself and the dictates of his own soul. Even his soul is fantastic in its constitution of fabricated circumstances and situations; it can be what it wants to be, and it can deny itself being anything in particular. When Vinzenz says that such people are "fantastic liars", peopl whose lies fit the facts, he is really hinting at Ulrich's "Möglicl keitsmenschen", people who retain within them, the possibility of fitting with every fact. Vinzenz, who in his ludicrous way, is as anxious to remain uncommitted as Ulrich, even lies about his being a confidence man in order to banish any possible distinguishing marks or characteristics from him. But he lacks totally Ulrich's ethical vision; far from making a genuine attempt to establish a basic morality, he is fooling with life for what he can gain from it. For him it is all a trite experiment. In fact, when he eventually establishes that he can gain nothing from it, but must submit himself to a reality which admits no fabrications, and which induces him to become a valet, he is not really in the least disillusioned. He has never sincerely believed that the intense metaphorical power of words could do anything to eradicate the basic rift. The most he could do was to allow words to inherit the fantasy of his soul, and so cast a film of deception over the crevices of his own experience. He had said in his early conversation with Bärli that "one can join together pieces which do not belong, so that nobody notices"; but he himself knew all along that this could only provide temporary alleviation of the ironic situation for him, that really, beneath the covering power of words, lay a chaos of dissociation, which in the end he would be forced to notice. A life based on deception could only bring about a farcical misrepresentation of what it really can be.

Vinzenz, like *Die Schwärmer* is an intellectual extract. In these two dramas, the attempt to unify opposing realities, to destroy ambivalence of experience, is made through the philosophy of the characters concerned, and indicates Musil's gradually increasing objectivity in his approach to the problem which in *Törless* had gripped his understanding in a vice, making him as much a victim of the deadly irony as Törless himself, and as ardent a seeker of its resolution. There was no objective distance between the author and the character he created, and the situation therefore suffered the further irony of the blind leading the blind. But as Musil develops as a writer, not just as a thinker, so the objective distance grows as he employs his literary craftsmanship to pummel a shape into the philosophies which in *Törless* had seemed so annihilating. In his first novel, language had been used simultaneously with thought, both being parallel expressions of the same ideas. Language described thought, and when thought ran out or hit against a brick wall, so did words, and were supplemented by the series of dots and dashes which probably earned *Törless* the Expressionist label it did not really deserve. By the time Musil published *Vereinigungen* (1911), the role of language had become integral to the total expression of the work. It was no longer a simultaneous reflection of the ideas and actions it set out to express, but rather a natural extension of them. It too, has become autonomous; an entity able to conceive and propagate ideas in its own right, but which draws its strength initially from the ideas of fusion and communication with which Musil is concerned. The result is a dramatic adhesion of form and content. From the point of view of taxing his abilities as a writer, this method of trying to assemble a total and integrated reality was probably the most difficult Musil ever undertook.

He was concerned in these two Novellen, with horizontalising the vertical reality of subjectivity, through language. He made concrete those abstract experiences of Törless which he had previously only been able to circumscribe, or else forced to interrupt with dots and dashes when they defied analysis, by forcing them into the limits of flexible verbal and compound nouns. He caught and held a series of motions or reflections or experiences in the tangible form of a single word, and yet allowed that word to contain the pent-up potential of the whole series.

> ". . . . . , sondern nur ein Gefühl, ... eine leere, unaufhörliche Bewegung des Spähens und Hinaussehens, . . . "(18)
>
> "Etwas Lockeres, Bewegliches und dunkel Empfindsames an einer Stelle ihres Verhältnisses, wo in der Liebe anderer Menschen nur knöchern und seelenlos das feste Traggerüst liegt. Eine leise Unruhe war in ihr, ein fast krankhaftes Sich nach-äusserster-Gespanntheit-Sehnen, die Ahnung einer letzten Steigerung."(19)

Sometimes a duality is introduced purely by the inference of the language as in this juxtaposition of physical and metaphysical, of the confined and the uninhibited.

> "Das leichte, gleichmässige Schwanken des Zugs, das Aufgelockerte, Tauende der Natur draussen, . . ."(20)

Very frequently the duality turns up in the form of a comparison, as here where Musil uses an explicit, direct comparison to supplement the inherent comparison of the verbal noun.

> ". . . . , als Mann blieb er mir so fremd wie alle, aber es war ein Hineinströmen in ihn, was ich mir plötzlich vorstellte, und zwischen den Lippen in Tropfen wieder Zurückfallen, ein Hineingeschucktwerden wie von einem trinkenden Tier, . . ."(21)

In their desire to live a unified existence the characters seem unwittingly to have exchanged their human properties for others from a more natural world, where they mingle together with greater ease and freedom. This desire for freedom of self-integration, the desire to attain a perfect state of balance, is something of which Claudine, heroine of *Die Vollendung der Liebe,* is acutely aware. Like Törless, she too unexpectedly senses the freedom and agility which the ironic circumstance could provide for her. She is given to looking back into the past, but on one particular occasion as the separate worlds of her past and present experience join, she notices something new and enormously free about their meeting.

> "In der letzten Zeit, manchmal vielleicht etwas häufiger, war dieses Zurücksehen ein stärkeres Sichzurückbiegen nach der Vergangenheit. . . . Claudinens Treue lehnte sich dagegen auf, gerade weil sie keine Ruhe, sondern ein Kräftefreimachen war, ein gegenseitiges Einanderstützen, ein Gleichgewicht durch die beständige Bewegung nach vorwärts."(22)

"Gleichgewicht", a state of perfect integration and balance, is the operative word not only for what Claudine senses, but for what all Musil's major characters hope to attain. It is the central concept which backs the whole of his literature. But his characters are not seeking a merely satisfied matrimony of body and soul, where neither is assaulted unduly by the other, but a state so deep, so central, so immovable, that it can only be the very fulcrum of their existence. Had Musil been well acquainted with depth psychology he might possibly have called it the "deep centre". But Musil stood at the beginning of this new system of designation, as a member of the *avant-garde,* although he is likely to have found the beginnings of such thought in the writings of Ernst Mach, about whom he had written his doctoral dissertation. He could only circumscribe in his way, that same devastating, ironic awareness of all things which he shared with Schlegel, Novalis, Solger, Kierkegaard, Nietzsche, Thomas Mann—to name only the most important. Each had his methods of circumspection, and Musil had his. In *Vereinigungen* and *Drei Frauen* he was perhaps more direct and more concentrated than any of them, for the density of these works is truly amazing. In his attempt to unite the ambivalent realities in *Vereinigungen,* he creates a complex world in which physical things take on abstract properties, and abstract things take on physical properties. But such an intermingling of the spheres is often too grotesquely frightening to be the longed-for harmonious synthesis. We witness, for example, Viktoria standing alone in her room as it comes to life about her.

> "Das ganze Gemach schien ein einziges Empfinden zu sein, ein leises Klingeln, wie es zur Weihnachtszeit durch ein Haus geht. Die Geräte wuchteten unverrückbar auf ihrem Platze, der Tisch und der Schrank und die Uhr an der Wand, sie waren ganz erfüllt von sich selbst und so fest in sich geschlossen wie eine geballte Faust, und doch sahen sie wie mit Augen auf und herab, . . ."(23)

Or the abstract formlessness of thought is suddenly endowed with such terrifying, physical proportions that it can crush the character from which it emanated in a passionate, human embrace.

"... krochen ihre Gedanken durch das Haus und füllten es mit sich und mit Liebe und Freundschaft wie mit einem weichen, klebrigen Leben, das sich lautlos in unaufhaltsamen Kreisen um Viktoria legte, enger und enger und schweigend wuchs und stumm sich schloss und langsam sich über sie schob . . . wie ein heisser, grauenhafter Leib und reglos sie niederdrückte."(24)

The reader feels himself being drawn into depths where inanimate objects become anthropomorphised, into a realm which appears to be a subtle integration of the physical and the abstract, and yet which proves itself a constantly vulnerable victim to the "unending, plenitudinous chaos" of Freidrich Schlegel's irony. It is an extreme world in which the characters play no active part and are forced to submit themselves to the complex functionings about them. Viktoria's intense passion takes over completely and she becomes nothing but a disembodied abstraction of herself, totally at its mercy.

". . . aber sie schritt durch eine andere Welt, und eine Lust, ihm weh zu tun, trug dort Viktoria wie eine leichte Luft, die sie mit bebendem Wittern einatmete, die sie erfüllte und hob, und in der ihre Gebärden ausfuhren, in die Ferne griffen, in der sich ihre Schritte mit einem leisen Druck vom Boden lösten und über Wälder hoben."(25)

Although the mental and physical aspects of this world are so freely interchanged, there is no real indication of that "Gleichgewicht" which is for ever being sought. For the deeply emotional world Musil creates here is a perversion, in which circumstances have taken charge of character; a destructive, misshapen setting in which man cannot possibly continue to exist. Ulrich, in *Der Mann ohne Eigenschaften* is to attempt to temper this destructiveness through a morality forged of man's own reckoning, which sets up man's will-power as his ruling force. Musil has not yet achieved the degree of objectivity necessary for such an approach. His characters still find themselves overpowered by the frenzy of an ill-synthesised existence from which they are unable to break free. They become conscious at these moments of a bewildering rhythm of movement which dominates the outside world and alienates them from all human responsibility. Viktoria remains statically aware of a rhythmic progression, advancing relentlessly, and seizing finally at her secret soul, to degrade it, and engulf it in a demoniac chaos.

"Es war ihr dabei, als rauschten auf den Strassen die Bäume, und dumpf in der Ferne stampften die Berge dazu, kleine Haare wehten flatternd auf ihrem Leibe, kribbelndes Ungeziefer wuchs ihr darauf, und eine in Seligkeit kreischende Stimme schrie in einem wilden, riesigen Atem hinein, der sie in einem Schwarm von Menschen und Tieren hüllten und an sich riss. . . ."[26]

Even amidst such violence as this Musil never lost the fundamental knowledge that the synthesis he had created here was far removed from the synthesis he sought. He realised that this world of Viktoria's was too terrifying and too perverted to be lived in, and totally incongruous with that perfect state of balance which was his prevailing ideal. He therefore rejected *Das Verzauberte Haus* in its draft form and published a revised version of it as *Die Versuchung der Stillen Veronika,* to accompany *Die Vollendung der Liebe.* His attempt to resolve the ambivalence which rends apart the experience of both Claudine and Veronika, employs not only the direct method of the skilful use of language implicitly (which we have discussed), but also the gentler, more indirect method of comparison explicitly. Perhaps it would be better to say that Musil, ridding himself of the terrifying proximity of Viktoria's world, is seeking here to bridge the rift between the reality of experience and the reality of cognisance rather than to resolve the dichotomy they present. For a comparison, by reason of its very nature, is *ir*resoluble since it must have two contributing factors which cannot meet, but which are joined by a common feature. If the two sides of a comparison are contracted together, then it ceases to be a comparison and becomes either a metaphor or a symbol. Musil was therefore using, in his battle for resolution, a weapon by definition irresoluble, but which, with a foot in each world, could provide a bridge from one to the other. The theory could possibly have worked, but in practice Musil lacks the courage of his convictions; perhaps it is because he has not yet fully recognised what he later admits in *Der Mann ohne Eigenschaften,* that the deepest happiness can only be the result of the deepest morality, and that morality must be universal. Here in *Vereinigungen,* Musil is still concerning himself with the individual without morality, which means, without a motivating power. The conditions may be perfect, but the characters still remain, quite literally, powerless, and unable to bridge the ironic rift in their lives. They are still condemned to live in an agonising awareness of two worlds which co-exist but cannot cooperate. Like the characters in *Die Schwärmer* they are often faced with a barrier which is only "paper-thin". This is particularly true of Claudine.

"Der Arm der Frau aber ragte von der Kanne weg und der Blick mit dem sie nach ihrem Manne sah, bildete mit ihm einen starren, steifen Winkel.

Gewiss einen Winkel, wie man sehen konnte; aber jenes andere, beinahe Körperliche konnten nur diese beiden Menschen in ihm fühlen, denen es vorkam, als spannte er sich zwischen ihnen wie eine Strebe aus härtestem Metall und hielte sie auf ihren Plätzen fest und verbände sie doch, trotzdem sie so weit auseinander waren, zu einer Einheit, die man fast mit den Sinnen empfinden konnte; . . . "[27]

The metaphorical bond between the husband and wife was "*beinahe* körperlich", and something which one "*fast* mit den Sinnen empfinden konnte". Indeed, Claudine is nearer to Ulrich than any others of Musil's characters in the respect that her final recognition is very close to the breakthrough which he makes with his relative moral scale. The union with her husband which she *almost* feels at the beginning of the tale, is fulfilled completely at the end of it in the moment of her making physical love with *another* man.

"Und dann fühlte sie mit Schaudern wie ihr Körper trotz allem sich mit Wollust füllte. . . . Und ganz fern, wie Kinder von Gott sagen, er ist gross, hatte sie eine Vorstellung von ihrer Liebe."[28]

She, whom her nameless lover significantly calls "du liebe, kleine Träumerin", has glimpsed a final perfection.

In a sense Musil uses these two Novellen as ground to bed out Ulrich's scheme of an infinite morality. In them we are first introduced to the subjunctive world of possibility; a way of comprehending made functional only by the comparitive forms "wie wenn" and "als ob".

"Ihr war, als lebte sie mit ihrem Mann in der Welt wie in einer schäumenden Kugel voll Perlen und Blasen und federleichter, rauschender Wölkchen."[29]

"Es war draussen alles noch so wie vorher. Aber . . . . —schal und unnachgiebig lag ein Widerstand darüber, als sähe sie durch eine dünne, milchige Widrigkeit hindurch."[30]

The characters live, comprehend and experience comparatively. Sometimes they themselves become meaningful only through the medium of a comparison, thus Johannes is "wie eine Kerze" which casts no light, but only deepens the darkness, and Viktoria is "wie ein Messer" and "wie eine Katze".

In *Drei Frauen* (1924) this literary device is contracted from a comparison to a symbol, as Musil's increasing objectivity draws the conditions of synthesis more tightly together. These symbols are so tight, that they do not merely represent, but replace. Grigia's cow is a reincarnation of herself, in "Tonka" the horse "gehört dazu", it belongs integrally to the young man's evocation of Tonka, and in *Die Portugiesin* the sick, mangy kitten is the counterpart of all three characters.

> "Fast mit Ehrfurcht sahen sie ihr zu; keiner dieser drei Menschen in seiner besonderen Lage bleibt von dem Gedanken verschont, dass es sein eigenes Schicksal sei, . . . "(31)

Neither the juxtaposition of symbol and reality however, nor the tight construction of these three tales, can approach the final resolution. They represent the most paradoxical of all Musil's writing, for the characters actually reside within that impenetrable region between mythology (in the very broadest sense of the word as a mysterious, inviolable unity) and logic; the women darkly representative of the one, and the men answerable only to the other. Each tale depends for its very existence on a primeval indecision, on a fundamental incapacity to find an explanation. Did Grigia escape from the cave, and was Homo left to die there? Was it even a real cave in which they found themselves, or is the whole situation a symbol? What or who was the little cat; could it really have been God as the Portugiesin suggests? Was Tonka guilty or innocent? Each question, the very axis of each tale, remains essentially unanswerable. The stories are not only a reflection, but a faithful representation of Musil's ambivalent attitude, although the close texture of the work, and the intricate manoeuvres, indicate that he has intervened with a greater objectivity than ever before. The characters are therefore less terrorised by the insoluble situations; Herr von Ketten even heralds something of Ulrich's willpower as he finally overcomes his illness and his suspicion. The dreadful immediacy of *Törless* has disappeared, as has the wandering formlessness of *Vereinigungen*. The three heroes are no nearer to explaining to ironic duality of their lives, but the intensity of their experience has decreased. Homo is left to die alone, but not in agony. Herr von Ketten is allowed to live on with his beautiful wife in their castle where "no noise penetrated beyond the walls". The nameless hero of *Tonka* looks back on the whole unexplained episode and realises the benefits with which the "tiny, warm shadow" of that past experience has endowed him.

Musil's experience of irony as expressed in all these works has been in some degree akin to the Romantic conception of it. This is not true of *Der Mann ohne Eigenschaften,* although the basic dichotomy still remains to be resolved, because between *Törless* and *Der Mann ohne Eigenschaften* Musil's field of vision had widened proportionately as the objective distance between him and his major characters increased. As he became less painfully involved with each of them personally, so a natural shift of emphasis ensued from the individual to society. The hero of *Der Mann ohne Eigenschaften* is a man whose concern for himself only stems from his far greater concern for society. The code he seeks for his own life shall be a pattern for others, and his search for it causes him to forego his own character in order that he might potentially incorporate all characters; he recognises " . . . dass man . . . am Ende vielleicht so zu leben hätte, als wäre er kein Mensch, sondern bloss eine Gestalt in eimem Buch, . . .",[32] for this code leads one curiously to personal integration because all unnecessary features are unportrayed " . . . damit sich das übrige magisch zusammenschliesse".[33] We are now forced to consider a different irony, one in which the centre of gravity has shifted from the individual to society. In Musil's main novel, as in those of his contemporary Thomas Mann, the use of irony is dependent for its pith on the author's observation of a decaying disintegrating society—in this case that of pre-First World War Vienna. The objectivity with which he now applies it incorporates the iron will of Zarathustra. His conception of irony has undergone a gradual change from the annihilating force which Törless experienced, and in the face of which man was powerless, to an element which can be made subservient to the totality of life. But in the last resort Musil could never have eradicated it altogether, because, with others like Thomas Mann and Nietzsche, he shared that fundamental knowledge that an awareness of irony was a pivot for human progress, analagous with the friction of two flints which will create a spark. "Träumer", people with such an awareness, have "den feurigen Tropfen" sparked off within their lives. At the origin of all things, Musil concludes, was an hermaphroditic idea, a quality which he refers to as the "Hermaphroditus der Urphantasie", which provided the world with the primeval spark, "den Feuerkern". It could have destroyed the world, and it still retains that potential, as Törless had discovered, but it can also be tamed to man's needs, which is what Ulrich attempts to do.

Over the years, the development of Musil's writing reflects that same development of a purposive dealing with the ironic paradox of life which is evident in the span of ironic writers between Friedrich Schlegel and Thomas Mann.* It ranges from a totally paralysed and incapacitated acceptance of the ambivalence of the human condition, to the broad ethical vision, forged of an unqualified acceptance of moral responsibility, which we find in *Der Mann*

* Beda Allemann has dealt with this span of writers in his book *"Ironie und Dichtung"*, Pfullingen, 1956.

ohne Eigenschaften. The plans for the novel were begun before the publication of *Törless,* and yet Musil died leaving it unfinished. He had entrusted his entire life to this monumental and precarious attempt to lay the ghost of polarity and dissociation, by taming his awareness of irony until it could be welded in as an integral part of an ethical, human pattern. It is doubtful whether he would have been able to do this without the courageous attempts of Solger and Kierkegaard to fight back the destructive fire of irony to a distance at which it could be contemplated and analysed. It is practically certain he could not have done it without the Nietzschean Übermensch having demonstrated the possibility of human supremacy over the ironic circumstance. But Ulrich is not in the clouds of Zarathustra's mountain, exhorting the people, he is down with them in the failing days of the Austro-Hungarian empire, living their daily life and thrusting an ethical purpose into it in an attempt to save it. He is not the all-capable Übermensch, but the all-possible human.

The work represents Musil's conscious experiment to subjugate the irony of human existence to the practical terms of an historical context. The scene is Vienna, the year 1913–14. Musil, like Mann, has hinged his broader, more objective ironic concept on a disintegrating society. More specifically, he has hinged it on a small representative group of that society, the members of the "Parallelaktion", who, blindly unaware of what is imminent about them, are planning to celebrate the seventieth year of the reign of Franz Josef as emperor with a jubilee year to prove the empire (Kakania, as it is called, a witticism drawn from the familiar "kaiserlich-königlich" (k. und k.) prefix of the Austro-Hungarian empire) a land of continued cultural and political significance. This is the vehicle for Musil's irony. Ulrich, who has taken "a year off from life" because he has become disillusioned with both his military and his mathematical career (a reflection of Musil's own life), becomes secretary of the Aktion, "Obgleich Ulrich mit allen diesen Personen immer nur gespielt zu haben glaubte".[34] Musil paints its members in comic vein, for this is the guise which irony has lately taken on as it orientates itself towards something external of itself, displaying one set of affairs, but cruelly indicating another. Musil is not really amused by them, but presents them rather with the fatalism of an artist who knows the catastrophe they herald.

It is while Ulrich is attending a meeting of the Parallelaktion, listening to the fatuous suggestions and retrogressive homilies of its members, that his mind begins to concretise the duality it has always experienced, and which has dogged all Musil's heroes, through the symbol of two trees. The characteristic feature of Musil's characters so far, had been a constant oscillation between two poles of comprehension and interpretation; "Schweben" had been the key word to the Romantic conception of irony. But as Ulrich strives to put society, instead of himself, in the centre of the universe, and involves the consequent shift of emphasis from an agonising irony imprisoned within its own purposelessness, to an active irony pungently and purposively hinged on a society in need of salvation, he finds himself having to tussle with a newly-emerging realisation which prompts the question "Wie könnte man übersehen, dass die Menschenwelt nichts Schwebendes ist, sondern nach gedrungenster Festigkeit verlangt, . . . "[35] Of the two symbolic trees, one incorporates all those passions which he had trained towards the normal world of "reality", and the other represents the "Schattenseite seines Wesens". For the first time in Musil's work the ironic problem is formulated with uncompromising and almost deceptive simplicity. The outcome is likewise almost deceptively mundane. Ulrich decides that he must come to a decision. He must determine at length, what this final "stability" is to be. But concurrently with this realisation, that the basic value of Ulrich's life lies in welding together the two opposing spheres of experience, rather than merely determining their existence (as Musil's other characters have done), comes the second, even more potent realisation that ". . . allein war er nicht imstande, das Auseinandergefallene von neuem zusammenzubringen".[36] With a sudden wild desire to be practical about his attempt to attain this ultimate stability Ulrich suggests to the Parallelaktion, the formation of "ein Erdensekretariat der Genauigkeit und Seele".[37] The idea meets, understandably, with uncomprehending frigidity. They cannot help him.

Ulrich was not a leader; he could not himself undertake to conduct the world to a point of perfect balance, he could only demonstrate through attaining the state within his own life. But even this he could not achieve alone, as he had recognised. It proved to be Agathe, his "twin" sister who was destined to help him towards the goal. She complements him exactly, and so makes him into a whole person. "Du bist meine Eigenliebe"[38] Ulrich tells her as he realises her utmost significance for him. Musil clarifies the sigficance in a note referring to a draft of the novel in an earlier form where he says that she "Gibt Ulrich Freude an sich selbst. Verleiht ihm also Eigenschaften".[39] She equips him to undertake with her "die Reise an den Rand des Möglichen" in a final attempt to overcome the duality which prompted Musil himself to remark of Ulrich, " . . . ein Mensch, der von irgend etwas gezwungen wird, gegen sich selbst zu leben".[40]* Musil describes the journey with the term "an den Rand des Möglichen" not because the venture strains our credulity or borders on the impossible in the usual sense of the word, but because Ulrich and Agathe are led to the limits of human cognisance when they are faced with the realisation that man's final stability can only consist of an infinity of possibility. Man must cast off the condition he recognises as "living" and strive to attain "den *anderen* Zustand" (the *other* condition); this means living entirely within the new context of possibility, "das Mögliche", and it is to the boundaries of this new region that Ulrich and Agathe are brought. It is an infinite realm cohabited by God and man.

> "Das Mögliche umfasst nicht nur die Träume nervenschwacher Personen, sondern auch die noch nicht erwachten Absichten Gottes".[41]

God, in fact, is the epitome of possibility, as Ulrich had dimly recognised even as a child at school, when he wrote in an essay that

> "... wahrscheinlich auch Gott von seiner Welt am liebsten im Conjunctivus Potentialis spreche ..., denn Gott macht die Welt und denkt dabei, es könnte ebensogut anders sein."[42]

And so, as Ulrich and Agathe approach the boundaries of "the other condition" of possibility, Musil is able to describe their search as "ein steigendes Verhältnis zu Gott".[43] They are aspiring towards

* Ernst Kaiser and Eithne Wilkins, after working for a very long time on the unpublished MSS insist that the "journey" undertaken by the brother and sister is purely spiritual, and condemn the commonly held view that they indulge in an incestuous union. However, it is also clear from the earlier drafts of the novel, which appear under different titles, that Musil had originally reckoned with physical incest. Indeed, it would be natural for his preoccupation with duality to express itself in his work through its concomitant physical forms, homosexual love (which he had used as a vehicle in *Törless*) and incestuous love. Musil may well have rejected, in his final plans, the physical incest of the brother and sister, but in any case the spiritual relationship of Ulrich with his *Eigenliebe* must ultimately also be regarded as incestuous. The synthesis of that relationship, which in fact never materialises in *Der Mann ohne Eigenschaften* as it now stands, would be an hermaphroditic unity. The hermaphrodite symbol is further embodied by Clarisse, Walter's wife, who is obsessed by a vision of herself playing an hermaphrodite role in the world, curiously endowed with the capacities of the Nietzschean Ubermensch, and destined to give birth to a saviour. But Clarisse, if not insane, was certainly the victim of severe nervous disorder, which would seem to indicate that the final synthesis of Ulrich and Agathe is not to be achieved within their normal frame of living. Certainly there is no final evidence of their triumph over duality, nor is a saviour likely to be born to Clarisse; the one event would almost certainly incur the other.

the supreme recognition that the world is eternally potential because its God is infinite possibility.

Somewhere within the region of possibility lies the deep centre of human experience, the ultimate balancing point of the Romantic "Schweben", the fulcrum of all life, the primeval Feuerkern. It is this point which Ulrich seeks to find. He is not satisfied with the temporary resolution of his duality through Agathe, not content with the knowledge that instead of his senses being divided into "die zwei Bäume des Lebens" he and his sister can now stand together "als stiegen sie aus einer Wurzel auf", because all this has been achieved without stepping over the boundary into the unknown territory of "das Mögliche". Musil may have made a marginal note in one of his drafts* to the effect that Ulrich and Agathe "in die entscheidende Phase getreten sind" and are learning "welches Glück es bedeutet, wenn alles Leben einen Mittelpunkt hat",[(44)] but it is significant that he never actually brings Ulrich to a point where he feels his search is over, even when he and Agathe do attain some sort of synthesis. For him, the *recognition* of a focal point to his life is insufficient if the final analysis of its mechanism, the mysterious moving cause behind it, continues to elude him. He admits:

> "Wir werden von dem Gefühl begleitet, dass wir die Mitte unseres Lebens erreicht haben, . . . dass wir an die Achse des Kreisels gelangt sind, . . ."[(45)]

but he has had to precede this admittance with another of much deeper resonance,

> "*Könnte* ich sagen, wir werden von dem Gefühl begleitet, in Einklang mit Gott zu leben, es wäre einfach; . . . "In Einklang" ist richtig, aber womit ist nicht zu sagen."[(46)]

Ulrich cannot merely accept the synthesis which they feel themselves to have attained; he feels himself propelled on in a supreme attempt to determine what that force is which has given them their sense of integration. He still feels uneasy.

The spiritual incest of Ulrich with Agathe, of rationalism with its own mythical counterpart, may have brought him to the supreme awareness of the potentially infinite magnitude of "das Mögliche", the twentieth century outcrop of Friedrich Schlegel's "unending chaos"; it may have brought him to the knowledge that love was the only code for existence within possibility, as he concluded in the diary he wrote and which Agathe found and read, but this

* The note has been indicated by Kaiser and Wilkins. It was made on a draft dated 1938–9

awareness never released him from the darkest knowledge which he constantly tried to suppress, that ultimately, the world of possibility could never totally coincide with the world of immediate reality, "das Wirkliche", or, as he finally admits, the *established* world, for it is power, he writes, which provides the progress for this world; and so his conclusion must be : "Das hiesse : die fertige Welt Sünde ! Die Mögliche : Liebe !"(47) Moosbrugger, the psychopath who killed and mutilated a prostitute, was representative of the established world; when, as a result of Clarisse's hare-brained scheme, he was secretly rescued from the asylum, he could only kill again. This was the only kind of "creation" mankind as a whole could achieve, as Ulrich had suspected when he first saw Moosbrugger, "Wenn die Menschheit als ganzes träumen könnte, müsste Moosbrugger entstehn." This was the way the world wanted to go. It was a mass, appetitive will which could never totally coincide with Ulrich's newly-integrated revelation. But even Ulrich, because his will cannot accept blindly what has been revealed to him, but drives him on to probe the very nature of it, fails to make the revelation coincide with his own human experience.

> "Ich glaube nicht, dass Gott da war, sondern dass er erst kommt. Aber nur, wenn man ihm den Weg kürzer macht als bisher."(48)

Ulrich, who stood on the very edge of "das Mögliche", could not take the one step necessary to make God's way shorter, although he recognised that one step would take him over the boundary. It was not only the years of exile in Switzerland, nor the straightened pecuniary circumstances which Musil suffered in his latter years, which condemned *Der Mann ohne Eigenschaften* to its mammoth, fragmentary state, but to a far greater extent, the simple fact that Ulrich's courage failed him. He could not make the leap in the dark into the unknown region because he needed *faith* to do so. Faith failed him. He believed in God, he even believed that man was set into the world "als Perle in die Weltmuschel",(49) but he had no faith in this belief. Like Musil, he was possessed of an incessant logic which could never allow him to take the one step over the boundary of possibility because he realised, that for a split second, as he did so, he would know nothing. It could not allow him to undertake the dangerous journey over Törless' bridge, because it had no supports in the middle. He could not risk that it might collapse, and only faith could assure him that it would not. Törless' youthful mind could span the abyss with a tottering but triumphant bridge of intuitive realisation and trust; Ulrich's logical mind cannot. In the final analysis, in spite of all his preparation, he cannot carry out the ecstatic instruction his sister had once given him,

> "Wirf alles, was du hast ins Feuer bis zu den Schuhen. Wenn du nichts mehr hast, denk nicht einmal ans Leichentuch und wirf dich nackt ins Feuer."[50]

Ulrich has to retain something which is his; the Feuerkern in which he believes, but which he does not have the faith to approach, must remain untouched and unexplained. He admires from afar those saints and mystics who have had the faith to do so, and who have consequently shared in the very process of creation, for they can speak:

> "Von Erkenntnissen, die so schnell sind, dass alles zugleich ist, und wie Feuertropfen sind, die in die Welt fallen."[51]

The weight of Musil's own confession about the novel, "Dieses Buch ist religiös unter den Voraussetzungen der Ungläubigen" now becomes almost unbearable with its suggestion that he recognised himself as a faithless believer. Unbearable too, is the realisation which he refuses to admit to himself as he struggles to terminate his life's work, that the irony which Törless knew in a welter of incomprehension, is far outweighed by that of Ulrich, whose supreme objectivity has clarified the ironic problem to the crystal contours of a "taghelle Mystik"[52]—into which he can never set foot, because the objective logic which unveiled it, cannot forsake itself and entrust itself to a subjective faith which could know it. Ulrich denies himself the freedom of that faith for which his every nerve and fibre yearn. The untouchable Feuerkern, the unbridgeable abyss, must remain untouched and unbridged; the ambivalence unresolved.

> "Also bis zu welchen Grad glaubst du?" wiederholte Agathe.
> "Ja und nein," sagte Ulrich.
> "Also nein," vollendete Agathe.

These words are wholly symptomatic of Musil's attitude to life. It is true that Ulrich speaks them well before the "end" of the novel, but they never ceased to hold true, for not only are they never resolved within his life, but they re-echo throughout that of his author. Of Musil's several sympathies, none of them was all-consuming. His "double-vision" may have belonged to a typically Austrian evolution, but he was more international than national; he admits to the influence of d'Annunzio, Hamsun, Flaubert and Dostoevsky. His style in *Törless* may have foretold something of the Expressionists, but Musil never followed in their footsteps. He could never have acknowledged fully their ideal of complete self-abnegation, even self-annihilation, for the preservation of mankind. Ulrich was too much of a realist to be a "neuer Mensch" of ideological Expressionist proportions; he believed in society as a working machine, and in himself as a relevant, perhaps even missionary, part of it, but he never regarded himself as a saviour. Musil was a mathematician, but his talent was constantly disjointed by a deeply mystic yearning. The explanation of God lay somewhere between the two. The developing schools of psychological thought in Vienna around the turn of the century, suckled by Sigmund Freud, Arthur Schnitzler, Franz Wedekind, and encouraged indirectly by the supposedly "absolute" philosophy of Ludwig Wittgenstein, attracted his interest, but they never persuaded him to accept them as a fundamental means of analysing the human psyche. Austrian, Expressionist, mathematician, psychologist, mystic; Musil was all of these and none of them. He lived in an eruptive era which suffered two world wars with all their inclusive chaos and fanaticisms. Musil steered a course through it, navigated entirely by his own conscience, which was indeed, the harshest judge of all that he undertook. Its iron rigours scrutinised his every thought and action, so that he could accept nothing unreservedly but was forced always to weigh up the merits of the opposing argument. It forbade him to join the ranks of any particular literary movement or political party, although he was never out of touch with current developments in these fields. A communal doctrine of which he could accept only a part could never become the mainstay of his life. Ultimately, the high integrity of his own conscience was the only code to which he could conform, and this owed obeisance to nothing which invaded it from without. It was a strong creed but a lonely one, which would not allow Musil to bow to the phases of popular taste. His work does not present the waxing and waning reflection of the so-called spirit of the age, but a constant drive forwards; he refused to ride the waves of circumstance, but tried to course his way through them. The only way he could be of use to others was by being intensely loyal to himself, and it was this mode of living and thinking which fashioned the extreme and brave individuality which was his, and around which increasing numbers of admirers have assembled. The inner dual which forms its well-worn cornerstone causes his writing to exercise a dichotomous fascination over its readers. On the one hand we can only stand in deep awe of his unerringly courageous attempts to pour his experience into a unifying mould of synthesis, whilst at the same time we feel ourselves dragged down into the vortex created by the insolubility of his cause. He fought his battle anonymously, but Musil's bravery has posthumously gained him a name which represents an unusual sanity and positive line of attack within modern German literature. Among those writing against the same background of events as he there were aesthetes, like George, Rilke and Hofmannsthal, who withdrew themselves into a realm where they could construct a private hierarchy, a secret intermingling of language and symbol; there were those, like Thomas Mann, who derided the disintegration of society in an attempt to make men come to their senses; some, like Berthold Brecht, were possessed of a political ardour and a burning sense of justice which condemned and attacked existing social structures; others, like the Expressionists, panicked as they envisioned the world precipitating towards an abyss, and they vomited up their fear and disgust in a literature of incomparably powerful themes and expression; others still, such as the Christian writers, wept and consoled in the face of despair, but hardly dared to whisper any words of salvation. Musil pretended to none of these, but he had the genuinely honest courage necessary to present himself, and his untiring inquiries into the ambivalence of his experience, as an example. Although deeply aware of the imperfections of the record he set down, he was willing to testify to its sincerity and to accept full responsibility for himself, so that, with almost pedantic stubbornness, he insisted at all times, on being Robert Musil.

TRANSLATIONS

1. I am downright uneducated all round.
2. One cannot say that Musil too, is seeking to synthesise intellect and emotion.
3. . . . despairing work.
4. . . . and he lived only in these letters.
5. At present I am reading Novalis, *Heinrich von Ofterdingen.*
6. . . . quite contrary to my usual practice, but because of an obvious need.
7. After four years of diffusion it shall provide me with an opportunity of discovering that direction of spiritual development which I consider to be mine.
8. I do not know, but it seems to me as though I can see two ways of attaining knowledge of man's existence. The one way, arduous and incalculable, the way of experience, the other, perhaps just one intuitive leap, the way of inner contemplation.
9. I know; things are things and always will be; and I shall go on seeing them first from this angle, then from that. Now with the eyes of my understanding, and now with my other eyes.

10. . . . a bridge, which has supporting pillars only at either end.

11. But these two are joined together by something which does not exist.

12. . . . that green grass is simply as green as grass.

13. . . . as close as the two sides of a playing card.

14. It (is) always the same pack of cards only shuffled and dealt differently.

15. Blood is surging through your heads. Your life-cells, as yet divided, grow in the depth of your bodies like a forest of coral. Images flow through it like the shifting meadows of variegated shoals of fish. Your beings force themselves mysteriously magnified, from the glassy spheres of your eyes. And your hearts thunder in time.

16. "den feurigen Tropfen"—the fiery drop.
"den Feuerkern"—the primeval spark of existence.

17. Nothing distinguishes them from themselves but a paper-thin feeling of a closed body and blood hammering behind it.

Note—In the cases of numbers 18–22 the structures of the German language cannot be transposed into the equivalent structures in English; any translation can therefore only be an approximation of the meaning, and can in no way convey the point of the present discussion, that the duality revealed in the Novellen is realised within the architecture of the words themselves.

18. . . . . , but only a feeling, . . . an empty incessant movement of glancing and looking out.

19. Something relaxed, mobile and darkly sensitive at a place in her relationship where the love other people know is supported only by something inflexible and soulless. A quiet unrest was within her; an almost morbid yearning to be tensed to the uttermost, the awareness of a culminating intensity.

20. The gentle, rhythmical swaying of the train, the sense of relaxing and melting in nature outside.

21. . . . as a man he remained as distant to me as any other, but I suddenly imagined myself being drawn into him, and falling back again as drops from his lips, a sense of being swallowed by a drinking animal.

22. Recently, sometimes a little more frequently perhaps, this looking back was a rather stronger leaning back to the past . . . Claudine's loyalty revolted against it precisely because it was not a repose, but a liberation of her strength, a mutual supporting of each other, a balance maintained by the constant forward movement.

23. The whole room seemed to be a single sensitive organ, a soft tinkling, like the sound that goes through a house at Christmas time. The furniture grew massive and immoveable in its place, the table and the cupboard and the clock on the wall were all filled with themselves and as tightly enclosed as a clenched fist, and yet they looked up and down with eyes . . .

24. . . . her thoughts crept through the house and filled it with themselves and with love and friendship as though with something soft, sticky and living which circled constantly about Viktoria, getting nearer and

nearer, and it grew silently and closed itself without a sound about her, engulfing her . . . like a hot, loathsome body, and without seeming to move, it forced her downwards.

25. . . . but she strode through another world, and a desire to hurt him lifted her up like a soft, balmy air, which she inhaled, quivering as she caught the scent, which filled her and lifted her up and in which her gestures reached out into the distance, in which her steps freed themselves from the ground with a slight thrust and carried her over treetops. . . .

26. At the same time it was as though trees rustled in the streets and in the distance the mountains joined in with stamping, tiny hairs stirred and waved on her body, creeping insects grew on it, and a voice screeching out in bliss cried into it with a single, wild, gigantic breath which enveloped her in a crowd of people and animals, and wrenched her towards itself. . . .

27. The woman's arm jutted up sharply from the teapot, and the look she cast towards her husband formed a rigidly firm angle with it.

It was certainly an angle, as one could see, but that other almost physical quality about it, could only be felt by these two people, to whom it seemed that something stretched itself between them like a strut made of the hardest metal, which was holding them fast to their seats, and which, although they were so far from each other, bound them into a unity which one could sense almost physically.

28. And then she felt with horror, how her body filled with desire, in spite of everything. And she had a very slight idea of her love, as slight as when children say of God, He is great.

29. It seemed to her that she lived with her husband in the world, as though it were a sphere full of pearls and bubbles and feathery, rustling little clouds.

30. Outside it was all as it had been before. But a resistance lay insipidly and unrelentingly over it all, as though she were looking through a thin, milky, repulsive substance.

31. They looked at it almost in awe; not one of these three people, in his particular situation, can escape from the thought that it is his own fate.

32. . . . that one . . . perhaps in the last resort, has to live as though one were not a person, but a character in a book. . . .

33. . . . so that the rest may magically seal itself together . . .

34. Although Ulrich had only ever considered himself to have played a game with these people.

35. How could one fail to see that that the world is not a thing of constant oscillation, but yearns for the most concentrated stability.

36. . . . alone, he was incapable of bringing together again that which had disintegrated.

37. . . . a General Secretariat for Precision and the Spirit.

38. You are my self-love.

39. Gives Ulrich joy in himself. Endows him with characteristics.

40. . . . a person who is forced by something to live at odds with himself.

41. The region of possibility does not only embrace the dreams of neurasthenic people, but also those designs of God which still lie dormant.

42. . . . that even God would best prefer to talk about his world in the subjunctive mood of potentiality . . . for God creates the world and thinks as he does so, that it could just as well be different.

43. . . . a process of growing nearer to God.

44. . . . have entered the decisive phase and are learning the joy brought about when the whole of life has a focal point.

45. We are accompanied by a feeling that we have reached the central point of our lives, . . . that we have attained the axis of the vortex.

46. *If* (the italic in the text is my own) I could say we were accompanied by the feeling of living in harmony with God, it would be simple. . . . In harmony is correct, but it is impossible to say with what.

47. That would mean: the established world, sin! The possible world: love!

48. If mankind could dream as a whole, Moosbrugger would surely arise.

49. I do not believe that God was there, but that he is yet to come. But only if man makes His way shorter than he has done so far.

50. . . . as the pearl in the oyster.

51. Cast all that you have into the fire, even your very shoes. When you have nothing left, give not a thought even to your shroud, but cast yourself naked into the fire.

52. . . . of perceptions which are so rapid, that they coalesce, and are like drops of fire which fall into the world.

53. . . . a daylight mysticism.

54. "To what extent do you have faith?" repeated Agathe.
"I have and I haven't," said Ulrich.
"Then you haven't," Agathe completed.

SELECTED BIBLIOGRAPHY

Translations into English

All these are by Eithne Wilkins and Ernst Kaiser

The Man Without Qualities.
Vol. I. London: Secker and Warburg, 1953, and New York: Coward and McCann, 1953.
Vol. II. London and New York, 1954.
Vol. III. London, 1960.

The Perfecting of a Love. Botteghe Obscure, XVIII (Autumn 1956).

The Portuguese Lady. Botteghe Obscure, XXV (Autumn 1960).

"Tonka" In *Modern Writing,* ed. W. Phillips and P. Rahv. New York, 1953.

Young Törless. London: Secker and Warburg, 1955. (Also available as Penguin) and New York: Pantheon, 1955.

Primary Literature

The only available edition of the collected works is edited by Adolf Frisé. It is this edition of *Der Mann ohne Eigenschaften* which has come under such heavy fire from Eithne Wilkins and Ernst Kaiser.

Tagebücher, Aphorismen, Essays and Reden. Rowohlt Verlag, Hamburg, 1955.
Prosa, Dremen, späte Briefe. 1957.
Der Mann ohne Eigenschaften. 1960. Reprinted 1962.

There are also Rororo paper-back editions of *Drei Frauen* (no. 64), and *Die Verwirrungen des Zöglings Törless* (no. 300).

Secondary Literature in English

BOENINGER, H. R. *The Rediscovery of Robert Musil*. In *Modern Language Forum*, XXXVII, 1952 (pp. 109–119).
BRAUN, W. Moosbrugger Dances. In *Germanic Review*, XXXV, 1960 (pp. 214–230).
BRAUN, W. Musil's Erdensekretariat der Genauigkeit und Seele—A Clue to the Philosophy of the Hero of *Der Mann ohne Eigenschaften*. In *Monatshefte*, XLVI, 1954 (pp. 305–316).
BRAUN, W. Musil's Musicians. In *Monatshefte*, LII, 1960 (pp. 9-17).
BRAUN, W. Musil's Siamese Twins. In *Germanic Review*, XXXIII, 1958. (pp.41–52).
BRAUN, *W*. Robert Musil and the Pendulum of the Intellect. In *Monatshefte*, XLIX, 1957 (pp. 109–119).
BRAUN, W. The Temptation of Ulrich. In *German Quarterly*, XXXIX, 1956 (pp. 29–37).
BRAUN, W. An Approach to Musil's *Die Schwärmer*. In *Monatshefte*, no. 4, April/May, 1962.
BRAUN, W. An Interpretation of Musil's Novelle *Tonka*. In *Monatshefte*, February, 1961.
BRAUN, W. Musil's *Vinzenz und die Freundin bedeutender Männer*. In *Germanic Review*, XXXVII, no. 2. March 1962. (pp. 121–134).
HERMAND, J. Musil's *Grigia*. In *Monatshefte*, no. 4 April/May, 1962.
HOLMES, F. A. Two Studies of Musil's *Der Mann ohne Eigenschaften*. In *German Life and Letters*, XX, April 1962, no. 3 (pp. 202–209).
KERMODE, F. Puzzles and Epiphanies. 1962.
MEYERHOFF, H. The Writer as Intellectual—*The Man Without Qualities* by Robert Musil. In *Partisan Review*, XXI, January, 1954 (pp. 98–108).
MCCORMICK, A. Ambivalence in Musil's *Drei Frauen*. In *Monatshefte*, no. 4, April/May, 1962.
PIKE, B. Robert Musil: An Introduction to his Work. Cornell University Press, 1962.

Secondary Literature in German

The most comprehensive and most recent publication, based on Musil's published and unpublished Mss is:

EITHNE WILKINS and ERNST KAISER. Robert Musil, Eine Einführung in das Werk. Kohlhammer Verlag, Stuttgart, 1962.

A very detailed study of Musil's satire in his main novel is provided in the following published thesis, which is very good, but purely analytical.

ARNTZEN, H. *Satirischer Stil:* zur Satire Robert Musil in *Der Mann ohne Eigenschaften.* (Bonner Abhandlungen 9), Bonn, H. Bouvier, 1960.

A collection of essays, excellent for the personal and biographical aspects of Musil, has been published under the official auspices of his birthplace.

DINKLAGE, K. (Ed.) Robert Musil. Leben, Werk, Wirkung. Amalthea-Verlag, Vienna, 1960.

Of the many articles, the following are perhaps the most penetrating.

BAUMANN, G. Robert Musil; eine Vorstudie. In *Germanisch-romanische Monatsschrift*, III, 1953 (pp. 292–316).

BAUMANN, G. Robert Musil: Die Struktur des Geistes und der Geist der Struktur. In *Germanisch-romanische Monatsschrift*, X, 1960 (pp. 420–442).

MICHEL, K. M. Die Utopie der Sprache. In *Akzente*, I, 1954 (pp. 23–35).

REQUADT, P. Zu Musil's Portugiesin. In *Wirkendes Wort*, V, 1954–55 (pp. 152–158).

Wolfgang Borchert

Wolfgang Borchert

by HANS POPPER

Wolfgang Borchert was born in Hamburg, on May 20, 1921, the son of Fritz Borchert, a primary school teacher, and of Herta, herself a writer and broadcaster of stories in her native Low German dialect (*platt-deutsch*). After a normal and quite undistinguished school career,[1] he was, on April 1, 1939, apprenticed to the old and extremely respectable bookshop of Heinrich Boysen.

He read widely—we hear especially of Shakespeare, Hölderlin, Rilke and the Expressionist poets,[2] such as Benn, Trakl, Lichtenstein, Toller, many of whose works were suppressed by the Nazi régime. We also know that he was acquainted with the French Symbolists, with the American novelist Thomas Wolfe and with Homer—all these in translation. Annotated copies of Nietzsche's *Thus spake Zarathustra* and Schopenhauer's *On Writing and Style*[3] have come down to us. He was also fond of music and the visual arts—Michelangelo and the Expressionist painters are frequently mentioned. He himself enjoyed painting and drawing, and even produced one painting of quite remarkable quality, *Klabautermann.*[4]

He disliked the conformism which was the product, both, of bourgeois respectability, and of fear of Nazi tyranny; thus he adopted eccentricities in dress and behaviour, as well as extravagances in his friendships and love affairs, such as are typical of the adolescent, who feels himself at odds with society as well as with himself. The Establishment tended to regard him with equal disfavour; he was a typical "outsider". His parents were known for their dislike of the government, but they were also hostile to established religion. His school, on the other hand, combined loyalty to the régime with efficient religious instruction. When, as an adolescent, he started writing verse, the actress Aline Bussmann (wife of the lawyer Dr. C. H. Hager) became his close friend and literary mentor. For her daughter Ruth the poet came to conceive the first great passion of his life; it was not reciprocated.

His first encounter with the Gestapo occurred, when, in April 1940, he was arrested and questioned on a charge of homosexuality,

> . . . "You are supposed to have carried on with a certain Rieke," the official said. "Rieke? Rieke?" Wolfgang racked his brains, who this could possibly be. He knew nobody by the name of Rieke. Suddenly it dawned on him: "Oh, you mean Rilke," he said, "he is a poet—but he is no longer alive. . . .[5]

The Gestapo continued to keep him under surveillance, and when, nearly two years later, he came into renewed collision with the government, he was already *persona non grata.*

The positive side of this reluctance to become simply a regular member of the German book trade was his unshakeable belief in his vocation as an artist.(6) Not only did he write poetry, but he entered the drama school of Helmuth Gmelin, under whom he studied for just over a year (1939–40). Having passed the examination and obtained the State Diploma in acting, he left the bookshop (December 31, 1940) and joined the touring company, "Landesbühne Osthannover". His career as an actor was short (March 3 to June 6, 1941), and perhaps the happiest period of his life. He worked hard, and met with some success. He had found his niche in society, where he was yet able to satisfy his demands for personal freedom and non-conformity, while he could fulfil his artistic aspirations without becoming a social outcast.

But this period of happiness and good health came to an end, when he was called up in summer 1941. After training in Weimar, he was sent to the Russian front (Kalinin) in December of the same year. If military discipline had seemed irksome from the start, his real sufferings were to start already in January 1942, with an attack of jaundice. Then, one day, he returned from patrol, wounded in the left hand, weeping with pain and terror. The wound, he said, had been caused by an accidental going-off of his gun, in the course of hand-to-hand fighting with a Russian soldier. He was sent to Schwabach military hospital. Accused of having himself inflicted the wound, he was arrested and put into solitary confinement in Nuremberg military prison. Conviction would have carried the death penalty with it. He was fortunate in being tried, not by a Nazi *Volksgericht* ("Court of the People"), but by a military tribunal, therefore according to the ordinary procedure of military law; he was defended by Dr. Hager, who obtained his acquittal. But immediately fresh proceedings were started against him, on account of spoken and written (letters to his parents and friends) pronouncements "against the State and the Party". The sentence of four months' imprisonment was changed to six weeks' solitary confinement, followed by immediate return to the Russian front.

After a short period in Saalfeld and the garrison at Jena, he was sent to Toropez in December 1942, where the fighting was at that time particularly intense. He acted as a courier, and was almost without arms. Again his health broke down. He passed through several military hospitals, had a period of home leave, during which he appeared in the well-known Hamburg cabaret, *Bronzekeller,* and was eventually to be discharged as unfit for military service (January–November 1943). On leaving the Army, he was to have joined a theatrical company for entertaining the troops.

Only a few weeks before this could come about, however, he was again arrested. Apparently he had parodied a Goebbels speech and had been denounced by one of his comrades. It was a foolish action on Borchert's part; denunciations of this kind were all too common in Nazi Germany, and of course encouraged by the government. This time Dr.

Hager could do little for the poet. He was condemned to a prison sentence of nine months, which he underwent in the Moabit prison in Berlin. During the heavy air raids of that year (1944), prisoners were not taken to any shelters, but simply left in their cells. He was released in September 1944, only to be immediately remobilised. In spring 1945 he was captured by the French Army. He managed to escape, but was again captured, this time by the Americans. But he was set free, on account of his record as a political prisoner. Later he avoided a further encounter with American troops by feigning madness.

Borchert was now definitely a sick man. Such medical treatment as he had received, had never been adequate; and during his terms of imprisonment no account had been taken of his physical state. He was never to regain health.

His great longing was for his native city of Hamburg, which he loved with that intense joy that was to find triumphant expression in the prose poems, *Hamburg* and *Die Elbe,* and which forms the background to most of his works. After a period of rest on a Westphalian estate, where he was hospitably received, he continued his trek back to Hamburg, always on foot and keeping close behind the advancing Allied troops. On May 10, 1945, he arrived at Curslack, completely exhausted, where his mother met him and took him back to Hamburg.

He now tried to resume his career on the stage and as a writer. He founded a cabaret with some friends (*Janmaaten im Hafen*), which had a strong local flavour, planned a Hamburg anthology,[7] participated in the launching of a small theatre (*Die Komödie*), and was finally asked by his old teacher Gmelin to assist in a production of Lessing's *Nathan der Weise*. But his health broke down completely

From December 1945 to spring 1946 he stayed in the Elizabeth hospital, Hamburg, without being cured. He returned home, and at first tried to lead a normal life, but eventually became completely bedridden. His physical sufferings increased as the hope of being cured waned. One last effort at restoration was made by some friends, who succeeded, after many difficulties, in getting him into the Catholic hospital of St. Clara in Basle.[8] A liver complaint was diagnosed, which had put one part of the liver completely out of action. Under-nourishment and bad treatment during his military service and the terms of imprisonment had weakened his constitution to such an extent, that a cure would have been nothing short of miraculous. He died on November 20, 1947, the day before the first stage performance of his play, *Draussen vor der Tür* (The Man Outside), at the *Hamburg Kammerspiele.*

AS far as we know, Borchert started writing at the age of fifteen. We hear of a number of plays, none of which have survived, and a staggering quantity of lyrical poetry. All the poems which were written before 1940—with the exception of those which had actually been published in newspapers and magazines—were subsequently suppressed by the poet. Of the poems produced between 1940 and 1945, only fourteen were included by him and Meyer-Marwitz in the collection, *Laterne, Nacht und Sterne* (published in December 1946). A further fifteen poems were included in a section, *Nachgelassene Gedichte,* in the Collected Works (*Das Gesamtwerk*).[9] Other poems were published by the poet in newspapers and magazines, or sent as gifts to friends (very often appended to letters). Some were published posthumously, appearing either in their own right,[10] or being quoted in the text of studies or monographs by Rühmkorf, Bussmann, Darboven and others. Many more pieces have survived, in manuscript or typescript. Very few of these would have been admitted by the poet himself, who destroyed a great number of them before he left Hamburg.

The majority of these poems are, in fact, very poor. A number of them do, however, reach real heights of emotional impact (e.g. *Draussen,* p. 296;[11] *Der Mond lügt: Moabit,* p. 293) or are able to charm and delight us by their simplicity and freshness of imagery (e.g. *Aranka,* p. 15; *Muscheln, Muscheln,* p. 18; *Der Wind und die Rose,* p. 19). Borchert was serving his apprenticeship, as a lyrical poet, mainly under Hölderlin, Rilke and the Expressionists. In the last phase of this period (1940–45) he was able to make himself independent of his models, to emancipate himself from the immediate emotional impact of the experience which would stimulate the writing of any one lyric, and to obtain clarity of thought and especially concreteness of imagery (*Versuch es,* p. 290; *Antiquitäten* p. 22).[12] But however highly we may regard those lyrics which really are of first-rate quality, we must agree with Meyer-Marwitz[13]—and not least with the poet himself—that his lyrical output served as a preparation for the really important works, which came into being in the period January 1946–November 1947: the prose pieces and the play, *Draussen vor der Tür.*

After January 1946, Borchert changed over *completely* to writing prose (apart from a few small dedicatory verses—*gifts* to friends, which he always delighted in sending out).[14]

Only two prose pieces had been written by him before that time, *Die Blume* (1941) and *Requiem für einen Freund* (1943).[15] They are hardly of any interest, except to the student of the poet's development.

> ... Where is life—thus the question from the decaying lips—where is meaning, where love—thus the question of the lost souls, the souls in confusion. Not knowing the nature of things, not understanding them—here lies the answer to everything. Bleeding and lamenting, the religions tore asunder, tore into shreds, and the merciless, the true face of the Nothing kept silence

through all space—and where is there comfort? thus the agonised prayer of the hearts. The Celestial Spirit smiled with pain, as he fell on the battlefield of Chaos—he had no question. . . .[16]

The mixture of Storm and Stress *gothique,* Hölderlin, Rilke and Expressionism is only too obvious in this and other passages. They do, however, contain some of the main themes of the poet's mature work. The dynamic absence of God (e.g. *Gottes Auge,*[17] where a child addresses the eye of a dead cod as God's eye, because mother has told him that it belongs to God; the child reacts to the eye's silence with fascination, exasperation, finally indifference); the adoration of nature to the point of uniting with it (concluding passage of *Die Hundeblume,*[18] which is reminiscent of a Gauguin picture of the South Sea Islanders); the theme of wandering, or journeying, which plays an important part in most works, from the drivers of milk vans, "these cowboys of the city",[19] in the third of the mature stories, *Alle Milchgeschäfte heissen Hinsch,* to Lieutenant Fischer's Via Dolorosa *(Die lange lange Strasse lang)* and the cuckoo's loneliness, whose home is the open road, because "our heart, our innocence, our mother, home and war are lost"[20] *(Im Mai, im Mai schrie der Kuckuck),* so that the soldier (who exemplifies this loneliness in the second half of the work) is too weary, even to take advantage of the woman, whose bed and services he has bought with a loaf of bread for the night!—written towards the end of the poet's career (summer 1947; the latter work is, in fact, the last which he wrote before he went to Switzerland).

The pose, which the poet adopts in *Die Blume,* is that of Hamlet, or of Hölderlin's Hyperion, flinging questions at Universal Existence and at Nothingness, alternating between ecstasy and despair, between a positive and a negative answer: " . . . Delivered up, at the mercy of the Remote, the Unspeakable, the Uncertain, the Dark . . . And our death is planned from the beginning . . .", at the mercy of Chance, suffering, lonely; "We live without God, without permanence in space, without promise, without certainty . . ."—yet on the other hand passionately in love with life, eager to experience all its vital impulses, aware of the monstrous jungle, which is any one of our cities, ". . . cruel, yet good. The city: silent, proud, stony, immortal.—And out there, at the periphery of the city, the new day dawns: with the purity of frost, utterly transparent." (*Gespräch über den Dächern.*)[21]

The Other One: . . . I am the voice that everybody really knows. I am the Other One, who is always present. The other man, the one that answers; the one that laughs, when you cry; that drives you on, when you get tired; I am the one to drive you on, I am the hidden depths, the irksome feelings. I am the optimist, who sees the good in the worst people and the lamplight in the blackest night . . . and the one that says Yes, when you say No—I am the one who says Yes. And the—

Beckmann: Say Yes as much as you like. Go away. I don't want you. I say No. No. No. Go away. I say No. Do you hear?[22]

The lyrics already contain many of the motifs, which Borchert was to work out more thoroughly in his prose pieces and in the play. And these two early prose pieces thus form a bridge between the two phases of the poet's work. In them we may also detect flashes of that concreteness in the presentation of setting and action, in the visual field, which makes his prose writing so effective. And we find beginnings of one of the most important characteristics of Borchert's style: the device of juxtaposing objects, or even words and short sentences, which appear, outwardly, to be totally disconnected, and which result in forming a rhythmic and visual pattern, having an atmosphere and a psychical unity of their own. But the relation to the observer—whether of such patterns, or even of single objects—is put on a new basis. Sometimes the poet uses, as it were, the style of a schoolchild's essay, or of an *ingénu,* so that the object the poet presents should be able to make its impact and impart its message, independent of our preconceived notions of it.

The following passage from *Requiem für einen Freund* is still far too close to the Rilkean model—

. . . Und dann vergess ich es nie, wie du nach tagelangem Marsch in dem zerschossenen Haus die kleine verschrumpfte Kartoffel aus der Asche nahmst, wie man eine kostbare Frucht, einen Pfirsich nimmt und voll Andacht ihren Geruch atmetest. —Erde und Sonne—sagtest du, und draussen waren es 48 Grad Kälte. . . .[23]

Let us now consider one of the last stories that Borchert wrote, *Maria, alles Maria,* in order to appreciate, how the poet's style and presentation had matured in a matter of less than four years. This is how the story opens—

Als er dann seine Stiefel auszog, hätten wir ihn am liebsten erschlagen.

Als er in unsere Zelle kam, roch es plötzlich nach Tier und Tabak und Schweiss und Angst und Leder. Er war Pole. Aber er war so geistlos blond wie ein Germane. Und diese blonden Männer waren immer etwas fade. Er auch. Und auch noch ein wenig fadenscheinig. Er konnte nur wenige Worte deutsch. Aber er hatte ein schönes buntes Abziehbild in der Tasche. Das betete er immer sehr lange an. Er stellte es dann auf seinen Schemel gegen den Trinkbecher. Er betete laut und auf polnisch . . .[24]

There follows an account of the picture—"a girl with a red scarf and a blue dress". She showed one breast, was "white and thin as a rake" ("reichlich mager"): altogether somewhat second-rate, as women go. But she had a few sunrays round her head.

> . . . Aber sonst sah sie ziemlich stur aus. Wir fanden das jedenfalls. Aber der Pole sagte Maria zu ihr. Und dabei machte er eine Handbewegung, als wollte er sagen : Na, is se nich n prächtiger Kerl ! Aber er meinte wohl etwas Zärtlicheres, wenn er uns angrinste und Maria sagte. Vielleicht sollte es ein sanftes frommes Lächeln werden, aber wir hassten ihn so sehr, für uns war das eben Grinsen. Er sagte : Maria.[24a]

This is alienation at its most brilliant. The primitive son of the earth is an outsider, his gaudy picture of the Virgin has become an extraordinary object, remote, colourful, yet unprepossessing, and his childlike devotion releases feelings with a personal quality about them, so that the life of the prison cell is revolutionised. Mary is in the centre, the prison bars are at the periphery.

If the poet wanted to dispose of a Rilkean icon by making the object of the Polish prisoner's devotion seem unattractive, the devotion itself emerges untarnished, while the other prisoners' hate, however intense, becomes more and more of an effort. His smile may be a *grin*—but he says : *Mary*. And gradually the prisoners come to realise that their hatred is not the superficial irritation, or even hostility, of the group against a foreign body, but that it has the intensely personal quality of a love-hate relationship. When he is taken away to be executed, two of the prisoners "said nothing. We knew, Liebig [another fellow-prisoner] was now sorry, that he had hated the Pole". (p. 110).

But that is not the end of the story. His childlike faith had shed a lustre on the degrading, impersonal quality of prison-life. With a mixture of such childlike faith and equally childlike cunning, he had fought the judicial system—and lost. Fear and bewilderment replaced his confident faith.

The end of the story occurs four months later, when one of the prisoners, who is also the narrator of the story,[25] is released, and, on his way out of prison, encounters the Pole, who is scrubbing the floor of the passage. He had had his death sentence commuted to fifteen years' imprisonment. "Remitted" : the German word "begnadigt" contains the meaning of having received mercy, or grace. This is certainly how the Pole takes it : "only fifteen years !"

...Und dann strahlte er und strich über seine Tasche: Maria, flüsterte er, alles Maria. Und dabei machte er ein Gesicht, als hätte er die Justiz ganz gewaltig übers Ohr gehauen. Er hatte es. Die Justiz der ganzen Welt.(26)

We see here the two sides of the Pole's character showing each other up. He is naïve, when he appears not to be so, and when his naïveté seems to be most manifest, his self-awareness warns us not to be taken in by what is apparently childlike simplicity. A pair of opposite, and superficially incompatible, qualities are put in dialectic relationship with each other. It is this which makes *alienation* possible, for it is in the nature of a dialectic relationship, that the pair of opposites are externalised forms of an original quality or existence common to both of them, and that this reappraisal of their common ground—which occurs, when they illuminate each other *ab extra*—should provide the dynamic for achieving a higher unity.

A study of Borchert's life and personality shows, that pairs of opposites in his attitudes, moods, thoughts and in his reaction to his environment are clear-cut to quite an extraordinary degree. This is also reflected in his manner of writing. Persons, actions, situations, are all set in a well-defined town- or landscape, and the events, with their motivation, are made manifest to the reader in the form of sense impressions. Yet by means of alienation we are taken to the very heart of the issues at stake—we relive the action, we re-experience its joys, its sorrows, its problematic.

This mastery of subject-matter and language is hardly more than a faint promise in *Die Blume* and *Requiem*. All the more astonishing is the fact that it breaks out, fully mature, when, on January 24, 1946, the poet writes his first major prose work, *Die Hundeblume*. And it is sustained, with surprisingly few lapses, right down to the last major work, *Im Mai, im Mai schrie der Kuckuck* (summer 1947), and the final manifesto, *Dann gibt es nur eins,*(27) which he wrote shortly before his death.

Hugo Sieker's, very early, warning(28) against "falling in love too much with single words", to the detriment of meaning, of the "solid core of substantial fact" (festen sachlichen kern") and Dr. Würzburger's recommendation in his letter dated October 24, 1947 (i.e. a month before the poet's death),(29) "that a more economic handling of the device of repeating the same expression, of continual playing with the same, often grey ball, would—with all respect for the truth-value of monotony—make the impact much more powerful"—these views are certainly relevant to a criticism of Borchert's prose—I am thinking especially of *Gespräch über den Dächern*. Yet it is surprising, how rarely his sense of timing fails him, even in such highly rhetorical pieces as *Die lange lange Strasse lang*, or *Im Mai, im Mai schrie der Kuckuck*. And the reason for this great buoyancy may be sought in the dialectic nature of the poet's attitude. For while the reader (or, in the case of the play, *Draussen vor der Tür*, the audience) is made to participate in the inner experience which the work in question presents, by watching and listening, even smelling and tasting, the poet himself moves in the *opposite* direction: he detaches himself, and views, even the most deeply felt sentiment, critically, even ironically. Let us take two examples. The first is from the story, *Der Kaffee ist undefinierbar*,[30] which is set in the desolate atmosphere of a station waiting-room. Men are reduced to mere functions designed to fill the gap between birth and death, hung over chairs and tables like drapery, playthings of a God without eyes and ears, simply covering, like cloth, the "chairs, bars, tables, gallows and immense abysses",[31] over which they have been hung ("hingehängt"). Their isolation from each other is complete. But their supreme desolation is due to their isolation from this God without eyes and ears, whose impotent playthings they are, who lets them breathe—just that and no more!—and who reduces their cries—by this very loneliness—to the thin-voiced tinkling of a bell.

The point at issue is this *absence* of seeing, communicating and hearing, the *remoteness* of man from man, so that the responsible coexistence of persons in community gets reduced to the chance togetherness of biological functions, and the *presence* of God, his vital breath, his powerful Word of Truth, gets veiled behind this cruel mask of deaf and blind facelessness. The *ruach adonai*, the *Logos* has become the mere originator and sustainer of bodies which breathe, which exercise their instincts "savagely, greedily, omnivorously" ("wild, gierig, gefrässig"). Four people sit at a table, three men and a girl. Suddenly, but in the most matter-of-fact way, the girl says that she is going to commit suicide. In this very situation, but also in the ensuing conversation, again and again, the opportunity presents itself of being truthful, of talking in a responsible, truly personal manner. The opportunity is missed every time, until the men discover that the girl has, in fact, carried out her intention. One of the characters, an intellectual ("der Buchmann"—"the man with the book"), suddenly recognises his and the other two men's irresponsible attitude: the girl had been lonely, and they had simply talked about her, then about their own concerns, as if she had not been present.[32]

> ...[the man with the book] looked into the empty cup. From the bottom of the cup a girl was looking at him. But he was no longer able to recognise her.

He is now seized with the full horror of this world of untruthfulness and desolation. And it comes home to him, through the atmosphere of the railway station, enveloped in night, with its fog, its misery and the smell of human breath. The coffee is wet and cold like the sweat of fear.

> ...The man with the book closed his eyes. The coffee is quite abominable, he heard the breadmerchant say. Yes, indeed, he nodded slowly, you are right: quite abominable....

The man with the book has reached a moment of truth: it is the picture of the girl, whom he can no longer recognise, that is real and important. The world around him has only one genuine fact which it can communicate: fear. The second of the three men, the breadmerchant, seems also to have arrived at a moment of truth. No longer is the coffee called "indefinable", it is defined, truthfully and exactly: "abominable".

But the third man, a soldier, breaks into the conversation, and restores the former state of irresponsibility and untruthfulness—

> ...Abominable this, abominable that, said the soldier, the fact is, that we have nothing else. The main thing is, that it is hot.

The soldier lets the glass tube, which had contained the girl's poison tablets, roll over the table and smash on the ground.

> ...(And God? He did not hear that small ugly sound. Whether it was a little glass tube that broke, or a heart: God heard nothing of all this. Remember, he had no ears. That was it; he had no ears.)

In this way the soldier gets back to the existential horror of the opening of this story. It is worth noticing—and here we come back to the question of Borchert's detachment—that this crowning horror is put in brackets and couched in conversational language. At the moment, where a heart breaks, and God is once again called deaf, the language is that of small-talk, and the whole passage treated as an aside. But there is also an example in this story of how a profound sentiment is treated ironically, until it becomes a real hindrance to the possible emergence of truth. It occurs for the first time near the beginning of the story,[33] when the three men first take stock of the indefinable quality of the coffee, and of the girl's declared intention to commit suicide.

The man with the book considers the impossibility of the girl drowning herself, because the cup is too small. The soldier, who has a *constitutionally* happy face, maintains that she must be mad. Something human stirs in the mind of the breadmerchant: the discrepancy between the soldier's face and what he says:

> ... Makes a Whitsuntide face and talks of murder....

A crisis seems imminent. The soldier is a man of whom one must beware, the breadmerchant continues. The door has been opened to some plain speaking—if to nothing else. But the man with the book knows the answer—and all further questioning is silenced. There is no need, in other words, to get excited over such discrepancies as a happy face and murderous talk—or of a cup that is too small for the girl to get drowned in. This is how the man with the book silences the argument and eases the uncomfortable tension:

> ... That is dualism, do you understand? typical dualism. We all have a bit of Jesus and of Nero in us, do you understand? All of us. Thereupon he made a grimace, pushed his chin and lower lip forward, narrowed the openings of his eyes until they were mere slits and inflated his nostrils. Nero, he said by way of explanation. Then he made a soft sentimental sort of face, smoothed down his hair and made eyes like a faithful dog, harmless and somewhat boring. Jesus, he explained this time....

Now, there is no doubt that Borchert was keenly aware of the tragic consequences of this dichotomy. He illustrates it in such stories as *Vorbei vorbei*,[34] the story of a young man at odds with himself, who is finally killed in war—his last cry "vinegar", recalling the Crucifixion; or *Jesus macht nicht mehr mit*,[35] the soldier with the "Jesus"-face, who is used for measuring newly dug graves, until he cannot stand it any longer; or *Billbrook*,[36] the Canadian Sergeant Major in the Air Force, who visits a bombed part of Hamburg, and is appalled by the destruction which his own people (himself included) have brought about; or Timm in *Vielleicht hat sie ein rosa Hemd*,[37] who crushes the dream of love and tenderness of a fellow-soldier on the Russian front, but cannot get away from the dream himself. This dualism, then, whether within one and the same person, or in the clash between personalities, or between a person and a system, is as basic as it is tragic. Yet here it is trivialised. What is the purpose?

I take it that Borchert was thinking of the harmful effect of a premature synthesis, which glosses over the conflicting issues, with which our present condition is, after all, burdened. He attacks the socially integrated, grown-up, secure people, whose maturity is, in fact, a façade, and whose authority makes it possible for them to send generation after generation of young people into war.

A playful instance of this pseudo-maturity occurs in *Die Küchenuhr*,[38] where a young man joins a group of people sitting on a seat in the sun. His house has recently been bombed out of existence, his parents killed. He has only rescued the kitchen clock from the universal wreckage. Its works are smashed, but the face is still intact. Its hands point to 2.30 a.m. As this appears to be important to the young man, one of these people, a gentleman, hazards an explanation.

> Then I suppose your house was hit at half past two, the man said, and *made his lower lip protrude with an air of importance*. I have often heard of that sort of thing happening. When the bomb comes down, all watches and clocks stop. It's caused by the pressure.

But the gentleman has missed the point completely. "You must not always talk of bombs", the young man replies, shaking his head with a superior air. He pricks the bubble of adult self-importance In spite of the important sound of such words as "bomb" and "pressure", and the impressiveness of a protruding lower lip (this occurs in a number of stories), the explanation is not merely irrelevant, it is quite wrong.

The hands of the clock *commemorate*, in fact, a scene that had been enacted night after night, before the bombs had destroyed the young man's family life : his coming home at 2.30 a.m., his mother's coming out into the kitchen and preparing a meal for him, barefoot, with a woollen cardigan and a red scarf on, with no other comment than : "so late again". This commemoration acquires the significance of a sacramental *anamnesis*, for through it the young man captures an intimation of "paradise".[39]

> ... And now I know, that it really was paradise. Well and truly : Paradise.

The other people are too embarrassed to look at him—they are, we might say, afraid of discarding the mask of adulthood. But the gentleman has also caught something of the young man's intimation. He looks at his shoes.

> ... But he did not see his shoes. He kept on thinking of this one word : paradise.

We turn now to the evil consequences of this pseudo-maturity. Borchert describes the characters, who think they are mature, with a mixture of envy and bitterness. They sit in their trams,[40] and they know where they are going (*Im Mai, im Mai schrie der Kuckuck*), so they must be happy! Their security under the wings of the ubiquitous watchfulness of the State is complete. They pay for that security in taxes, or with an amputated leg as a result of war—although war invalids are only charged half fare! Being good actors, they are as convinced as nine-year-olds, of the helpless, important, ageing of their childish faces. They play at being grown-ups, although, in secret, they would prefer to make pellets out of their tram tickets and bombard each other with these. For, as with ex-accountant Erwin Knoke, who is also the ex-convict No. 1563 (*Von drüben nach drüben*), they have no notion of a community of persons, bound together by love. Examples of the latter are: *Die drei dunklen Könige* (a Nativity-type); *Das Brot* (not as close to Eucharistic *anamnesis* as *Die Küchenuhr*); *Schischyphusch* (the author remembers from his childhood an encounter between his uncle and a waiter, who share the same speech defect. Pride and fear are overcome by true humanity).[41] Their ideal, as that of Erwin Knoke, is the Wild West, as depicted in the Winnetou stories of Karl May, with their projection into eternity of hunting-grounds, where thrills may be had without effort, without intermission and without expenditure of emotion, and adventures do not have to be paid for in terms of danger.

> ...(...the eternal hunting-grounds still kept haunting his brain, since he lacked any other notion of eternity. This had been his one modest little vice.)[42]

Erwin Knoke, the victim of the all-powerful State and its protégés, the ageing children, who play at being grown-ups, is treated with sympathy and pity (like the waiter in *Schischyphusch*). But he shares with them the same longing for an *Ersatz* Heaven. The whole of their life is one vast game of make-belief. That is its deadly danger. As scientists, they write a few figures on a piece of paper—and two grammes of the product can liquidate a thousand people (*Lesebuchgeschichten*);[43] as generals, they draw a red line and a dot on a map and that signifies a village in flames (*Die Katze war im Schnee erfroren*);[44] as N.C.O.s they liquidate "86 Iwans" with a few bursts of machine-gun fire (*Die lange lange Strasse lang*);[45] as teachers, they put on their dark suits, hold a farewell celebration, with hymns, poetry and prose in praise of God and Fatherland (*Lesebuchgeschichten*),[46] sending their pupils off to the front; as fathers they see them off at the station with the usual clichés: be a good soldier, my boy—show courage to the last breath!—waving their hats, all to the tune of E. M. Arndt's battle-hymn, "God, by whose decree steel sprang up on this earth" (*Im Mai, im Mai schrie der Kuckuck*).[47]

> When the war was over, the soldier came home.
> But he had no bread to eat. Then he saw a man
> who had bread. He killed him.
> But you must not kill people, said the judge.
> Why not, asked the soldier.
>
> (*Lesebuchgeschichten.*)[48]

A great deal of Borchert's writing is concerned with the showing up of the assumptions on which political and social life is based; many of these are not the result of experience and thought which have attained maturity and preserved depth in balance, but are simply an escape from the challenge of truth and moral responsibility in personal living. The family, the state, daily routine, books, shopping, social conventions, the military machine, prison (on *either* side of the locked door)—all these can offer false security and the most pernicious dehumanisation. Morality becomes obedience to a system, truths—even important, deeply cherished ideas and attitudes—are reduced to clichés.

I come now to the second example of how even the poet's own attitude can be viewed critically and with irony and detachment. It is scene 4 of *Draussen vor der Tür*,[49] the one play that Borchert wrote in his mature period of production.

Beckmann, ex-soldier, ex-prisoner-of-war, comes back from three years' Siberian captivity, and tries to return to normal civilian life. But his son has been killed in the air raids, his wife has deserted him and his old colonel is completely insensitive to his predicament. In scene 4 he has an interview with the manager of a cabaret. He is first treated to a harangue on the needs of contemporary theatre: it is to be sober, devoted to truth, sensitive to the needs of the age and full of the vigour of youth. No profundities, no mature balance, no detached objectivity, but the immediacy of the cry of the heart—questing, hoping, hungering! The great need of the day: men who will depict "the grey, living, suffering face of our time".[50]

Now, this statement would appear to be quite impressive. The embracing of "truth" and the refusal to be "profound" need not be self-contradictory, because by the latter is meant stability, balance, intellectual validtiy. In literary history—indeed in the history of all the arts, as in that of society generally—periods of reasoned balance and formal decorum have always alternated with revolutionary phases, where devotion to truth has led to an abrogation of serenity in attitude and exquisiteness in aesthetic style. The sufferings, hypocrisies, absurdities, which disfigure the social scene and render the predicament of the individual critical, are then shown up with prophetic frankness. Indeed, Borchert himself had presented his own contemporaries with a profile of the harassed, restless generation of young people, who were afraid of personal feeling, because neither the present nor the past contained anything of lasting significance, any real ties; their life was movement without pattern, story without plot.

> Our existence is filled with encounters, encounters which do not last and which terminate without farewell—like the stars. They approach each other, stand next to one another for some light-seconds, then move away from each other: without trace, without tie, without farewell.
>
> (*Generation ohne Abschied*)[51]

They had no homecoming, so they were looking forward to an arrival on a new star, a life under a new sun, "zu einem neuen Lieben, zu einem neuen Lachen, zu einem neuen Gott" ("to a new loving, a new laughing, a new God").[52]

Later, Borchert was to deepen this picture of the *hectic* age, and to call on the poet to invent new rhythms, new harmonies, to capture the truth regarding contemporary existence, the tremendous *ugliness* of its agonies, the need for starting in a vacuum for building a community of persons, whose life was rooted in a love which took suffering as its starting-point and was all-embracing: *Das ist unser Manifest*,[53] written in late spring 1947. A shorter piece, *Der Schriftsteller*,[54] is a product of the same period. In this, the writer's prophetic duty is outlined. He is to present the *sober truth*—

> The writer must *name* the house, which all men are engaged in building. He must also name the different rooms.... He must not call the cellar "the beautiful room".

—and when the house is in danger, he must "blow the trumpet, until his lungs burst"—an obligation, which the man with the book is on the verge of realising, when he *closes his eyes* (*Der Kaffee ist undefinierbar*), and which the poet himself realised: with literal clarity—

> ...Our German word *Krieg*, war, is written with a *g* at the end. G like *Grube*, a ditch or grave....
>
> (*An diesem Dienstag*)[55]

with satire—

> When in the year 5000 a mole peeped out from under the earth, he felt reassured, as he remarked:
> The trees are still trees.

> The crows still croak.
> And the dogs still lift up their hind-legs.
> ......
> And occasionally—yes, occasionally one comes across a human being.
>
> (Last of the *Lesebuchgeschichten*)[56]

and with apocalyptic force, when he exhorts people in all walks and conditions of life to say No, if they should ever be called upon to harness their skills to the promotion of war: in his final manifesto, *Dann gibt es nur eins,*[57] written in Basle a few days before his death. The climax of this work occurs in the second half, where the poet describes what would happen, if mothers did not say No, when called upon to bear children, in order to have nurses for military hospitals and soldiers for new battles.

> Then the last man will wander around, his entrails in shreds, his lungs festering, diseased—at a loss for an answer, lonely, the rays of the sun beating down on him with poisonous heat, the stars above him swaying senselessly; lonely, lost among an unending expanse of mass graves and the cold idols of the cities, whose gigantic blocks of concrete spell desolation. The last man—his body dried up, insane, blaspheming, lamenting and accusing: WHY?—and his terrible lament, this accusation, will drain away in the wasteland, unheard and unheeded. . . .[58]

Perhaps Dr. Würzburger is right[59] when he links this passage with chapter one of Genesis, which the poet was reading, when he visited him five days before his death: "Perhaps Borchert decided to find out", he says, with reference to verse 2 ("And the earth was without form, and void . . . "), "what is involved in the realisation of the possibility—all too imminent and within the bounds of human feasibility—of making the earth once again 'without form and void' ". Meyer-Marwitz[60] thinks that this manifesto was an appeal to the conscience of the world, "with Hiroshima in mind". It is in any case the climax of a series of manifestoes, in which the poet is faithful to his mission of "presenting", as the manager in scene 4 of *Draussen vor der Tür* says, "the grey, living, suffering face of our time". The manager's remarks, then, would appear to form a link between *Generation ohne Abschied* (written before December 1946) and *Das ist unser Manifest* (late spring 1947—*Draussen vor der Tür* was written in January 1947). But let us look at the text more closely. The manager is really holding a monologue. Beckmann's remarks go unheeded, and it is only by association with the word "face" ("leidvolle Gesicht . . . Übrigens bei Gesicht fällt mir ein:

. . ."—"suffering face . . . Talking of face, it occurs to me . . .")[61] that his attention returns to Beckmann, and he asks him about his glasses. Beckmann's remarks, on the other hand, are in each case a comment on some detail in the manager's harangue. He agrees with the manager about the need for sobriety—only he is thinking, not of the young Schiller, Grabbe, or Heine, but of Siberia, his dead son, his unfaithful wife, and the river Elbe, who, in *The Dream*—the scene preceding scene 1,[62] had disillusioned him about her character: she is a self-respecting woman, not a romantic girl, "type Ophelia", and she throws him back on the riverbank, refusing to allow him to commit suicide, sending him back into the rough and tumble of life (". . . If somebody kicks you, kick him back! . . .").

Beckmann's next agreement is on the subject of hunger. The manager is inveighing against mature, rounded off works of art.

Manager: . . . Let it be a cry, a crying out, uttered from the very heart: question, hope, hunger!
Beckmann (to himself): Hunger—oh, yes, we are certainly hungry!

The third agreement occurs, when the manager speaks of *presenting* the face of the time—

Manager: . . . What we lack are the *avant garde* writers, who present the grey, living, suffering face of our time.
Beckmann (to himself): Oh yes: always "present"—present faces! present arms! present ghosts!—Something is always presented!

The manager speaks of hunger as an aesthetic experience, a quest —Beckmann is simply hungry; the manager is speaking of the power of the word—Beckmann recalls the military machine and his pangs of conscience. Perhaps the manager knows Toller's play, *Die Wandlung*, which has a Prologue, where, even in death, the skeletons go on parade: the military machine has even swallowed up death in war. But Beckmann's experience of a parade of skeletons is not a stage set, but a genuine nightmare, haunting him (scene 3), as it surely did Toller and Borchert, who were poets with sufficient courage to be genuinely devoted to truth.

The poet sees it as his prophetic task to explore and interpret, even the most agonising experience. Beckmann is unable to do so; he simply suffers, and all he would really like to do is to sleep or to die. Or, on the other hand, he would like to rediscover what it is like to love and be loved, to speak and to listen in a real encounter. For the moment, however, he would simply like not to be hungry and out in the cold. Now, the manager has seen to it that his nest is feathered. He is concerned, not with sleep, death or hunger, but with their stark presentation on the stage. He is not after *real* experience, but after *moving* experience. In the list of characters, the poet comments that the manager "would like to be courageous, but in the end prefers being a coward".[63] This would suggest that there had been a time when he had aspired after truth. But by the time Beckmann arrives, the aspiration has fossilised into a set piece of literary salesmanship. Beckmann frightens him, in fact, by singing a song, in which the "grey, living face of our time" shows up with stark truth. And it is at this point, that it transpires that the manager is not even concerned with a moving experience, but merely with pleasing his audience. It is no use feeding the people with rye bread, when they ask for pastry.[64] The manager now recommends Beckmann the detachment of a Goethe, who wrote an operetta by the camp fire,[65] the positive approach of Mozart, of Schiller's *Jungfrau von Orléans* (a play about St. Joan), of Wagner, Schmeling, Shirley Temple;[66] polish and experience[67]—as if Siberia had not been an experience!—"discreet *piquancy* in eroticism"—but also ethics and profounder wisdom of life.[68]

Now, it is true, that Borchert found Goethe unendurable. In letters and conversations he made it quite clear that he could abide neither his sensibility (the eighteenth-century *Empfindsamkeit*), nor his achievement of balance, and, worst of all, the Olympian pose! On one level, therefore, Borchert is here ridiculing maturity. But it is the sort of maturity which will have nothing to do with truth. Art, he finally tells Beckmann,[69] has nothing to do with truth. You don't get very far with truth; truth only makes you unpopular.

The manager, then, praises *avant-garde* immaturity, and classical maturity; single-minded devotion to truth and elegant, "positive" art; agony and detachment; *piquancy* and rounded-off wisdom and ethics—but he is committed to all of them only in so far as they are box office draws. Borchert sees that even his most deeply held convictions become ridiculous, when they are merely clichés. As for maturity, this is admissible only when it is existentially true. Thus in a letter to Hugo Sieker (Jena, October 20, 1944)[70] he speaks of the positive effect that the Army and the war might have: that of making a person "even more sensitive (in the good sense of the word)!" ("noch empfindlicher (im gutem Sinne)"); and he goes on:

> ... And it is not only we who undergo a severe test—Mozart, Hölderlin, Van Gogh must also show us, that their value goes beyond simply filling in our leisure hours and giving us entertainment!—

And in a letter to Dr. Gantz (Hamburg, February 27, 1947), in answer to a criticism of his play, he writes[71] of the change that takes place in the growing person's religious outlook, as the child's naïve notion of a God, as a super-person, always at the beck and call of anybody who prays, ready to ward off all evil and danger, if called upon, is destroyed by more mature experience. He continues:

> ... But tell me now: How is a young person of our day, who recognises, that his childish conception of God is a false one, who is going through *such* a war, *such* a peace, as has fallen to our lot—how is he to believe in the good, the divine? Such a faith is only possible, where there is a high degree of inner maturity and steadfastness in character and outlook—as well as a certain stability and integration in a person's social orientation. And it is these very qualities that a young person cannot and ought not to have.

Borchert sees, then, quite clearly, that maturity is the state, which a person achieves with more advanced years. To act, as if one had attained it, to mistake a certain façade of poise and authoritativeness for the balance which is achieved through suffering, through facing truth, is as pathetically, tragically false as the refusal to envisage anything but rebellion: to be *merely* a monk or an adventurer (or alternating between the two)[72] results, not only in permanent exile from society, in perpetual loneliness, but above all in the exclusion of the most precious of all qualities: love. Borchert had envisaged the rebuilding of Germany, through the rediscovery of love in the very desolation of bombed cities and the brutality of daily living: loving Germany "as the Christians love their Christ: for the sake of his suffering".[73] The inability to love, in the typical manner of the *generation without farewell,* is depicted in such simple, yet powerful, stories as: *Marguerite*[74] (still gentle—one of the earlier pieces, in which the pleasure of reminiscing seems to predominate), *Später Nachmittag* and *Die traurigen Geranien*[75] (stories in which flight prevents even the possibility of a genuine encounter), *Bleib doch, Giraffe,*[76] in which love-making, even at the animal level, is vitiated by a sense of fear, due to loneliness and guilt, so that it is cut short by the soldier, who leaves the girl, lonely and desolate; and above all in the second half of *Im Mai, im Mai schrie der Kuckuck,*[77] where the mouth of the sleeping soldier tells the woman of the brazenness that is there to cover up the rootlessness, which she in her heart would rather not remember.

The fact is, that Borchert had already looked beyond the immaturity of the young person, who is disillusioned, both, about the social and religious security of the child, and about the false security of the passengers in the yellow tram,[78] who play at being grown-ups, but in reality have no better notion of eternity than the hunting-grounds of Winnetou, obedient servants of the state, whose success consists in wars, into which they send the younger generation with enthusiasm. In *Draussen vor der Tür*, the colonel and the manager exemplify these types very clearly. The child's God in the shape of the old man, in whom nobody believes any longer, as we keep on hearing, is also shown up. But Borchert has also seen through another notion : the reverting to a primeval state of primitive harmony with all nature—frequent enough in the lyrics, magnificently expressed at the end of *Die Hundeblume*.(79) Not that Borchert wants to give up his sense of kinship with the stones of the city, the wind, the forests—all objects, all life, such as he had loved from the earliest lyrics on.(80) In fact, cosmic breathing and cosmic speech recur a number of times throughout the prose works.(81) But he realises now, that a flight into primeval or subhuman forms of primitive existence does not in itself lead to a discovery of the divine or the good. We can see this in the relationship between Beckmann and the Other One.

In scene 1, from which we have already quoted, where the Other One first introduces himself to Beckmann, he is told to go away, *because he has no face*. He answers that he has a *thousand* faces—but that is really the same thing. He represents the natural vitality of the human species, always hoping, always persevering in this business of living. But the nature of man's predicament, in its moral, personal aspect is beyond his scope.

It is he who, in scene 1, draws Beckmann's attention to the girl, who is walking along the banks of the Elbe, while Beckmann, only just washed ashore and awakened from his suicide dream, is still reluctant to get up and face life. The girl offers Beckmann pity, then love—and thereby, both, reminds him of his guilty act during the war in Russia, and involves him in guilt now. For just as Beckmann had found his wife in the arms of another man, so he now takes the place of the girl's husband, who has also just returned from Siberia and now finds himself an intruder in his own home. He also it is whom Beckmann had commanded to "hold his post to the last" (scene 2),(82) which had cost the man one of his legs. It is the Other One, too, who advises Beckmann to visit his old colonel, in order to return to him his responsibility (Scenes 2 and 3)(83) for the twenty men whom he had been ordered to take out on reconnaissance east of Gorodok, and for whom he had been given the responsibility; eleven had not returned.

Then there is Death, the great devaluer of all life, himself a devalued entity: a prosperous undertaker *(Vorspiel)*,(84) who eats up dead humans "like flies", and who has their devotion by a perversion of the Theological Virtues: Faith, Love, Fear; or the roadsweeper, employee of the undertaking firm Garbage & Decay, ex-general, sweeping up human corpses like so much rubbish—this death always has his door open (scene 5),[85] and Beckmann hankers after going down to him. But the Other One heads him off.

The Other One thus provides the framework, into which Beckmann can build his quest for personal existence and moral values. But he does no more. To him humans are essentially "the two-legged species", who can be revived, no matter how sick unto death they may feel.

> . . . Simply on account of a few curls, a piece of white skin and a whiff of some woman's body. There they are, up again from their deathbed and healthy and strong like ten thousand stags in February. . . . (end of scene 1)[86]

So it is not surprising, that to him life is good, men are good, only death is to be avoided (second half of scene 5);[87] for life to him has the splendour of the ten thousand stags in February. But when Beckmann faces the dilemma of God and moral responsibility, the Other One has left him and Beckmann is alone. "Where are you now, you, the one who always says yes? Answer me now! Now I need you!... But you have gone all of a sudden!" (end of scene 5),[88] thus he harangues him. But the Other One's vital energy, necessary as it is to provide an organic basis for life, does not bear evaluation on the moral and spiritual planes—on these it is merely shallow optimism.

Beckmann's wife had first made him aware of his dehumanised state, when she had ignored his Christian name.

> . . . Beckmann—that was how my wife addressed me. Simply Beckmann . . . just as one calls a table, "table". Piece of furniture Beckmann. Put it away somewhere, the piece of furniture Beckman. . . . (scene 1 : dialogue with the Other One)[89]

And what he now learns—in his appeals to the colonel and the manager—is, that society is in no better state—worse, in fact, for as soon as the danger of an inconvenient truth looms on their horizon, they erect a barrier of clichés, supported either by naïve robustness or by smooth professionalism—but in any case quite impenetrable.[90] The self-deception and moral irresponsibility of these attitudes are shown up in great detail in the later prose pieces, and we have already considered them. To some extent Beckmann shares these attitudes. This is brought out very clearly by the symbolic use of his and the manager's glasses. The latter has three elegant pairs, which (scene 4)[91] are *quite essential* to him. He depends on them for his ideas, the effect he has on the public, his moods ("Einfälle . . . Wirkung . . . Stimmungen"). Beckmann's normal, civilian pair had been "shot to smithereens" in the war, as he tells the girl in scene 2.[92] He now wears a pair of gas-mask spectacles, which reduces even his face to a "grey uniform-face . . . a tin-robot-face" ("so ein graues Uniformgesicht . . . So ein blechernes Robotergesicht"). And without it he is ". . . lost without hope. Really, utterly helpless"—so he tells the girl (scene 2 : *ibid*). And to the manager he says:

> . . . That is my salvation. After all, there is no other salvation —no other glasses, I mean (scene 4).[93]

Now, the girl takes off his glasses, so that Beckmann's vision becomes blurred (scene 2):[94] "I think you wear such gas-mask spectacles inside, as well as on your nose . . ." she says to him. Without them, he has to reorientate himself as a human being—towards love, and towards awareness of his own guilt. The manager's glasses are expensive and of his own choosing: he can deceive himself. Beckmann's pair were issued to him. Their ugliness shows up the immorality and spiritual emptiness of the System of which they are a product. The clarity of vision which they give may be deceptive; but the sense of security—however tyrannous and false—makes them as indispensable as the manager's three pairs or the colonel's naïve Prussianism. Beckmann, then, is at the cross-roads. He seeks out, then discards, a society which has no use for him, and therefore discards him. Bereft of the security of the military machine, of his former family life, of post-war civilian society, he tries to return to his mother (scene 5). But both his parents are dead. His dream about them is shattered—they had been too involved in Nazism, and committed suicide. His childhood now appears as an unreal dream, just as death is not the Romantic fusion with the elements—"type Ophelia". He is told this by Frau Kramer, who is hard and cynical enough to quote her husband's comment on the suicide of the parents, that the gas, with which they had gassed themselves, would have done for a whole month's cooking.[95] Her indifference is, in fact, a vulgar version of that of the rest of society: a trivialising of emotion into sentimentality, a hardening of the instinct of self-preservation, until moral sensitivity is stifled.

> *Frau Kramer* (robust, so as not to howl with weeping): . . . Certainly, it touches my heart—but where would we be, if we went round, crying over all the tragedies of people? . . . otherwise even one's little bit of margarine goes rancid that one has on the bread . . . (scene 5, second half)[96]

Beckmann is thus completely alone. All normal bonds of family and society are severed. His one possibility of loving and being loved is overshadowed by guilt; for if he can ignore Frau Kramer's remark,[97] that he must have *known* of his father's fanatical anti-semitism, he cannot side-step the girl's husband, whom he has "killed"[98] by taking his place by the girl's—his wife's—side, just as Beckmann himself had been "killed" by the indifference of his own wife and her lover. The girl's husband asks Beckmann not to forget him, his victim, and Beckmann promises not to do so.

With that, the vicious circle of evil-doing and indifference is broken. Beckmann not only acknowledges his active involvement in the evil of the world in general, but he takes upon him the burden of his particular share of responsibility, and in his own individual, personal terms. But that makes his situation a tragic one. Neither romantic or childish dreams, nor social ties and rationalisations give him any support. He has discarded the childish notion of a God who preserves him from evil by continuous *tours de force*—either of miracles, or of human sophistries as to why no miracles occur, in the absence of faith. And the optimism which arises from sheer vital energy likewise breaks down. How is he to measure up to this loneliness?

Robespierre, in Büchner's play, *Dantons Tod (The Death of Danton,* 1835),[99] compares his loneliness with that of Christ in his suffering, but side-steps the realisation that their very loneliness could be a bond between them. With stoical resignation he crucifies the Son of Man within him, and undertakes the programme of political mass-liquidation, which will take evil out of the hands of the people.

Beckmann cannot thus be resigned, either to his loneliness, or to the apparent necessity of evil-doing. Nor is he able, as Lucile does at the end of Büchner's play, to break through the vicious circle of self-deception and inhumanity by an act of self-sacrifice, actuated by pure love. So the play ends on a series of questions, regarding this moral predicament, culminating in the question—since the Other One, as well as the Old Man who calls himself God, are both gone—whether there is *anybody* who will give him an answer. "Is there nobody, nobody who will give an answer???" This question, with which the play ends, is on the verge of being rhetorical. But the agony of the three question-marks shows that Beckmann is really waiting for a response.

We must now return to the letter to Dr. Gantz, to which we have already referred. In the penultimate paragraph he comments on the end of his play. Beckmann, the poet says, does not throw himself into the Elbe, but cries out for an answer, asks after God, after love, after the neighbour, after the meaning of life on this earth.

> ...And he does not receive an answer. No answer exists. Life itself is the answer. Or do you know of one?

"No answer exists" is almost dynamic. The paradoxical "Life itself is the answer" is a retrograde step. It suggests the same immanentism as appears in the previous paragraph, which we considered above, and which appears again and again throughout the poet's work. It has its value, but is inadequate. Here we may again refer to Dr. Würzburger's extraordinarily perceptive criticism, in the letter to the poet, to which we have already referred.[100]

> If urged to express any criticism with regard to your pieces of writing [lit. "jottings"—but Würzburger here simply takes over Borchert's expression, although he obviously considers these writings to be fully-fledged works], then I would direct it principally against those few passages where there is something like a flash of hope—a hope which plays with life, as if life only were life, properly and meaningfully speaking, when it is *lived to capacity*. You are actually closest to me when you are utterly deprived of hope; when you give up everything, because you stretch out your hands in front of you and you perceive nothing but fog, then I begin to hope for you.

If we translate this criticism back into Borchert's symbolism, then we must say that the opposition between the prison, which human society has built (*Die Hundeblume*), with its locked doors, its barred windows, and its uniformed guards on the one hand, and primitive nature on the other, is of only secondary importance. It is true, the prison yard, where the *planks* in a human *fence* go round and round, *encompassed* by *barking dogs* (Ps. 22, 16),[101] is the very antithesis of living growth, even of such a humble plant as the dandelion, which convict No. 432 manages to pluck surreptitiously one day, to have in his cell as a token of the universal breath of life. Again, earth is good and tastes sweet *(Radi)*;[102] but snow is, again and again, described as nauseating, giving rise to anxiety—even disorienting one's whole sense of time and space (esp. *Mein bleicher Bruder* and *Der viele viele Schnee*).[103] "Rain is an angel" *(Liebe blue graue Nacht)*,[104] but wind is cunning and destructive (*Die Mauer, Tui Hoo*);[105] and the combination of physical strength with the instincts unleashed in man can crush a sensitive soul as effectively as the indifference of the men round the coffee table in *Der Kaffee ist undefinierbar:* Elsie in *Alle Milchgeschäfte heissen Hinsch.*[106] As for self-sufficiency, the spider in *Die Hundeblume* is the perfect example. It produces its own scaffolding by excreting the necessary substance, and it would seem that the motto of the story: "And who catches us in mid-air? God?" is quite inapplicable. Furthermore the spider's web is a symbol for prison-bars, already in the *Moabit* lyric included in the section, *Nachgelassene Gedichte,* in the *Gesamtwerk: Der Mond lügt;*(107) in *Das Holz für morgen* the glass roof over the top of the landing of a block of flats is covered with wire netting, which looks like a spider's web,(108) breaks up the light, obscures it. The hero of the story notices it at the beginning, when he intends to commit suicide. At the end, when he has given up the idea, because he has discovered that he is wanted and loved by his family, it is no longer noticed.(109) It seems, in fact, not to harbour, but to *exclude* the divine quality in life. And in *Im Mai, im Mai schrie der Kuckuck*(110) it adds its touch of dreariness and neglect to the institutional green of the lampshades, which the all-powerful All-Provider, the Fatherland, has placed in railway stations and lavatories for the benefit of its children.

It is true, on the other hand, that when personal community (*Das Brot*) or divine hope (*Die drei dunklen Könige*) is experienced, the terms must be those of natural or human objects and of personal living. And yet its dynamic transcends nature. It is rooted in the human soul (*Nachts schlafen die Ratten doch*),(111) but again, its provenance is as mysterious as the sweetness and brightness of the burning timber, or the spontaneous giving and receiving of hospitality together with the presenting of gifts, which has nothing to do with that resentment that makes the father of the new-born child wish he had somebody's face to push in (*Die drei dunklen Könige*).

And ultimately, the problematic of life is not to be found in among the elements, plants, animals, or even the actions and sensations of the human world, but in the loneliness for which there are no words, to an awareness of which we are recalled by the cry of the cuckoo. This is the true "vocabulary" of the world, before which all else must keep silent. (*Im Mai, im Mai shrie der Kuckuck.*)(112) But its full realisation in human terms is rare and full of terror. We find it in the child's impotence when faced with the cod's eye (*Gottes Auge*), which, although supposed to belong to God, is utterly inactive and unresponsive. We find it again in *Die Kegelbahn,*(113) when two soldiers obediently liquidate piles of enemy lives, until the realisation of what they are doing costs them their sleep. So they talk about it, and their argument sways to and fro: they had been commanded to do so. But they had done it. It had been terrible. But sometimes it had been real fun. God had made them that way, the first soldier objects.

But God has an excuse, said the other one, he does not exist.—He does not exist? asked the first one.—That is his only excuse, answered the second one.—But we—we exist, whispered the first one.—Yes, we exist, whispered the other one.

The two men, who had been ordered to destroy as many heads as possible, did not sleep at night; for the heads rolled softly like thunder.

After that conversation the order comes through and they get ready for another bout of slaughtering unknown people. The gun they use had been invented by somebody who had been rewarded for it.

And somebody—somebody had ordered it.

Here the non-existence of God is linked with the existence of men, with moral responsibility. The word *existence* is charged with the same potential force, as when Borchert tells Dr. Gantz, that no answer *exists.* It tears down such idols as "our good German truth", or the "impregnable civilian prosperity" of the Colonel and the Manager respectively (*Draussen vor der Tür,* scenes 3 and 4),[114] and drives Beckmann into a void, where he asks questions, to which he does not receive an answer; for God, to change the metaphor (*Der Kaffee ist undefinierbar*), is without face. The man with the book *closes his eyes* and realises that the girl, whose face he can no longer visualise, has killed herself because she had been bypassed in conversation. Her absence exists as powerfully as the deafness of the God, who does not hear the glass tube drop on the floor and smash. And this deafness reappears, even more terrifyingly, at the end of *Dann gibt es nur eins,* in the above-quoted passage, where the last blasphemy, the last accusing "Why?" drains away in the wasteland, because man has been as irresponsible as the soldier in *Der Kaffee ist undefinierbar* when he lets the glass tube roll across the table till it smashes on the floor.

This is as far as the actual text of the works takes us. Attempts at making Borchert either into a "nihilist"—except in the very special meaning of the word as used in *Das ist unser Manifest,* where love is seen to be rooted in suffering and evil; or, on the other hand, into a *positive* writer with a comforting message, are one-sided. The poet certainly intended his work to be read as a message—hence his series of manifestoes. But the comfort is no more than a hope. God is hidden. And the only trace of the Logos is in the poet's utter truthfulness in his statements regarding human responsibility in the face of this hiddenness.

NOTES AND TRANSLATIONS

Abbreviations: *G*=*Gesamtwerk* (ed. Meyer-Marwitz), tr. Ger.=*Die traurigen Geranien* (ed. Rühmkorf). Rühmkorf=Item 6 (Section B) in the Bibliography.

N.B.: All translations are my own.

1. He left the *Oberrealschule* (similar to a non-classical type of grammar school, or Technical High School) at the age of seventeen, after completing the *Obersekunda* (roughly equivalent to the first year of a three-year Sixth Form course).

2. He would certainly have known the classic anthology of Expressionist poets, edited by Kurt Pinthus, *Menschheitsdämmerung—Symphonie jüngster Dichtung* (1st edn.: 1920)—of esp. *Rühmkorf,* p. 36; on Ringelnatz, *ibid.,* pp. 48, 77, 92.

3. *Über Schriftstellerei und Stil.* cf. Rühmkorf, p. 40.

4. Reproduced in *Rühmkorf,* p. 62.

5. Quoted from Aline Bussmann, p. 7; cf. also *Rühmkorf,* pp. 29–30. The word "misdemeanour", used by Joseph Mileck in this connection, is unwarranted: cf. his biographical sketch, printed in *German Quarterly,* vol. XXXIII, May 1960, No. 3, p. 233, and in *Monatshefte für deutschen Unterricht,* vol. LI, Dec. 1959, No. 7, p. 328.—In most of the biographical accounts—including even those of Aline Bussman and Meyer-Marwitz (the latter in G, pp. 349–75)—there are many inaccuracies. Rühmkorf's monograph is the first (and so far the only) accurate major study of the poet's life. A chronological table appears on pp. 169–70 of that work. The Introduction (pp. 9–57; biographical sketch: pp. 9–13) in Dr. P. B. Salmon's edition of *Draussen vor der Tür* (London, 1963) is also reliable.

6. cf. on this *Rühmkorf,* p. 38.

7. His own prose piece, *Hamburg,* was later to be included in the Hamburg anthology, edited and published by his friend, Bernhard Meyer-Marwitz, *Hamburg, Heimat am Strom* (1946).—*Hamburg:* G, pp. 81–3; *Die Elbe:* G. pp. 103–7.

8. He was to have continued the journey to a convalescent home, but his physical state was so poor, that he had to be kept in Basle.

9. ed. Meyer-Marwitz, Hamburg, 1949, reprinted many times.

10. e.g. in *Akzente,* vol. 2, 1955, p. 120.

11. All references in this section are to G.

12. cf. the study of the poet's development in *Rühmkorf,* esp. pp. 34–6, 80, 117–20.

13. G, p. 363.

14. The two poems quoted by Anna-Maria Darboven on pp. 22 and 23 of her essay were *not* written "kurz for seinem Ende" ("a short time before his death"—p. 22); for correct dating cf. Aline Bussmann, p. 10. This, again, is one of the many inaccuracies that we find in the secondary literature.—Rühmkorf thinks, that the last *poem* (i.e. apart from private dedi-

catory verses) is the single verse, quoted by him on p. 117, in which Borchert reacts against the ghastly whiteness of the ward in the Elizabeth hospital, where he was lying at the time.

15. Discussed and extracts quoted in *Rühmkorf*, pp. 67–74: *Die Blume* (in connection with *Die Hundeblume*) and pp. 81–4: *Requiem für einen Freund* (in connection with *Das ist unser Manifest*).

16. Quoted from *Rühmkorf*, p. 68.

17. G, pp. 331–2.

18. G, pp. 40–1.

19. tr. Ger. p. 28; the whole story: pp. 25–31.

20. G, p. 253; the whole work: pp. 247–64.—*Die lange lange Strasse lang*: G, pp. 265–86.—cf. esp. *Rühmkorf*, pp. 14–15.

21. G, pp. 51–60; my quotations and paraphrases from pp. 52–53, 56–57, 59–60.

22. *Draussen vor der Tür*, scene I: in G, pp. 118–19.

23. Quoted in *Rühmkorf*, p. 82. . . . And then I shall never forget, how, after marching for many days, you would pick the small shrivelled potato out of the ashes, under the shell that had once been a house; you would pick it up, as one does a rare fruit, a peach, and you would draw in its fragrance with reverence and devotion.—Earth and sun, you would say. Outside the temperature was 48° below freezing. . . .

24. tr. Ger., pp. 102–3; the whole story: pp.102–10. But when he took off his high boots, we really felt like murdering him on the spot.

When he entered our cell, it suddenly started smelling of animals and tobacco, sweat, fear and leather. He was a Pole. But with his flaxen hair he wore the looks of one of those dreary Teutonic types. The flaxen-haired males always were a bit drained of colour. He too. And what is more, he seemed to be a bit worn thin. He only knew a few words of German. But in his pocket he carried a picture, made from a transfer, which had lots of gay colours in it. He always used to pray to it for a very long time. He would prop it up against his beaker on his stool. He would pray in a loud voice and in Polish . . .

24a. *ibid.*:. . . But apart from that she looked rather a dull person. At least that is how she struck us. But the pole addressed her as: *Mary.* And he accompanied this with a movement of his hand, as if he wanted to say: Well, isn't she terrific!—Of course, he really wanted to say something a little more tender, when he looked at us with a grin on his face and said *Mary.* Perhaps it was meant to be a smile full of gentle devotion, but we hated him so much, that to us it was simply a grin. He said: *Mary.*

25. This, and another prison story, *Unser kleiner Mozart* (G, pp. 225–31) are set in the same prison cell in the Moabit prison in Berlin, where Borchert had spent his second term of imprisonment. The prisoners, apart from "Mozart" and the Pole, are the same. The geography is fixed by the station announcer's call, *"Lehrter Strasse"*, at the beginning of *Unser kleiner Mozart* (p. 225). *Ching Ling, die Fliege* (tr. Ger. pp. 95–101) must refer to the period of close arrest prior to being sentenced to imprisonment in the Moabit prison, judging by the veiled reference to the charge (pp. 95–6). *Die Hundeblume* (G, pp. 27–41) refers to Borchert's

solitary confinement in Nuremberg military prison: cf. Borchert's letter to Cordes, quoted in *Rühmkorf,* p. 67.—*Von drüben nach drüben* (G, pp. 321–7) describes the death of an ex-convict, almost immediately following his release. There is no indication, as to which prison is meant. In the only other prison story, *Ein Sonntagmorgen* (tr. Ger., pp. 84–94), there is also no clue as to the locality of the prison.—Examples of the high degree of biographical content in the prose works may be found again and again in *Rühmkorf.* It is not difficult to demonstrate, where the evidence has been preserved, that the poet observed, remembered and remoulded the items of his experience in new patterns. He hardly ever invented freely. An example of this is given by Rühmkorf on pp. 63–5.

26. tr. Ger., p. 110: the end of the story. . . . And then his face radiated happiness and with his hand he stroked his pocket: Mary, he whispered, all of it Mary. And as he said this, he made a face, as if he had *pulled a fast one* over the judicial system. So he had. The judicial system of the whole world.

27. G, pp. 344–7.

28. Letter dater April 23, 1940, quoted in *Rühmkorf,* p. 37.

29. Karl Würzburger, *St. Clara-Spital. Zimmer 200 (Besuch bei Wolfgang Borchert)*: Typescript text of a broadcast on the *Süddeutscher Rundfunk,* Stuttgart, May 25, 1961. The text of this letter: pp. 5–8; the passage to which reference is here made occurs at the end of the letter, on p. 8.

30. G, pp. 213–19.

31. p. 213.

32. pp. 218–19, also for the whole of the following discussion.

33. This part of the discussion refers to pp. 215–16.

34. G., pp. 73–5.

35. G, pp. 191–4.

36. G, pp. 84–102.

37. G, pp. 223–4.

38. G, pp. 220–2; I am quoting the first para. on p. 221 (my italics).

39. p. 222.

40. G, pp. 251–2.

41. G, pp. 200–2, 328–30, 308–20, resp.

42. G, p. 327; the whole story: pp. 321–7.

43. G, p. 340: the whole series: pp. 340–3.

44. G, p. 195: the whole story: pp. 195–6.

45. G, p. 276.

46. G, p. 341.

47. Paraphrased from G, p. 260. The attempt at translating "Der Gott der Eisen wachsen liess" shows up the grotesqueness of these sentiments.

48. G, p. 342.

49. G, pp. 109–75; sc. 4; pp. 140–8.

50. p. 140.

51. G, p. 64; the whole work: pp. 63–5.

52. p. 65.

53. G, pp. 333–9.

54. G, p. 307.
55. G, p. 207; the whole story: pp. 207–10.
56. G, pp. 342–3.
57. G, pp. 344–7.
58. p. 346.
59. Test of broadcast, p. 9. But cf. also *Thus spake Zarathustra,* the end of Part I: p. 115 in Borchert's edition (Alfred Kröner Verlag 1918); p. 84 (Alfred Kröner Verlag, 1960): "Und das ist der grosse Mittag, da der Mensch auf der Mitte seiner Bahn steht zwischen Tier und Übermensch . . ."—the poet's marginal note: "Gott!" (Annotations date from 1939.)
60. In G, p. 373.
61. G, pp. 140–1.
62. pp. 116–17.
63. p. 111.
64. p. 145.
65. *Ibid.*
66. p. 142.
67. p. 145.
68. *Ibid.*
69. p. 146.
70. Published in *Akzente,* vol. 2, 1955, p. 117.
71. *Ibid,* p. 118.
72. Letter quoted in *Rühmkorf,* p. 79.
73. G, p. 338.
74. tr. Ger., pp. 111–18.
75. tr. Ger. pp. 11–13 and 7–10, resp.
76. G, pp. 70–2.
77. G, pp. 253–64.
78. G, pp. 250–2.
79. G, pp. 40–1.
80. G, p. 339; cf. also Meyer-Marwitz's account, *ibid.,* pp. 372–3.
81. Cosmic breathing seems to occur more in the earlier works: tr. Ger., p. 63 (in *Tui Hoo*), G, 105–6 (in *Die Elbe*); cosmic speech—more especially in relationship with human fear—more in the later works: G, p. 196 (in *Die Katze war im Schnee erfroren*), but supremely in *Im Mai, im Mai schrie der Kuckuck,* esp. G, p. 249.—Cosmic laughter: G, p. 106; also G, p. 52 (in *Gespräch über den Dächern*).
82. G, p. 128.
83. G, pp. 128, 135, resp.
84. pp. 113–15—on the devaluation of death cf. Martini's remarks, pp. 92–3, in his contribution (*Das Drama der Gegenwart*) in the volume *Deutsche Literatur in unserer Zeit,* ed. Wolfgang Kayser.
85. pp. 160–1.
86. p. 122.
87. pp. 152–71.
88. p. 175.
89. p. 119.

90. For the Colonel cf. sc. 3 and part of sc. 5 (pp. 163–5: incomprehension through sheer indifference), but esp. towards the end of sc. 3: p. 137: naïve Prussianism; for the Manager, cf. sc. 4 (esp. p. 146: abrogation of truth; p. 141: abrogation of social responsibility) and part of sc. 5 (pp. 166–7; cowardice hardening into indifference).

91. pp. 141–2.

92. p. 123.

93. p. 141.

94. pp. 123–4.

95. p. 152.

96. p. 169.

97. p. 151.

98. For the discussion that follows cf. the end of the play, pp. 172–5.

99. I am referring especially to the monologue at the end of Act I (pp. 31–2 in the Insel Verlag edition of Büchner's works, 1953).

100. Text of broadcast, pp. 7–8.

101. G, pp. 29–30.

102. G, pp. 203–6.

103. G, pp. 188–94, 185–7, resp.

104. tr. Ger., p. 48; the whole piece: pp. 40–8.—cf. also the poem *Versuch es,* in G, p. 290.

105. tr. Ger., pp. 53–7, 58–71, resp.

106. tr. Ger., pp. 25-31.

107. G, p. 293.

108. tr. Ger., p. 20; the whole story: pp. 18–24.

109. p. 24.

110. G, p. 252.

111. G, pp. 236–9.

112. G, p. 249.

113. G, pp. 181–2; the quotations are from p. 182.

114. G, p. 130: "Wir wollen doch lieber bei unserer guten deutschen Wahrheit bleiben." p. 141: "Wir haben doch längst wieder das dickste Zivilleben!"

SELECT BIBLIOGRAPHY

A. THE WORKS

No complete bibliographical account is as yet in existence. Lyrics, the play and prose works appeared singly, often in newspapers and journals, even in the poet's lifetime, and continued to be published, or reprinted—often also in anthologies and other larger works—after the poet's death. (cf. item 10 (a) and (b) below, for some letters and poems.) The number of such items is very large, and it has so far been impossible to trace them all. Smaller collections of works, beginning with *Laterne, Nacht und Sterne* (1946), constitute a continuous series to the present day.

The following are at present available:

1. (a) Wolfgang Borchert, Das Gesamtwerk. Mit einem biographischen Nachwort von Bernhard Meyer-Marwitz.
First impression: published jointly by *Verlag Hamburgische Bücherei* and *Rowohlt Verlag Hamburg,* 1949. From 1952 onwards many reprints by *Rowohlt Verlag,* who now have the full rights.
(b) An East German edition, by licence from the *Rowohlt Verlag,* was published by *Mitteldeutscher Verlag,* Halle/Saale, in 1957.
2. *Selection from the Gesamtwerk:*
Wolfgang Borchert, Draussen vor der Tür und ausgewälte Erzählungen. Mit einem Nachwort von Heinrich Böll.
rororo Taschenbuch Ausgabe. Rowohlt Verlag, Hamburg, 1956 (and reprinted many times).
3. Wolfgang Borchert, Die traurigen Geranien und andere Geschichten aus dem Nachlass.
Herausgegeben mit einem Nachwort von Peter Rühmkorf. *Rowohlt Verlag, Hamburg,* 1962 and reprinted.
4. *Draussen vor der Tür* by Wolfgang Borchert. Edited with an introduction, notes and a select vocabulary by P. B. Salmon, M.A., Ph.D., Lecturer in German at Royal Holloway College, University of London. *George G. Harrap & Co. Ltd., London, Toronto, Wellington, Sydney,* 1963.
5. In English:
The Man Outside. The prose works of Wolfgang Borchert. Translated from the German by David Porter. Introduction by Stephen Spender. *Hutchinson International Authors Limited, London, New York, Melbourne, Sydney, Cape Town,* 1952.
(This volume is out of print, but available in the libraries. It contains all works which appear in the *Gesamtwerk,* except the verse).

Das Gesamtwerk and *Die Traurigen Geranien* account for a fraction of the verse written 1940–5, the play, and all the important prose works, *except* the two early works, *Die Blume* and *Requiem an einen Freund,* as well as *Das Nasenbein,* which has been lost. Of the projected novel, *Persil bleibt Persil,* only the chapter headings and the beginning (about a page long, a prose poem entitled *Unser Pusteblumendasein* were written and have not been published. *Strandgut* (item 42, p. 24 in Christa Urban's Bibliography) I am unable to identify. A chronological table of the prose works, incomplete, but taken from one of Borchert's notebooks, appears on pp. 132–3 of Rühmkorf's monograph.

Photocopies and typescript copies of a number of items, important for research, but difficult or impossible to obtain, are deposited at the Institute of Germanic Studies, University of London; the German Department Library, University of Bristol; and the Library of the University College of Swansea.

B. SECONDARY LITERATURE

6. Wolfgang Borchert in Selbstzeuguissen und Bilddokumenten Dargestellt von Peter Rühmkorf. (*Series:* rororo Bildmonographien.

Rowohlts Monographien, herausgegeben von Kurt Kusenberg. *Rowohlt Taschenbuch Verlag, Hamburg,* 1961 (and reprinted several times).

Despite its modest title and small size, this monograph is the most important work on the poet and his work that has appeared so far. It is of fundamental importance for any serious study in this field.

7. (a) Karl Würzburger, St. Clara-Spital, Zimmer 200. (Besuch bei Wolfgang Borchert).
   (*Typescript of broadcast on:* Süddeutscher Rundfunk, Stuttgart, May 25, 1961.)
   (b) Karl Würzburger, Begegnung mit Wolfgang Borchert. 10 (1950), Konfirmandenheft.
   (I have not seen this; it is listed in Christa Urban's Bibliography: item 157, p. 33.)
8. Erinnerungen an Wolfgang Borchert von Aline Bussman. Zur zehnten Wiederkehr seines Todestages am 20. November 1957. *Rowohlt Verlag, Hamburg,* 1957.
   (This work is out of print. Photocopies at: Institute of Germanic Studies, University of London; German Department Library, University of Bristol; University College of Swansea Library).
9. Wolfgang Borchert. Der Rufer in einer Zeit der Not. von Anna-Maria Darboven. *Norddeutsche Verlagsanstalt. O. Goedel. Hannover und Frankfurt/M.* (Goedelbuch Nr. 302), 1957.
10. Material published in *Akzente,* vol. 2, Stuttgart, 1955.
   (N.B.: Although (a) and (b) really come under Section A, I have listed all the items which occur in this volume together for convenience.)
   (a) *Letters.*
      p. 116: to his parents—Saalfeld, October 25, 1942.
      p. 117: to Hugo Sieker—Jena, October 20, 1944.
      pp. 118–19: to Dr Max Gantz—Hamburg, February 27, 1947.
   (b) *Two poems.*
      p. 120: Gedichte aus dem Nachlass—
         Im Kreis.
         Wir sind im Kreis.
   (c) *Critical studies.*
      pp. 121ff.: Alfred Bourk, Zur Dichtung Wolfgang Borcherts. Generation ohne Abschied.
      pp. 128ff.: Herbert Seliger, Wer schreibt für uns eine neue Harmonielehre?
      pp. 139ff.: Siegfried Unseld, An diesem Dienstag. Unvorgreifliche Gedanken über die Kurzgeschichte.
11. Der Deutschunterricht:
   (a) Jahrgang VII, Heft I. Stuttgart, 1955.
      pp. 13ff.: Rober Ulshöfer, Die Wirklichkeitsauffassung in der modernen Prosadichtung. Dargestellt an Manns "Tod in Venedig", Kafkas "Verwandlung" und Borcherts Kurzgeschichten, verglichen mit Goethes "Hermann und Dorothea".

(b) Jahrgang IX, Heft I. Stuttgart, 1957.
pp. 36ff.: Ruth Lorbe, Die deutsche Kurzgeschichte der Jahrhundertmitte.

12. Interpretationen zu Wolfgang Borchert. *R. Oldenburg Verlag, München,* 1962. (*Series:* Interpretationen zum Deutschunterricht an den höheren Schulen. Herausgegeben von Rupert Hirschenauer und Albrecht Weber.)
The contributors are: Karl Migner, Rupert Hirschenauer, Manfred Horst, Helmut Christmann, Hans Grassl, Hans-Udo Dück, Albrecht Weber.
(Page references are to the *Gesamtwerk* and the *rororo Taschenbuch Ausgabe.*)

13. (a) Werner Zimmermann, Deutsche Prosadichtungen der Gegenwort. Interpretationen für Lehrende und Lernende. *Pädogogischer Verlag Schwann, Düsseldorf.* Teil I: 1956; Teil II: 1956; Teil III: 1960. (Interpretations of stories by Borchert: Pt. II, pp. 119–35; Pt. III, pp. 221–8.)
(b) Wirkendes Wort 5 (1954–5). pp. 97–105: Werner Zimmermann, Deutsche Prosadichtungen der Gegenwart als Gestaltganzes dargestellt an einer Kurzgeschichte von Wolfgang Borchert.

14. Monatshefte für deutschen Unterricht, deutsche Sprache und Literatur, vol. LI, December 1959, No. 7.
pp. 328–36: Joseph Mileck, Wolfgang Borchert: "Draussen vor der Tür": A Young Poet's Struggle with Guilt and Despair.

15. Modern Language Quarterly, vol. 17, Washington, 1956.
pp. 153–65: Karl S. Weimar, No Entry, no exit. A study of Borchert with some notes on Sartre.

16. Etudes Germaniques. IIe année, 1956. Janvier-Mars, No. 1.
pp. 36–44: Michel Pinault, Wolfgang Borchert et l'angoisse du temps présent.

17. Deutsche Literatur in unserer Zeit. Mit Beiträgen von W. Kayser, B. von Wiese, W. Emrich, Fr. Martini, M. Wehrli, Fr. Heer. *Vandenhoeck & Ruprecht, Göttingen.* 3. Auflage, 1959; 1961.
pp. 80–104: Fritz Martini, Das Drama der Gegenwart.

C. BIBLIOGRAPHIES

18. Wolfgang Borchert. Ein bibliographischer Versuch. Prüfungsarbeit der Hamburger Bibliotheksschule vorgelegt am 15.8.1958 von Christa Urban. (Staats-und Universitäts-bibliothek Hamburg.)
(Typescript copy in Hamburg State and University Library. Microfilm in Swansea University College Library.)

19. The German Quarterly, vol. XXXIII, May 1960, No. 3.
pp. 233–9: Joseph Mileck, Wolfgang Borchert: Bibliography.

20. *In:* Rühmkorf (item 6 above): pp 173–6.

21. *In:* Draussen vor der Tür, ed. Salmon (item 4 above): pp. 59–62.

22. *In:* rororo Taschenbuch Ausgabe (item 2 above), [p. 2] facing title page: *Zu diesem Buch,* end para.: *Literatur.*

23. *In:* Interpretationen zu Wolfgang Borchert (item 12 above): in footnotes in various places, by the individual contributors.

D. REFERENCE HAS ALSO BEEN MADE TO THE FOLLOWING:

24. (a) Kurt Pinthus (ed.), Menschheitsdämmerung, Symphonie jüngster Dichtung. *Ernst Rowohlt Verlag, Berlin,* 1920.
This book is now available as:
(b) Menschheitsdämmerung. Ein Dokument des Expressionismus. Mit Biographien und Bibliographien neu herausgegeben von Kurt Pinthus, *Rowohlt Verlag, Hamburg,* 1959–60. (*Series:* Rowohlts Klassiker der Literatur und der Wissenschaft. Herausgegeben von Ernesto Grassi unter Mitarbeit von Walter Hess. Deutsche Literatur, Band 4).

25. Georg Büchner, Werke und Briefe. Gesamtausgabe. Herausgegeben von Fritz Bergemann.
Erschienen im Insel-Verlag. Wiesbaden, 1953.

26. Ernst Toller, Prosa, Briefe, Dramen, Gedichte. Mit einem Vorwort von Kurt Hiller. (*Rowohlt Paperback.*) *Rowohlt Verlag, Hamburg,* 1961.
pp. 235–85: Die Wandlung.
pp. 287–330: Masse-Mensch.
pp. 391–435: Hinkemann.

27. Friedrich Nietzsche. Also Sprach Zarathustra . . . 180–204. Tausend. [1918]. (The poet's note on p. [478]: " gelesen: 1939. W.B.") Keinen. Miteinem Nachwort von Alfred Baeumler. Alfred Kröner Verlag, Stuttgart [1960].

Max Frisch

Max Frisch

by MARTIN ESSLIN

Max Frisch was born in Zürich on May 15, 1911. His grandfather on the paternal side had come to Switzerland from Austria; he was a saddler. On the mother's side his great-grandfather had come to Zürich from Württemberg; his name was Wildermuth and he was director of the city's Arts and Crafts School. After two years of reading German and Philosophy at the University of Zürich, the death of his father, who was an architect, compelled him to start earning a living. So, at twenty-two he became a journalist. As a freelance reporter he travelled widely in Eastern Europe. Having written a first novel, he was, at the age of twenty-five, enabled by the generosity of a friend, who undertook to support him for four years, to resume his studies. He decided to become an architect and gained his diploma at the Eidgenoessische Technische Hochschule (ETH) at Zürich. While still studying he was called up at the outbreak of the Second World War and spent some time guarding the frontiers of his native country to protect its neutrality. After the fall of France he was able to get back to work, completed his studies and married. In 1943 a novel, *J'adore ce qui me brûle oder die Schwierigen*, appeared and had a favourable reception from some of the critics. Among the reactions was a letter from Kurt Hirschfeld, then the *Dramaturg* of the Zürich Schauspielhaus, suggesting that he might try his hand at writing a play. At about the same time Frisch won an architectural competition for a public building—the Municipal Swimming Baths at Letzigraben in Zürich—and was enabled to open his own office as an architect. This in turn gave him the freedom to arrange his own time and to devote more time to writing. In 1947–8 Frisch befriended Bertolt Brecht who had temporarily settled near Zürich after his return from the United States and before he decided to go to East Berlin. Frisch has travelled widely: in 1951–2 he spent a considerable time in the United States and Mexico. After attaining fame as a writer he gave up his architect's practice. His marriage has been dissolved and he now lives mainly in Rome.

WHEN German civilisation collapsed in 1933—and it is a matter for argument whether the rise of Hitler was the cause of this collapse or merely its chief symptom—only one German-speaking area of Europe remained untouched by this calamity: German Switzerland. It is therefore no coincidence that some of the best writers now active in the German language are Swiss—members of that very generation which has remained totally sterile in Germany itself, the generation born between 1910 and 1920 whose formative years fell into the Nazi period. Among these Swiss writers, two, Friedrich Dürrenmatt and Max Frisch, have attained world fame.

Dürrenmatt is the scion of an old Bernese patrician family, Frisch the grandson of an Austrian immigrant. Yet it has rightly been pointed out that this makes Frisch the more typically Swiss; a higher percentage of present-day German Swiss citizens have an ancestry like Frisch. While Dürrenmatt comes from a family of statesmen, professors and parsons, Frisch has a background of artisans and "artists". He himself has described the artistic pretentions of his maternal great-grandfather, who "called himself a painter, wore a considerable cravat which was much bolder than his drawings and paintings. . . . My mother, to see the great wide world, once worked as a governess in Czarist Russia; she has often told us about it. My father was an architect. Being the son of a saddler he had not been able to afford a professional education and so it was his ambition to see his sons as university graduates."(1) So Frisch has the more artistic background, yet he has striven much harder than Dürrenmatt to find a place in his society: as an architect he is a technologist and a very typical embodiment of our contemporary world, a world where construction and production play so decisive a part. In discussing his position with one foot in the camp of literature, the other in the camp of scientific technology, Frisch clearly reveals that he sympathises with some of the men he worked with who considered his writing as a somewhat crazy aberration: "Having a dual profession as a writer and as an architect is, of course, not always easy, however many fruitful effects it may have. It is not so much a question of time as of strength. I find it a blessing to work every day with men who have nothing to do with literature; some of them may know that I write, but they don't hold it against me, so long as my other work is all right."(2)

And yet for Frisch writing has always been a necessity, an almost compulsory activity, an effort at self-exploration. In a brief note, headed *About Writing*, in his published diary he gives a fascinating and ruthlessly sincere insight into the motives of his work as a writer: "Years ago, in my capacity as an architect, I once visited one of those factories where our glorious watches are being made; my impression was more shattering than any I have ever received in a factory; and yet I have never succeeded in conversation to reproduce this experience, one of the strongest of my life, in such a way that it was relived by my interlocutor. Once it has been talked about, this experience always remains trivial or unreal, real only for the one who went through it, incommunicable like any personal experience—or rather: every experience remains basically incommunicable so long as we hope to express it through the real example that actually happened to us. Real expression can be found for me only through an example that is as far removed from my own self as from that of the person listening: that is, the fictional example. Communication is essentially possible only through the fictitious, transformed, reshaped instance; and that is also why artistic failure is always accompanied by a feeling of suffocating loneliness."(3)

Frisch has enabled us to follow the process of transformation of his experience into fiction through a series of autobiographical writings, mainly journals and diaries, which are among the most remarkable writers' notebooks of our time. *Blätter aus dem Brotsack* (1940) is his diary of military service at the outbreak of war; *Tagebuch mit Marion* (1947) was later reprinted in the wider *Tagebuch 1946–49*.

His first novel *Jürg Reinhart* which deals with a young man's attainment of maturity during a trip to Dalmatia, has clearly autobiographical character. (Frisch travelled in south-eastern Europe before the war as a freelance journalist.) The delightful novella *Bin oder die Reise nach Peking* which describes the lyrical musings of a young man who holds long conversations with Bin, his alter ego or second romantic self, on an imaginary journey to Peking, the ever unattainable goal of the German romantic tradition, also barely rises above the level of autobiographical statement. In Frisch's later plays and novels the transmutation of the material into truly fictional terms is far more complete, but the basic connection with the author's quest for his own self nevertheless always remains clear.

Frisch's origin and background account for some of the main themes of his writings: to be Swiss means to be a citizen of a relatively small, self-governing community with its inevitably petty local politics that tend to loom very large in the foreground even in times of world upheaval; the sensitive, artistic temperament tends to react against this by a violent yearning for the great, wide world: Frisch spent his *Wanderjahre* as a journalist in south-eastern Europe before the war, he has since travelled widely in the United States and Europe: the yearning for exotic climes, romantic distant islands is a recurring theme in his plays and novels; and so is scorn against the narrowness and pettiness, the complacency and arrogance of a small, self-contained community which feels itself free from the taints and crimes of other, less fortunate countries. For to be Swiss also means to be the citizen of a country that has escaped two world wars. *Andorra,* Frisch's most widely performed play, is among other things, an attack on this Swiss complacency. Andorra in the play is a small, mountain country, proud of its freedom, proud of being better and morally superior; convinced that this moral superiority makes it immune to any foreign attack: "As Perin, our great poet once said: Our weapon is our innocence. Or the other way round: our innocence is our weapon. Where else in the world is there a republic that can say this? I ask you: where? A nation like ourselves who as no other can appeal to the conscience of the world, a people without guilt. . . . Andorrans I tell you: no nation on earth has ever been attacked without someone having been able to reproach them with a crime. What can they reproach us with? The only thing that could happen to Andorra, would be an injustice, a gross and open injustice. And that they will not dare. Tomorrow even less than yesterday. Because the whole world would defend us. At one fell swoop. Because the conscience of the world is on our side."(4) And yet Andorra is attacked, and the Andorrans sacrifice young Andri, whom they believe to be a Jew, to the anti-Sematic invaders. They have prided themselves on being free from the sins of those powerful neighbours, but they have carried the seeds of the same moral corruption within themselves all the time. They have been free from the crimes that great powers become guilty of, only because being a small power they have never exercised any responsibility, they have never taken an active part in history; their innocence springs from their insignificance, from their pettiness, from their provincialism, from their bourgeois respectability. One of the impulses behind Frisch's writing is the passionate resolve *not* to feel himself free from the guilt and responsibilities of his age, to detect within himself the seeds of the crimes that sully the record of the great powers: in the plays *Nun singen sie wieder* (1945) and *Als der Krieg zu Ende war* (1949) as well as in *Andorra* (1961) he comes to grips with the problem of the extermination of the Jews; in *Die chinesische Mauer* (1946) the problem of the atom bomb is boldly confronted: "The flood can now be manufactured by man!" And the young poet, the "contemporary man" (and thus undoubtedly an image of the author himself) who has come to inform the Emperor of China and all the great figures of history of this fact reveals himself as not only unable to act to defend the suffering people; having delivered an impassioned plea against the bomb, having uttered a terrible warning to the Emperor, he is awarded a prize for fiction and ignored. Because he is helpless to change the course of history the poet, the intellectual, who knows the horrors to come and cannot act effectively, shares in the final guilt.

To be Swiss also means having been brought up to an ideal of bourgeois rectitude, to have lived in a small community where neighbours know each other only too well and where one has to do one's utmost to maintain a façade of strict, puritanical respectability. This respectability is merely another aspect of the features of Swiss life against which a sensitive, artistic personality like Frisch is bound to react strongly: the narrowness of local politics, the righteous complacency of guiltless and petty neutrality it will appear to such an individual as a refusal to face the world and human life as they really are, an escape from responsibility, from guilt, from temptation—and therefore from life itself. For such respectability is bought at a terrible price: by running away from any valid experience, by hiding behind barriers of timidity and moral cowardice.

This is one of the main themes of *Biedermann und die Brandstifter* (1957–8) (known in England as *The Fireraisers* and in the United States as *The Firebugs*). Biedermann (in German the name is also a generic term for a complacent, respectable citizen, a *faux bonhomme*) is a ruthless businessman, he has just driven an exploited employee to suicide; yet he prides himself on the fact that his daily life is amiable, well-ordered, superficially that of a "good man". And that is why he cannot believe that the two sinister characters who have infiltrated themselves into his house can really be plotting to use the drums of petrol and the bales of inflammable stuff they are hoarding in the attic to burn down Mr. Biedermann's respectable house, and the whole respectable city he inhabits. For, after all, Biedermann manages to be on friendly conversational terms with them, he has invited them to dinner even, that shows that he is human, friendly, benevolent, free from guilt and therefore he cannot, he will not be attacked (exactly as the citizens of Andorra are convinced that nobody can attack them because they are innocent of ever having furnished any good reason to be attacked). And so he even offers the incendiaries the match with which they will blow up his world. His false values, the inauthentic life and the lack of awareness, of consciousness they entail, lead Biedermann directly to destruction.

The Fireraisers also has a direct political implication, quite different incidentally from that imposed upon it by a number of performances in Britain, notably Lindsay Anderson's production at the Royal Court. Far from being a play about the atomic bomb which we are having in our attic and which will blow up our world, *The Fireraisers* deals—or dealt originally—with the Western world's inability to see through Communist tactics of infiltration. In Frisch's published diary for 1946–9 the idea for Biedermann is noted immediately after the entry about his consternation at the Communist take-over in Czechoslovakia. "Worries about our friends. And to all this the glee of my acquaintances towards whom I have always presented Czechoslovakia as an example of a Socialist democracy; and all this topped by the general conceit: such a thing could not happen here!" These words are clearly the germ of the idea. . . . Only if the fireraisers can be seen as revolutionaries threatening the bourgeois world will the play make sense. And it is significant that the other interpretation which will fit the play and at which Frisch hints in the Epilogue in Hell that he added after the success of the original radio version refers to the inability of the German bourgeoisie to see the rise of Hitler in its true significance. Frisch despises the bourgeois precisely because having forced himself into the image of *bonhomie* (which is a lie for it is merely a mask for the cruelties of a system based on exploitation, merely a refusal to see the obvious hardships and sufferings of our world), having suppressed the spontaneous human reactions by a dry, heartless and calculating respectability, he has become incapable even of defending the values on which his well-being is founded.

How is one to react against bourgeois respectability and its dangers? The conventional reaction is to fall into Bohemianism, to flaunt one's defiance of respectable values. Swiss cities like Zürich have their own brand of Bohemian, artistic communities. And Frisch certainly frequented this world in his youth. But if anything these small enclaves of Bohemianism are even narrower than the narrow bourgeois world they defy. Hence the Swiss nostalgia for the romantic, the exotic and the far off. In Frisch's earliest published play *Santa Cruz* (1944) everything revolves round the conflict between the respectable and narrow circle of everyday lives, and the mysterious pull of distant and exotic lands. The Cavalry Captain and his wife Elvira have lived together in a humdrum marriage for seventeen years. And all that time Elvira has been dreaming of the vagabond whom she once loved and who may be the father of her daughter; and all that time the Captain has been dreaming of the friend with whom he once planned to roam the world and to visit the Southern Seas. Pelegrin the vagabond comes to visit them, as he is about to die, and the ageing couple recognise that they have been dreaming of the same man, the same romantic ideal. But they also recognise that the real flaw of their lives was that each concealed his secret longing from the other. It is not the escape to remote romantic islands that is the solution, but the courage to be oneself and the courage to love. This question, the problem of identity, the problem of how man can find his true self, an authentic existence, is the central pivot around which most of Frisch's work revolves. It is also the main problem of existential philosophy and although there is no evidence that Frisch has ever been preoccupied with the work of writers like Camus and Sartre, his approach to it coincides with many of their ideas. For Frisch is above all appalled by the influence that the opinions of other people have on our own identity: "Some fixed opinion of our friends, our parents, our teachers . . . may weigh upon us like an ancient oracle. Half a lifetime may be blighted by the secret question: will it come true or will it not come true. . . . A teacher once said to my mother she would never learn how to knit. My mother often told us about this assertion; she never forgot, never forgave it; she became a passionate, extraordinarily skilful knitter; and all the stockings and knitted caps, all the gloves and pullovers I ever received, in the end I owe them to that objectionable oracle. . . .! To a certain extent we really are what others see in us, friends as well as enemies. And the other way round: we too are the *authors* of the others; in a mysterious and inescapable way we are responsible for the face they show us. . . ."(5) We create the others in the image we make ourselves of them. And this for Frisch is the ultimate sin, the extinction of their authentic existence, the origin of all the troubles of our time. For the image that we thus make is a fixed, a dead thing, an imposition that can kill. If thus "being-for-others" by fixing an image reduces human freedom, love that accepts a human personality as "being-for-itself" creates freedom: "Love frees from all images. That is the exciting, the adventurous, the truly suspenseful thing about love, that with those human beings we love we never reach an end: because we love them; as long as we love them. Listen to the poets when they are in love: they search for similes, as though they were drunk, they grasp for all the things in the universe, flowers, animals, clouds, stars, and oceans. Why? Just as the universe, God's inexhaustible spaciousness, is boundless, so boundless, pregnant with all possibilities, all mysteries, unfathomable is the human being we love. . . . If we think we know the other, that is the end of love, every time; but perhaps cause and effect are reversed . . . not because we know the other person is our love coming to an end, but the other way round: because our love is at an end, because its strength is exhausted, we have finished with the other person. . . . We deny him the claim of all living things, which must remain unfathomable, and at the same time we are astonished and disappointed that our relationship is no longer alive. 'You are not', says the disappointed man or woman, 'what I took you to be.' And what did one take the other for? A mystery, that man, after all, is, an exciting riddle we have become tired of. Now we make ourself an image. That is the loss of love, the betrayal."(6) This beautiful passage in Frisch's published diaries for the years 1946–9, the most fruitful, formative period of his creative life, certainly is the key to a great deal of his subsequent work. It defines the subject of his great novel *Stiller* (English title: *I'm not Stiller*) (1954) and of a number of his most interesting plays.

Anatol Ludwig Stiller, a successful sculptor at Zürich had disappeared without a trace for more than six years when a man resembling him in all particulars was picked up at the Swiss frontier because his passport, made out in the name of White, was obviously not in order. Is the stranger Stiller? He refuses to acknowledge his identity, any identity, and the bulk of the novel is taken up by this unidentified man's diaries in prison. He denies that he is Stiller and yet in the end he has to accept the fact that he is Stiller. He wanted to escape from the image that was constricting him, but the world with all its powers of official and sentimental pressure (through his wife, family and friends) effectively puts a stop to any such attempts. Seen from one angle the hero of the novel is a clinical case of split personality, seen from another he is a human being trying to assert his uniqueness, his freedom to choose himself (in Sartre's sense); and, moreover, he is also a legendary hero, a Rip Van Winkle, who returns to his former surroundings as a changed man. (Frisch has written a radio play on the theme of *Stiller* which has the title *Rip van Winkle*.)

As a novel *Stiller* is a remarkable *tour de force*. We are made to witness the gradual rediscovery of his self by a man who has rejected not only the world's former image of his personality, but his own image of himself. And at the end we feel with him that, although he must bow to the overwhelming evidence of his physical identity with Stiller, mentally and spiritually he remains as unconvinced as ever. He returns to his image as we slip back into an old suit we had discarded; the self the world imposes on Stiller is an alien, dead thing. He tried to discard his former self because he felt himself a failure as an artist and as a husband. Now he is pushed back into these roles and again he therefore must end up as a failure.

And yet, perhaps, Stiller's failure is an even deeper one: he refused to accept the image of himself that society imposed on him, but he also could not make up his mind to be himself. As Stiller's wife lies dying, the public prosecutor, who conducted the case and later became Stiller's friend, tries to sum up the lesson of his life: "As far as I know your life, you have again and again thrown everything away because you have been uncertain of yourself. You are not the truth. You are a human being and you have often been ready to abandon an untruth, to be uncertain. What else does this mean, Stiller, but that you do believe in a truth? A truth, that is, which we cannot alter and which we cannot even kill—which is life itself. . . . Again and again you have tried to accept yourself without accepting something like God. And that has turned out to be impossible. He is the power that can help you to accept yourself truly. All this you have experienced! And in spite of it you say that you cannot pray . . . you cling to your own powerlessness which you take for your personality; and yet you know your own powerlessness so well—and all this as though from stubbornness, only because you yourself are not the power . . ."[7] Stiller himself makes no comment on these observations and the question remains open. We merely learn that Stiller's return to his wife, the renewal of his failed marriage, in the end killed the woman he loved and that after that he lived on as a broken man. And yet Stiller, who refuses the world's image of himself, who is unable to accept his own image of himself, is, and this is the subtlest turn in the labyrinthine complexity of this brilliantly conceived novel, himself a maker of images, a sculptor: "Whether there is not something inhuman in the mere attempt to make a picture of a living human being, that is a big question. It essentially concerns Stiller", says the public prosecutor in his commentary that forms the final part of the book. Thus Stiller stands for the artist in general—and for his own creator, who, as a playwright and novelist, has also embarked on the dangerous and perhaps deadly pursuit of making images of human beings.

Stiller is a deeply serious, searching and philosophical work. In a lighter and more ironical vein Frisch has dealt with the same subject in the play *Don Juan oder die Liebe zur Geometrie* (1953) which was written almost at the same time. Don Juan is here shown as a man whose ruthless determination to be true to himself creates a wholly false image. Far from being a seducer or voluptuary, he really is only interested in geometry. Betrothed to Donna Anna, and truly in love with her, he refuses to pronounce the marriage vows merely because he feels himself morally unable to pledge his future conduct so far ahead, for after all we can only know what our present self intends, never what may be the sincere feelings of our future selves. Having killed Donna Anna's father and having acquired the reputation of a wicked voluptuary as a result, he is so much sought after by the ladies that he finally decides to end it all by staging his own death in the most gruesome circumstances: the arrival of the dead Governor's statue and the swallowing up of Don Juan by the mouth of hell are elaborately stage-managed at his own expense in the presence of a multitude of his mistresses. It seems as though Don Juan, now believed to be in hell, could safely start a new life (just like Stiller after he had shed his old self) and devote himself to his true love, geometrical research. But one of the ladies who loves Don Juan knows his secret and so she can blackmail him into a life at her side—marriage and domesticity. This is boring and irritating, but at least Don Juan *has* shed his former image. But no—as the play ends a visitor arrives with a book, the newly published comedy about Don Juan, the seducer of Seville. The image has become immortal and will outlive the real Don Juan.

But the problem of man's identity has other facets as well: it is not merely a question of the image that the outside world imposes on us. It is also one of which of the multitudinous potentialities in ourselves is our real self. Are we what we appear to be in our self-controlled, conscious waking hours; or are we the wild wishes and violent desires of our dreams. In *Graf Oederland* (first version 1951, third and final version 1961) Frisch approaches this problem in a play which is probably his most intriguing virtuoso performance. An official of the utmost respectability, a public prosecutor, one day finds that he is identifying himself with the murderer whose trial he has been conducting in court—a humdrum little man who killed without motive, merely because he could not endure the deadly routine of a pointless existence. The public prosecutor helps the murderer to escape, takes to the woods, becomes the leader of a revolutionary force of outlaws which overthrows the legal government and thus the dictator of his country. Having entered the capital at the head of his victorious forces he returns to his own house and finds himself there in exactly the same position and situation as at the moment when the whole fantastic sequence of events began. In a flash, and greatly relieved, he realises that it has all been a nightmare, the wild fantasy of a man dreaming by the fireside at the end of a hard day in court. The public prosecutor, and the audience with him, can now see the whole violent sequence of events in all its extravagant improbability. Of course, it *was* all a dream! But then the maid asks: "Do you want me to take off your muddy boots?" And the public prosecutor looks at his boots: the nightmare was reality after all. It was *not* a dream. Or is it merely part of the nightmare that we ask ourselves whether we are dreaming and still are so deeply immersed in the dream that we must answer that it is reality after all . . .? Frisch has here brilliantly succeeded in putting a most elusive human situation on the stage: the situation when we are going through some terrible event and hope it is a dream, or when we are dreaming and are hoping it is a dream and yet cannot but accept the dream as real. But beyond the mere virtuosity of recreating such a highly ambivalent psychological state, Frisch here says something very important: namely, that dream or not, each human being really *is* what his hidden desires represent, as much as he really *is* the well-behaved and respectable shell that he presents to the outside world. The public prosecutor followed his *real* desires when he became an outlaw and it is therefore relatively irrelevant whether at the end of the play it all turns out to have been a fantasy or whether it all really happened; the violence was potentially present from the very beginning.

The public prosecutor's nightmare adventure merges into myth, the myth of Count Oederland, a fairy-tale figure that has been haunting the public prosecutor. And indeed our subconscious wishes and fantasies are closely akin to myth, in which the archetypal fears and desires of human beings have found lasting form. In the novel *Homo Faber* (1957) Frisch has attempted another *tour de force*—to recreate an ancient myth in the terms of our technological age. Walter Faber, the hero of this tale, which Frisch has subtitled "A Report", is a technologist, an engineer. But he is also a modern Oedipus, a man fated to become the bridegroom of his own daughter. The role of the blind fate which drove Oedipus into guilt in the Greek myth is here played by the pitiless, impersonal directing force of our own lives: the workings of our mechanical civilisation. Faber's fate is shaped by engine failures of aircraft, by a slight defect in his electric razor: if a bit of nylon thread had not stopped the razor he would not have been at home when the shipping line phoned to confirm his booking and would not have been able to take the boat on which he met the girl with whom he fell in love and who later turned out to be his own daughter. The engineer who prides himself on controlling machines is constantly controlled by the whims of minute pieces of machinery. And what is more: the further we are removed from the true sources of human feeling, the more isolated we seem from the raw, primeval workings of humanity, the more certainly we are thrown back into the primeval human situation—subjected to the blind workings of an impersonal fate, involved in monstrous guilts. The image of Auschwitz in which technological man could be seen as merely a more monstrous, because more powerful, repetition of the Stone-Age savage, stands behind the subtle and delicate imagery of *Homo Faber*.

In *Andorra* Frisch returned to the problem of human identity, but he put it against the background of this terrible guilt of our age. The play is about anti-Semitism, but it also deals with the existential situation of man as the product of the opinions of his neighbours. Andri, the hero of the play, is the illegitimate son of an Andorran schoolmaster and a woman from beyond the borders of Andorra, 'the country of the Blacks.' Ashamed to confess his transgression to his wife the schoolmaster has taken the boy into his home by pretending that he is a Jewish orphan, a victim of the anti-Semitic excesses of the Blacks. The schoolmaster is an idealist who wants to teach his countrymen a lesson about racialism. When the boy is grown up and generally accepted as a Jew he will reveal that he is his own son and no Jew and this will prove the fallacy of all racial prejudices and theories.

But Andri is not only regarded as a Jew; being looked at as a Jew imposes on him the patterns of Jewish character. The carpenter to whom he is apprenticed, for example, simply will not believe that he likes making furniture; he forces him to become a salesman because that suits his Jewish talents. Andri has fallen in love with Barblin, the schoolmaster's daughter. When he asks his "fosterfather" for her hand, he meets a horrified refusal—and he is convinced that this is due to his Jewishness. When the schoolmaster tells him the real reason he simply cannot accept it. Having been seen as a Jew by the others, he has now *become* a Jew and cannot but *be* a Jew. And so he goes to his death as a Jew when the Blacks invade Andorra and demand a scapegoat for the murder of a Black woman (who is none other than Andri's own mother) at the hands of the xenophobic Andorrans. The image we have made for ourselves has killed the real human being, and now we kill the image *and* the man who bears it.

Andorra tells the story of Andri in retrospect. Each scene is prefaced by the self-justification of one of "the others" from a witness box—or is it a dock?—at the side of the stage. None of us wants to have been responsible afterwards, when the consequences of our thoughtless actions have resulted in tragedy. Undoubtedly Frisch has here been influenced by the *epic theatre* of Bertolt Brecht, with whom he had been linked by ties of close friendship since Brecht's Zürich period (after his return from the United States in the late autumn of 1947). Frisch has left an unforgettable pen picture of Brecht at this period of his life in his published diaries. Yet, in spite of this obvious link, Frisch's style as a dramatist does not bear many direct marks of Brechtian influence and technique. The fluid, argumentative construction of plays like *Die Chinesische Mauer* or *Nun singen sie wieder* (in which the dead mingle with the living) owes more to the example of Thornton Wilder, whose *By the Skin of our Teeth* made a tremendous impact when it was staged in Zürich towards the end of the war. And in the ironic retelling of a myth like the Don Juan legend there is also clearly discernible the influence of Shaw, Cocteau or Giraudoux. Frisch's existentialism owes more to Kierkegaard than to the French or German schools of our own time. In his preoccupation with the need for self-realisation he acknowledges the influence of the great Swiss novelist of the nineteenth century Gottfried Keller, and his masterpiece, *Der grüne Heinrich.* In his two major novels he is deeply concerned with the technical problem of telling the story through the eyes of a narrator who is himself largely unaware of the implications of what he is telling. It might be possible to detect the influence and example of a writer like Faulkner in this preoccupation.

But however eclectic Frisch might appear if he is thus summed up in terms of literary models and influences, he is, basically, a highly original and personal writer, who has always strenuously refused to be classified or classed with any school or ideological grouping. And this precisely is what singles him out among most German-speaking writers of his generation : where most of them indulge in wild and woolly generalisations, Frisch always remains concrete and direct; where they go in for *Weltanschauung,* Frisch remains ideologically uncommitted; where they are baroque and excessive in their style, Frisch is simple, direct and yet full of lyrical power. Where they tend to offer panaceas and infallible solutions Frisch merely wants to define some questions that ought to be asked : "As a playwright I would consider my task to have been thoroughly fulfilled if one of my plays could succeed in so posing a question that from that moment on the audience could not go on living without an answer—without their own answer, which they can only give through their own lives. The general demand for an answer, a general answer, which is so often made so movingly, so reproachfully, perhaps, after all it is not as honest as those who ask it themselves believe. Every human answer as soon as it transcends a personal answer and pretends to general validity will be questionable, we know that all too well; and the satisfaction we find in disproving other people's answers consists in making us forget the question that bothers us; and that would mean : we do not really want answers we merely want to forget the question. So as not to become responsible."[8]

NOTES

1. Frisch: *Tagebuch 1946–1949,* Suhrkamp, 1950, p. 275.
2. *Ibid,* p. 282.
3. *Ibid.* p. 411.
4. *Andorra,* scene 8 in Stücke II, pp. 258–9.
5. *Tagebuch,* pp. 33–4.
6. *Ibid.* pp. 31–2.
7. Frisch: *Stiller,* Suhrkamp, 1958, p. 570.
8. Frisch: *Tagebuch,* pp. 141–2.

SHORT BIBLIOGRAPHY

PLAYS

Max Frische, *Stücke,* 2 vol. Suhrkamp, Frankfurt, 1961.

Vol. I contains: *Santa Cruz, Nun singen sie wieder, Die chinesische Mauer, Als der Krieg zu Ende War, Graf Oederland.*

Vol. II contains: *Don Juan oder Die Liebe zur Geometrie, Biedermann und die Brandstifter, Die grosse Wut des Philipp Hotz, Andorra.*

In English: Max Frisch, *Three Plays,* Methuen, London, 1962.

Contains: *The Fireraisers, Count Oederland, Andorra,* translated by Michael Bullock.

NOVELS

Stiller, Suhrkamp, Frankfurt, 1954.

English translation: *I'm not Stiller* (Penguin Books).

Homo Faber, Suhrkamp, Frankfurt, 1957.

English translation: *Homo Faber* (Penguin Books).

AUTOBIOGRAPHY

Tagebuch 1946–1949, Suhrkamp, Frankfurt, 1950.

ON FRISCH

Eduard Stäuble, *Max Frisch, Ein Schweizer Dichter der Gegenwart,* Bodensee Verlag, Amriswil, 2nd ed. 1960.

Hans Baenziger, *Frisch und Duerrenmatt,* Francke, Berne and Munich, 1960.

Michael Kustow, *No Graven Image* in *Encore* May–June 1962.

Friedrich Dürrenmatt

Friedrich Dürrenmatt

by H. M. WAIDSON

Friedrich Dürrenmatt, born on January 5, 1921 at Konolfingen, Canton Berne, is the son of the pastor Reinhold Dürrenmatt. When the family moved to Berne in 1935, Friedrich Dürrenmatt continued his secondary education there. In 1941 he began studying, in Zürich and then in Berne, and soon began writing; at one time he also thought of devoting himself to painting. He did not complete his university studies, but spent the years 1946–8 as a freelance writer in Basle. His play *Es steht geschrieben* was first performed at the Zürich Schauspielhaus on April 19, 1947. He married, in 1947, Lotti Geißler, an actress, and now lives at Neuchâtel with her and his three children. Apart from stage-plays, he has written mostly radio-plays and novels. (For biographical information, see especially the studies of Hans Bänziger and Elisabeth Brock-Sulzer.)

ALTHOUGH understandably reluctant to offer any direct and complete interpretation of his work, Friedrich Dürrenmatt has made a number of comments on his own plays, mostly in the form of short epilogues, and has written two essays primarily concerned with dramatic theory. Acting, magic and play, he says in the epilogue to *Frank der Fünfte*, are the origins of drama:

> Der Ursprung jeder Dramatik liegt vorerst im Trieb, Theater möglich zu machen, auf der Bühne zu zaubern, mit der Bühne zu spielen. Theater ist eine Angelegenheit der schöpferischen Lebensfreude, der unmittelbarsten Lebenskraft.(1)

He maintains that he does not interpret the world, for that is not the function of the creative writer, except incidentally and subconsciously. The correspondence, if any, between what is shown on the stage and the outside world, is no business of the dramatist as a creative writer, but it is the duty of the critic to point to the existence of these two worlds and to show how far they are related to one another.

> Der Realität muß im Theater eine Überrealität gegenüberstehen. . . .
>
> . . . Dies alles enthebt den Kritiker jedoch nicht der Pflicht, gerade das zu tun, was ich mir verbiete, die Welt in meinen möglichen Welten zu entdecken.(2)

The assertion is then, roughly, that Dürrenmatt's plays originate in a series of "Einfälle", motifs or devices, but not in anything so formulated as an idea. In the comments at the end of *Die Physiker* Dürrenmatt states:

> Ich gehe nicht von einer These, sondern von einer Geschichte aus.[3]

He seems to be illustrating this method of imaginative writing in the construction of the radio-play *Der Doppelgänger*. Here the "author" tells the "producer" that he has a story to tell that lies close to his heart:

> Doch muß ich gestehen, daß ich nicht viel mehr von ihr weiß als das Motiv. Es macht dies aber nichts: Eine Handlung stellt sich immer zur rechten Zeit ein.[4]

The producer, the practical man with an eye to the expectations of the listeners, proceeds to try to persuade his author to name his hero, to give him a geographical setting, and generally to coax the action into common-sense shape; the author regards most of the producer's demands as irrelevant, but on the whole conforms to them, though without enthusiasm or conviction.

While emphatic in his belief that play-writing consists essentially in the dynamic urge of imaginative material in the dramatist's mind, and that a rigid structure of dramatic or philosophical theory is not part of the dramatist's essential craft, Dürrenmatt has made a number of theoretical statements which clearly have relevance to his creative writing. His essay on Schiller (1959) shows the affinities of his own writing to that of the earlier dramatist; the fact that Dürrenmatt had the occasion to make this speech (having been awarded the Schiller Prize by the city of Mannheim), he says, indicates that the civic advisers were already aware of this affinity. Dürrenmatt joins the name of Schiller with that of Brecht, and the links that he finds between them inevitably reflect some of his own dramatic preoccupations. Both Schiller and Brecht he sees as concerned with dramatic theory and its relationship with creative writing. He says of Schiller:

> Seine Dramatik beruht auf einer durchaus sicheren, handfesten Dramaturgie. . . . Diese Dramaturgie zielt auf das Rhetorische. Der Mensch wird in Szene gesetzt, um rhetorisch ausbrechen zu können. Operndramaturgie.[5]

Operatic and rhetorical elements are present in Dürrenmatt's work, as in that of Schiller and Brecht. The way in which Schiller brings about the downfall of his heroes is summarised in words which could apply equally to a number of Dürrenmatt's own plays :

> Der Mensch scheitert am unnatürlichen Zustande der Welt. . . . Der Mensch geht schuldlos zugrunde. Sein Opfer bleibt nur in einer inneren Weise sinnvoll.(6)

Dürrenmatt compares and contrasts Schiller and Brecht in their attitude to the state and to the idea of revolution, and in expressing his concern about the impotence of the individual in face of a mass-organised world, he is also reflecting situations from his own work :

> Für den Einzelnen bleibt die Ohnmacht, das Gefühl, übergangen zu werden, nicht mehr einschreiten, mitbestimmen zu können, untertauchen zu müssen, um nicht unterzugehen. . . .(7)

By implication therefore Dürrenmatt sees himself as closer to Schiller and Brecht than, to quote the names he mentions in this context, Shakespeare, Molière and Nestroy.

The earlier essay *Theaterprobleme* (1955) emphasises the spontaneous nature of drama writing and the subordinate position of dramatic theory and ideas :

> Die Bühne stellt nicht für mich ein Feld für Theorien, Weltanschauungen und Aussagen, sondern ein Instrument dar, dessen Möglichkeiten ich zu kennen versuche, indem ich damit spiele.(8)

If it happens that his characters are concerned with problems of faith and philosophy, it is because Dürrenmatt finds it tedious to depict "lauter Dummköpfe", nothing but fools, and because human beings do concern themselves with such problems. Any dramatic theory, he says, will have only relative value, since it is bound to a specific environment. This is claimed to be true of Brecht as well as of Aristotle; if Brecht builds his dramatic theory into his philosophy of life, it often happens, and should happen, that "Der Dichter Brecht dem Dramaturgen Brecht durchbrennt".(9)

Theaterprobleme treats of a number of "practical problems" ("arbeitspraktische Probleme") which correspond to various devices that are used in Dürrenmatt's plays. One issue in the essay however, which is repeatedly relevant to his own writing is the question of the possibility of creating tragedy for the modern stage. (It is echoed also in the query raised in the introduction to the tale *Die Panne* as to whether narrative is capable of existing today :

> Die Ahnung steigt auf, es gebe nichts mehr zu erzählen, die Abdankung wird ernstlich in Erwägung gezogen, vielleicht sind einige Sätze noch möglich. . . .(10))

Dürrenmatt points out that the hero of tragedy traditionally comes from the highest social class and arouses our pity. With Lessing and Schiller the hero could come from the middle classes, and in the eighteenth century there was special emphasis on the element of pity; in the case of Büchner the implication seems to be that Woyzeck is the last tragic hero in German drama. Historical "Staatsdrama" in the manner of *Wallenstein,* it is argued, is impossible today because the state has lost its shape; political power has become so gigantic and uncontrollable that it ceases to be effective as drama. Tragedy depends on "Schuld, Not, Maß, Übersicht, Verantwortung" ("guilt, sorrow, proportion, perspective, responsibility"), but Dürrenmatt argues that these qualities are absent today, since events are on such a vast unpredictable scale that no individual can be held responsible.

> Unsere Welt hat ebenso zur Groteske geführt wie zur Atombombe.(11)

Comedy then has more chance of success than tragedy, for it is formed on a social basis. It may be more effective to ridicule the tyrants of today than to criticise them by means of tragic pathos.

Dürrenmatt's first two plays may be seen as experiments in tragedy. There is a considerable quantity of clowning and parody in *Es steht geschrieben,* but the general treatment of its theme and the element of "Das Rhetorische" seem to point to tragedy, or at least to no conscious intention to avoid tragedy. *Der Blinde* is perhaps Dürrenmatt's most consistent tragedy. The blind Duke retains his faith in a supra-natural, ideal world in face of the destruction of his outward happiness and security, in a way that recalls Schiller's idea of the tragic hero in *Über das Erhabene.* Elisabeth Brock-Sulzer points out that *Der Blinde* was criticised at the time of its first production as being essentially undramatic; it is indeed a martyr-drama, with no outward opposition to the villain Negro da Ponte. She reminds us, however, that the element of theatre plays a large part in this play, though more as spectacle than as drama. Negro da Ponte causes a whole series of dramolets to be enacted before the unseeing eyes of the Duke; thus there is a set of plays within the play. But it seems as though Dürrenmatt became dissatisfied with the martyr-drama in this form; *Der Blinde* was withheld from publication for more than ten years, and in the meantime the author has hesitated to use the word "tragedy" with reference to his own plays. (*Der Blinde* is described in the published version as "Ein Drama".) The conscious evolution of a theory and practice of comedy on Dürrenmatt's part seems to have taken place after the first performance of *Der Blinde.* With *Romulus der Große,* the sunniest of Dürrenmatt's stage-plays and the closest to the traditional structure of drama, martyr-tragedy has merged into martyr-comedy; the hero, alone in his conflict with the evil and folly in himself and in the world at large, has now become the subject of comedy. But even so the possibility of his achieving tragic quality, of a traditional nature, cannot be excluded. Dürrenmatt writes in a note to *Romulus der Große*:

> Menschlichkeit ist vom Schauspieler hinter jeder meiner Gestalten zu entdecken, sonst lassen sie sich gar nicht spielen. Das gilt von allen meinen Stücken.[12]

However, his quality of humanity, though never absent from the author's intentions, is evidently expressed more sympathetically in some figures than others, and the mood of a play is indicated to some extent by the importance of the role assigned to the hero, the humane and suffering figure.

Es steht geschrieben has elements of horror, absurdity and vulgarity, plenty of action, plenty of speeches often containing paradoxical rhetoric, a variety of stage devices, great vitality. In the *Theaterprobleme* Dürrenmatt refers to a tendency on his part to attempt too much in the framework of one play:

> Es ist meine nicht immer glückliche Leidenschaft, auf dem Theater den Reichtum, die Vielfalt der Welt darstellen zu wollen. So wird mein Theater oft vieldeutig und scheint zu verwirren.[13]

This is particularly applicable to Dürrenmatt's first play, where it may be some time before it is recognised that Knipperdollinck is the hero (in the sense here of a model personality, with whom we may be expected to feel sympathy), since the outward action is often dominated by Bockelson, the newcomer to Münster who so violently affects its fate. It is Knipperdollinck, the rich merchant with settled domestic habits, who considers most closely the central theme of the play which is indicated in its title; literal obedience to the Bible's injunctions causes him to seize as an opportunity the importunate arrival of Bockelson at his house, to be impelled to divest himself of his possessions:

> Da steht geschrieben:
> Verkaufe was du hast und gib's den Armen, so wirst du einen Schatz im Himmel haben. . . .[14]

Knipperdollinck asks God for an answer: "Herr, du schweigst, und ich brauche eine Antwort", explaining his bewilderment: "Ich habe keinen Glauben, ich habe Gold".[15] (This statement anticipates the author's development of the theme in *Der Besuch der alten Dame* and *Frank der Fünfte*.) As the action proceeds, the two men change their parts; Knipperdollinck, the man of substance, gives away everything and in the practice of patient suffering acquires faith, while the beggar Bockelson steps into Knipperdollinck's discarded possessions and becomes further confirmed in his cosmic despair. There is a remarkable scene as the two men dance on the roof-top waiting for their city to fall to the Roman Catholic troops. In anticipation of certain death the two men let fall their differences and the driving force of their personalities and beliefs, and enjoy the dance in an aesthetic lyricism that includes the clumsy and ridiculous. If the main conflict of the play is on a personal level between Knipperdollinck and Bockelson, the wider tension is between the Anabaptist community and the established Empire and Church. The Anabaptists are all, in the context of this play, tragic-comic heroes and fools. Knipperdollinck and Bockelson are both clowns, swept on by living in a world where literal interpretation of the Bible is of prime importance. Thus Dürrenmatt's first play, while glorifying in Knipperdollinck the hero as martyr, at the same time contains strong elements of comedy, parodying the martyr as fool and clown.

Der Blinde is more unified in mood, a morality play, retelling the story of Job in the setting of the Thirty Years War. The Duke is close to Knipperdollinck, sharing his humility and his determination not to move away from the position he has taken up; both suffer deprivation from their possessions and then the loss of those members of their families closest to them, and at the end of each play both men still affirm their faith.

In *Romulus der Große* the situation of the martyr-hero confronted by vicissitudes of fortune is re-interpreted in the manner of comedy. Romulus, as last Roman emperor before the invasion of the Germanic barbarians, might be considered as the suitable central figure of a classicist tragedy, but Dürrenmatt depicts him as an anti-hero and clown. It seems as if the decaying Roman Empire is in conflict with the might of the advancing barbarians, but this apparent, outward, political conflict is shown ultimately as paradoxically non-existent. The contrast between the mood of the play's exposition and that of high tragedy is indicated in the scene where Phylax endeavours to instruct Rea to absorb the role of a tragic heroine, Antigone. The essential dramatic conflict is between Romulus and his own family and supporters. Much of the first three acts is on a level of persiflage and light banter, the witticisms and deliberate disrespectfulness of the Emperor arousing the indignation of his wife, daughter and entourage. The fourth act shows the elevation of the play, after comedy and then melodrama, in the attempted assassination of Romulus, to seriousness, as Romulus now contemplates the fulfilment of his self-appointed role of unheroic martyr. He differs from Knipperdollinck and the Duke in being free from a tendency to take himself too seriously in his role as sufferer. Romulus expects execution twice, but is spared the first time by sheer chance (as is also the case with Bockelson), the second time because he himself also has a conventional conception of the Germani. Apparently the first version of the play was consistently on a level of light comedy, but in the revised edition Dürrenmatt rewrote the last two acts to give Romulus greater dignity and heroism. As Dürrenmatt indicates in his postscript to the play, Romulus passes judgment on the Roman world in act three; but judgment is passed on him later when he is frustrated of his desired martyrdom, so that tragedy might be found in his inability to attain the dignity of this aim and in his being presented with comedy and pensioning-off. His wisdom lies in his willingness to accept an unheroic ending and to refuse to dramatise himself. As a character Romulus is much more rounded, warmer and more human than either Knipperdollinck or the Duke. What is more, his character gradually emerges as the play proceeds, undergoing development and purification.

Dürrenmatt takes up again in *Die Ehe des Herrn Mississippi* something of the grotesqueness of *Es steht geschrieben*, though in this instance he is more firmly determined to interpret it in a spirit of comedy. Elisabeth Brock-Sulzer regards *Die Ehe des Herrn Mississippi* as "sentimentalisch", that is, not spontaneous and evocative through direct human characteristics, but as "konstruiert", since its main characters are embodiments of ideas. It has been pointed out that Mississippi, Saint-Claude and Bodo von Übelohe may represent faith, hope and charity. These three main characters are united in their search for an absolute, in their desire to change the world and in their dissatisfaction with the policy of preserving the existing situation which is manifested in the figure of the minister Diego. Thus they are united by a gleam of what is regarded by others as fanaticism and folly, and hold together, symbolically at least, like the Anabaptists in face of the traditional forces of Church and Empire, or like the Duke when confronted by Negro da Ponte. Bodo von Übelohe resembles Knipperdollinck, the Duke and Romulus when he strips himself, or is stripped, of his riches until, possessing nothing, he embodies the ideal of poverty and powerlessness. Knipperdollinck and the Duke, in holding fast to rigid attitudes are tragic martyrs; Romulus and Übelohe have no illusions about themselves, are willing to be regarded as clowns, and thus (from

Dürrenmatt's point of view as apparently implied in these plays) can speak for ideals of wisdom or love. If Mississippi realises that the action he is taking part in during a certain scene is comedy, he resents this and finds it humiliating:

> Wie lange soll diese für beide Teile entwürdigende Komödie noch abspielen, gnädige Frau?[16]

Mississippi's role seems to be anticipated in a phrase from the early prose narrative, *Das Bild des Sisyphos*:

> ...auch schien unter seinen Worten jener Fanatismus zu glühen, den wir bei Menschen antreffen, die entschlossen sind, ihrer Idee die Welt zu opfern.[17]

Übelohe does not appear until the first section, previously dominated by Mississippi and Saint-Claude, is more than half over; subsequently he has a larger part to play and is allowed to survive, after Mississippi and Saint-Claude are dead, and to speak the epilogue. His desire to help mankind ("Dein Urwaldspital in Borneo"—"Your hospital in the primeval forests of Borneo") has crumbled, and his last illusion about mankind, his love for Anastasia, is soon lost:

> Allein die Liebe ist geblieben. Die Liebe eines Narren, die Liebe eines lächerlichen Menschen.[18]

Übelohe's appearance finally, as Don Quixote in battered armour tilting at a windmill, sums up his conception of the play:

> Eine ewige Komödie
> Daß aufleuchte Seine Herrlichkeit
> genährt durch unsere Ohnmacht.[19]

Romulus der Große, where the hero dominates most of the time, is more unified in its plot, theme and mood than the more disparate *Die Ehe des Herrn Mississippi.*

Ein Engel kommt nach Babylon, Dürrenmatt informs its readers, was intended as the preliminary action of a work which should culminate in the building of the tower of Babel, and is therefore sub-titled a "fragmentary comedy". As in *Die Ehe des Herrn Mississippi,* the stability of the state is threatened by revolution, though the rising is thwarted and the old order finally remains in control. The appearance of the Angel, with his bland belief in the perfection of earth as a planet, brings confusion and no visible improvement in the lot of the majority of Babylonians; his final leave-taking from the earth and the bewildered Kurrubi recalls the departure of the three gods in Brecht's *Der gute Mensch von Sezuan.* From the events in the first act especially our attention is directed to the figures of two comic beggars: Akki, the last surviving beggar in Babylon, and Nebukadnezar, the king who has assumed the guise of beggar for a short period. Dürrenmatt introduces an element of paradox into his conception of these two men. Akki, as a highly proficient beggar, is patron of numerous poets, and for a time becomes an unconventional executioner; here we are reminded of Brecht's Azdak in *Der kaukasische Kreidekreis*. The gift of Kurrubi is intended for Akki; as the Angel says to her:

> Die geringsten der Menschen sind die Bettler. Du wirst demnach einem gewissen Akki gehören, der, wenn diese Karte stimmt, der einzige noch erhaltene Bettler der Erde ist.[20]

But Kurrubi is presented to Nebukadnezar, who desires her, as she now desires him. In one sense this is due to an error on the Angel's part, but in another sense (cf. Elisabeth Brock-Sulzer) it is fitting that Kurrubi should be linked with Nebukadnezar, for as king he is the first, and therefore the last man, while as a beggar he appears comic and clumsy in his efforts to compete with Akki; his power, though apparently unrestricted, shows itself in the third act as close to impotence. To realise the happiness offered by this gift of divine grace, Nebukadnezar would have to forego all wealth and power and become a humbler and also more comic character than Akki. The king has the most important and critical decision to make in the action of the play: to accept or reject Kurrubi. At the end of the first act he refuses her in favour of gaining power over ex-king Nimrod, while he loses her to Akki in the final act because he is unwilling to accept her unless she becomes his queen. Nebukadnezar is both tyrant and victim of his own tyranny, and some words of Mississippi seem to have relevance in this connection:

> So fielen wir, Henker und Opfer zugleich, durch unsere eigenen Werke.[21]

The play has a light, fairy-tale mood and a delicacy of charm in addition to satirical humour.

The situation of the action in *Der Besuch der alten Dame* is comparable to that of earlier plays in that a powerful figure comes from outside and with his or her entry into a previously static community brings about confusion and conflict before disappearing from the scene at the end of the play. Claire Zachanassian brings the gift of her wealth, after having deliberately impoverished the community, as the Angel brought Kurrubi; or she can be seen as inflicting fear upon Ill, just as Negro da Ponte brought tribulations to the Duke. External forces start the action of these plays, and each of them contains a quality of irresponsibility and indifference to the needs and welfare of the community they disturb. The dissolution of the conventional world is threatened by Mississippi and Saint-Claude too, but is not achieved. The execution of Ill by his fellow-citizens at the orders of Claire Zachanassian recalls the death of Knipperdollinck and Bockelson in *Es steht geschrieben.* Claire Zachanassian is a static character, because she is outside the normal human order with her wealth and sense of purpose:

> Doch da sie sich außerhalb der menschlichen Ordnung bewegt, ist sie etwas Unabänderliches, Starres geworden, ohne Entwicklung mehr, es sei denn die, zu versteinern, ein Götzenbild zu werden.(22)

Like the Angel in *Ein Engel kommt nach Babylon* the millionairess is remote from the people of Güllen. But Ill develops in the course of the action, while the citizens of the town change too. He becomes purified through guilt and suffering, but his family and fellow-townsmen become compromised through their guilt towards him. Up to the age of sixty-four Ill has lived unthinkingly, until Claire Zachanassian's ultimatum shocks him into a new awareness:

> Zauberhexchen! Das kannst du doch nicht fordern! Das Leben ging doch längst weiter!(23)

Anastasia and the Minister, in *Die Ehe des Herrn Mississippi,* succeed in preserving the *status quo* that lets them live in the present, but Ill is forced out of this position in the first act of *Der Besuch der alten Dame.* The second act shows the undermining of Ill's confidence and of his fellow-citizens' support of him and of the cause of "humanity". The crisis and turning-point occurs at the end of this act when he is unable to take the decisive step of entering the train:

> Einer wird mich zurückhalten, wenn ich den Zug besteige.(24)

By the third act he has overcome his anxiety and has turned from fear to readiness for repentance and atonement not through the compulsion of the other Güllen citizens, but through his own choice. In the first act Ill is identified with Güllen, subsequently he becomes separated from the other inhabitants of the town by his fear, while in the third act he acknowledges his guilt and is willing to accept death. The more surely he becomes resigned and ready, the less certain do the people of Güllen become, realising something of the new guilt that is coming upon them. The Bürgermeister invites Ill to commit suicide to save the community from responsibility for his death:

> Es wäre doch nun eigentlich Ihre Pflicht, mit Ihrem Leben Schluß zu machen, als Ehrenmann die Konsequenzen ziehen, finden Sie nicht? Schon aus Gemeinschaftsgefühl, aus Liebe zur Vaterstadt.[25]

But Ill, now stronger than the Bürgermeister in his newly found defencelessness, resembles Romulus standing alone against his family:

> Bürgermeister! Ich bin durch eine Hölle gegangen. Ich sah, wie ihr Schulden machtet, spürte bei jedem Anzeichen des Wohlstands den Tod näher kriechen. Hättet ihr mir diese Angst erspart, dieses grauenhafte Fürchten, wäre alles anders gekommen, könnten wir anders reden, würde ich das Gewehr nehmen. Euch zu liebe. Aber nun schloß ich mich ein, besiegte meine Furcht. Allein. Es war schwer, nun ist es getan. Ein Zurück gibt es nicht. Ihr *müßt* nun meine Richter sein. Ich unterwerfe mich eurem Urteil, wie es nun auch ausfalle.[26]

In his final *tête-à-tête* with Claire Zachanassian, Ill is cool and factual, much more her equal in the strength of his personality than in their first encounter in act one. He has become a suffering hero in the course of the action, having wrestled with himself for this quality in painful solitude. For Romulus, this quality was present all the time, but it was only fully revealed when his fellow-Romans left him. Ill begins as one of the drifting, conventional crowd, but is compelled to undergo a complete reversal of fortune and change of character. As Ill dies, he becomes the sacrificial victim so that the people of Güllen may be temporarily saved from poverty. The period of prosperity to which they proceed may only be an interlude before their judgment of Ill is caught up in a larger execution that may befall the whole community.

Humour in this play, which is sub-titled a "tragische Komödie", is for the most part demonstrated in the minor characters. There are the satellites of Claire Zachanassian, who have no personality since they have become humiliated to complete subordination to her will; hardly human, they are an extension of her personality and power. There are Ill's family and the other citizens of Güllen, whose gradual yielding to the will of the millionairess is satirically demonstrated. It could be argued that Ill is a tragic hero who has to undergo a searching process of emotional purification. At the same time Dürrenmatt has emphasised that comedy is integral to his conception of the play; as he writes in the "note" at the end of *Der Besuch der alten Dame*:

> Man inszeniere mich auf die Richtung von Volksstücken hin, behandle mich als eine Art bewußten Nestroy und man wird am weitesten kommen. Man bleibe bei meinen Einfällen und lasse den Tiefsinn fahren. . . Die alte Dame ist ein böses Stück, doch gerade deshalb darf es nicht böse, sondern aufs humanste wiedergegeben werden, mit Traur, nicht mit Zorn, doch auch mit Humor, denn nichts schadet dieser Komödie, die tragisch endet, mehr als tierischer Ernst.(27)

Frank der Fünfte, "opera of a private bank" culminates in the killing of a bank magnate by his own son, after an exposition of the many crimes in which all members of the firm have been implicated. It is an essay in dynastic melodrama, and the parodistic prologue spoken by the personnel manager Egli draws a parallel with Shakespeare, insisting that a modern business milieu is as capable of showing "royal" action as any sixteenth-century play:

> Ein Relikt wie du, einer besseren schöneren Welt
> Stehn wir fürchterlich vor dir
> Henker zwar doch Götter schier
> Minder groß und blutig nicht
> Als die Helden von Shakespeare.(28)

The bank of Frank the Fifth has been left over from an earlier epoch, and finally when his régime is terminated his son is to modernise the undertaking by "a few years of brutal honesty":

> Ich werde die Bank meiner Väter retten. Von jetzt an wird legal gewirtschaftet, einige Jahre brutaler Ehrlichkeit und wir tanzen wieder im Reigen der Großbanken mit.(29)

In an environment of total unscrupulousness there is little room for sympathy; the feigned death of Frank the Fifth is as melodramatic as his final disappearance at the end of the play. The illustrations of the bank's methods are indeed presented as being simplifications, since a detailed account, it is said, would be impossible to reconcile with the requirements of drama. In his desire to confess his past misdeeds Böckmann corresponds most closely to Ill in *Der Besuch der alten Dame* and to the earlier martyr-heroes. His discovery that he has cancer and that Frank the Fifth and Ottilie have been unwilling to permit the operation advised two years earlier, that they have children while he has remained alone, opens his eyes to a new interpretation of the world about him. Later, on his death-bed, Böckmann asserts his need to turn away from the life behind him:

> In jeder Stunde hätten wir umkehren können, in jedem Augenblick unseres bösen Lebens. Es gibt kein Erbe, das nicht auszuschlagen wäre und kein Verbrechen, das getan werden muß.[30]

This last wish is effectively frustrated by Ottilie and her husband. For Böckmann there is little or no opportunity to escape from the way of life he has lived so long; in this respect he differs from Ill.

In *Die Physiker* Möbius corresponds in some respects to Böckmann in *Frank der Fünfte,* though Möbius has a much more developed and significant part. Just as Böckmann finds it impossible to escape from his ties to the bank, so Möbius is apparently wholly identified with his fellow-inmates of the sanatorium "Les Cerisiers". The first act offers an exposition in which the three scientists appear to the audience as hardly differentiated in their roles. Beutler ("Newton"), Ernesti ("Einstein") and Möbius ("King Solomon") live together, are physicists with seemingly similar delusions, and as the act closes Möbius follows his companions' example when he too murders his nurse. Earlier in the act the separation from his children and his wife, who is newly married to a missionary, has allowed for Möbius' introduction to the audience as a character in the tradition of the suffering, clumsy figures in Dürrenmatt's previous works. A stage-direction describes him as:

> ein vierzigjähriger, etwas unbeholfener Mensch. Er schaut sich unsicher im Zimmer um . . .[31]

and he feels that as a father he has been inadequate:

> Ich bin froh, daß die Buben einen tüchtigen Vater gefunden haben. Ich bin ein ungenügender Vater gewesen.[32]

He attempts, in act two, to give himself up to the police-inspector, but with his two fellow-physicists realises that "Les Cerisiers" has become increasingly like a prison. When he realises the identity of "Newton" and "Einstein", Möbius knows that he has been threatened with abduction from the agents of the two opposing major powers in world politics. He is an outstanding physicist, and thereby is liable to become the victim of the social-political consequences of his own discoveries; even if he "escapes" from the sanatorium, he will only become a prisoner of one of the two great states. As he explains his career to "Newton" and "Einstein", Möbius shows that he deliberately assumed the fool's cap, like King Romulus, believing that only through the assumption of madness would the world have a chance of being saved:

> Es gibt Risiken, die man nie eingehen darf: Der Untergang der Menschheit ist ein solches. Was die Welt mit den Waffen anrichtet die sie schon besitzt, wissen wir, was sie mit jenen anrichten würde, die ich ermögliche, können wir uns denken.[33]

It is Möbius who persuades his two colleagues to give up their political missions and to remain voluntarily with him in the sanatorium. In this way, and no other, is there a remote possibility that the world may be saved, he argues, and that the murders they have committed may not be without meaning:

> Sollen unsere Morde sinnlos werden? Entweder haben wir geopfert oder gemordet. Entweder bleiben wir im Irrenhaus oder die Welt wird eines. Entweder löschen wir uns im Gedächtnis der Menschen aus oder die Menschheit erlischt.[34]

The three hope to be "mad, but wise, captive, but free, and physicists, but innocent". At this point the play attains a dignity comparable to the meeting between Romulus and Odoaker, and Möbius too may be seen as making a gesture of heroic self-sacrifice. But Dürrenmatt ends *Die Physiker* on a note of sharp disillusionment. As "Einstein" says:

> Die Welt ist in die Hände einer verrückten Irrenärztin gefallen.[35]

Dr. Mathilde von Zahnd is a much more immediate danger to mankind than Odoaker's nephew in *Romulus der Große*. But Möbius is allowed the last words in the play, to confirm the central importance of his function in it; if Bodo von Übelohe concludes *Die Ehe des Herrn Mississippi* by seeing himself as Don Quixote, Möbius speaks as a King Solomon whose realm has lost all life:

> Ich bin Salomo. Ich bin der arme König Salomo. Einst war ich unermeßlich, reich, weise und gottesfürchtig. Ob meiner Macht erzitterten die Gewaltigen. Ich war ein Fürst des Friedens und der Gerechtigkeit. Aber meine Weisheit zerstörte meine Gottesfurcht, und als ich Gott nicht mehr fürchtete, zerstörte meine Weisheit meinen Reichtum. Nun sind die Städte tot, über die ich regierte, mein Reich leer, das mir anvertraut worden war, eine blauschimmernde Wüste, und, irgendwo, um einen kleinen, gelben, namenlosen Stern, kreist, sinnlos, immerzu, die radioaktive Erde. Ich bin Salomo, ich bin Salomo, ich bin der arme König Salomo.[36]

In opposition to Dürrenmatt's passive heroes stand the tyrants, executioners and men of ceremony. Together heroes and villains are absorbed by the problematic nature of life and by a strong desire to make it different, or at least not to accept it; the majority of people, of course, are not directly involved in the conflicts Dürrenmatt describes, and it may be part of the comedy that the dramatic tension often lies between people who, while violently in conflict with one another, have something in common which separates them from the unthinking majority. In *Es steht geschrieben* Charles V is shown as someone to whom the government of a vast empire brings none of the excitement that Bockelson acquires from his short-lived reign as "king" of Münster. The Bishop of Münster believes it to be his duty to persuade Charles V to destroy the Anabaptists, and in so doing asserts the right to sit in judgment over their state; but Dürrenmatt makes it clear that final judgment may take some quite other shape. Romulus is judged and condemned by his family and entourage; they are drowned as they try to escape, and Romulus remains alone. Mississippi and Saint-Claude are both executioners who are fanatically devoted to their cause. Nebukadnezar and Nimrod, as a pair of tyrants, are inexorably linked together. *Frank der Fünfte* shows the execution of an executioner. In this play, as also in *Der Besuch der alten Dame* and *Die Physiker,* the major antagonist to the suffering hero is an "old lady". Claire Zachanassian, it may be argued, has ultimately and in spite of herself, an ennobling effect upon her victim Ill. Frank the Fifth is supported and directed by his wife Ottilie; since during the course of most of the action he is ostensibly dead, she assumes leadership of the firm. She describes herself to Böckmann thus:

> Böckmann! Ich bin aufgerieben wie du von unserem Geschäft, eine alte Frau, die sich seit Jahren nur noch mit Morphium durch ein ekelhaftes Leben schleppt.(37)

Ottilie finally asks the President of the state, once her lover, to mete out justice and wind up the bank's affairs, but this is refused to her. As the President says to her:

> Nein, nein, erwarte von mir keine Strafe, erwarte von mir nur noch Gnade.(38)

Dr. Mathilde von Zahnd has a minor and apparently harmless role in the first act of *Die Physiker.* As last heiress of an old family, she may perhaps be eccentric, but in no wise dangerous:

> Schicksal, Voß. Ich bin immer Alleinerbin. Meine Familie ist so alt, daß es beinahe einem kleinen medizinischen Wunder gleichkommt, wenn ich relativ für normal gelten darf, ich meine, was meinen Geisteszustand betrifft.(39)

Her final revelation, that she is the sole possessor of Möbius' discoveries and thereby the most powerful person in the world, brings her into close kinship with Claire Zachanassian.

In a speech to the audience Übelohe gives some hint as to the author's identity and purposes in *Die Ehe des Herrn Mississippi*:

> So ließ der Liebhaber grausamer Fabeln und nichtsnutziger Lustspiele, der mich schuf, dieser zähschreibende Protestant und verlorene Phantast mich zerbrechen, um meinen Kern zu schmecken . . . um mich nicht als Sieger, sondern als Besiegten . . . in den Tiegel seiner Komödie zu werfen: Dies allein nur, um zu sehen, ob denn wirklich Gottes Gnade in dieser endlichen Schöpfung unendlich sei, unsere einzige Hoffnung.[40]

In *Ein Engel kommt nach Babylon* this gift of grace is available to the beggar but not to the monarch. Nebukadnezar recognises this already on first encountering Kurrubi:

> So schlage ich zu Boden, was ich mehr liebe denn je einen Menschen, so trete ich dich mit Füßen, du Gnade Gottes, von der meine Seligkeit abhängt . . .[41]

Nebukadnezar has wished to found a state on a combination of power and reason alone, with himself as its ruler:

> Ich trachtete nach Vollkommenheit. Ich schuf eine neue Ordnung der Dinge. Ich suchte die Armut zu tilgen. Ich wünschte die Vernunft einzuführen. Der Himmel mißachtete mein Werk. Ich blieb ohne Gnade.[42]

Augias *(Herkules und der Stall des Augias)* presents to his son the "garden of his resignation" which he has cultivated in the midst of the all-pervasive dung, and tells him that the fruition of human endeavour is dependent upon grace, the presence of which cannot be compelled. These are a very few examples of the relevance in Dürrenmatt's work of the subject of grace, and the importance of this aspect has been shown by Fritz Buri in his essay in *Der unbequeme Dürrenmatt*.

One unifying theme that runs through most of Dürrenmatt's stage-plays is the passive hero, who embodies love and humility, often linked with ridiculousness. As Werner Oberle says *(Der unbequeme Dürrenmatt)*: "Finally, the hero must have love, not a deluded love, but a love in spite of everything." What has been attempted above is to draw attention mainly to this facet of Dürrenmatt's work. It is by no means the only aspect of his writing, of course. Beda Allemann has traced the relationship of executioner and victim, taking as his starting-point *Es steht geschrieben*. In *Der unbequeme Dürrenmatt* Reinhold Grimm has analysed the nature of the grotesque in Dürrenmatt's work, and Hans Mayer has emphasised the relationship with Brecht. There is no doubt that there are many approaches to this writing which, with its strength and vitality, provides plenty of material for discussion, challenge and appreciation.

TRANSLATIONS

1. The origin of all dramatic art lies in the first place in the urge to make a performance possible, to practise magic on the stage and to play with the stage. A theatrical performance is a matter of the creative enjoyment of life, of the most direct vital energy.

2. In the theatre reality must be confronted with a supra-reality. . . . However, all this does not relieve the critic of the duty of doing precisely what I do not allow myself to do, that is, of discovering the world in my potential worlds.

3. I do not start from a thesis, but from a story.

4. Yet I must confess that I don't know much more about it than the motif. But this doesn't matter: a plot can always be found at the right time.

5. His dramatic art rests upon a completely sure and practical dramatic theory. . . . This dramatic theory aims at a rhetorical effect. A character is put on the stage so that he can break out rhetorically. Dramatic theory for opera.

6. Man founders because of the unnatural situation of the world. . . . Man is destroyed in innocence. His sacrifice retains meaning only in an inward manner.

7. For the individual there remains impotence, the feeling of being passed over, of no longer being able to intervene and to have influence, of being compelled to go underground in order not to go under. . . .

8. The stage does not represent for me a vehicle for theories, views of the world and pronouncements, but an instrument the potentialities of which I am attempting to get to know by playing with them.

9. Brecht the creative writer runs away with Brecht the dramatic theorist.

10. The misgiving arises that there is nothing more to relate, abdication is taken into serious consideration, perhaps a few sentences are still possible. . . .

11. Our world has led to the grotesque just as to the atom-bomb.

12. The actor is to discover humanity behind each one of my characters, otherwise they cannot be played at all. This is the case with all my plays.

13. It is my not always felicitous passion to try to depict the richness and multifariousness of the world on the stage. In this way my playwriting often becomes ambiguous and seems to bewilder.

14. It is written: sell what you have and give it to the poor, and you will have treasure in heaven.

15. Lord, You are silent, and I need an answer. . . . I have no faith, I have gold.

16. How much longer is this comedy, which is so degrading for both sides, supposed to go on, madam?

17. Beneath his words it also seemed as if that fanaticism was burning which we meet in people who are determined to sacrifice the world to their idea.

18. Only love remains. The love of a fool, of a ridiculous person.

19. An eternal comedy, so that His majesty may light up, nourished by our impotence.

20. Beggars are the least among mankind. Consequently you will belong to a certain Akki who, if this map is right, is the only surviving beggar on the earth.

21. Thus we fell, executioner and victim at the same time, through our own works.

22. However, since she moves outside the human order, she has become something unalterable and inflexible, without any further development, unless it were to become petrified and to turn into an idol.

23. Little witch! But surely you can't ask for that! After all, life has been continuing on its way for a long time now!

24. Somebody will hold me back if I get on the train.

25. Now after all it is really your duty to terminate your life, to draw conclusions as a man of honour, don't you think? Even if only out of a communal spirit, out of love for your native town.

26. Mr. Mayor! I have been through hell. I saw how you all ran up debts and I felt death creeping more closely with every indication of prosperity: If you had spared me this anxiety and this horrible fear, everything would have turned out differently, we could be talking differently and I would accept the weapon. For your sakes. But now I shut myself in and overcame my fear. Alone. It was difficult, but now it is over. There is no going back. You *must* be my judges now. I submit to your judgment, whatever way it may go.

27. My work should be produced in a manner reminiscent of popular plays, I should be treated as a kind of self-conscious Nestroy, and that will take us furthest. Stick to my fancies and let the profundity go. . . . The *Old Lady* is a wicked play, but precisely on that account it should not be played in a wicked manner, but in the most humane way possible, with grief, not anger, but also with humour, for nothing injures this comedy, which has a tragic ending, more than brutal earnestness.

28. A relic, like yourself, of a better and more beautiful world, we stand in our fearfulness before you, executioners, it is true, but almost gods, no less great and bloody than the heroes of Shakespeare.

29. I shall save the bank of my fathers. From now onwards everything will be run in a legal manner; a few years of brutal honesty and we shall once more take our part in the dance of the big banks.

30. We could have turned back at any hour or moment of our evil lives.

There is no inheritance that may not be refused, and no crime that has to be committed.

31. A forty-year-old and somewhat ungainly man. He looks round the room uncertainly. . . .

32. I am glad that the boys have found a good father. I have been an inadequate father.

33. There are risks which one may never take: the destruction of humanity is one. We know what the world can do with the weapons which it already possesses, and we can imagine what it would do with those which I make possible.

34. Are the murders we have committed to become meaningless? Either we have performed sacrifices or committed murders. Either we stay in the asylum or the world becomes one. Either we blot ourselves out from the memory of men or mankind is blotted out.

35. The world has fallen into the hands of a mad doctor of mental diseases.

36. I am Solomon. I am poor King Solomon. Once I was immeasurably rich, wise and God-fearing. The mighty trembled at my power. I was a prince of peace and justice. But my wisdom destroyed my piety, and when I no longer feared God, my wisdom destroyed my wealth. Now the towns over which I ruled are dead, the kingdom which was entrusted to me is empty, a blue-shimmering desert, and somewhere the radio-active earth is circling senselessly and continually around a little yellow nameless star. I am Solomon, I am Solomon, I am poor King Solomon.

37. Böckmann! I am worn out by our business just as much as you are, an old woman who for years has only dragged her way through a repulsive life with the help of morphia.

38. No, no, don't expect any punishment from me, expect from me only mercy.

39. Fate, Voss. I am always the sole heiress. My family is so old that it almost seems a small medical miracle if I may be considered to be relatively normal, I mean, as far as my mental condition is concerned.

40. So the lover of dreadful fables and worthless comedies who created me, this tough-writing Protestant and lost dreamer, had me broken in order to enjoy my essence . . . in order to throw me into the crucible of his comedy . . . not as victor, but as one who is defeated: he has done this in order to see if God's grace, our only hope, really is infinite in this finite creation.

41. Thus I throw to the ground what I love more than any human being, thus I stamp on you with my feet, you grace of God, on which my salvation depends.

42. I aimed at perfection. I created a new order of things. I tried to destroy poverty. I wanted to introduce reason. Heaven disregarded my work. I remained without grace.

SELECT BIBLIOGRAPHY

Dürrenmatt's chief publications to date (these have appeared mostly in the Verlag der Arche, Zürich, or in the Benziger Verlag, Einsiedeln and Cologne):

Stage Plays:

Es steht geschrieben, 1947.
Der Blinde, 1948.
Romulus der Große, 1949 (edited by H. F. Garten, London, 1962).
Die Ehe des Herrn Mississippi, 1952.
Ein Engel kommt nach Babylon, 1953.
Der Besuch der alten Dame, 1956 (edited by Paul Kurt Ackermann, London, 1961).
Frank der Fünfte, 1959.
Die Physiker, 1962.

Radio Plays:

Der Prozeß um des Esels Schatten, 1951.
Nächtliches Gespräch, 1952.
Stranitzky und der Nationalheld, 1953.
Herkules und der Stall des Augias, 1954.
Das Unternehmen der Wega, 1955.
Abendstunde im Spätherbst, 1957.
Der Doppelgänger, 1960.

Novels, stories, essays:

Der Richter und sein Henker, 1950 (edited by Leonard Forster, London, 1962).
Der Verdacht, 1951.
Die Stadt, 1952.
Grieche sucht Griechin, 1955.
Theaterprobleme, 1955.
Die Panne, 1956.
Das Versprechen, 1958.
Friedrich Schiller. Eine Rede, 1960.

Some Writings on Dürrenmatt:

Beda Allemann, *Es steht geschrieben.* In: *Das deutsche Drama,* edited by Benno von Wiese, vol. 2, Düsseldorf, 1958.
Hans Bänziger, *Frisch und Dürrenmatt.* Berne and Munich, 1960.
Elisabeth Brock-Sulzer, *Dürrenmatt. Stationen seines Werkes.* Zürich 1960.
A. J. Harper, *Dürrenmatt. A Way of Approach.* In: *Germania,* vol. 2, no. 1, 1962.

Joachim Müller, *Max Frisch und Friedrich Dürrenmatt als Dramatiker der Gegenwart*. In: *Universitas,* vol 17, no. 7, 1962.

Therese Poser, *Friedrich Dürrenmatt*. In: *Zur Interpretation des modernen Dramas,* edited by Rolf Geißler, Frankfurt am Main, Berlin and Bonn, n.d.

Morality Plays. In: *Times Literary Supplement,* January 11, 1963.

Der Unbequeme Dürrenmatt, a collection of essays. Basilius Presse, Basle, 1962.

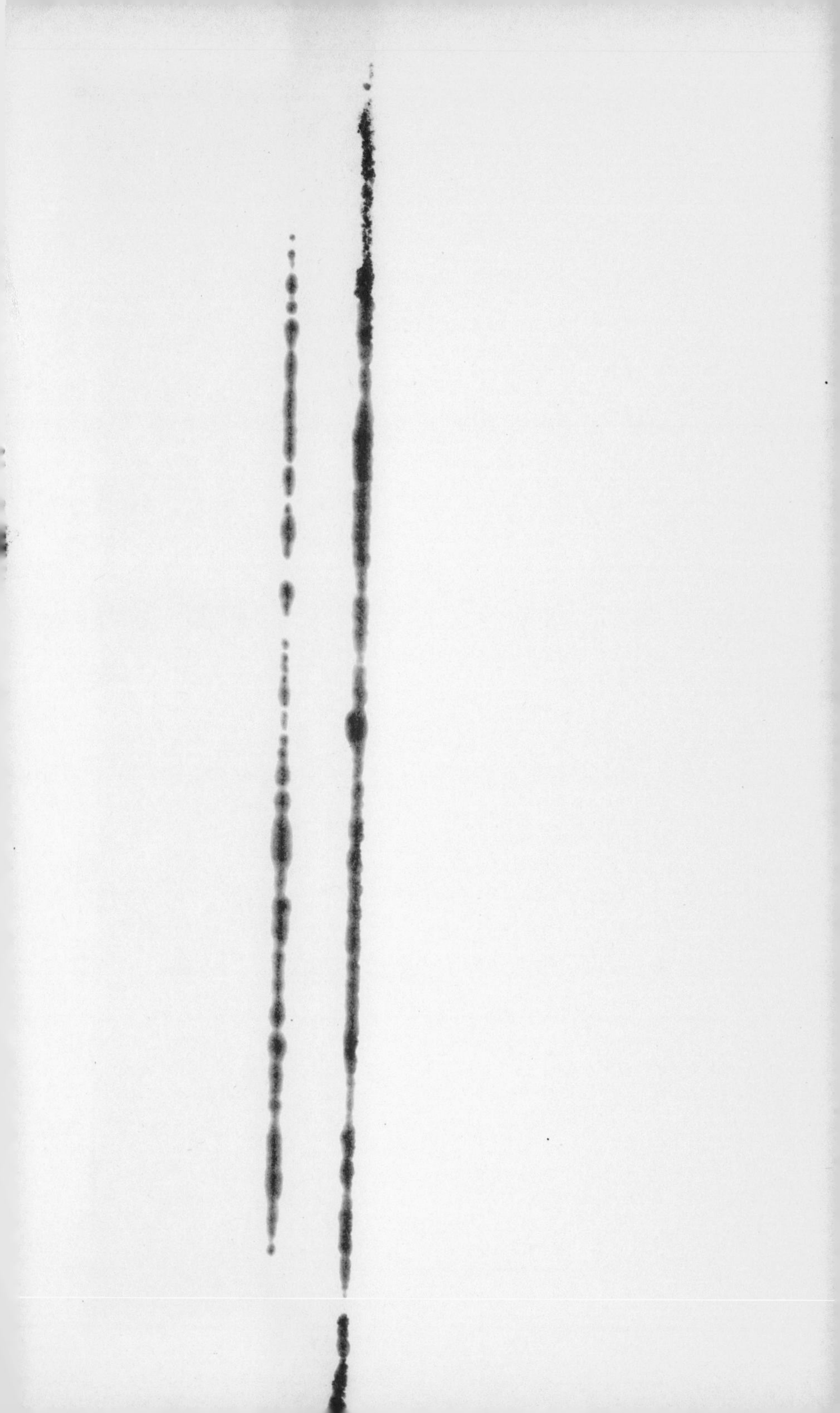